THE GOSPEL WORKING UP

Recent titles in
RELIGION IN AMERICA SERIES
Harry S. Stout, General Editor

Saints in Exile
The Holiness-Pentecostal Experience in
    African American Religion and Culture
Cheryl J. Sanders

Democratic Religion
Freedom, Authority, and Church Discipline
    in the Baptist South, 1785–1900
Gregory A. Willis

The Soul of Development
Biblical Christianity and Economic
    Transformation in Guatemala
Amy L. Sherman

The Viper on the Hearth
Mormons, Myths, and the
    Construction of Heresy
Terryl L. Givens

Sacred Companies
Organizational Aspects of Religion and
    Religious Aspects of Organizations
Edited by N. J. Demerath III, Peter
    Dobkin Hall, Terry Schmitt,
    and Rhys H. Williams

*Mary Lyon and the Mount Holyoke
    Missionaries*
Amanda Porterfield

Being There
Culture and Formation in Two
    Theological Schools
Jackson W. Carroll, Barbara G. Wheeler,
    Daniel O. Aleshire, Penny Long Marler

The Character of God
Recovering the Lost Literary Power of
    American Protestantism
Thomas E. Jenkins

The Revival of 1857–58
Interpreting an American
    Religious Awakening
Kathryn Teresa Long

American Madonna
Images of the Divine Woman in
    Literary Culture
John Gatta

Our Lady of the Exile
Diasporic Religion at a Cuban Catholic
    Shrine in Miami
Thomas A. Tweed

Taking Heaven by Storm
Methodism and the Rise of Popular
    Christianity in America
John H. Wigger

Encounters with God
An Approach to the Theology of
    Jonathan Edwards
Michael J. McClymond

*Evangelicals and Science in Historical
    Perspective*
Edited by David N. Livingstone,
    D. G. Hart and Mark A. Noll

*Methodism and the Southern Mind,
    1770–1810*
Cynthia Lynn Lyerly

Princeton in the Nation's Service
Religious Ideals and Educational Practice,
    1868–1928
P. C. Kemeny

Church People in the Struggle
The National Council of Churches and the
    Black Freedom Movement, 1950–1970
James F. Findlay Jr.

Tenacious of their Liberties
The Congregationalists in Colonial
    Massachusetts
James F. Cooper Jr.

Nothing but Christ
Rufus Anderson and the Ideology of
    Protestant Foreign Missions
Paul William Harris

The Gospel Working Up

Progress and the Pulpit in
Nineteenth-Century Virginia

BETH BARTON SCHWEIGER

New York   Oxford

Oxford University Press

2000

Oxford University Press

Oxford   New York
Athens   Auckland   Bangkok   Bogotá   Buenos Aires   Calcutta
Cape Town   Chennai   Dar es Salaam   Delhi   Florence   Hong Kong   Istanbul
Karachi   Kuala Lumpar   Madrid   Melbourne   Mexico City   Mumbai
Nairobi   Paris   São Paulo   Singapore   Taipei   Tokyo   Toronto   Warsaw

and associated companies in
Berlin   Ibadan

Copyright © 2000 by Beth Barton Schweiger

Published by Oxford University Press, Inc.
198 Madison Avenue, New York, New York 10016

Oxford is a registered trademark of Oxford University Press

Library of Congress Cataloging-in-Publication Data
Schweiger, Beth Barton.
The gospel working up : progress and the pulpit in
nineteenth-century Virginia / Beth Barton Schweiger.
p.   cm. — (Religion in America series)
ISBN 0-19-511195-8
1. Virginia—Church history—19th century.   2. Baptists—Virginia—
Clergy—History—19th century.   3. Methodist Church—Virginia—
Clergy—History—19th century.   I. Title.   II. Series: Religion in
America series (Oxford University Press) 13.
BR555.V8S38   2000
277.55'081—dc21   99-17992

1 3 5 7 9 8 6 4 2
Printed in the United States of America
on acid-free paper

to Tom,

and in memory of Kevin,

who did not go gentle

Preface

"Up" may be the wrong direction.

—*Wendell Berry*

The renowned nineteenth-century evangelist Sam Jones's grandmother read the Bible through thirty-seven times on her knees. In Flannery O'Connor's view, the South—rural, small town, and city—was "made up of descendants of old ladies like her. You don't shake off their influence in even several generations." I began this book in the belief that Sam Jones's grandmother experienced something about the South that is missing in its histories. And in studying the sources, I found that what we know about the mystery and manners of Southern religion we have learned more from writers like O'Connor than from historians.

This book describes one of the main religious manners of the nineteenth-century South. The Gospel "worked up"—that is, converts thought it improved everything it touched. They believed that it worked up mysteriously of itself, like a physical principle. True religion not only brought progress, it was the main source of progress in their world—spiritual, moral, and material—and it did not encourage converts to distinguish between the three. But the Gospel "worked up" in another way. It stirred people to act. The men and women in this study worked very hard. Though they considered their work "Southern," like most other Americans they never asked whether "up" was the right direction.

The goal of their work was not the top of society. Their aspirations had clear limits, mainly because they succeeded so well. By the end of the century, church leaders were largely satisfied with their own progress up and out of the fields. Their main worry was over the rural rank and file they left behind.

Nor did pastors work up together. The nineteenth-century pastorate embraced a variety of men and motives. It hinged on negotiation—between themselves and those in the pew. Clerical authority in the South was fraught with tension. It required constant vigilance in congregations where the boundaries between leader and people were permeable. This is not a story of institutional religion versus popular religion, priests versus people. Instead, it is a story of popular institutions headed by pastors who wielded an authority rooted in consensus. Many in the pew shared pastors' belief in religion as progress, but not all pastors had equal influence in the institutional church. Power both within the larger denomination and within individual congregations was fluid in ways that disturbed these leaders, who strove for order and stability in their churches and in their own professional lives.

The belief in religion as progress brought instability beyond dividing white pastors and congregations. It also widened the breach between already estranged white and black Protestants. The very success of the Gospel among slaves and free blacks—for whom, most whites were convinced, religion could bring neither social, intellectual, nor material progress—raised troubling questions among those for whom racial inequality was just as firm a principle as progressive religion. Ironically, white Southern preachers became the victims of their own success. By the end of the century, the wealthy denominations that they believed would widen their authority in Southern society only limited it. Pastors found that they administered increasingly insular bureaucracies that choked off their influence in society at large.

Much that is important about religion in the South does not appear in these pages. I have not fully explored how religion may have shaped the aspirations of African-Americans or women. The growth of religious institutions on both sides of the color line shows, as so many things in Southern life do, how black and white Southerners moved in the same direction separately. That religion was a critical source of aspiration for Southerners of all races, and that it moved them in the same direction, is a point for further study. Although the male clerical profession gained a new, more systematic kind of control in religious life, women (who were two-thirds of the congregations) and what they understood to be "women's concerns" increasingly defined the terms of that control. A fuller understanding of how these changes affected women and how women shaped their churches awaits further study. Other Protestant traditions—particularly the Presbyterian and Episcopalian—were, of course, crucial to the religious culture of the South. But their generally higher social status meant that they were not as eager to better themselves as the Methodists and Baptists I have studied here.

It is a genuine pleasure to thank the many people who have helped me with this book. My research was supported by the Corcoran Department of History at the University of Virginia, the Congregational History Project of the Divinity School at the University of Chicago, the Institute for the Study of American Evangelicals at Wheaton College, and the Pew Program in Religion and American History at Yale University.

I relied on the diligence and expertise of archivists and librarians at Alderman Library of the University of Virginia, McGraw-Page Library at Randolph-Macon College, the Virginia Baptist Historical Society and Boatwright Memorial Library at the University of Richmond, the Virginia Historical Society, the Library of Virginia, the Southern Historical Collection at the University of North Carolina, William Smith Morton Library at Union Theological Seminary of Virginia, and Ferrum College.

Edward L. Ayers was an exemplary mentor over the long course of this study, and he has seen it through with grace and good cheer. I am grateful for the exacting standards of humane scholarship he set for me from the beginning. Many friends and colleagues generously read and commented on conference papers and drafts: Donald G. Mathews, Ted Ownby, Janette Thomas Greenwood, John C. Willis, Lawrence Hartzell, Gaines Foster, Bill J. Leonard, Samuel S. Hill, Samuel C. Shepherd, Robert D. Cross, Joseph F. Kett, James Davison Hunter, Catherine O'Brion, Harry S. Stout, Eugene D. Genovese, Lendol Calder, Timothy Hall, Anne Loveland, James O. Farmer, Charles Reagan Wilson, and David G. Hackett.

I am grateful for conversation and correspondence with E. Brooks Holifield, R. Stephen Warner, John Boles, Mark Noll, William A. Link, Robert M. Calhoon, John Quist, Anne Rubin, Bertram Wyatt-Brown, Daniel Stowell, Jewel Spangler, Briane Turley, Gregory A. Wills, Michael O'Brien, Steven M. Stowe, David Moltke-Hansen, Daniel Woods, and the historians' seminar of the Young Scholars in American Religion at the University of Notre Dame— Karin Gedge, Phil Gleason, Eugene McCarraher, Linda Przybyszewski, Kathleen Riley, James Treat, Roberto Trevino, Beth Wenger, and David Yoo.

A gifted and kind cohort of historians who make their homes in Richmond or who did research here have offered conversation and encouragement at critical times. I thank Hampton Carey, Peter Carmichael, Michael Fellman, Tony Iaccarino, Gregg D. Kimball, John Kneebone, Blair A. Pogue, Brent Tarter, and Sandy Treadway.

I have my grandparents, John Allen and Edna Gist Barton, and my parents, John Allen and Patricia Lawshe Barton, to thank for Central Texas tombstones and George Washington's dentures. Their insistence that the past matters took deep root and has borne fruit in this work. Mitchell Snay, Tatiana van Riemsdijk, and Paul Harvey amiably plowed through large chunks of this study in amazingly short time and offered both practical advice and enthusiasm. Suzanne Wolk edited the manuscript, and it is much better for her exacting care. Cynthia A. Read and MaryBeth Branigan of Oxford University Press have been skilled guides through the perils of publishing.

I met Kurt Berends in the final stages of this work, but his friendship and expertise have proven invaluable. David L. Chappell has proven his mettle mainly through his relentless reading of what I have written. Mary McLaughlin has helped me to see differently. Elisabeth W. Sommer has been unfailingly interested in my ideas for many years, and I have benefited much from her knowledge, encouragement, and friendship. Elizabeth Kurtz Lynch provided clean linens, hot coffee, and regular updates on her own work on Susanna Wesley, in addition to her uncommon good sense about the past and many other things.

Thomas A. J. Schweiger has lived with this book from its beginning and has been the bedrock supporting it in so many loving ways. Margaret Eleanor has lived with this book from *her* beginning and has been a stumbling block in its path, to my great joy. Kevin M. Wilson told me that I would write a book long before the idea had occurred to me or to anyone else. I am indebted to his astonishing vision, and I trust that he would be pleased with what I have done.

B. B. S.
Richmond, Virginia

March 1999

Contents

Introduction: Religion in the
    Nineteenth-Century South 3

ONE   Country Preachers 11

TWO   City Pastors 35

THREE   Reading, Writing, and Religion 55

FOUR   Sectionalism and the Rise of Denominations 77

FIVE   Pastors and Soldiers 91

SIX   Reconstructing Religion 109

SEVEN   The Ministerial Profession 129

EIGHT   A Call to Order 149

NINE   The Divided Mind of New South Pastors 171

Epilogue: Religion and Progress in the
Nineteenth-Century South   195

Appendix: A Note on Sources and Methods   197

Notes   209

Selected Bibliography   245

Index   257

THE GOSPEL WORKING UP

Introduction

Religion in the
Nineteenth-Century South

In 1836, the self-educated son of a Virginia overseer received a call to First Baptist Church in Richmond. Jeremiah Jeter's congregation soon moved into an elegant Greek Revival church designed by the architect of the addition to the U.S. Capitol. Jeter's position in Richmond society led him to fault his wife for her plain dress, telling her it stung his pride for her to appear in public in dress "out of keeping with her position." The style of his new life bred open distaste for the simple religious practices of his youth. After less than a decade in Richmond, he visited several "country meetings" and publicly proclaimed his great disappointment in them as "one accustomed to the almost perfect order of city meetings."[1]

Almost forty years later, another young pastor moved to the same city to head one of its leading Methodist congregations. Son of a Mississippi farmer, Samuel Steel came from Charlottesville, where he had served briefly as chaplain at the University of Virginia. The twenty-five-year-old pastor immodestly declared in 1875 that there was "already enough romance in my life to make a thrilling tale." Just five years earlier, he exulted, he had been a "regular field hand, plowing and sweating in the hot cornfields." Now he was the "pastor of the largest and finest of our city churches, with my life, my associations, my tastes, my all, completely changed."[2]

The ranks of the nineteenth-century ministry were filled with young men who left their fathers' fields and workshops to find an opportunity for self-improvement in the clerical profession. Although neither Jeter nor Steel ever became particularly well known outside a small group of peers, their lives paralleled those of many nineteenth-century Southern pastors who found a place among the professional classes.

To a greater extent than historians have acknowledged, men like Jeter and Steel succeeded in changing the associations and tastes of congregations across the South. The possibilities of progress, achieved by an ancient faith channeled into new bureaucratic forms, defined the work of Baptist and Methodist pastors in the South throughout the nineteenth century. Their vision of spiritual, social, and material improvement was inspired by a faith in progress, and they energetically built their denominations as shrines to the possible, rather than to the past. Their God was an innovator and their churches changed the face of the nineteenth-century South.

Historians, however, have not considered Southern pastors or their churches on these terms. Viewed as bastions of premodern and antimodern sentiment, churches have figured in Southern history as havens of old-time religion for those fleeing the clatter of modern life. Whereas scholars have regarded Protestant Christianity to be a source of innovation in the lives of Americans in other regions of the country, they have interpreted Southern Protestantism largely as a conserving—even reactionary—element of Southern society and culture. In light of this, they have argued that religion unified the South. Indeed, the story of white "Southern evangelicalism" has long provided one of the primary explanations for why this varied and conflicted region hung together during the Civil War.

Focusing on religion through the lens of proslavery Christianity, Confederate nationalism, and the Lost Cause, historians have portrayed white evangelical churches as captives of their culture, mired in consensus, and doggedly withstanding even the most aggressive assaults of modernity. Life in the South, scholars have argued, was on simpler terms than in the North, its society not so complex. While nineteenth-century Northern Protestantism spurred the growth of industrial capitalism, we are told, Southern Protestant belief and practice were grounded in a peculiarly traditionalist, reactionary message. Scholars on both sides of the furious debate over whether the antebellum South participated reluctantly, or at all, in the market revolution, have simply assumed that religion resisted change and thwarted innovation on all fronts. According to this view, pastors and proslavery Christianity foiled capitalism and secularization at once, while planters looked on approvingly. Religious leaders and institutions, then, maintained the South as a sacred society throughout the nineteenth century.[3]

The story of religion in the South, as in the rest of nineteenth- century America, was far more nuanced than this stark choice between modernity and tradition suggests. The continuing and even growing influence of religion in the late twentieth century has discredited the view that modernization inevitably secularizes and hence that traditional societies inevitably remain religious. Instead, scholars have argued that modern life itself creates situations where traditional religious belief and institutions can thrive.[4] Religion flourished in the nineteenth-century South, as it did in the rest of the United States, for reasons far more complex than a simple distaste for modernity and industrial capitalism. Indeed, Protestant belief bloomed most furiously in the New South, creating the Bible Belt in a place and time when the region was most deeply affected by industrialization and urbanization.[5]

The social and cultural context of Southern religious life changed enormously over the course of the nineteenth century, but it did so in the context of Southerners' abiding ambivalence about change. In the South, as in the nation as a whole, Protestants embraced some modern ideas and forms even as they rejected others. Many Southern Protestants displayed apprehension about liberal theology that bore no relation to their embrace of modern bureaucratic methods. The assumptions and structures of both white and black institutional Protestantism in the nineteenth-century South were distinctly modern.[6] The professional values and aspirations of the clergy, as well as the sprawling denominational bureaucracies they created, bespeak a reverence for efficiency, innovation, and social mobility. Southern pastors built denominational bureaucracies that challenged the efficiency, wealth, and size of those in the North even before the Civil War. They evangelized the nineteenth-century South through organization, printing presses, strategic planning, and settled institutions, rather than through the revival preaching long hailed by historians.

The story told here differs from other approaches to nineteenth-century Southern religion in other ways as well. Scholars have stressed both consensus among white Protestants and continuity in their story after they formally embraced slavery early in the nineteenth century. The majority of white Protestants, Samuel S. Hill and others have argued, languished in "cultural captivity" from about the 1820s until the mid-twentieth century.[7] While Southern historians have created a rich and sophisticated literature rooted in debates about whether and how deeply emancipation and Confederate defeat changed old patterns of Southern life, few have disputed the continuity of religious belief and practice.[8]

This study tries to recover a sense of the conversation that occurred between religion, culture, and society in nineteenth-century Virginia. The search for the roots of Southern injustice has led, with good reason, to white churches. But proslavery Christianity and religion's role in building Confederate nationalism and in sustaining the Lost Cause have overshadowed the very issues of religious life that pastors and those in their congregations held most dear. It is well that historians have developed a sophisticated critique of a religious culture that was often blind to its own limitations, especially on racial issues. But too often inquiries into Southern religious life have been narrowed to a single question: why did the white Southern church fail? Southern religion has borne a peculiar moral burden in historical scholarship that has prevented the imaginative study it deserves, and that has stripped religious people and their institutions of agency in Southern history.[9] This study begins not with questions about these churches' failure, but rather by asking simply how did they work?

In a region virtually barren of the schoolhouses in which generations of Northern children learned the arts of democracy and respectability, churches were the schools of the South for a long stretch of the nineteenth century. In worship services and revivals, Sunday schools, sewing circles, deacons' meet-

ings, and prayer groups, nineteenth-century Southerners learned and practiced the social manners, values, and aspirations that defined the lives of the
professional and mercantile classes and those who aspired to them. Denominations linked cities and towns to the most remote rural areas, and they institutionalized the conviction that Christianity elevated manners, morals, and
tastes. James Taylor, the preacher son of an immigrant cabinetmaker, "loved
to see how the Gospel worked up—improving men's circumstances and in
every respect elevating their character."[10]

Interest in such matters among Virginia pastors and their congregations
was muted in earlier times. As Rhys Isaac and others have shown, eighteenth-
century dissenters embraced a style that was a conscious counterpoint to that
of the Anglican gentry. The defining characteristic of eighteenth-century
Methodist and Baptist congregational life was its alienation from the world.
By the first decades of the nineteenth century, however, Methodists and Baptists began to recast the social customs of their belief, as the appeal of alienation from society was replaced by their desire to influence it.[11]

This book traces the long transformation of the social customs of belief
from alienation to influence through the experience of Southern Methodist
and Baptist clergy. Pastors were particularly sensitive to what Nathan O.
Hatch has called the "allure of respectability." They transformed themselves
from self-educated stump-speaking revivalists early in the century into professionals who valued seminary degrees and polished pulpits. In a society devoted primarily to agriculture, they made the pastorate an avenue of social
mobility. It attracted young men who turned to self-improvement in their
search for a way off the farm. That very few men won posts that could match
their aspirations did not hinder the profession's bent toward respectability. The
poverty and isolation of many rural congregations even at the end of the century only strengthened pastors' resolve to remake them.[12]

Education and denomination building lay at the heart of this professional
ethos. Once he discovered his calling to preach, a young man's first desire was
to get an education. Early in the century, this often meant self-education or
an informal apprenticeship to an older pastor. By the 1830s, Virginia Methodists and Baptists had established colleges to educate their pastors. These
were not primarily schools of theology, which most ministers believed was best
learned directly from the Scriptures, but places in which young ministers
might learn the genteel literary arts. Many aspiring young ministers scrimped
and saved their way into these schools. More than half of the young men
ordained in the missionary Baptist and Southern Methodist churches of Virginia in the 1850s had received some college training, a level that would be
sustained for the rest of the century.

Along with education, the denomination defined the clerical profession.
From his decision to enter the pulpit until ill health or old age forced his
retirement, a pastor was surrounded by men who pledged loyalty to a denominational tradition. They followed one another's successes and failures, shared
ideas about how to go about their work, encouraged one another through
letters and visits, and sometimes quarreled bitterly.

If Southern pastors generally denounced modernism and liberalism in theology, in their denominations they created a religious bureaucracy that exalted organization and efficiency. These bureaucracies challenged the efficiency, wealth, and size of those in the North. Southern pastors filled pages of their publications with scorn for the old-fashioned and praise for new organizational strategies; they hungered after innovation and progress with every committee meeting and each new brick church. By the end of the century, the connectional work of the denomination so overshadowed the life of individual congregations that some pastors felt inclined to defend their very existence. Their language often betrays their sense that congregations had become, more than anything else, a means to the larger end of denomination building.

Education and denomination building transformed religious life for those in the pews as well. The clergy's long love affair with education shifted the focus of religious experience from the camp meeting to the classroom, eroding the importance of revivalism, particularly for the middle class. Churchgoers' reluctance to support public education after the Civil War only underscored their stubborn conviction that education was properly a religious endeavor. They contributed millions of dollars to raise and sustain denominational schools and colleges at the same time that they spurned tax-supported public schools.

Like education, the bureaucratization of religious life involved every church member, many of whom enthusiastically supported new committees and programs. These bureaucracies lay at the heart of efforts to create a religiously inspired social consensus in the postwar South. The denomination eroded the localism that had characterized antebellum religious life and gave the laity a leading part in denominational works of religious benevolence. Women in particular benefited from the new expanded bureaucracy. Traditional limits on women's leadership in congregations were discarded as they assumed a public role in denominational committees and agencies. Through this growing network of denominational agencies, church members from the most isolated Virginia communities learned and practiced habits of organization that anticipated the reforms of the Progressive era.

Like other Americans, nineteenth-century Southerners lived under the "rule of religion" whether or not they participated in the organized church.[13] The letters and diaries that Virginians left behind suggest that church was one of the most durable institutions in their lives. Whether out of conviction, convention, or curiosity, many rarely missed a Sunday preaching.

Religion's authority was not a faceless one; in communities across the South, it dwelt in the person of the local preacher. He deeply affected both the private convictions and public expressions of their faith. The scrutiny, loyalty, and criticism pastors aroused rivaled that paid to elected officeholders. Indeed, throughout the century, Virginians identified the local clergyman as a public figure. They gossiped about his family life and criticized his sermons. They "pounded" him annually, bringing barrels of flour, salt pork, and dried apples to his home on Christmas Day. They quarreled and parted with kin and lifelong friends over his appointment. They bought him a new frock coat, invited him for Sunday dinner, and boarded him in their homes for years at a time. They sent for him when their children were sick and dying, and he sat up with grieving families far into the night.[14]

Because most Southern clergymen publicly supported slavery, secession, and the Civil War, an understanding of their role is particularly important to interpretations of the region's, and the nation's, history. Yet few social historians of either North or South have taken up the nineteenth-century clergy, and none has published a social history of the ministry that spans the Civil War. Southern historians have generally focused their attention on religion in the Old South. Whether concerned with the Old or the New South, scholars have rarely ventured beyond the published works of a few well-known men. The Southern clergyman's popular image rests somewhere between that of an ill-educated demagogue and a puppet of the planter elite.[15]

What follows is a history of three generations of Baptist and Methodist clergymen and, through them, of their congregations and communities. These eight hundred pastors baptized, married, and buried three-fourths of all Virginia church members and preached to even greater numbers who attended services on a regular basis between the Second Great Awakening and the beginning of the twentieth century. They encompass the whole spectrum of the clerical profession, from those who labored and died in obscurity to those who gained a national reputation.

The story of Virginia pastors is crucial to the story of pastors across the South and the nation. Virginia's religious folkways became those of the early nineteenth-century American frontier. If westward migration hindered growth in church membership for a time, it also multiplied Virginia's influence. By 1850, almost 400,000 Virginians were living in other states. Virginia Baptists, Methodists, Presbyterians, and Quakers settled Indiana, Kentucky, Ohio, Missouri, Mississippi, Alabama, Louisiana, Texas, and Arkansas. Virginia clergymen, too, moved west. In the old Southwest alone, Virginia supplied almost half of the ministers between 1780 and 1830.[16]

These eight hundred pastors provide one angle of vision on the changes in nineteenth-century Southern life. As scholars have lately insisted, there were many Souths. There were many churches and many clergies as well. Virginia clergymen were divided along lines of class, income, educational background, and doctrine. The sons of yeomen, overseers, merchants, lawyers, and planters, they preached in piedmont, town, and plantation districts to the daughters and sons of slaves, planters, industrialists, free blacks, and yeoman farmers. They were united only in their advocacy of Protestant Christianity and their firm opposition to sin, and they often disagreed on how to define both of these. Neither did they think of themselves as representatives of something that historians have labeled "Southern evangelicalism," a phrase that they have so often invoked in such varied contexts that it has lost any meaning.

"Southern evangelical" refers to an imaginary, homogeneous group that would have been a mystery to the subjects of this study. It is avoided in the pages that follow.

This study traces several themes through the lives and careers of these three generations of pastors. Chapter 1 begins with the rural church, describing the local character of antebellum religious life and the central role of the congregation in choosing pastors. Chapter 2 contrasts the rural experience with that of the antebellum urban clergy and shows how the allure of respectability and upward mobility influenced the configuration of city churches both socially and spiritually. Urban pastors saw education as a critical part of their profession and mission. Chapter 3 discusses the central role of literacy and education in early denomination building. Chapter 4 addresses the growing prominence of the denomination after the Methodist and Baptist schisms of the 1840s dramatically accelerated denominational growth and gave Southern clergymen a platform from which to assert a broad influence on public life. The Civil War offered an unparalleled opportunity for Southern clergy to expand their denominations to accomplish what they viewed as the chief task of the wartime church: evangelization of the army. Chapter 5 explores their service as chaplains and examines the role of denominations in evangelization of the army, particularly through print. After the war, pastors expected religion to create social consensus in the postwar South. The most striking and immediate result of the war, the departure of blacks from their churches, had surprisingly little impact on the direction of their thinking, even if it represented a tremendous loss of authority in Southern society. Characteristically, pastors turned to education to bolster their influence, and they applied their energies to charitable education for Confederate veterans and orphans. Chapter 7 examines the clergy's professional status in the New South and the new meaning of their salaries. One of the most important changes in postwar religious life was the new role of the laity in denominational benevolence. City churches created this movement, but rural congregations eagerly took up the spirit of connectional work in an effort to throw off provincialism in the New South. Chapter 8 examines how women, in particular, benefited from this new lay authority and expanded their influence in denominational committees even as their leadership role in congregations continued to be restricted. Their stunning success in foreign missions was the best example of how the denomination empowered the laity and compromised the importance of the local congregation. Chapter 9 examines the rise of a new generation of pastors in the 1880s. These pastors had an ever larger and wealthier bureaucracy to oversee, but the denominational empire they administered was an increasingly insular one. Ironically, it diminished their authority outside of their churches. Many Virginians viewed denominational interests as narrow and irrelevant, and ambitious clergy found a new outlet for their energies in the temperance and Southern progressive movements.[17]

CHAPTER ONE

Country Preachers

When Noah Carlton Baldwin took up a pen in 1850 to begin his diary, he turned to the first page and wrote an account of his conversion twelve years earlier. Although twenty-one years old at the time, Baldwin considered it the day that his life began. "At length, my sleepy soul was awakened in a most powerful manner to its sense of danger," he wrote.

> I saw myself instantaneously a guilty and justly condemned sinner . . . [and] soon after this my mind was seriously impressed with the belief that it was my duty to preach Jesus Christ to sinners. But from [the] discharge of this duty I shrank, under the burden of my ignorance and inability. . . . At length however after many painful struggles I consented in my mind to spend my time and tallents, the remnant of my days for him who had done so much for me. As soon as I consented in my mind . . . I felt a sensible change in my feelings, and was again enabled in some degree to rejoice in Jesus.

Baldwin wrote almost daily in his diary until his death in 1903, recording almost every significant event in his life as a pastor. Four months after his conversion in 1838, he preached his first sermon. Soon he moved with his wife into the antimission stronghold of the Virginia mountains, where he preached a missionary Baptist message for more than sixty years. He worked in a particularly contentious and remote area, without recognition from his peers. Throughout his career, Baldwin suffered what he called "unbrotherly personal treatment" for his doctrinal views. Three of his churches dismissed him over doctrinal controversies, and he once narrowly escaped tarring and feathering. His financial fortunes changed virtually overnight, he saw his farm and house burned to the ground by Union troops, and he buried three of his four wives.[1]

Yet Baldwin's sense of calling never wavered. He was not a preacher by his own choice, he said, but because he had been compelled to obey God's calling. By the age of seventy-seven, bruised and weary from the work, he was counting the costs of that obedience. He had drawn down the initial reserves of energy and enthusiasm he had found in his conversion and baptism. "I now confess humbly before my maker that if I had my life to live over and were left to myself to make a choice of a profession, I never would choose the *office and responsibilities* of a pastor," he wrote in 1894. Yet his frustration did not weaken his conviction that he had lived that life in reply to God's call.[2]

Like Baldwin, most men who took up preaching in nineteenth-century Virginia hungered for a challenge bigger than keeping the furrows straight as they followed a plow. Some of their accounts record their entrance into the ministry against considerable odds, and nearly all testify to a life of hardship after they did so. Young and often poor, some entered the ministry against family advice or by abandoning a more lucrative career. Nineteenth-century Baptist and Methodist preachers earned little money, traveled many lonely miles to preach, and, like Noah Baldwin, usually won little recognition for their lives of hardship. Neither could they easily give up their calling if they became discouraged or displayed a lack of ability or motivation for the work. Preachers were bound to the office, and unless forced to leave the pulpit in disgrace, one who became a preacher in antebellum Virginia would be a preacher for the rest of his life.[3]

Yet preaching was more than a calling. Even as he acknowledged it was rooted in the call of God, Baldwin called preaching a "profession." Accepting the call had temporal consequences. The call determined where Baldwin lived, whom he married, his financial fortunes, and how he spent his evenings. It made him good friends and bitter enemies. It influenced his political views, first as a Whig and later as a Readjuster. It made him an ardent supporter of temperance and an ardent opponent of abstinence, and to the day he died he quietly indulged in his morning toddy. It encouraged his love of music, giving him a huge repertoire of hymns to play on his fiddle and a reason to dance his jigs. His decision to become a Baptist, rooted in his conviction that infant baptism was in error, broke his family's long attachment to the Methodist church, and probably left troubled relations in its wake. Likewise, his ardent support of missionary societies and Sunday schools cost him dearly in a region infused with antimission spirit. Preaching cast the life and fortunes of Noah Baldwin just as it did for hundreds of men across nineteenth-century Virginia.[4]

Noah Baldwin's native state stretched from the close backwaters of the Tidewater's Northern Neck to the clearer air and soaring heights of his own mountainous southwest.[5] Virginia lay north of the great Southern cotton belt, and its agriculture was more diversified than that of the states of the Deep South. Through the century, tobacco dwindled and grain, especially wheat and rye, took its place. An important producer of fruit and livestock, Virginia also boasted the largest manufacturing sector of any Southern state by the 1850s.

This diversified economy made Virginia much like other states of the mid-Atlantic region. The difference was slavery. Traditional plantation slavery endured in the eastern Tidewater region and increasingly pushed into the Southside, where labor-intensive cultivation of tobacco flourished. Yet Virginians worked in a staggering variety of settings, from manufacturing to oystering and fishing.

The profits of slavery made Virginia overwhelmingly rural for the span of the nineteenth century. In 1850, just 9 percent of all Virginians, white and black, slave and free, made their homes in one of the thirty-four towns and cities in the state. Only four of these cities—Richmond, Norfolk, Petersburg, and Wheeling—had more than ten thousand inhabitants, and eleven of the total had fewer than a thousand. Half of these thirty-four "cities" were in the region that later became West Virginia.[6]

After Nat Turner's rebellion of 1831, Virginians' uneasy embrace of slavery became more self-conscious. Nervous legislators passed measures to restrict slaves' movement and their ability to gather and to read. In the same decade, economic decline began to mark the state with empty fields and unkempt and abandoned houses, particularly in the long-cultivated region of the Tidewater, where tobacco had long since exhausted the soils.

Economic malaise was matched by political decline, as Virginians streamed into the trans-Appalachian west, taking the state's political influence with them. Representation in Congress dwindled as the rate of population growth fell behind other states. Antebellum Virginia politics seethed with controversy as the state split into eastern and western factions. White easterners enjoyed the fruits of slavery and wrote policies that supported it while westerners with few slaves agitated for equal representation and constitutional reform.

Historians have characterized antebellum Virginia as a place gripped by nostalgia, its leaders yearning for the mythic influence of the Revolutionary generation. According to this view, Virginians took a stance later to be embraced by the South as a whole, "that of a conscious and declining minority within a young and growing nation."[7] The fortunes of Baptists and Methodists in antebellum Virginia, however, followed a strikingly different pattern. If Virginia gentry fretted about the state's declining influence, preachers like Baldwin were not inclined to notice. Their angle of vision highlighted growth and success rather than dissipation and decline. Methodist and Baptist denominational organizations flourished, particularly during the 1850s, instilling in their leaders a sense of achievement and progress.

Virginia had a long history of influence in the Methodist and Baptist traditions in the United States, and that influence grew in the early nineteenth century. This was particularly true of Methodists. If "American Methodism developed in the South and has had a Southern accent ever since," then that accent resonated in the nineteenth century with the peculiar vowels of Tidewater Virginia. Virginia Methodists' early cooperation with the evangelical wing of the Anglican Church partly accounted for its prominence in the Methodist movement. Francis Asbury, later the first American bishop, traveled a Virginia circuit for the first time in 1775. By 1800, Virginia had more Methodists than any other state. Western migration and sectarian splits combined to slow membership growth, but during the 1840s Virginia's Methodist membership grew at a faster rate than the state's population—more than *three times* faster between 1845 and 1859.[8]

Virginia also occupied a central place in Baptist history. Although fiercely committed to the independence of their churches, Baptists joined together in the cause of foreign missions, and early missionaries had intimate ties with Virginia. Several Virginians went to Siam or China. Luther Rice, an early missionary in India, developed a close relationship with Richmond Baptists, and black Virginians such as Lott Carey took a leading role in early missionary work in Africa. Like the Methodists, Baptist church membership far outpaced state population growth.[9]

By 1850, Methodists and Baptists overwhelmed their closest competitors, the Presbyterians and Episcopalians: for every Virginian who belonged to an Episcopal or Presbyterian congregation, four belonged to a Methodist or Baptist congregation. Baptists and Methodists were about 13 percent of the state's population overall. Although historians have made much of the success of these denominations on the antebellum frontier, in 1850 their strength in Virginia remained in the long-settled areas east of the Blue Ridge Mountains. Baptists accounted for 12 percent of the state population in the Tidewater, 8 percent in the Piedmont, and only 3 percent in the west (see Appendix, Table 1).

Virginia also gave birth to several of the tumultuous sectarian rivalries of the antebellum period. Alexander Campbell, whose followers later formed the Christian Church, was a charismatic leader and resident of what later became West Virginia. The mountains of southwest Virginia were an important center of the antimissionary Baptist movement. Methodists, too, experienced a schism sparked by Virginia leadership. James O'Kelly, who traveled circuits in Southside Virginia and North Carolina, initiated a serious challenge to the Methodist episcopacy with his Republican Methodist movement in 1792.[10]

Antebellum Baptists and Methodists confirmed Virginia's continuing importance by locating their denominational agencies and colleges there. Baptists established the Virginia Baptist Seminary and the Baptist Foreign Missions Board in Richmond, and American Methodists obtained a charter for their first permanent college, Randolph-Macon in Southside Virginia, in 1830. Also during the 1820s and 1830s, newspapers that would remain influential voices in the region throughout the century, the Baptist *Religious Herald* and Methodist *Richmond Christian Advocate*, began publishing in Richmond.

The rapid growth of antebellum Baptists and Methodists was rooted in their adaptation to the rural landscape of early America. From fewer than seventy thousand members nationally in 1800, Methodists grew to more than 1.1 million members in 1844. Baptists, meanwhile, grew by a factor of ten from 1776 to 1806, and they doubled their numbers again in the decade between 1802 and 1812.[11] Growth of both denominations in Virginia was comparable to that in the nation at large; while state population grew by one and a half times between 1810 and 1860, the number of Virginia Baptists tripled, and Virginia Methodists doubled (see Appendix, Table 2).

Historians have credited camp meetings and revivals for this astonishing rate of growth. These meetings did succeed overwhelmingly as a means of mass persuasion in the young nation's sparsely settled landscape. In the early 1840s alone, Virginia Baptists claimed that revivals brought in twenty thousand members over a 2-year period.[12] Denominational leaders shared responsibility for these neighborhood events, known to the faithful and irreligious alike by names such as "Protracted Meetings of the Big Preaching." These meetings were "protracted" because the harvest of souls they reaped often compelled the preachers to keep preaching. Revivals embodied a spontaneity that was as attractive to the pious as to the merely curious, who expected to witness spiritual revelations at these all-day meetings. Yet the fiery preaching could not entirely dim the appeal of the flesh. After long hours of preparation, churchwomen customarily served a huge noonday meal at one long table to their church family, friends, and strangers.

As the primary source of new members early in the century, revivals fashioned early rural congregations in their own image.[13] Young and old, wealthy and poor, slave and free—all attended revivals and church meetings and were baptized and welcomed into fellowship. Doctrinal convictions cut across social distinctions in the antebellum South as often as they reinforced them. With only one Baptist or Methodist congregation in each neighborhood, church congregations included all sorts of people, from planters to merchants' wives to yeomen to slaves, united by their doctrinal convictions. In virtually every church, women far outnumbered men.[14]

African-Americans, mostly women and children, crowded back pews, galleries, and churchyards across antebellum Virginia. Their place at the margins of worship services, whether they were slave or free, reflected their role in the official church life. Yet their growing and eventually overwhelming numbers in most congregations demanded the attention of white church leaders at the same time as the first angry cries of abolitionists arose in the North.

Race relations in antebellum congregations mirrored the controversy and contradiction, cruelty and kindness that characterized the relations of slavery generally. Former slaves sometimes recalled their preacher masters bitterly, remembering some as unconscionably cruel and others as hypocrites. "Marser daid now an' I ain' plannin' on meetin' him in heaven, neither," Armaci Adams recalled in the 1930s. "He were too wicked. Marse was an' ole Methodist preacher an' de las' time I seed 'im he was comin' in f'om a revival drunk." Interviews with former slaves are riddled with disdainful assessments of white preaching. They scorned the choice of "slaves, obey your masters" as the chief text of white sermonizing. Others spoke of white preachers and Christian masters with genuine affection, recognizing the ties that bound them, however tenuously, in the Kingdom of God.[15]

White pastors themselves were both reassured and troubled by growing numbers of black faces in their pews. They read these overwhelming numbers as a sign of the Gospel's success in their era, yet they also knew that African Americans sometimes mocked them. Horace Tonsler, born a slave in 1857, recalled that there was no room for slaves and free blacks in his neighborhood church, so they would gather under the trees outside to listen to the preacher through open windows. Every so often, Tonsler recalled, the preacher would stick his head out and yell something at those gathered outside. But instead of straining to hear his argument, they mocked the preacher. "Den sometimes ole nigger would git up outside an' start in to preachin' right along wid preacher Woodson. Softlike, of course, wid a lot of handwavin' an' twistin' of his mouth widdout makin' no noise. We would sit up an' listen to him an' laugh when he say just what the white preacher say."[16] The irreligious—both black and white—who used church meetings as an opportunity to socialize and to sell their wares displayed contempt for the preacher's authority and took comfort in their profits.

Necessity as well as choice dictated a simple style in churches in rural Virginia. Congregations worshiped together in old wooden houses or even in clearings in the woods, and they baptized new members on muddy creek banks. Jeremiah Jeter described the early antebellum churches in his Bedford County neighborhood as "built of log or framed, without plastering, ceiling or stoves, fitted merely as shelters from sun and rain." Many buildings were so poor that they could not accommodate winter meetings, forcing worshipers to gather in private homes. In the 1850s, many rural churches remained primitive. Frederick Law Olmstead described a rural Virginia meeting house with a crude shed near the entrance where outdoor services were held. Inside "was a square, unpainted pulpit and on the floor were rows of rude benches. The house was sufficiently lighted by crevices between the upper logs." Other congregations had neither the land nor the money to build even such a simple structure as this. They met in schoolhouses or churches of other denominations.[17]

If rural congregations could afford to build only rude log houses, they endowed these cramped, dark, and cold spaces with spiritual significance. All who attended learned to equate simplicity with spirituality. The gentry, too, acquiesced in the simple, even spartan, style of worship and community life. The deacon of a Northern Neck Baptist congregation served as commissioner in his county chancery, suggesting some wealth and social status. Yet in his church, "a plain, country congregation," "everything was done and conducted in cheap, simple style. There was no high-sounding organ, no hired choir, and no costly pulpit ornaments."[18] There is little evidence that the conversion of significant numbers of Virginia gentry in the early nineteenth century altered the simplicity of rural church life. Hard benches and cold feet discouraged shallow religious commitments. In their impulse to spiritualize simplicity, rural Virginians spiritualized the trials of their way of life.

Many of the young men ordained in the Methodist and Regular Baptist churches in the first half of the nineteenth century marked the beginning of their Christian lives in a revival meeting. There they experienced the intensity and intimacy of Christian community for the first time. Harvey and William Hatcher, grandsons of a Baptist preacher and sons of a slaveholder, grew up in Bedford County at the foot of the Blue Ridge in the 1840s. There they gained reputations as impious and boisterous young men. Harvey was known for his passion for hunting and riding. "We were twelve miles from the county seat, had mail once a week, and church once a month when the weather was good," William recalled. The two boys attended the neighborhood Sunday school but remembered it as "most unattractive; the teachers and scholars stammered through long chapters of the Bible, the prayers were long, and there was no singing."[19]

In the early 1850s, however, both experienced conversion together under the preaching of William Harris. The Hatcher boys had been reared in church, but still their conversion seemed to them starkly significant. "The old house was of wood, long and rather narrow," William Hatcher recalled. "The house was packed. . . . Elder Harris walked down from the pulpit. . . . He began in soft, gentle tones, but his heart was on fire and he rapidly kindled, and for half an hour he poured forth a torrent of eloquence that I have never heard equaled." Harris, known for his shoulder-length white hair, homespun dress, and pipe smoking, was not reported to be a gifted preacher. Yet he baptized more than thirty Virginia Baptist pastors in the antebellum period. During Harris's lifetime, Bedford County was the center of the Strawberry Baptist Association, a western stronghold of Baptist sentiment in Virginia.[20]

Rural pastors usually held a baptismal service every few months. On the appointed day, friends, family, and often the entire congregation gathered on the bank of a nearby stream. The Hatcher brothers were baptized along with eighteen other young men, probably all converts from the same revival. After the service, the company returned to the church, where Harris preached and the congregation sang hymns before extending the hand of Christian fellowship to the new members. "All came to us and bade us welcome among the Lord's saints," William Hatcher remembered. "And the pastor came also, and what delight beamed in his eye as he took his children in the Lord by the hand."

As the Hatcher brothers' experience suggests, baptism was a community ritual in the South. Those who observed this spiritual rite of passage reaffirmed their own baptismal vows even as the convert recited his or hers for the first time. "Let plenteous grace descend on those, Who hoping in thy word, This day have solemnly declared, That Jesus is their Lord," the congregation sang together, declaring that the Christian pilgrimage was not to be made alone.[21]

News of a conversion and baptism caught the attention of even those beyond the community of the saved. A change of heart, and presumably of habit, especially in one never reckoned to be so inclined, set friends and family buzzing. When the lawyer father of Herbert Bacon experienced conversion in 1845, a lively series of family letters commented on the event. "I was very much surprised to hear that your Pa had joined the church for when I last saw him I thought he had as little notion of doing such a thing as any person I ever saw," a cousin frankly wrote to Herbert, who himself would later be ordained. "I was much surprised at its being through the Methodists, knowing his great prejudice against that sect—I hope, however, he is indeed a *new man*," his aunt pointedly observed.[22]

If pastors shared the conversion experience with other Christians, the call to preach clearly set them apart. Sometimes brought on by months of soul searching or depression, sometimes by miracles, most pastors identified the call simply as a deeply felt conviction to preach the Gospel. It usually accompanied conversion, or followed soon after. Women, especially mothers, deeply influenced the piety and calling of many pastors. Walter Sawyer, a minister born to a North Carolina Methodist family in 1855, remembered that after he went on particularly raucous escapades with his five brothers, his mother "would take him into the parlor, and having shut the door, would kneel with him in fervent prayer." A mother's influence lingered after her death, as young men sometimes made deathbed promises to enter the ministry.[23]

If the means of hearing the call varied, there were patterns in antebellum Virginian conversion narratives that recalled those of Protestant ministers in other times and places. Convention dictated that the appropriate response to the call was fear, humility, and even denial. "The man who entertains just views of the Christian ministry shrinks from its responsibilities," a Baptist observed in 1840. Initially the young man felt himself unworthy of the task and was tormented at the prospect. After he resigned himself to preaching as a duty, however, doubts were dispelled and peace restored, often immediately.[24]

Conversion narratives recounted a private spiritual battle, but no man took an antebellum pulpit without the support of his elders. The Christian community called a pastor just as surely as God himself did. Young men entered the ministry only after being urged to do so by older Christians or other ministers. In their judgment of the young man's gifts, his elders tested his outward signs of calling such as prudence and tactfulness. In 1840, a Baptist suggested that the call would be evident in a young man who exhibited a desire for work, "attachment to the Redeemer," a praying spirit, a willingness to endure persecution, an aptitude for teaching, a knowledge of language, and an ability to communicate. The call to preach entailed both desire and ability. As one preacher explained to his son, "of the one *you* must be the judge—of the other—the *church*." If a young man did not receive the consent of his congregation, he either gave up his ambition to preach or left the church to join, or in some cases establish, another one.[25]

Congregational authority in judging a man's calling to preach underscores the importance of women in church life. Women's authority in the calling of a pastor was generally implicit rather than formalized. Yet that authority was real. Many congregations allowed women a vote *only* when calling a pastor, viewed as the most important decision of church life. When the church judged a prospective minister's gifts, women exercised a real, if limited, spiritual and social authority over male leadership.[26]

But men were more valuable church members than women were—largely because they were less likely to be church members. Strictures on women's formal leadership meant that the very survival of a congregation depended on a steady supply of pious and prudent white male leaders. The Christian community lavished attention on young male converts and, in many cases, brought considerable pressure on them to become church leaders, if not to preach. In a society steeped in the traditions of honor, and in which piety was conventionally judged to be a feminine trait, congregations prized young men. Throughout the nineteenth century, more than two-thirds of Southern church members were women. Yet their overwhelming presence sometimes threatened the very life of their churches. A dearth of men was often taken by pastors as a clear sign that a congregation should be dissolved. Baptist leader dissolved Pettsworth Church in Gloucester County in 1846, for example, because the church had only "two white male members, neither of whom were calculated to manage its concerns." Mathews Church, with two white male members, suffered the same fate. Ironically, the successful evangelization of Southern women and slaves threatened the very existence of their churches.[27]

The carefully preserved records of pastors' conversion and calling focus, not surprisingly, on the spiritual motivation for their decisions. But if preachers considered the call primarily a spiritual matter, they did not choose preaching in isolation from other considerations. Their accounts either leave out altogether or only vaguely suggest the rich social context of their decision: coming of age, family ambitions, a distaste for a father's profession, love of study, the desire to win the favor of a certain pious young lady, or a promise to a dying mother.

Conversion alone did not solve the central problem of a young man's life—his need to choose a vocation. With few exceptions, Virginia pastors experienced conversion in the context of coming of age. Most of those ordained in the nineteenth century experienced conversion when they were between 15 and 19 years old, and almost all prospective pastors experienced conversion by the age of 25 (see Appendix, Table 3).

Families customarily took an interest in a young man's choice of a career, and they carefully weighed the desirability of the ministry. As one man struggled with the decision to become a preacher, an aunt frankly told him she wanted him to become a "plain *clod hopper* [more] than anything else," but she knew that farming "would not meet your Papa's views, as he always wished you to be a professional character." R. N. Sledd, on the other hand, recalled that his father took his entry into the ministry very hard.[28]

Preaching rarely provided a steady income in antebellum Virginia, one reason that some parents may have discouraged their sons from taking the pulpit. Few men could hope to maintain a family on the meager salary paid by rural congregations. These modest salaries reflected the view that preaching was a calling, not a profession. While professional salaries represented the value of specialized knowledge, rural antebellum pastors did not expect their income to bear much relation to the value of their work. Only those rural pastors who inherited or married into wealth could expect a life free from financial cares.[29]

Yet young Virginians recognized advantages of the office other than financial reward. Many who entered the antebellum ministry did so with the blessing of their fathers, who were preachers themselves. The tendency of some Virginia clans to become identified with the ministry for several generations increased over the course of the nineteenth century. Where one-third of the men ordained before 1850 were pastors' sons, half were preachers' sons by the end of the century. At least twenty-eight father-son pairs appear among the pastors studied here, in addition to six families in which more than one brother became a pastor. Joseph E. Potts, ordained in 1853, saw all four of his sons ordained into the Methodist ministry. His brother, too was a pastor. At times, a pastor's interest in seeing his son take the pulpit eclipsed all other considerations. *"You must make a preacher,"* a senior Baptist pressed his son in 1860. "Think and pray and dream of it . . . and let it be *the one idea* of your life—but not for worldly end—Oh no! *Let it be to please the Master."*[30]

The sons of pastors grew up in homes ruled by piety and the rhythm of the church year. Children observed firsthand the trials of the ministry—calls in the middle of the night, disputes over doctrine and church policy that dissolved into personal quarrels, the often-demeaning dependence on the congregation for a salary. Yet they also knew its peculiar rewards—annual "poundings," when congregations showed their appreciation with barrels of food and clothing, the esteem in which preachers were often held, the security that grew out of pastors' assurance that their work was significant. Preachers' sons grew up with fathers who embodied a masculine piety in a society where religious sentiment was often associated with women. Their fathers also knew, often personally, professors and senior pastors who might smooth the young candidate's path.

If many young men followed their fathers into the pulpit, about one-third were the sons of farmers (see Appendix, Table 4). These young men were unfamiliar with the daily life and unwritten rules of the ministry. Their desire to preach represented a conscious break from the lives of their own fathers. This impulse may be traced in ministers' choice of a career before they began to preach. More than half of the pastors ordained in Virginia before 1861 were former teachers, while just 3 percent were the sons of teachers themselves. Whereas one-third were farmers' sons, fewer than 10 percent of antebellum ministers took up farming before they entered the ministry. These pastors abandoned the work of their farming and tradesmen fathers, choosing vocations like teaching, business, law, or printing before they entered the ministry (see Appendix, Table 5). The antebellum Southern pastorate often attracted young men who intended to make a living with their heads, not their hands.[31]

An aspiring minister's first obligation was to serve his own congregation. Church leaders deemed Sunday school teaching and administration, or visiting church members as appropriate tests of the call. Most important, leaders invited prospective pastors to "exhort" the congregation. Exhorters took the pulpit after the sermon to underscore the pastor's message. As a forum for informal and extemporaneous speaking, exhortation provided an opportunity to test a young man's ability to preach, as well as his success in persuading his audience to repent or to inspire religious feeling. Success at exhortation usually yielded an invitation to preach in earnest. Most young men delivered their first tentative sermons to congregations that included childhood friends and family. Edgar Pritchett remembered the stinging embarrassment that came from "preaching of the Gospel among the people . . . who are familiar with our past lives as sinners." When Benjamin Tennille gazed out from behind the pulpit for the first time, the terrified young man bolted down the aisle to his seat, tripping en route over a kneeling board, "like a blind horse over a heap of rocks amidst the unrestrained titters of the congregation."[32]

Church leaders scrutinized the young man's performance in these duties before allowing him to advance to a period of apprenticeship to an elder pastor. Methodists required a one- to two-year apprenticeship before ordination. Baptist preachers, too, began a period of junior ministry. These young helpers traveled with their elders, observing their work and doing simple tasks. Sometimes the experience proved trying. Lemuel Reed, a Methodist, recalled the indiscretion of his young partner of 1853. He "had plenty of cheek, was impulsive and heady and would fight if he had half a chance, talking of thrashing anyone who crossed his path." After spending a year with the young man, Reed declined to recommend him for ordination.[33]

Apprenticeship was the only formal preparation many antebellum ministers received. A tiny number traveled out of state to attend theological seminaries, but most viewed such intensive and specialized preparation as unnecessary. In their view, the Bible's meaning was largely self-evident and could be discovered by any Christian minister of average ability through careful study. Pastors did not belittle general education, however. Those who could afford to do so, or who won financial help from other church members, enrolled in local private academies or what Virginians called "old field schools"—the rare and rudimentary neighborhood schools. About one-third of the pastors ordained before 1850 attended college for at least a time, where they received a general education considered more than adequate for preaching (see Appendix, Table 6).

The first few years in the ministry determined to a large degree a minister's success. For conscientious young pastors, these were anxious years. They learned to compose and preach sermons, negotiate with lay leaders, arbitrate congregational disputes, travel long hours in the saddle, and make do with the meager salaries provided by their flocks.

Young pastors depended on the advice of their elders. In the tight-knit "brotherhood" of the ministry, personal connections proved invaluable. Older pastors scrutinized young licentiates for signs of promise, and competition for the best and most lucrative pulpits was fierce. If a preacher's speaking skills alone could not land him a fashionable church, he could usually depend on connections with key ministers or laymen for a good position. Often the pastor who baptized him became a lifelong friend and mentor. Friendships between these men, bound by the same calling, were often intense. Ministers routinely made pacts with their peers, promising that whoever survived the other would preach his funeral sermon. Yet the difficulties of ministerial life also tested such friendships. The disputes were sometimes vindictive, the wounds deep and lasting.[34]

Other relations proved more amenable. Courtship and marriage were part of nearly every young man's early career. Although elder ministers often discouraged a young man from marrying too early, most arrived at their first church determined to marry. Taking a congregation far from home became a singular opportunity to court a new group of young women, and many men married the daughters of senior colleagues or laymen.

The devout nineteenth-century marriage entailed both romantic love and practical considerations. A happy domestic life and a wife fully committed to her husband's calling were assets, both personal and professional. Pastors, like others, carefully considered marriage even while curious family members and friends showered them with advice. Like most Virginia bachelors, pastors sought financial resources, as well as physical and emotional comfort, from their wives.

Nineteenth-century wedding vows charged men to protect, love, and cherish their wives. Women promised to fulfill their calling as helpmeet and to submit to the man as the head of the family. Beyond these roles, however, lay the more critical spiritual dimension of marriage, its ability to nurture religious piety. But marriage could also be a stumbling block to the Christian life. Marital relationships were often more than carefully calculated obligations, and one danger of a particularly happy union was idolatry. "My fear is that I shall idolize my wife and give to her that devotion that is due God alone," one pastor worried a few weeks after his wedding.[35]

Over the course of the century, being a pastor's wife became a vocation in its own right. Manuals described in detail the qualifications, duties, trials, and rewards of marrying into the ministry. Thomas Sydnor proposed to Sarah Chapin in a sober and formal letter in 1838 in which he set out clear expectations of the companionate marriage many preachers and their wives enjoyed. "In soliciting your hand, Miss Sarah . . . it has been my object to seek an auxiliary in the work to which I hope to devote my life. . . . If I am faithful to Him whom I serve, my life must be a life of laborious effort. I ask you to be a coworker with me."[36]

The life of an itinerant preacher's wife was particularly difficult. Pastors rode the circuit for weeks at a time, and if they often lamented the necessity of separation, their sense of calling might temper their regrets. Long separations could be unbearably lonely and even life-threatening for women. In times of illness and pregnancy, they were forced to find companionship and help with parents, in-laws, and neighbors. Grave illness and even death came while husband and wife were separated, and many surviving letters between pastors and their wives reveal the sharp anxieties of separation. "Went to see my poor wife a corpse, having died a short time before my arrival [in childbirth]. Very awful and mysterious. I am crushed with sorrow," Robert Burton wrote in March of 1857. "Owing to pressing engagements," Burton had not seen his ailing wife for nearly four weeks before her death.[37]

Children brought both joy and a sober sense of responsibility. "What a priceless gift! Lord God, by whom, and for whom are all things; as thou has given us this child help us to give it back to thee by our faithful instruction, prayers, and example," Burton prayed several years earlier, at the birth of his first daughter. A young Presbyterian pastor's wife deferred to the rigors of Calvinist discipline when she handed her firstborn son to his father. "Here is another sinful creature for you to pray for," she told him.[38] Yet childrearing was not so much a private matter of prayer as a public expression of parents' faithfulness, particularly in preachers' families. An orderly household was a sign of a man's suitability to preach, and his family was open to scrutiny by the religious and irreligious alike. Few topics sent more tongues wagging than tales of the preacher's children.

Few rural pastors expected to work as full-time ministers. Some had an independent income from a farm either inherited or gained by marriage. More often, preachers earned their living by using skills they had learned before they entered the ministry, such as teaching, trades, or farming. They routinely preached at several "appointments" over long weekends. Some never lived in their own homes, boarding with church members instead. The pattern of engaging in several occupations was common even among those outside the ministry in the nineteenth century, and ministers often used their wits to juggle several sources of income.[39]

Like many other nineteenth-century Americans, pastors' financial fortunes could change virtually overnight. Financial security was rare. Unlike others, however, they were burdened with trying to balance their responsibilities between preaching and the vocations that fed their families. "Secular pursuits are very unfavorable to preaching, yet it is very necessary for ministers to have a home and a family," one man sighed in 1852. Those who spent too much time working outside the pulpit to feed and clothe their families were open to charges of neglecting their flocks. Yet a minister was also subject to the burdens of maintaining a certain standard of respectability. Pious and impious neighbors alike scrutinized everything from his speech to the cut of his jacket. Rev. William Broaddus, a Virginia Baptist who had removed to Kentucky in the 1840s, returned from a trip to find "everything in utter confusion. My salary was too high, my sermons too pointed, my language too lofty, my hair too long, my visits too seldom, my reproofs too severe, my discipline too rigid, my wife's cap too fine, my daughter's dress too costly, my sons too high minded, my horse too fat, & a thousand other things had been conjured up to show that I was not the man for Lexington."[40]

Indeed, strict notions of propriety accompanied the preacher's office. There were few respectable means of supplementing a pastor's small salary. Vocations that "tended to lessen ministerial dignity" included keeping a grocery that sold ardent spirits, running a tavern, "or book selling, unless he makes it secondary to the Gospel," a Baptist observed in 1850.[41] Some solved the problem by serving several congregations. Methodist circuits entailed responsibility for many congregations, often more than a day's journey apart. Baptists, too, preached to congregations thirty miles or more apart. Weddings and funerals provided one of the best opportunities to earn money. Fees were left to the discretion of the family, but most pastors earned one or two dollars for their trouble. Weddings provided significant income for city pastors. Philip Courtney, a Richmond pastor and schoolmaster, performed dozens of weddings per year, and in 1834 alone, collected more than $200 in wedding fees, a sum that exceeded the annual salary of many rural pastors.[42]

Regardless of whether a young minister attended an old field school, private academy, or college, when he arrived at his first charge, he was likely to be the most bookish man in the congregation. A preacher studied, in an oft-quoted Bible phrase, "in order to show himself approved" by God. For nineteenth-century evangelical Protestants, ideas had consequences. Studying the Bible, praying, and listening to sermons changed how people lived.

Many pastors were former teachers, and their teaching skills served them well. Above all, they remained students themselves. Those fortunate enough to live near a college or university often attended lectures in their spare time. Indeed, after a chaplaincy was established at the University of Virginia, Methodists and Baptists coveted the position for the opportunities it afforded for study. Edward Wilson, a Methodist of modest education who began preaching in 1841, enthusiastically attended lectures on "criticism, sublime in writing, beauty," and "structure of language." Zealous laity also challenged pastors to publicly defend their doctrinal positions, and they usually did so eagerly.[43]

Preachers worked diligently to build personal libraries. "I have not a large but a select and valuable collection of religious books, having purchased and read them as my exigencies required," Baptist Cornelius Tyree wrote. Itinerants carefully carried in their saddlebags their small collections of books, including Bibles, Greek or Hebrew lexicons, texts on preaching, and well-worn devotional volumes by Charles Wesley or the English Puritan William Law. The search for good books was a lifelong pursuit. On Baptist recommended that pastors collect books in no fewer than twelve categories, including historical, controversial, biographical, literary, devotional, philological, and scientific works.[44]

The office of preaching was unique in its demands even upon men with little formal training in producing original sermons. Delivering a weekly sermon, or even several sermons per week, required pastors to be crafters of language, and many were able and articulate writers. Even self-taught pastors often wrote eloquently in prose that was shaped by the exalted phrasing of the King James Bible. Their writing also reflected a wider acquaintance with poetry and devotional classics. Pastors spent a large part of each week preparing sermons, which they carefully recorded in notebooks and indexed for future use. They kept up a lively correspondence with church members, other clergymen, and family because their preaching assignments and clerical assemblies required frequent travel, sometimes for weeks at a time. The office required less creative writing as well. Pastors collected money for a variety of denominational causes and kept small notebooks filled with careful notations of finances and appointments, suggesting that the office attracted men of meticulous habits. Many wrote daily in small leather-bound diaries.

They also spent long hours reading. Chiefly, of course, they read the Bible for their own benefit as well as for their sermon preparation. Yet they also read widely in other religious and popular literature. Biographies, especially of great Christian men, were a favorite genre. Pastors found security in their reading. They scrutinized the Bible and other works for models for their own ministry. "Spent most of the day in reading the history of the labors and trials and defences of St. Paul, as given in the Acts of the Apostles," one man confided to his diary in 1856. His reading of Paul's life reflected his own ambitions. "A man of true genuine courage and uncompromising integrity. Of good birth, great talents and fine cultivation, he might have acquired fame and wealth. But he sacrificed all for the name of the Lord Jesus."[45]

Some pastors were sensitive spirits who constantly fretted over the state of their own souls. Noah Baldwin spent his entire ministry unsure of his own salvation and frequently lamented the poor state of his life and spirit. "Fear that I have no grace, for surely no one having Grace in their heart would be as full of evil as I am," he wrote in July 1850. Even happiness distressed Baldwin. "Today I have possessed a reading and meditating disposition and feel for the most part calm. I fear rather too much so, for after a few days of tranquility I have generally found something to annoy me and make me unhappy."[46] Many took their spiritual temperature every day, recording in diaries their feelings about God, their fears that they had lost their faith, and vague allusions to besetting sins. Some displayed through the years a despair that suggested they suffered from severe depression.[47]

If most did not match Baldwin's melancholia, pastors often confessed uncertainty about their work and spiritual state. Their laments reflected more than a concern for the conventions of the office. "I sometimes feel that I have little to live for here and but slight hope of a happy eternity, but . . . from what we read in the Psalms and in the biographies of great and good men I suppose such states are not peculiar to me," a Staunton pastor wrote in the late 1850s.[48] Pastors felt keenly the burden of serving as an example to their congregations, convinced that they would be held accountable for the souls they shepherded. "How awful that the carelessness of one minister may result in the Eternal loss of many souls," Richard Fox told his congregation. "There can be no doubt that a great deal of the sin, both in the world *and in the Church*, is owing to the neglect and sins of pastors," another wrote in 1851. "For when they fail to do their duty; or fall into sin it at once gives licence to others to do it likewise."[49]

The sheer physical demands of the work exhausted and discouraged them. Edward Wilson traveled a mountain circuit in the early 1840s with twenty-two preaching appointments in twenty-eight days. For his trouble he received $75 annually. Thomas Goggin, ordained at age twenty-three in 1838, farmed from Tuesday to Friday of each week before leaving his new wife to preach three or four times at schoolhouses, private homes, and even clearings in the woods. One of his appointments was thirty-seven miles from his home. Goggin did much of his preaching without any compensation. W. P. Harrison's first circuit consisted of twenty-one churches and seven schoolhouse preaching appointments; he traveled three hundred miles every month on a circuit with eighteen hundred members. Baptists did not ride formal circuits; they usually stayed closer to home. Fluvanna County resident George Snead lived his entire life in Fork Union, preaching and practicing medicine, and he was reportedly bound by blood or marriage to almost everyone in the section.[50]

The travel required of a Southern preacher was not always merely exhausting; it often lent interest and a sense of broadened horizons to his life and calling. Ten-year-old George Bagby climbed aboard a stagecoach in Lynchburg in 1838, quivering with excitement over his first trip to Richmond. He settled in for the two days' journey, only to notice "there was an unnatural preponderance of preacher to boy—nine of preacher to one of boy" inside the coach.[51] No doubt the Methodists were traveling to a ministerial assembly in Richmond. Pastors' public and private writings brim with accounts of their journeys. For many, preaching afforded them the first long trips of their lives. Pastors traveled to the next county to preach at revivals, to the Valley to attend a burial, to Richmond and Petersburg to meet with other Virginia ministers, and to Baltimore and New York City to meet with other American pastors. Like their taste for study, these journeys gave preachers, even the plainest among them, a worldly air. They had seen more of the world than those in their pews, particularly as most of their members were women who could only dream of such journeys. Independent travel by respectable conveyances was a privilege of men of means in the nineteenth century, and such indulgences underscored the authority of Virginia pastors.

These journeys shaped pastors' view of their place in the world, and that of their congregations. Pastors were grateful for the new experiences and acquaintances that preaching afforded them, and the people they met and places they saw made their way into their sermons and conversations. In this sense, pastors often opened the world to their members, much as eighteenth-century itinerants urged their congregations to transcend their narrow boundaries and to envision their place in a wider world. The ministry thus became a metaphor for opportunity for both pastors and their congregations in antebellum Virginia.[52]

Grand visions of a wider world, though, were often hedged in by the thorny concerns of congregational life. Young pastors labored under heavy expectations from their congregations, and they found the office of the preacher fraught with controversy. The clearest lines of conflict were drawn between the faithful and the worldly. Pastors expected conflict with those outside the church. Still, when it came, it was unsettling.

Joseph H. Amiss rode a remote mountain circuit, where he regularly preached in an old tavern that had been converted into a schoolhouse. On his second visit there, he met a local man, Mr. M. As they watered their horses, Amiss noticed he had a "common water bucket on his arm, about half full of liquor." "I have a little here to drink—won't you take some with me? I haven't taken but one or two drams since I saw you last," Mr. M. said. When the preacher declined, Mr. M. told him he had come out expressly to hear him preach. When the arrived at the church, he took a seat near the back of the congregation, leaving his bucket outside the door.

After Amiss began to preach, Mr. M. became restless and left, taking several men with him. A few minutes later, loud and angry oaths interrupted the service. Mr. M. appeared in the door. "Sir, you can't damn me," he shouted. "Nobody but my Saviour can damn me." "The men looked serious," Amiss wrote, "and many of the women trembled and wept." Mr. P., "an influential man of the mountains," rose and rebuked the drunken man, charging him with violating both the law of God and man. Mr. M. took his seat and Amiss resumed his preaching.

But the peace did not last. "On making some statement [in the sermon] Mr. M. said 'No such thing, Sir!' " Amiss recalled. "I did not notice him but kept on. Soon he said, 'Bah! Who believes that?' I saw it was not worthwhile to continue the service." After Amiss dismissed the congregation, several of the "respectable" men threatened to arrest Mr. M. More angry words were exchanged, and Mr. M. even threatened Amiss's life. "I said nothing to him, and the congregation quietly dispersed. He did not come to hear me preach again until nearly the close of the Conference year, and then not until he had

sent me word that he was heartily sorry for his conduct." Amiss sent word
that he forgave him, and "hoped that he would be a better man."[53]

Irreligious behavior routinely challenged religious authority in the antebellum South. The preacher's authority was sometimes revered, and even a
plain man of the cloth could shame a man of status. Rev. John O. Turpin, a
silversmith, was present one day when a "distinguished lawyer" used an oath.
When he realized a pastor was present, the man immediately turned to apol-
ogize. Turpin acknowledged him merely by pointing skyward and saying, "Ask
pardon up yonder."[54] Yet just as often, pastors were required to stare down
those, like Mr. M, who felt no particular respect for a man of the cloth. Was
Mr. M. a member of the church where Amiss preached? Clearly, he was known
in the neighborhood and could marshal support from some of the local men.
What was his motivation for attending church services that morning?

The complex relations of slavery also compromised a white preacher's authority, not only over African Americans but also over white church members.
White preachers had good reason to suspect that outward deference did not
necessarily translate into respect, particularly among slaves. And a white pastor could shrug off disrespect for his office as a sign of black inferiority, but
it could be a particularly galling reminder of the fragility of the clerical office
in antebellum Virginia.

Beverly Jones of Gloucester recalled that at a service presided over by a
Reverend Johnson, "de slaves were sittin' dere sleepin' an' fannin' theyselves
wid oak branches, an' Uncle Silas got up in de front row of de slaves' pew an'
halted Reverend Johnson. 'Is us slaves gonna be free in Heaven?'" he demanded. "De preacher stopped an' looked at Uncle Silas like he wanta kill
him 'cause no one ain't 'sposed to say nothin' 'ceptin' 'Amen' whilst he was
preachin'." Johnson stared at Silas but gave him no answer. The old man
repeated his question, yelling it this time. "Old white preacher pult out his
handkerchief an' wiped de sweat fum his face. 'Jesus says come to Me ye who
are free fum sin an' I will give you salvation,'" he replied. "Gonna give us
freedom 'long wid salvation?" demanded Silas. "'De Lawd gives an' de Lawd
takes away, an' he dat is widdout sin is gonna have life everlastin',' preached
the preacher. Den he went ahead preachin', fast-like, widdout payin' no 'ten-
tion to Uncle Silas." But, Jones recalled, "Uncle Silas wouldn't sit down; stood
dere de res' of de service, he did, an' dat was de las' time he come to church."
He died before the next appointed preaching.[55]

Amiss's and Johnson's encounters suggest that clerical authority in antebellum Virginia turned on a delicate balance between the inherent authority
of the office and the consent of the congregation. A tradition of lay authority
tempered the pastor's role as preacher and interpreter of the Word of God,
just as it directed his entry into the ministry. "As a denomination, we hold the
opinion pretty generally that . . . the pew is more to be relied upon than the
pulpit in reference to things of Christ's kingdom," a Baptist pastor wrote in

1842, apparently willing to concede this point to the pew.[56] In day-to-day congregational life, wise pastors kept an ear carefully tuned to their congregation. Amiss's authority alone was not enough to challenge Mr. M. in his mountaintop church; he needed the help of leading laymen as well.

Even the wisest pastors could not avoid conflict. Nineteenth-century Protestant life was fraught with strife at every turn. More telling than discord with the unsaved were disputes among the saved. Nineteenth-century Southerners, like other Americans, were ambivalent about sectarianism. Although they often claimed to care little for it, they engaged in sectarian battles with revealing frequency. By their examples, pastors encouraged their congregants to take up doctrinal controversies; willingness to argue was taken as a sign of commitment and intelligence. Especially important for a pastor was an ability to make a ready and extemporaneous defense of his beliefs when challenged. Yet unrelenting doctrinal conflict also tore apart congregations, neighbors, and even families.

Sectarian conflicts in the South reflected the honor-bound culture of the region. Though women showed great interest in doctrine, public theology remained a masculine domain, sometimes deteriorating into personal attacks and even physical threats. In 1855, Noah Baldwin was "turned out" of a congregation he founded ("Friendship Church," ironically) in southwest Virginia. Just five years later, he was "cast out" of another church and threatened with tarring and feathering.[57] Another Baptist pastor, Littlebury Allen, who was known for his "directness," recorded an incident with a young man who attended his church. Angry at something Allen had said, the young man threatened him. Allen invited the young man to walk out into the woods with him. "I'm not here to fight, but to preach the Gospel of peace," he told him. "If, however, you attack me, I shall give you the soundest drubbing you ever had. I am able to do it and I will do it." A particularly dramatic dispute broke out in a small Methodist congregation in 1847. The congregation was divided in its support of the pastor, and one Sunday morning several men were prepared to bar Samuel Moorman from the pulpit. His supporters, numbering near twenty, armed themselves, taking communion with "deadly weapons upon their bodies." Antebellum piety had little trouble reconciling religion with honor.[58]

Pastors found themselves as often at the mercy of these disputes as at the head of them. Even among Methodists, a pastor's authority in the church was largely consensual; that is, it depended on the congregation's confidence that he acted in their interests and on their behalf. To maintain a cohesive community, the most agile pastors learned to defer to the congregation. They had plenty of opportunity to sharpen their diplomatic skills. Those with harder opinions suffered almost constant conflict with lay leaders. This pattern of shared authority complicated congregational life and compromised the preacher's autonomy. Conflict raged at the expense of unity, and schisms were common.[59]

Disputes arose over doctrine, moral issues, discipline, church practice, and policy. Young pastors learned early to defend their positions on controversial issues with Biblical texts. Better-known ministers published treatises that added to the mountains of controversial literature published in the nine-teenth century. These were, in turn, answered by their opponents in print. If the Scriptures did not suggest compromise, compromise was not possible, and pastors usually stated their positions in absolute terms. With the stakes so high, conflicts erupted with more fury than the bitterest political battles, yield-ing harsh words and personal attacks that broke up lifelong friendships, ruined business partnerships, and rent families in two.

Other issues also caused conflict in antebellum congregations. These were always fragile communities, and they were rarely untroubled. Pastors quar-reled with laity, and lay leaders bickered. "Our choir leader was turned out for habitual cruelty to his wife. Our clerk was found to be spending many of his nights at the card table. Our senior deacon . . . had his drunken sprees . . . and the most prominent woman of the church had almost infinite genius for breeding disorders," one pastor wrote of his unhappy flock. William Broaddus's conflict with his Kentucky congregation turned on his views on temperance. His opponents, nearly all women, prevailed. They eventually ousted him from their pulpit.[60]

The appointment of a new pastor presented a fine opportunity for those eager to stir up strife. In principle, Baptists and Methodists differed over the appointment of pastors, but in practice pastors of both traditions found themselves subject to the laity. Senior Methodists routinely consulted local church leaders before making recommendations to the bishop. As a Meth-odist Presiding Elder wrote to a prominent Richmond layman in 1849, "I [hope] to get some impression of your opinion and that of the stewards rela-tive to the return of Bro. Fields. If you think he will succeed . . . I will return him, if not, I will send you another."[61] Sometimes, however, the wishes of congregations were ignored. When, in 1844, stewards at a Richmond congre-gation told the Methodist bishop that they were "sorely grieved at the ap-pointment" of Thomas Crowder, the bishop declined their request for another man. Crowder stayed in Richmond for just one year of strained relations with his congregation.[62]

Church discipline could either bind a congregation together or break it apart. Discipline demanded strong loyalty to church and pastor, loyalty beyond that of friendship and blood relations, because it required reporting the secret deeds of friends and family.[63] Antebellum clergymen and congregations ex-tended the power of the religious community to address transgressions of civil law, and church trials mixed civil and religious language and procedure. Civil authorities routinely certified written testimony for use in church trials, and the pastors and laymen who presided over the procedures were often trained in legal procedures, as either justices of the peace or lawyers.[64]

The fragile order of congregational life was most threatened when pastors themselves stood accused. A pastor's career depended on his reputation, and at times he was at the mercy of his congregation to preserve it. As one told his accuser, "Jim, you have got my character and my family in your hand and you can ruin them if you choose to do so."[65] Often the subject of gossip, pastors agonized over rumors that might sully their character. After learning of rumors regarding his character, Baptist Robert Burton exclaimed, "My God! Thou knowest that I am clear in this matter . . . o give me grace to be prudent in disproving this most unexpected slander."[66] Once begun, rumors were almost impossible to squelch. "For a time I never dreamed that I could outlive it," one wrote of a story that had him frequenting Richmond bar rooms. "In my simplicity I believed that everybody would believe it and I had hours of entirely unnecessary anguish about it."[67] Church trials against pastors usually convened only after a preponderance of rumors forced the issue into the public eye.

Most pressing and scandalous were accusations of sexual offenses. Surviving records of ministerial disciplinary trials suggest that pastors were frequently sullied by such charges. John Davis Williams, born in 1800 on the North Carolina–Virginia border, wrote an anguished letter that begged forgiveness and admitted his guilt after he was turned out of a church for improper relations with a young convert, Laura Buckley.

> The thought of returning to the world was more gloomy to me than the grave. I cannot live in this world. I want to be with a people who relish religion, that love to talk of the ordinances of God's house, of the way to heaven and of Jesus. . . . I sometimes retire into the solitary wood and tell my grief to the unfeeling trees. . . . And if I take myself to prayer, often the heavens seem plated with brass to keep my poor petitions from reaching the ear of Jehovah, and shame covers my face. If I read in the Bible and find any comfort, I am afraid it is false peace. When I go to the house of God everything condemns me. I beseech you dear Church of the living God, try and forgive me. I want the forgiveness of all. Yes, of the least esteemed African as well as the others.

The church clerk duly recorded Williams' letter in the church minute book. The congregation eventually received Williams back but refused to install him as pastor. Despondent, he left the neighborhood and eventually took up preaching miles away in Petersburg to Gillfield Baptist Church, the well-known black congregation. African American churches sometimes provided a pulpit to estranged white pastors, as in the case of a Norfolk Baptist who opposed slavery and married a black woman in the 1830s. Yet white pastors found their position even in these churches tenuous, for they rarely wrested complete control from black lay leaders.[68]

The explosive nature of sexual charges could shatter the most guarded congregation when news of them fell into eager public hands. Rev. C. G. Griswald of Centenary Methodist in Richmond faced public complaints in 1852 that he had visited a "house of ill fame" and that he had been seen on the street "under circumstances that excited suspicion." After a public church trial, church leaders "sustained" both complaints. Although they judged that he was not involved in "criminality," they did find that Griswald had exhibited a "degree of imprudence unbecoming a Christian minister." By sustaining the complaint, church leaders essentially agreed with it, although they declined to remove Griswald from his post. Surviving records suggest this was a common finding when pastors were charged with offenses judged to be less than crippling to their ministry.[69]

Relations between preachers and their congregations usually turned on more mundane matters. The custom of ministerial "visitation" obliged pastors to make regular, formal calls on church members at home. Many church members took this duty quite seriously and felt slighted if the minister did not pay them a regular call. Visitation was intended to encourage the faithful, mildly rebuke those who had not attended church for a few weeks or months, and shame into repentance those who openly defied church discipline. Laymen also made visits, sometimes spending as many as two or three evenings a week visiting non-Christians or backsliding members. Writing to his son at seminary in 1859, the Rev. Robert Ryland explained, "The people will soon love you if you go among them and *be of them.*" He urged his son to visit the poor in particular. A Baptist editor complained about the usual subjects of conversation on his visits—"the country, the peach buds, best time to plant corn, qualities of my dog, how to make sorghum syrup, will poplar trees make good rails, how do you like the schoolmaster. . . . Brethren and Sisters," he chided, "you ought to cultivate habits of religious conversation."[70] Relationships in church congregations in nineteenth-century Virginia were fraught with high expectations and disappointments, jealousies and acts of grace.

Antebellum pastors took up the work of a preacher in the close context of the Christian community. Family and friends carefully nurtured and assessed their conversion and calling to preach. They practiced a vocation that allowed them some freedom—in what they preached, in where they went—but their autonomy was limited by their accountability to the local congregation. Although their calling to God's work set them apart, an egalitarian ethos underlay the relationship between pastors and their congregations. A man was called not because of his special abilities or his status, but by virtue of God's grace alone.

Yet even in the early years of the nineteenth century, Virginia pastors began to test the community bonds that restricted their autonomy. Some expected more from their vocation than rides on dusty back roads to visit households that extended a mean hospitality. Edward Portlock Wilson, a Methodist in Southside Virginia, frequently complained about his hosts. "Went to old Sister Hobsons," he wrote of a trip in the 1840s. "I found her a great scold, and though she is quite wealthy she thinks she is poor." At Sister Wright's, Wilson wished that "they would be more particular about cooking for it is somewhat a struggle to eat coffee, mean biscuits half cooked they are not as clean as they ought to be." His second morning there, too, was awkward. "This morning up early as great a struggle as ever to eat breakfast. If people are poor let them be clean and neat."[71]

Wilson was a young man of humble birth without formal education. At the time of his visit to Sister Wright's, the twenty-four-year-old pastor had served only remote circuits. His words betray his expectation that religious people should aspire to a certain respectability and, in particular, that a preacher of the Gospel deserved better than "mean biscuits."[72] If those who expected religion to breed respectability were often disappointed in the Virginia countryside, however, they found a more hospital welcome in the city.

CHAPTER TWO

City Pastors

By the 1840s, the experiences of pastors in Virginia's towns and cities had begun to differ sharply from those in the countryside. Rural churchgoers continued to worship in simplicity and self-denial, while those in the city began to link religion with social respectability. Rural congregations consisted overwhelmingly of farmers, but urban churches attracted a growing number of merchant and professional families. Free and slave families mixed in country churches, while city congregations began to segregate.

The day-to-day tasks of pastors reflected these distinctions. The work of rural pastors changed little from the eighteenth to the nineteenth century. Most had more than one church, and they divided their days between farming, visiting members, conducting services at odd hours and places. Their churches were log cabins or simple sheds, and their small salaries reflected their modest lives and their sense of preaching as a calling. Town and city pastors, meanwhile, took responsibility for a single congregation that worshiped in a stylish church. The building and its furnishings reflected the tastes and aspirations of its congregation. Instead of long days in the saddle, city preachers spent hours in their studies, lingered with church members over tea, or met with sewing circles and missionary societies. They drew large salaries, and the burden of their responsibilities made work outside the pulpit impossible. At the center of growing denominational organizations, with their own bureaucratic structures and chains of authority, these city and town pastors sought to make the ministry a full-time profession.

By the 1840s, leading Southern ministers had shifted their interest away from the revivals of an earlier era. Whereas an earlier generation of pastors had built its reputation on revival preaching, by the 1840s ambitious pastors staked their fortunes on the energy and connections of city life and the modest denominations they began to build there. In Richmond, Alexandria, Petersburg, Norfolk, and Fredericksburg, pastors wrote and published treatises and newspapers, led denominational assemblies, established schools, and built commodious churches. These men had different tasks from their rural peers, and they worked in a different material and social context. City pastors had decisive influence in a rural society, and they shaped the young Southern religious institutions in their image.[1]

Cities and towns were the birthplace of the ministerial profession and hence the starting place for nearly all of the ideas about organized religion in nineteenth-century Virginia. The key to this apparent paradox lies in the role of voluntary associations, which historians have long viewed as strongly connected with urban life. Southern religious voluntary associations—denominations—grew at astonishing rates in the 1840s and 1850s, and they embodied a bureaucratic style and discipline that was foreign to the rhythms of rural life. This is not to say that the rural religious style capitulated to the city's in antebellum Virginia. On the contrary, many Virginian churchgoers had never visited a city. Indeed, they were quick to indict city people as less godly, or at least as hedged in by greater temptations, than themselves. But though revivals filled rural church pews in the 1810s and 1820s, and though the Methodist genius for evangelism was seated in the circuit rider's saddle, the builders of Southern religious institutions did not linger in the countryside. They soon found their way to town. The predominance of city men instilled in denominations a certain bent toward urban values and style in the antebellum South. By the 1840s, these pastors had begun to spin tales of a rural, determinedly agrarian, and traditional South out of their urban nostalgia.

That denominations went to town raises questions about the place of religion in antebellum Southern society. How was it that denominations and their leaders, defenders of slavery all, cast their fortunes with Southern cities and towns? How did the habits of mind fostered by these organizations affect Southern life beyond the church door? How did religious institutions bridge the cultures of city and country in the antebellum South?

Jeremiah Bell Jeter was born to a farmer, Pleasant Jeter, and a preacher's daughter, née Jenny Hatcher, at the foot of the Blue Ridge in 1802. When Jeter was seven, General John Preston hired his father as overseer on his Montgomery County plantation, and the family moved the fifty miles southwest from Bedford County. Pleasant Jeter was not an educated man, but he did not object to his son's attendance at school for a brief time. The neighborhood school met in a crude log house, where a small group of students suffered the temperamental teaching of a man much given to whipping. Jeter enjoyed the spelling bees but admitted he did not learn much at school. He soon returned to the fields.[2]

As a boy, Jeter worshiped in a setting that reflected his parents' simple life. He sat on hard benches in log houses "without plastering, ceiling or stoves" listening to sermons that sometimes stretched to three hours. When Jeter was eleven, he heard the celebrated Lorenzo Dow at a revival in neighboring Botetourt County. But he did not find faith himself until he was nine-teen. On an August evening in 1821, Jeter and a friend felt shamed when "big, unbidden tears began to drop" down their faces during a revival meeting. They both left the meeting "determined to be Christians."

Jeter accepted a plain Gospel at the hands of a plain people, but religion demanded the sacrifice of even the simple affectations of a young farmer. One of Jeter's first acts of piety was to give up wearing his hair curled, with po-matum, on his forehead. The namesake of his grandfather preacher, he deliv-ered his first sermon on the banks of the creek where he had been baptized moments earlier. He had found his vocation. "I preferred being a preacher," he wrote, "poor, despised, persecuted—to being a king or an emperor." In the first years after his conversion, Jeter traveled throughout his native region, preaching for Christ and against antimissionists, whom he described as "ear-nestly and successfully devoted to doing nothing."

In 1823, Jeter's journey to the organizational meeting of the Baptist Gen-eral Association in Richmond took him farther from home than he had ever been before. The Tidewater differed from Bedford both socially and politically, and during the 1810s and 1820s, westerners' demand for liberalization of the franchise reflected their frustrations with eastern domination.[3] But young Jeter was impressed by the east. "The city of Richmond seemed to me to be of passing grandeur," he wrote. "The capitol exceeded all my conceptions of ar-chitectural greatness and beauty . . . [and] made an impression on my youthful imagination." Appointed a missionary of the association, his course in life was now firm. A year later he was ordained.

Jeter never again made his home in the west. After assisting a pastor in southeastern Virginia, he took a church on the Northern Neck, where he married the daughter of a slaveholder in 1828. Jeter described the deacons at Morattico Church as men plain in habit and dress. One had "elevated himself from a humble condition to a state of independence and respectability" to become the county sheriff. Another, a slaveholder, called the fashion of collars a form of hypocrisy inappropriate for a Christian, "for it appears you have on a clean shirt when you haven't." While at Morattico, Jeter continued to visit the city, usually in connection with professional obligations. In 1829, he at-tended the state constitutional convention in Richmond, and later that year he sailed to Baltimore. "I returned to my plain country home quite impressed. . . . [Baltimore] was certainly the most magnificent place that I had seen." In 1832, he made the long journey to New York City to attend the Baptist triennial convention.

In 1836, Jeter received a call to First Baptist Church in Richmond, and his eager acceptance was a sign of his ambition.[4] His new position was a prominent one—perhaps the most prominent—in the Virginia General Asso-ciation, and both in his own mind and in the estimation of his peers, Jeter had advanced far beyond his beginnings as the son of an overseer. Soon after moving to Richmond, he faulted his wife for her plain apparel, telling her it stung his pride for her to appear "in a dress out of keeping with her position." City life bred in him an open distaste for the simple religious culture of his youth. In 1845, he visited several "country meetings" and proclaimed his great disappointment with them in the pages of the Baptist newspaper. "To one accustomed to the almost perfect order of city meetings," he wrote, "there are some things which rather painfully arrest my attention." His list of grievances included the passing of pitchers of water among the ladies by slaves, bringing little children to services, and the selling of cakes, candies, and toys in stalls outside rural churches.[5]

After just nine years of city life, Jeter had cast aside his early preference for the simple religious tastes of the country. When the pastor stood behind his polished pulpit, his glance fell first on respectable white merchants and professionals and their families. His conviction that faith flourished in an atmosphere of simplicity evaporated. Social respectability and religion had called a truce in Jeter's mind—more than that, they had become allies. Although rural religion had demanded that he give up curling his hair to become a "poor, despised, persecuted" minister of the Gospel, the mores of First Baptist mandated that he adopt manners "in keeping with his position."

What led this former Bedford farm boy to entertain such pretensions? What persuaded Jeter to cast his lot with the strife and noise of the commercial capital of Virginia? Jeter himself provided a quick answer, without reflection or qualification: God himself had led Jeter to the city and, in so doing, had given his life a meaning, purpose, and direction far grander than that he could have achieved in quiet Bedford County. His call to the city gave Jeter's life its central theme: that of steady social progress wrought by God's calling. In contrast to Noah Baldwin's long struggle in southwestern Virginia, which left him nearly where he had begun, Jeter's life traced a steady progression away from the plow toward the refined relations of a city preacher.

In describing the career of his lifelong friend and fellow Baptist minister, Daniel Witt, Jeter made his feelings plain enough. Converted side by side at a Bedford revival, Witt and Jeter initially worked together, but Jeter later went east to Richmond, while Witt settled into a long ministry in Prince Edward County in Virginia's isolated Southside. Jeter's relief at having escaped the fate of his friend was palpable, and his biography of Witt is tinged with apology that a plain country preacher's life might be worth even setting down. "It is very difficult to write, in a satisfactory manner, the life of a country pastor," Jeter wrote. "The history of a long rural pastorate must, like the life itself, be monotonous. The journal of one week is that of another week. . . . For almost a century [Witt] lived in the same house; traveled over the same roads; preached at the same places; labored among the same people, or their descendants; proclaimed not indeed the same sermons, but the same gospel; pursued the same wearisome round of toil; and was subject to the same anxious cares." While this uniformity was "sometimes broken" by a revival, a visit from another pastor, a trip to the springs or out west, in the main Jeter felt Witt's life to be "remarkably uniform and quiet." Witt himself confirmed his friend's judgment. Writing after the war, he admitted to a friend that while Jeter had worked in an "eminent sphere," he himself had been called to "an humbler sphere" in the congregation to which he preached for forty-five years.[6]

The contrast between the preaching careers of these two lifelong friends—who were born just one year apart, reared in the same neighborhood, and converted at the same revival, and who labored together as the first missionaries of the Virginia Baptist General Association—is particularly dramatic. The records they have left of their experiences and their feelings about each other are rare. But their conviction that the work of a city preacher was more visible, more eminent, and ultimately perhaps more useful than that of a country pastor was shared by many pastors in antebellum Virginia. Even those who were fiercely loyal to country work saw the antebellum ministry divided into two classes: those who lived in town and those who did not.

This distinction lay at the heart of the typical narrative of the ministerial life of nineteenth-century Baptists and Methodists: steady social improvement. Preaching, along with the modest organizational work of Baptists and Methodists that began to creep across Virginia in the 1820s and 1830s, provided a chance for young men like Jeter and Witt to escape the cramped life of their fathers into a sphere of "wider usefulness." It is difficult to imagine a comparable route of escape for a young man of energy and vision in a place and time when the ambitions of most Virginians were hedged in by isolation, lack of opportunity, and the exhausting and mind-numbing work of farming.

From the beginning, this escape had a spatial dimension. Religion provided an opportunity for men of modest means to travel. To attend the revival at which he was converted, Daniel Witt left his own neighborhood for the first time in his life. His reputation as a preacher soon yielded an invitation for the twenty-one-year-old to travel 150 miles to Richmond, where his connections opened a "wider door of usefulness." After his stay in the state capitol, Witt "preached myself back to my home with my saddle-bags filled with books and my pockets with money."[7]

These pastors' lives followed a pattern that was very familiar to antebellum Americans but has not figured in scholarly accounts of the antebellum South. The image of a raw, country youth finding his fortune in the city symbolized the aspirations of the young nation in these years. Jeter's own experience paralleled that of many young white men who sought their fortune in antebellum Richmond with carefully folded letters of introduction in their pockets. Young pastors, like young clerks, could make their way in the city. Their aspirations embodied the notion that, in the words of two Virginians, "all the promise of life seemed to us to be at the other end of the rainbow—somewhere else—anywhere else but on the farm."[8]

Jeter's experience bore a remarkable similarity to that of other ministers of his generation across the country. Nathan Bangs, the self-educated son of a blacksmith, made his way to a New York City Methodist pulpit, where he became one of the most influential pastors of his generation. James Henley Thornwell, the eminent Southern Presbyterian, was, like Jeter, the son of an overseer. By the 1840s, leading Baptist and Methodist clergymen across America had abandoned the desire to separate their new communities of faith from society; instead, they began to take on the task of building institutions that worked deliberately to bend society toward Christ. Instead of measuring the distance between church and world as a sign of the church's purity, a new generation of ministers took it on themselves to narrow the gap.[9]

Their plans to accomplish this mission took them to the city. Virginia Baptists and Methodists disagreed with New York Unitarians and Princeton Presbyterians on nearly everything but agreed with them on the importance of the city to the interests of religion. Princetonian Samuel Miller urged religious people to devote themselves to cities, for "a happy impulse given here, will vibrate, and be beneficially felt to the remotest bounds of the social body." In 1836, the year that Jeter moved to Richmond, an influential New York Unitarian published an essay called *The Moral Importance of Cities*, containing a similar argument.[10]

Residents of antebellum Virginia's cities and towns were intimately acquainted with the marketplace and its demands for discipline and a vision for the future. Market habits worked themselves into the lives of ministers as they did for others in town. The ministry counted in its ranks men who shared the moral imperative and self-made dreams of other antebellum Americans. Many were gifted fund-raisers and organizers, and they harnessed their faith to the standards of efficiency and professionalism that townspeople celebrated. Men like Jeter and Bangs led their congregations away from what they now viewed as the tasteless excesses of revivalism toward the more sedate and respectable goals of opening colleges and academies and building brick churches with rented pews.

Historians have overlooked the importance of city and town pastors to religious institution building in the South. Not all ministers carried equal weight in their burgeoning profession: the city pastors were "the mighty weights" in their profession.[11] From early in the century, the most influential Baptist and Methodist pastors were city men like Jeter who believed that religion did not exist in isolation from the social world but should be used to influence it. They promoted an educated ministry and argued that pastors should work full-time for denominational causes. Those who led denominational colleges, presses, and agencies preached from pulpits in Richmond, Petersburg, and Norfolk. City pastors made their churches the center of both denominational administration and wealth.

Religious institution building in the antebellum period provides a novel perspective on the relation between countryside and towns and cities in the Old South. Religious institutions provided one of the most important conduits between town and country in the nineteenth century. Yet early on, leading city pastors established the pattern that would prevail for the rest of the century. Their authority and influence flowed in just one direction: from the city into the surrounding countryside.[12]

Richmond, the city of "passing grandeur" that so impressed young Jeremiah Jeter in 1823, was the commercial as well as the political capital of Virginia.

The city's economic expansion coincided with the appearance of a distinctively Southern identity in reaction to Nat Turner's rebellion and the first angry cries of Northern abolitionists. Richmonders engaged in a variety of enterprises, from canal and railroad building, to flour milling and iron manufacture, to tobacco processing and waterworks.[13]

To the astonished eye of young Jeter of Bedford, the city's streets were a roiling mass of teamsters, mud, carriages, coal smoke, and costermongers. In the city's lower sections, near the river, tipsy seamen spilled out of grogshop doorways into the path of hired slaves hurrying on their errands. City docks and wharves swarmed with workers unloading tobacco and grain from dugouts and bateaux.

The city was a jumble of buildings scattered on a series of hills above the James River. To the disapproving eye of Charles Dickens, who visited in the early 1840s, the disorder and poverty of some sections were a metaphor for slavery itself. "There are pretty villas and cheerful houses in its streets, and Nature smiles upon the country round; but jostling its handsome residences, like slavery itself going hand in hand with many lofty virtues, are deplorable tenements, fences unrepaired, walls crumbling into ruinous heaps." Richmond slaves labored at many tasks. City life stretched the institution into shapes that barely resembled the plantation slavery that dominated the countryside.

High on Shockoe Hill, Jefferson's serene capitol building sat above the fray. Around Capitol Square ranged the homes of Richmond's leading families. They included some planting families, but an increasing number of the city's leaders had come from elsewhere to make their fortunes in mercantile enterprises or law offices. The malaise that almost paralyzed Virginia elites in this period, the yearning for the influence of the Revolutionary generation, and the angst about the state's declining political influence and economic weight were more apparent in the drawing and dining rooms of the gentry than they were in the bustle of Richmond's streets. Jeremiah Jeter himself did not sympathize with such concerns, if he was aware of them at all. He was absorbed by the success and energy of the merchants and middling professionals. The South that de Tocqueville encountered, one that turned "its melancholy gaze inward and back to the past, perpetually fancying that it may be suffering oppression," was not a South that Jeter knew well.[14]

From very early in the nineteenth century, city congregations like Jeter's wielded more influence than their rural counterparts in the organized work of Baptists and Methodists. In part, this was true simply because membership rates were higher in cities. In 1850, for example, Baptist church members were 10 percent of the population in Norfolk, 16 percent in Richmond, and 24 percent in Petersburg, but just 6 percent of the state population overall.[15] They also wielded greater influence because of the higher status of their members. Cities were the seat of success for a variety of nonagricultural pursuits in the antebellum era—especially trade and the bar. Though a majority of antebellum Baptists and Methodists were plain, rural people, their leaders in denominational affairs were city merchants, printers, and lawyers. Like successful pastors, the elite among the Baptist and Methodist laity was concentrated in city churches, and these families gave generously to the cause of religion.

Although nine of ten antebellum Virginians lived in the countryside, Virginia was the most urban of the Southern states. Virginia's cities, like cities elsewhere, carried a significance that far outweighed their population. As centers of commerce, culture, and education, cities attracted more than their share of people who sought the new, the exciting, and the sophisticated. Time seemed to pass more quickly in the city, fashions to change more easily. By 1835, one writer decried the departure of Richmond's leading classes from what he called the frank, simple, and unostentatious manners and customs of the old Virginia character.[16]

Attention to image and style likewise defined church life in the city. By the 1840s, city churches worshiped very differently than rural churches. Rural Virginians continued to associate spirituality with simplicity. City churchgoers learned to connect it with order, beauty, and social respectability. Decorated with thick carpets, pew cushions, and sweeping curtains, their churches reflected the members' tastes in home furnishings. They bought expensive organs and paid their choirs. Like their country brethren, city church members endowed their church buildings with spiritual significance, and their tasteful furnishings symbolized to them the powerful union between spiritual and material progress. Their elegant buildings, usually built before they could afford them, enhanced the "perfect order" of their meetings, setting a tone of worship that proclaimed the refinement not only of church members but also of their God. Because most of these buildings plunged their congregations into consuming debt, they represented the highest aspirations of their members, underscoring the distance these congregations wished to maintain from both their eighteenth-century forebears and their rural brethren. City church buildings embodied antebellum Southern Protestant aspirations.[17]

The trappings of refinement did not win the hearts of Virginia evangelicals without a fight. Virginia Methodists and Baptists had their own version of the style wars that Richard Bushman has described among Unitarians, Congregationalists, and Episcopalians farther north. Notable, however, at Jeter's First Baptist was the absence of conoversy sparked by the church's remaking of itself in the 1840s.

First Baptist Church of Richmond provides an instructive example of how changes in the material context of worship both reflected and prompted changes in the social context of antebellum religious life. The first building occupied by the congregation, built around 1798, was "a small wooden house with a shed at either end" that the congregation used, according to one observer, "for want of a better place of worship." They baptized members in the nearby Penitentiary Pool and later in the city canal. By 1802, the congregation had built a new, larger church building, low and simple in style, without a steeple. Through additions and renovations over the next four decades, this building became the largest assembly hall in antebellum Richmond. As the church opened for political assemblies, entertainments, and other town meetings, it was familiar to many residents. For a month, delegates to the celebrated Virginia Constitutional Convention of 1829–30 met there.[18]

Shortly after Jeremiah Jeter arrived in 1836, the congregation installed a baptistry in the church. This "domestication" of the baptismal ceremony—its move from a muddy pool to the regulated confines of an indoor baptistry—marked a momentous change in attitudes toward the central ritual of Baptist life. Nineteenth-century rural Baptists took pride in the simplicity of creekside ceremonies, commonly baptizing willing converts even in midwinter. Noah Baldwin baptized his brother-in-law, who was ill with consumption, in the cold waters of Cherokee Creek in November 1860. "Every doctor said it would kill him," he scoffed, but Baldwin was certain that the man's obedience would prolong his life.[19]

What possessed a people, reared on such a custom, to exchange their muddy riverbank for a mechanical pool with rolling floors and dressing chambers? How did those eager to find Scriptural precedent for nearly everything come to view an artificial pool as a setting fit for the most meaningful ritual of their lives? Baptism in the frigid waters of a wild creek or a sluggish river recalled that of their Lord. The embrace of the baptistry marked more than a desire to be immersed in warmer water; it suggested an openness to technical innovation and an aspiration that was not afraid to leave tradition behind.

More momentous than the baptistry was the building of a new church a few years later. In 1841, the congregation literally reinvented itself by constructing a new $40,000 house of worship on prestigious Shockoe Hill. The imposing structure, built on a prime lot on the corner of Twelfth and Broad Streets, was designed by the architect who later designed the new dome and wings of the U.S. Capitol building. The severe Greek Revival structure contrasted sharply with the old church, a low and steepleless building that dated from the turn of the century.[20] In a gesture that underscored the humble appearance of the old church, the congregation gave it to the new First African Baptist Church. First Baptist Church, then, segregated its members upon construction of the imposing new building. How eagerly African American members welcomed this news, and exactly what role they took in the affair, is not recorded. Many may have welcomed the opportunity for separate worship; they may even have suggested it.

Writers in the local press lavished praise on the new building. The sparkling white walls and ceiling set off the deep blue of the pew cushions nicely. A quilted blue damask hanging centered with a brilliant white star graced the front wall, and the Bible rested on a matching damask cushion. The most striking new feature was the practice of selling and renting pews, apparently adopted by the congregation with little controversy. A professional auctioneer sold pews on a late Tuesday afternoon in 1841 for amounts ranging from $50 to $500 paid in installments. Profits were used to retire debt on the building. Church leaders drew up a careful plan, with free pews located near the pulpit and in the gallery. The most expensive pews were at the center of the center aisle, and leading members of the congregation, including Archibald Thomas, a deacon and merchant who was one of the largest creditors of the church, paid $500 apiece for the privilege of sitting in them weekly. Unsold pews were rented for an annual fee that helped to pay the pastor's salary.[21]

The sale of pews completely altered the social context of worship for the formerly biracial congregation. The majority membership of slaves and free blacks was gone, and the sale of pews imposed a visible social hierarchy on the white worshipers who remained. The new system embraced this hierarchy, not least because the church became dependent on the money of the unsaved. Church leaders expected nonmembers to purchase pews and welcomed their contribution, even while assuring members of more modest means that these pew owners would have no formal voice in church affairs.

The building was a financial departure as well. Congregations like First Baptist plunged unapologetically into debt in order to build what they considered a suitable house of worship. At a time when many Protestants considered personal indebtedness sinful and customarily cited St. Paul's call to "owe no man anything" as a first rule of Christian life, city congregations resorted to collective indebtedness with few reservations. One congregation's desire for a fine brick church was so strong that after it was built they had no money left to pay their pastor. Such desires often forced pastors to plead their case to those outside the church. In addition to collecting subscriptions from members, church leaders solicited money from wealthy patrons who were not members of their church, nor sometimes of any other. The patrons' willingness to give and the congregation's willingness to ask underscored the assumption that a fine church building served the public interest.[22]

Many subscribers, even church members, failed to pay up. Building sometimes began as soon as enough cash was in hand to do so, and defaults on subscriptions left church leaders in an awkward position. Such was the situation facing the trustees of Centenary Methodist Church of Richmond in 1842. With creditors pressing them, they voted to begin renting pews in a somewhat desperate attempt to pay for their handsome new $20,000 church building. Pew renting marked a significant departure from the historical position of Methodists, who had found the practice among Anglicans particularly repugnant. Centenary trustees argued, however, that their transition from a "free church" was not only necessary but also desirable. In a letter to their members, they explained that rented pews would advance the cause of religion, extending the Gospel to "a class of hearers who are averse to visiting Methodist Churches simply because they cannot procure a seat of their own." Few church members publicly objected, and pews were sold for amounts ranging from $5 to $150. The church did reserve some free pews for slaves, the poor, and the elderly.[23] In spite of the sales, Centenary remained in debt for its new building for another nine years, during which time the church also gained a paid choirmaster, curtains and cushions, and a parsonage with more than $600 worth of furnishings. Official church records did not mention the storm of controversy raised by the episode, but about forty members, among them many prominent families, withdrew to join the Clay Street Methodist Church. There they pointedly posted a sign in the church vestibule that read The Seats in This House Are Free.[24]

The debate over church furnishings at Centenary Methodist mirrored debates in congregations around the country. What should the social and material context of religious life and worship be? As Richard Bushman has demonstrated, at the heart of the dispute was a deep ambiguity as to whether, and how much, refinement was required of Christian people. For many church members, the embrace of ornamentation and wealth compromised spiritual purity. Arguments appeared in support of both elegant churches and plain meeting houses. In 1843, a Portsmouth Methodist congregation passed a resolution against "anything like an appearance of exclusive seats either by renting or by placing cushions in the seats" or by carpeting their church. In 1852, Baptist James Powell publicly lamented the pride and vanity associated with costly churches. Powell criticized the elaborate dedication ceremonies for new churches because they fostered "a superstitious reverence for the house. . . . The time was when our houses of worship were called meeting houses. Now they are called churches . . . [and] the seats in them are sold or . . . rented to the highest bidder," he complained.[25] Critics like Powell understood how these practices altered the nature of worship. Another Baptist decried paid choirs, arguing that performances were "contrary to the spirit of the New Testament and practice of the apostles" because they made members passive observers in services that depended upon rehearsed performance. In his view, the point of such worship was no longer the spontaneous inspiration of the Spirit, which had been so central to the camp meeting. He despaired of rationalized worship and ornamented church buildings.[26]

The dispute remained unresolved before the Civil War. An extended debate on church furnishings appeared in the Baptist newspaper in 1858. In a series of letters, a bold correspondent who took the name Progress argued that rented pews and elegant churches extended the influence of the Gospel to a better class of people. "The great wail is that such methods drive out the poor," he wrote impatiently. "Are the houses of God to be erected exclusively for the poor? It is easier and better to seek to raise the poor to a higher level than to bring other more numerous classes to a lower."[27] Progress waved aside the reply of another reader, who argued that congregations should mix rich and poor so that they might benefit each other. The arguments of both Progress and his opponent focused on the social benefits of religion.

Progress assumed that religion should raise humble people and open to them the pleasures of respectability. He even assumed that churches had succeeded at this task so well by the late 1850s that the respectable classes were the majority of churchgoers. Such a view was probably rooted in his own experience in a city church. Yet by the 1850s, there were signs that urban tastes had begun to influence small towns and rural areas as well. Even small congregations began to yearn for brick churches, making their pastors fundraisers, much like their city peers. When the resources of the congregation could not match its tastes, pastors turned to wealthy patrons. These men and women were not necessarily members of the church or even of the denomination that solicited their support. In May 1851, Methodist pastor Alfred Wiles penned a long and anxious letter to the Honorable John Young Mason, explaining the "pecuniary embarrassment" in two churches on his Westmoreland circuit. Mason was a prominent Richmond lawyer and Jacksonian Democrat who had served as a state legislator and member of Congress, as well as a cabinet member in the Tyler and Polk administrations. "The brethren and friends have done their utmost at both places, but they still fall short of raising the requisite sums," Wiles wrote. "The debt must be paid or the church will be sold for the man to whom the debt is due is not a member of any church, and I am told has but little regard for religion and will in all probability execute his threats." In the second church, which was "quite small," Wiles had been "compelled to preach in the grove. We want to build a frame church, not to cost us over $1,200 as we are not able to build a brick, and we will be very thankful to get any kind."[28]

In 1842, three well-known Virginia Baptists called for the professionalization of the ministry by urging pastors to stop supporting themselves with secular work. Like legislators, lawyers, physicians, teachers, merchants, and farmers, they argued, pastors' work demanded their full attention. Pastors had "heavy responsibilities" and were obliged to devote an increasing amount of time to "benevolent efforts," including committee and board meetings, Sunday schools, and other speaking engagements. These pastors placed organization and administration at the heart of their definition of professionalism, setting up the ideal of the ministry as that of the city, not the country, pastor. Just a few years later, leaders anticipated that their appeal was being answered when they celebrated the "new race" of young ministers who had recently visited the pulpit of First Baptist Church.[29]

  The position of a preacher in the towns and cities of antebellum Virginia was indeed different from that of a rural pastor. Most rural congregations worshiped with an ordained pastor only every few weeks, which encouraged ambitious lay leaders to take a strong hand in church affairs. Indeed, lay preachers were a fixture of rural religious life. Among Methodists, lay preachers outnumbered regular preachers until the 1860s, and their presence compromised the arguments of those who urged professionalism among the clergy. City pastors, meanwhile, only rarely shared the pulpit with lay leaders (see Appendix, Table 7).

  Their position was also far more stable than that of rural pastors, who often traveled from church to church. City pastors preached from the same pulpit every Sunday, and this continuity of leadership reinforced their authority over the congregation. Although Baptists often held the same pulpits for decades, rural Methodist pastors spent an average of just two years in each circuit. As newcomers, they were often unschooled in the channels of established authority in the congregation and depended on the laity for direction. Antebellum Methodist leaders routinely complained that they had not enough qualified men, as opposed to men of "ordinary talent," to fill urban pulpits.[30] Some urban Methodist pastors managed to be reappointed to the same congregation for many years at a time, eliminating the disadvantages of the circuit system and raising the ire of some rural men who noticed the trend.

Doctrine also meant different things in town and country. In sparsely settled Virginia counties, each neighborhood typically supported a single congregation for each denomination. A rural woman in agreement with Baptist doctrine, for example, was obliged to attend services at her neighborhood church or risk an awkward journey to another church. By contrast, in Richmond by the 1850s, a Baptist woman could attend services at any of seven churches with little hardship. City churches reflected the social status of their neighborhoods in the growing city, and made the choosing of a church a matter of aspiration as well as of proximity.

This development greatly complicated the religious landscape of the antebellum South. The tendency of well-heeled churches to develop "missions," usually in poorer areas of town that eventually became churches in their own right, further encouraged drawing social distinctions between congregations. For pastors, this meant that some appointments were more socially desirable than others. By the late antebellum period, denominational lines did not neatly parallel social distinctions in Southern towns and cities.[31]

Denominations were progressive institutions in the Old South. Their raison d'être was to organize and mobilize churches across the state and nation in works of religious benevolence. The differences between those who supported such organization and those who opposed it yawned wide, especially among Baptists. Disagreements about religious benevolence fueled much of the sectarian strife in the antebellum South. Missionary Baptists viewed predestinarian Antimissionary Baptists as a compelling example of what progressive religion was not—against organization, religious benevolence, and education. In Virginia, the paths of missionary and antimissionary Baptists began to diverge as early as 1821. Discord between the two groups actually dated to eighteenth-century disputes between Separates and Regulars. After a temporary truce, the controversy erupted with a vengeance during the 1820s and 1830s, a time of heightened interest in foreign mission societies, Baptist state conventions, temperance, and Sunday schools. Antimissionists refused to participate in these works, insisting that the congregation alone was the only agency for church work sanctioned by New Testament writers. In 1827, the first antimissionary Baptist association denounced "all Missionary Societies, Bible Societies and Theological Seminaries, and the practices heretofore resorted to for their support, in begging money from the public." Antimissionary pastors preached without salaries, lectured their churches on the evils of contributions for religious benevolence, and opposed ministerial education; Regular Baptists preached the virtues of foreign missions, Sunday schools, and ministerial education. By 1840, formal schism had created two Baptist sects, missionary and antimission or Primitive Baptists.[32]

In the South, sectarian conflict was more than just disagreement over the fine points of doctrine. Although they shared some doctrinal views, Regular and antimissionary Baptists differed socially and culturally. Missionary leaders defined religious benevolence as the natural activity of the redeemed, placing its agencies at the center of congregational life. "Preached on the subject of industry in business," Noah Baldwin noted in 1852. "My object was to stimulate system in business, so that something might be accumulated and given to the cause of benevolence."[33] Pastors like Baldwin used every opportunity to ridicule those who opposed such projects as backwards and unsophisticated, even characterizing their differences as those of enemies on the battlefield.[34] In the end, missionary Baptists won the long war. By 1890, only 45,000 antimissionary Baptists remained in the South, while missionary Baptists numbered more than 1 million.[35]

Even as Baldwin struggled to support the cause of religious benevolence in the southwest, it flourished in other parts of Virginia. Even the relatively modest social networks of Virginia's small cities provided a fertile environment for women and men to create a variety of organizations dedicated to improving residents' lives by preaching the Gospel. Interest in voluntary organizations and reform often grew out of religious revivals. City churches transformed the revival technique so successful in the countryside by replacing camp meetings with Sunday schools and church societies. Church women, in particular, enthusiastically organized for a wide variety of causes. Because it was considered unseemly for women to meet on their own "publicly," pastors attended and often presided over these meetings.[36]

From the beginning, clerical professionalism focused on encouraging works of religious benevolence, and city pastors took up works of religious benevolence more often than rural pastors.[37] Cities formed natural hubs for the fledgling denominational work of both Baptists and Methodists from the eighteenth century, and church leaders made their homes there. Methodists divided the state into regions that bore the names of towns and cities. In 1860, nine districts comprised the Virginia Conference of the Methodist Episcopal Church, South: Richmond, Fredericksburg, Washington, Charlottesville, Lynchburg, Danville, Farmville, Petersburg, and Norfolk. Denominational colleges in Richmond and Washington, D.C., drew the most ambitious young pastors. Taught by professors devoted to the professional ideal of the ministry, they grew accustomed to the more stimulating social and intellectual environment, wealthier congregations, and the ease they found there. Even pastors in rural areas read weekly newspapers that were edited and printed in cities.

Antebellum Southern religious institutions fostered urban habits of mind. Those who were most devoted to institution building were those who led the denominations in college classrooms and urban pulpits. And their view, shared by other professionals in nineteenth-century American cities, was that rural churches should follow the lead of urban innovation.

The association of clerical professionalism with urban life emerged clearly in the large clerical assemblies that met annually in cities from the late eighteenth century on. The highlight of the year for many pastors, these meetings fostered an intimate link between cities and the professional culture of the nineteenth-century ministry. As they had for Jeremiah Jeter and Daniel Witt, trips to meetings in Richmond, Baltimore, and New York City provided for many young farmers their first opportunity to visit a city, and some of them found it powerfully attractive. Pastors relished these assemblies for fellowship and gossip as they gathered for a week to report on the progress of their labors and to plan denominational strategy. They shared the difficulties and pleasures of their work and their spiritual struggles. In the antebellum period the proceedings of these meetings were reported in detail, or even in their entirety, in local newspapers, evidence of the social significance of clerical assemblies. Interest and participation in these meetings were not confined to the members of the hosting churches. On the contrary, pulpits across the city were opened to the visiting preachers, and city residents hosted pastors and lay families. Women showed great interest in the preaching and proceedings and attended in large numbers as well.

The festive atmosphere did much to ease the loneliness of the itinerant pastor's life. Methodists in particular suffered not only the trials of travel from church to church on their circuits but also reassignment every two years to a new congregation. Friends were always being left behind, and pastors often had the chance to renew their relations only at clerical assemblies. "One of the lights, or joyful circumstances of itinerancy is the meeting together and mutual comforts of the preachers," Elijah Woolsey recalled. "One of the shadows, sorrowful circumstances [of itinerant life], is the separation and solitary sufferings." One of the most important tasks of the Methodist conference was the announcement of new assignments, a moment of "profound suspense," as one preacher remembered. One year he feared that he would be assigned to "a certain mountain mission, the very hardest place in the Conference." Instead, he received his appointment to a "large, pleasant circuit" with great relief.[38]

The generous salaries earned by those in urban pulpits underscored the centrality of the city to professional prestige. Throughout the nineteenth century, city congregations paid their pastors far more than rural congregations. Churchgoers voluntarily paid these salaries, of course, and their impulse to pay a particular amount was a congregational decision. In the antebellum period, pastoral salaries, which were widely publicized, were taken as a sign of the tastes and status of a congregation. City pastors sometimes earned ten times more than their rural peers did, and urban salaries rapidly increased in late antebellum years. A prominent Richmond Methodist congregation increased its pastor's salary fivefold between 1830 and 1844 alone, when it reached $1,000 annually. By 1852, that church paid its pastor more than $1,600 a year.[39]

These salaries were a significant source of clerical wealth in the antebellum South. In a pioneering study, Brooks Holifield found that Southern urban clergy held considerably more wealth than their Northern peers. He attributed the difference to slaves gained through inheritance and marriage. But the urban clergy's wealth may not have rested solely on slaves acquired through inheritance and marriage, but on their generous salaries. This suggests a fluidity of opportunity in the Southern clerical profession that historians have been reluctant to grant.[40]

Those who prospered in the pulpit, however, tried to be discreet about their success. There were upper, as well as lower, limits to taste and discretion among pious Methodists and Baptists in antebellum Virginia. If a pastor valued his reputation, he was obliged to avoid all appearance of profiting from religion or flaunting his wealth. Those with surplus cash turned to investment. "I know of no safer and more quiet way of making something of my surplus funds, than good six per cent stocks," Methodist James Riddick assured his financial advisor in 1858.[41] Nevertheless, profit some did, even directly from their ministry. Methodist Bishop John Early of Lynchburg, for example, acquired land in Texas on his visits to congregations there. At his death, he left his heirs an income of almost $1,000 annually.[42]

The high urban salaries and liberal resources of city congregations contrasted sharply with those of rural churches. But they also suggested that salaries meant something entirely different to urban ministers. Urban pastors drew salaries that represented the value not only of their work but also of themselves, the very point of professional status. This was a departure from the traditions of the rural ministry, where pastors earned little for their trouble and did not equate their earnings with the value of their work. Those pastors who managed to keep an urban pulpit for even a relatively short time discovered the great financial advantage of their position.

Like the financial context, the social context of city church life differed sharply from that of rural churches. City pastors routinely socialized with lawyers, doctors, merchants, editors, and political leaders. Not only did the sheer expense of their churches and parsonages force city pastors to be more attentive to financial matters than many of those in rural churches, these pastors found themselves among people with high expectations of their preacher. Even those in small towns yearned to see their own aspirations reflected in the man in the Sunday pulpit. Methodists in Staunton, a prosperous town in the Shenandoah Valley, complained incredulously to their bishop in the 1830s after he sent them an unsuitable candidate, there was "no place more important anywhere." A fine town church demanded nothing less than a very fine preacher.[43]

Although most antebellum Methodist and Baptist pastors were from modest rural backgrounds, those who made their way to the city quickly adapted to the more sophisticated way of life. Like many city residents, they felt nostalgia for some aspects of country life. The place of their childhood may have been backward, but it was morally pure. The city offered sophistication, but it was tainted with the lure of worldliness. In April 1844 a Richmond pastor visited a couple in rural Powhatan County and welcomed the escape to a place of simpler tastes. "Having been much used to the society of those who looked upon accumulation of wealth as the chief end of life, and having often desired a quiet retreat from such, this scene of rural life was altogether congenial," he wrote. Even so, condescension tinged his description of the country woman's "artless simplicity" and "unsuspecting demeanor."[44]

The exclusion of blacks, slave and free, from church meetings in fine new churches such as Richmond's First Baptist marked one of the most dramatic distinctions between rural and urban congregations. Whereas eighteenth- and early nineteenth-century rural Southern Protestants generally shared their services, buildings, and preachers with black slaves, by the 1840s, segregated services, even in rural churches, became more common. Segregated churches increased in number during the 1840s and 1850s, and they sharply distinguished between the social context of urban and rural worship.[45] After the establishment of First African Baptist Church in Richmond, for example, white Baptists in that city could view segregation as a sign of social sophistication. Segregated congregations had appeared throughout the South since the eighteenth century, but they were the exception. Religion was an important means of maintaining control over slaves, and slaveholders considered the opportunity for slaves to observe the piety of masters and mistresses during a church service essential to public order. Membership in white congregations, one leading Baptist pastor noted in 1848, removed "the ignorance and superstition of the colored race" through contact with preachers and "intelligent white members."[46]

Nevertheless, city congregations generally created separate black services when the number of black members began to far outnumber whites.[47] In 1836, when Jeremiah Jeter arrived in Richmond, First Baptist Church counted 1,700 members, of whom more than three-quarters were slaves and free blacks. Jeter soon claimed that he could not meet the needs of both blacks and whites, and First African Baptist Church was organized in 1842. Mindful of legal restrictions on black assembly, Jeter persuaded the Rev. Robert Ryland, president of Richmond College and a slaveholder, to lead it, although the church included several ordained black preachers and exhorters. The new congregation was initially controversial, in that blacks had been barred from meeting together since the Turner rebellion in 1831. The congregation met only in the daytime and only in the presence of white leadership. First African Baptist solved the "problem" of a black majority for white members of Second Baptist Church as well, for by 1843, two years after First African opened, that congregation voted that "no coloured members would be received except under peculiar circumstances." After 1841, then, white Baptists in Richmond no longer expected to worship with blacks.[48]

The growing estrangement of black and white members in traditionally biracial churches was rooted in both the social aspirations of an increasingly prosperous white membership and the growing conviction among white leaders that churches should distinguish between the intellectual abilities of black and white churchgoers. If white and black Southerners could be saved by the same preaching in the eighteenth century, by the 1840s whites were inclined to expect that blacks would not respond to the teaching that they themselves found inspiring. In their view, of course, it was they who had moved, not their

African American brethren. Their own tastes increasingly ran toward sermons that were "refined and intellectual," and educated pastors embellished them with literary references that they felt were lost on uneducated people.

The refined image projected by First Baptist's costly building in Richmond was not one to which white church members wished slaves or free blacks to aspire. Its architecture embodied whites' conviction that true religion refined and elevated its adherents, something that could not hold true for Christian slaves or free blacks. At the very least, whites suspected that Christianity could refine and elevate African Americans only in sharply limited ways. Chiefly, religion could improve a black woman's character, as well as assure her a place in heaven. Christian slaves were better slaves; Christian free blacks were presumably more honest and trustworthy than the irreligious. But whites' expectation that religion would refine and uplift white Virginians—socially, culturally, and materially—was out of the question for black Virginians. If white Baptists intended to raise their social status, they could not worship in a church filled with slaves. Being known as a "slave church" was surely a social stigma. By the 1840s, white members of First Baptist found it increasingly difficult to reconcile their vision of a refined and refining religious sensibility with the experience of the black Christians around them.

Publicly, white Baptists placed the reasons for segregation squarely in a practical context. They argued that segregated services were a necessity because black Christians, women and men, slave and free, required a simpler style of teaching and preaching than whites. Robert Ryland, the white pastor of First African Baptist, preached "an eminently plain, instructive, and practical" message to that congregation. "His aim was to make his hearers think rather than feel, and to act rather than to speculate." Meanwhile, Jeremiah Jeter noted that "the style of preaching demanded by the white congregation was not well adapted to . . . colored people."[49]

The view that slaves and free blacks could not be saved or sanctified by the same preaching as whites marked a significant shift in how white Southern Protestants viewed church life. Several themes came together in this shift. It revealed the quixotic hope among white people that black people were inherently simple, probably too simple to be discontented with their station in life, and that they needed white supervision. But it also suggested that laws banning slave and free black literacy created self-fulfilling prophecies. There is evidence that many white Protestants subverted the restrictions on slave literacy (usually out of religious conviction) and were sometimes publicly condemned for doing so. Yet they could not escape their entanglement in the perceptions fostered by those laws. In the end, the ban on teaching slaves encouraged the conviction among Southern whites that black people were unworthy of being taught in the first place.

Low estimates of black intellectual ability also coincided with the growing interest in the use of catechisms to teach religion to children. Church leaders and Sunday school teachers systematized approaches to teaching in Sunday schools at the same time that they embraced the mission to the slaves. Protestants like Robert Ryland wrote catechisms for blacks even as they began to use them to instruct their own children. Catechizing slaves was not just a necessity; whites began to suspect that it was the only effective way to teach an adult population with the intellectual ability of children.

In the main, however, arguments about the intellectual inferiority of blacks marked a profound shift in whites' thinking about the very nature of salvation. It suggested that they were beginning to rely less on the capricious mysteries of the Holy Spirit's saving grace and more on their own ability to teach people to become Christians. The metaphor that most pastors began to prefer was that of church as school, pastor as schoolmaster, and Bible as textbook. Revival religion remained central to the experience of many Southern Protestants in the nineteenth century, but the meaning of revivalism changed in light of their growing fascination with teaching and learning about the faith.

Segregation of churches underscored the growing gap between urban and rural churchgoers. Men like Jeter and Ryland did not urge rural congregations to segregate. In part, this was a pragmatic matter; rural churches did not have the same resources as most urban congregations. Yet Jeter and Ryland also assumed that country churches could remain integrated in part because the simpler sermons of rural pastors suited the needs of both uneducated whites and African American slaves. Many rural churches did hold separate services or Sunday schools for blacks, usually on Sunday afternoons, but rural churches in Virginia were far more likely to continue biracial worship services. City pastors viewed this as natural, and it measured the distance between themselves and their rural brethren. Like the argument that black Christians needed simpler teaching, their views suggested that they had left rural churches behind.

Jeremiah Jeter remembered the preaching of his rural youth as overly controversial and polemical. He charged his elders with spiritualizing texts unnecessarily, with taking "plain historical passages and drawing from them lessons which their authors never dreamed." Over the course of the century, sermons shrank in length from more than one hour to between thirty and forty minutes. They also became less polemical and controversial and more narrative by the end of the century. In 1859, at the newly opened Southern Baptist Theological Seminary, a professor lectured to a small class that included Robert Ryland's son, Charles. He counseled his students that "the character of the times demands [careful sermon preparation]—not as formerly—knowledge now runs in broader if not deeper streams. The people are not satisfied with commonplace ideas and words."[50] But his advice, directed to a small class of seminarians who were likely to take distinguished pulpits, did not address the experience of most Virginia pastors. On the contrary, Cornelius Tyree wrote that he was "compelled to preach to plain people, and being often thrown into meetings where the object was to bring men to Christ, I was led by degrees to prepare and deliver plain, simple sermons, addressed mostly to conscience."[51] Indeed, pastors like Tyree found that in some places in Virginia, too much education could be a disadvantage for a preacher, or even grounds for dismissal.[52]

By midcentury, Methodists and Baptists began to settle into the respectable patterns of religious practice they would follow for the rest of the century. Church colleges, elaborate churches, and segregated congregations all signaled the gentrification of these denominations. City congregations represented the social, intellectual, and material "best" that both Methodists and Baptists had to offer. Their style of worship, architecture, and attitude suggested that true religion and respectability were no longer adversaries but firm allies.

Jeremiah Jeter's impulse to forsake not only his childhood home in rural Virginia but also the religious culture of his youth symbolized the professional promise that the city held out to antebellum pastors. Even before the Civil War, pastors wed their professional standards and status to the institutions and way of life in Virginia cities and towns. In a society dominated by the agricultural economy of slavery, the ministry offered a singular path of social mobility to some farmers' sons in the city, and the increasingly urban bias of professional custom in the ministry emphasized divisions between rural and urban religious life.[53] Yet all over Virginia pastors were trying to bridge the gap. Convinced of the power of religion to refine and uplift people, town and city pastors eagerly spread their cultured religion to the most remote corners of Virginia. The chief instrument in their campaign was the printing press.

CHAPTER THREE

Reading, Writing, and Religion

The majority of pastors in antebellum Virginia were the sons of pastors, yeomen, and artisans, and many were poor. These young men could not hope for careers that would bring them the power and honor of slaveholders. However, they could aspire to greater things than their fathers had. The poor yet ambitious among them had to forgo the traditional basis of Southern gentility—control over slaves and property. Determined to become "gentlemen pastors," they found in education an important means of social mobility. And in their embrace of education for themselves, pastors shaped churches that placed literacy and education at the heart of their work.

James B. Taylor, who became a leading Southern Baptist pastor, pursued self-education into a world apart from that of his cabinetmaker father. Born in 1804, he grew up in Mecklenburg County in Southside Virginia, where his attendance at Sunday school and the books he found there were an important influence in his early life. At thirteen, he began to learn his father's trade, but religion soon eclipsed his interest in cabinetmaking. He began to preach when he was sixteen. Soon after founding a congregation in nearby Clarkesville, he opened a school because many in his congregation could not read, and he eventually taught more than a hundred students there.

In 1824, Taylor became a missionary for the new Baptist General Association of Virginia. Two years later, he moved to Richmond to take the pulpit of the Second Baptist Church, "a feeble band" of generally poor and uneducated people. Using his own example as inspiration, he encouraged church members to "improve themselves" through self-education. He distributed tracts and encouraged benevolent societies even as he eagerly sought out books for his own benefit. Taylor's connections to the countryside led those who moved to Richmond to seek him out. One destitute young apprentice joined Taylor's church after he heard him preach and donated generously to the congregation after he made his fortune.

Like other ministers, Taylor's work often required travel to such cities as New York and Baltimore. By 1833, he had purchased a house in Richmond for $1,600. His skill as a fund-raiser for the new Baptist seminary in Richmond, as well as his interest in other benevolent causes, prompted the American Sunday School Union to invite him to become its agent in Virginia, a post he declined. His chief benevolent interest lay in foreign missions, and in 1836 he became president of the State Board of Missions, a position he held until his death.[1]

In 1839, Taylor was appointed chaplain at the University of Virginia, where he met regularly with professors. During his year there, he wrote his second book, a biography of missionary Luther Rice. Taylor then returned to Richmond, where he took the pulpit at Grace Street Baptist and within a few years won the salaried position of secretary of the Southern Baptist Foreign Mission Board. In 1855, this self-educated cabinetmaker's son received an honorary doctorate from Columbian College in Washington, D.C. Taylor's position brought him financial as well as social benefits; by 1856, he was a director of Richmond's New York Life Insurance Company.[2]

James Taylor's experience highlights the possibilities the ministry offered to enterprising young men of humble status in antebellum Virginia. Central to his vision of self-improvement was his love of reading. From Taylor's earliest recollection, learning to read and getting religion occurred simultaneously, and he eagerly proclaimed the benefits of reading to his congregation.[3]

Taylor's social aspirations were apparent in the opportunities that he provided for his son. George Taylor, who also became a Baptist minister, led a childhood much different from that of his father. James placed learning at the center of his son's life, and books abounded in the Taylor home. When he was fourteen, George enrolled at Richmond College, and on his fifteenth birthday, his father presented the young scholar with a copy of Chambers's *Encyclopedia of English Literature*. George's matriculation at the University of Virginia marked his status as an aspiring gentleman.

The society in which James and George Taylor lived did not easily bestow gentility on preachers. By the 1840s, many Southern gentlemen considered piety an essential trait of their class, but the relationship between gentlemen and preachers remained an uneasy one, even among Presbyterians and Episcopalians. To them, the very idea of an educated Baptist would have seemed a contradiction in terms. Few Baptist or Methodist pastors owned many slaves or large tracts of land or had distinguished family connections. Taylor and his peers, however, did not aspire to a place in the drawing rooms of James River plantations. They considered their acceptance among urban professionals and merchants evidence enough of improvement, and there they found their niche.[4]

In rural Virginia, most Baptist and Methodist pastors had little hope of entering the privileged world of the planter. The few wealthy families whose homes became "preacher's homes," or places where traveling pastors were routinely welcomed, were especially prized. "I not only felt free; I felt rich," a Baptist wrote of his visits to a layman's plantation in the central Piedmont.

"For the time, I seemed to be the owner of a large house and 1,200 acres of land; everything about me was mine to use and enjoy."[5]

James Taylor's entrance into the ministry was a way for him to feel free and even rich. This son of a tradesman took firm hold of the course of his own life even as he preached of a world ruled firmly by God. He reconciled his own avid pursuit of an education and self-improvement with his understanding that God was sovereign. Like many of his peers, Taylor's life in the ministry combined meaningful work with professional success, a divine calling with the pleasant, if modest, life of an educated and esteemed pastor. James Taylor loved the things of Christ, but he suspected that they included the finely bound volumes of essays and poetry that lined his shelves.

Taylor's experience suggests how education, even self-education, could smooth the path to an urban pulpit in the antebellum South. In a place and time where most young white Southern men had little chance of leaving the farm, college education remained part of an exalted world. Most considered those who attended college or university as gentlemen.[6] By encouraging prospective young ministers to value and pursue education, Virginia Baptists and Methodists pushed the democratization of gentility deep into the Southern countryside.

The ministry offered men like Taylor a means of social mobility in the slave South. James and George Taylor's search for respectability placed them squarely in the tradition of Americans of their day, where "almost every man consider[ed] himself a gentleman." There was nothing particularly Southern about their hunger for self-improvement and social respectability. In the South as in the North, Americans tended to equate financial success with genteel respectability, and educated Virginia pastors, particularly those with a generous salary from an urban church, were no exception.[7]

In the 1850s, the number of young ministers who attended college rose dramatically over that of earlier generations. Although those ordained in the 1820s and 1830s could find their way into prominent pulpits without formal education, during the 1850s it became a virtual prerequisite for acceptance into the best ministerial circles. Those who aspired to professional excellence knew that they must educate themselves. Almost two-thirds of Methodist and Baptist pastors in Virginia ordained during the 1850s, or twice as many as in the previous generation, attended college (see Appendix, Table 8).

Overall, Baptists attended college in greater numbers than Methodists, particularly for the earlier generation. Among pastors ordained before 1850, more than one-third of Baptists and one-fifth of Methodists attended college for any period of time. These numbers jumped to more than two-thirds of Baptists and just over half of Methodists for pastors ordained in the 1850s. Baptists were also far more likely to attend college out of state, although Methodist pastors were more likely to attend the University of Virginia.

By the 1850s, leading Methodist and Baptist pastors had embraced the ideal of the educated clergyman. Neither denomination required a college degree for ordination until the twentieth century, but this was a pragmatic concession to the realities of Southern life rather than a cherished principle. Leading pastors highly esteemed education, and they tirelessly promoted the virtues of an educated ministry.

Debates about education's place in clerical training were tied to a wider public debate.[8] Politicians and voters briefly exhibited interest in education reform in the late 1830s and 1840s. Educated Virginians were embarrassed by reports of high white illiteracy rates, and clergymen were among the staunchest supporters of reform. "Intelligence is necessary to the preservation of our liberties," a Baptist argued, asking pastors to attend a meeting of educational leaders in Richmond. Another was more to the point. "So long as a single county in Virginia contains . . . freemen unable to read and write . . . so long will the same page that records her glory also record her shame. We would make the Legislative halls of Virginia now to echo long and loud: Educate, Educate, EDUCATE the People."[9] Legislators did levy a tax to pay for free primary education, but opposition to tax-supported public schools meant the measure went unenforced. The failure of this initiative in spite of fervent support from the state's leading clergymen suggested their limited political influence. In mid-nineteenth-century Virginia, education remained a privilege for those who could pay for it, as it had been since the colonial period.[10]

Debates about clerical education within Virginia congregations, however, reflected deep ambivalence about the nature of the ministry itself. At the heart of the dispute was the question of whether God made pastors or whether the ministry was a profession. Throughout the nineteenth century, missionary Baptists and Methodists associated education with self-improvement and worldly pride. The former was to be sought, the latter to be avoided at all cost. At issue was not basic literacy; even those who opposed clerical education as unbecomingly worldly did not oppose universal white literacy, and some thought slaves should learn to read the Bible as well. What many did question was the value of a classical education to a preacher of the Gospel. Knowledge of the classics had long been regarded as the mark of a gentleman. Although a few Methodist and Baptist clergymen did attend the University of Virginia and similar schools, most did not consider such places appropriate training grounds for future ministers. Ministers did not need an intimate acquaintance with ancient pagans; the Bible alone was the proper focus of a Christian mind. Education puffed a man up, and an educated minister might rely on the folly of his own mind rather than the guidance of the Holy Spirit. Virginians should not despise ministers who had no education, one seventy-year-old "old-fashioned preacher" argued in 1852, because the Apostle Peter had none.[11]

Others who opposed a formal educational requirement, however, did support ministerial education. They expected that their pastors should spend hours studying the Scriptures, theological works, and even secular literature. In 1844, the small Beulah Baptist Association cited study as the "second point of necessity for a preacher." The Bible was the premier text, of course, but "the book of Nature may be studied, too. All science and nature may be made tributary to religion."[12] Methodists had a long tradition of examining their ministerial candidates and tested their lay preachers on theological texts as well as on the Bible and the Methodist Discipline.[13] They encouraged any young man who could afford to go to school to do so. But in their view, *requiring* college education for a minister was simply impractical in a state with no public school system. "I go for educating the masses," a Methodist pastor wrote to a friend in the late 1850s. "Let our people generally rise with the advance of education and God will always call the right class of men."[14]

Senior ministers sometimes counseled young men against attending college when they knew of an empty pulpit. Joseph Amiss, ordained in 1854, encountered opposition from some pastors when he requested ordination because he lacked schooling. Yet they later ordained him and even counseled him against further formal study. "I think one of the great mistakes of my life was yielding to the advice of some of the elder preachers," he later wrote. "I was not prepared and should have gone to school longer." James Lumsden also yielded to the advice of an elder to leave college but later regretted doing so. Lumsden, a Scottish immigrant and former gunsmith's apprentice, also spent the balance of his career in rural pulpits.[15]

In fact, by the 1850s, in denominations that raised up fine brick churches and college endowments, the definition of the "right class of men" had changed. Even in the 1830s and 1840s, notions of a self-educated ministry were under attack by church leaders, who wished to establish the professional credentials of the ministry and to appeal to a more refined audience. A tiny number of ministers did attend theological seminaries in these years, primarily at northeastern schools, and were rewarded with top positions. When Southern Baptists opened their seminary in South Carolina in 1859, Virginia supported the school with enthusiasm by sending the most young men of any Southern state. Charles Hill Ryland, son of the president of Richmond College, was one of several students who attended the first session in Greenville. His notebooks reveal the wide range of studies offered, ranging from pastoral theology to instructions about negotiating a salary. On balance, Ryland received more instruction that year in practical matters than on theology. Instructors cautioned Ryland's class, for example, not to offend members of their congregations and told them to decline a salary offer if they deemed it too small.[16]

But leading pastors recognized the impropriety of pushing their new ideas too far among potentially resistant older generations and rural congregations. The decision to forgo educational requirements was thus a savvy compromise. Although leading pastors refused to institute education as a formal requirement, they embraced it as an informal one. By doing so, they avoided charges of elitism even as they groomed ministers to become gentlemen professionals.

Education dominated discussions of professional standards during the 1850s. Before that time, talented men without college training could still advance into the upper ranks of the ministry. James Taylor and Jeremiah Jeter, as well as other Baptists, rose to prominent positions with little if any formal education. But by the 1850s, some congregations, particularly urban ones, would take nothing but educated men. Taylor and Jeter, although self-educated, took great care to display refined manners and ardently supported ministerial education. Occasionally senior ministers even held back young men destined for careers in small rural churches for want of an education.[17] Even as leading ministers and congregations rejected a formal educational requirement for the ministry, they made it clear that ambitious young men should meet one.

But getting an education in antebellum Virginia, especially for men of typically poor or modest means, was not easy. Lack of support from friends and family, lack of adequate preparation, and above all, lack of money, proved formidable barriers to even the most ambitious among them. "If [ministerial candidates] are indigent—and such the Holy Spirit most frequently moves to assume this office," a Baptist explained in 1851, "it is [the churches'] province and privilege to contribute generously to their comfort."[18]

Financing ministerial education thus became a priority. Those who desired an educated ministry realized that denominations needed their own schools with a new philosophy of education. The appearance of denominational colleges throughout the South marked a unique experiment in the use of education to refine and uplift farmer's sons.

Ministerial training was the impetus behind the establishment of Methodist and Baptist colleges in the region during the 1820s and 1830s. Virginia Baptists had a long relationship with Columbian College in Washington, D.C., founded by missionary Luther Rice in 1822. Rice and other Baptists felt an educated ministry was needed to support their missionary enterprises. Virginians raised much of the money for the college's operation, although it soon fell on hard times. During this lull, Virginia Baptists decided that the state needed its own school. In 1830, James Taylor and other state leaders organized the Virginia Baptist Education Society, which opened a simple boarding school at the large Powhatan County plantation of Mrs. Ann Hickman. Six students took a simple course of study and worked on the farm to support themselves. Support for a seminary grew, and in 1832 Baptists purchased a farm four miles north of Richmond. By 1833 the college supported twenty students—of whom sixteen were given free tuition because they were approved for entry into the ministry. Two years later, the school moved to a farm just west of Richmond, where sixty students enrolled.[19]

Virginia Methodists decided to build their seminary in 1825. They chose a remote site in Mecklenburg County, Boydton, after that county made the most generous offer to win the school. Methodists spent about $14,000 to purchase 240 acres and build their school. Randolph-Macon College was chartered in 1830 and opened its doors to students in 1832. By 1838, the school enrolled more than one hundred students.[20]

Yet even while church leaders established these schools to train ministers, they de-emphasized theology in their course offerings. Even the most enthusiastic advocates of an educated ministry in antebellum Virginia did not regard theological training as a requirement for the pulpit. They regarded the conversion experience as the primary spiritual preparation needed by most pastors; enough theology could be gained through individual study.[21] State legislators were also reluctant to charter a theological school. Both Baptists and Methodists prized their state charters, which allowed them to cast their schools as beneficial to the broader society. Neither Randolph-Macon College nor Richmond College, therefore, ever planned a course in theology. Nathan O. Hatch has noted that the leader of the Christian Church, Alexander Campbell, "gained a charter for his Bethany College from the state of Virginia with the curious provision that no professorship of theology ever be established." Although Campbell's disdain for the "priesthood" undoubtedly influenced the school's curriculum, the state charter would not have been granted had the school included a theological curriculum. The focus on general education was also prompted by practical and financial considerations: administrators had neither the money nor the students to offer a full theological course. The solvency of these schools was tenuous, and they operated solely on a tuition basis. They could survive only by offering a general educational course.[22]

The focus on general education was risky, however, because a general education could be acquired at other schools. Ministerial candidates whose aspirations outstripped the modest offerings of Richmond College and Randolph-Macon College could attend a better-known school, and those who did so were usually rewarded with prime pulpits. Although the number of ministers who attended college jumped by 50 percent in this period, the percentage of young men who attended the state's denominational colleges saw only a modest increase. One-third of ministers attended state denominational schools in the 1850s, twice the number from the earlier generation, while the percentage of those who attended the University of Virginia in the 1850s tripled to 15 percent. By 1861, some Baptists complained that many young men at Richmond College were transferring to more prestigious schools.[23]

Church leaders realized that they would need to recruit aggressively if they hoped to keep their schools open. Even while convinced of education's social and moral benefits, they were aware that, in the end, education was also a business. Both Baptists and Methodists invested heavily in education during the 1850s.[24] They worked hard to keep costs down to attract students from families of modest means. The first president of Randolph-Macon College, for example, affirmed the school's desire to "reduce the charges of education to the lowest possible amount" to ensure a place for students from families of modest means.[25]

Even these measures, however, did not bring costs low enough to benefit many of the young men who wanted to enter the ministry. To aid such men, Southern pastors began a system of educational charity for prospective ministers that continued into the twentieth century. It became one of the most important determinants of who entered the ministry. Ministerial students either paid no tuition or paid sharply reduced rates. Some young men enlisted the aid of a wealthy benefactor; others benefited from special fund-raising efforts in their own congregations. In the postbellum period, denominations lent tuition money to ministerial students, expecting them to pay back the money after they were employed. By all of these means, churches offered an education to young men who could not otherwise afford one, making the ministry an attractive choice for ambitious young men of modest means. For schools that were struggling to stay open, the decision to sponsor ministerial students free of charge or at reduced rates made little financial sense, but it did underscore Virginia Baptists' and Methodists' fierce commitment to an educated ministry.

Not only were denominational colleges more accessible than other schools, their philosophy of education differed from that of the old field schools, classical academies, and state universities. Teachers in rural schools struggled to make poor students barely literate, and professors of elite schools polished young Virginia gentlemen. At denominational colleges, by contrast, education was a tool of self-improvement and service to the community. "Live to be useful, rather than illustrious," a Methodist bishop exhorted students at Randolph-Macon College in 1844.[26]

Virginia's pastor-professors delighted in taking raw, intelligent farmers' sons and pushing them up the social ladder by refining their sensibilities and sharpening their intellects. Their enthusiasm for religious schooling overwhelmed even their vision of the necessity of church congregations. As a Virginia Baptist pastor declared in 1853, the fulcrum at which to stand if one wished to overturn the world was "the District School, the Academy, the College. Let me govern them, and I will revolutionize the world." It was a telling slip of the tongue. By the 1850s, leading Baptists and Methodists had committed themselves to turning their world upside down through the school rather than the church.[27]

Schools were poor instruments of revolution, however. The few hundred young Virginians who attended Randolph-Macon and Richmond College before the Civil War learned the manners and tastes of gentlemen, not of revolutionaries. At a time when college students were considered gentlemen, even those who managed to stay in school for only a brief time were shaped by the experience. The very nature of these schools, with their general educational offerings, bent young men toward genteel expressions of piety and away from the manners they had learned to associate with religion in their plain churches. The new pastors eagerly took these habits with them when they returned to their small congregations, if they were not quick or lucky enough to win a more prized position.

The majority of ministers, however, remained self-educated.[28] That left the minority who attended college or seminary with few rivals in defining the ideals of the young clerical profession. "The churches . . . should unanimously and at once discourage from preaching all *young* men who are unwilling to pursue a course of liberal study," the Virginia Baptist Educational Society soberly declared in 1851. "We have little confidence in the integrity of any *young man* who, professing a great love for souls, is yet too indolent or too self-conceited to toil for the acquisition of that knowledge that is so needed to win souls."[29] And if knowledge was the key to ushering souls into the Kingdom of God, then surely an educated ministry was a necessity rather than a

luxury. "The minister of Christ should neglect no opportunities for improvement, and should strive to become at least respectable in every branch of
human learning," one pastor argued.[30] The rising number of young men who
received an education during the 1850s suggests that many heeded such arguments.

Education did more than shape the prospects of aspiring young ministers;
it also provided a few of them an income after ordination. Denominational
colleges established in the 1830s flowered during the 1840s and 1850s, when
the cause of public education languished and died in Virginia, and Baptists
and Methodists raised $100,000 endowments in voluntary contributions for
each of their state colleges. The president of Richmond College argued at its
founding that the school would become the center of intellectual life in Richmond and compared it to schools like Brown and Harvard. If his predictions
were grandiose, by the end of the 1850s, Richmond College did boast six professors, a building, a library, and a scientific apparatus. The school had more
than doubled its enrollment of twenty years earlier to 161 students. In addition,
Virginia Baptists provided two of the four professors and the largest number
of students of any Southern state for the first session of the Southern Baptist
Theological Seminary in Greenville, South Carolina, in 1859. Virginia Methodists, too, saw the interests of Randolph-Macon flourish during the 1850s.
By 1858, 165 students were enrolled. Additionally, an unprecedented number
of church-affiliated academies for men and women opened between 1845 and
1861. Pastors and laity also opened private academies, and in some cases,
congregations established their own schools. These schools provided a few
sought-after teaching jobs.[31]

The themes of reform, gentility, and the city all came together in women's
education. Southerners exhibited growing interest in women's education during the antebellum period, and churchgoing people supplied much of this
attention. Churchgoing women had long viewed education as a special area
of responsibility. Religious women read as much as, and perhaps more, than
men did. But beyond its ability to cultivate spirituality in individuals, education
afforded women a means of influence in society as a whole. The women of
First Baptist Church in Richmond formed the Maternal Association in August
1842, for example, with the purpose of affording "mutual aid in the education,
and especially the religious education, of our children." They declared, "It is
a question . . . whether the mother of a household of children or the governor
of the Commonwealth has the more weighty and responsible office to sustain."[32] Likewise, pastors and laymen argued that churches needed educated
women to promote religious benevolence. "Throw yourselves into the current
of virtuous action," John Wright told the young women at Robert F. Stubbs's
Female School. "Women are the greatest educators of mankind," Jeremiah
Jeter wrote in 1858, no mean compliment from a man thoroughly committed
to the virtues of education. He continued, "True, men and women are called
to labor in different spheres . . . but do not females need an education to fit
them to occupy, with grace and usefulness, their important position in society."
Pastors and their wives often opened female schools, and one congregation

even founded a school. Antebellum Virginia Baptist women could attend Valley Union Seminary (later Hollins College), Albemarle Female Institute, or Richmond Female Institute.[33]

The Richmond Female Institute was the most ambitious denominational project for women's education in antebellum Virginia. Baptists opened their elegant, debt-laden Italianate brick school with much fanfare in 1854. President Basil Manly Jr. had traveled to eight Northern cities to observe the operations of no less than thirty women's schools. From the beginning, Baptists conceived the school as an academy for the most genteel young women of the state. Trustees turned a deaf ear to complaints that the $280 annual board and tuition was too high for most Baptist families. Tuition could not be reduced without the "sacrifice of style and quality," they argued.[34] Neither could they offer students a board that was "genteel, nutritious and palatable . . . be afforded at a price materially less." They built an elaborate $60,000 building in the center of the city that plunged the enterprise into embarrassing debt. Like men's schools, the institute offered a general educational course without reference to sectarian religious principles, in the hopes of drawing the largest possible constituency.

The city setting of the school was unique, as most women's academies of the era were located deep in the countryside to shelter students from temptation. In a striking departure, Baptist leaders proclaimed the city a fit setting for women's education. "A young lady completing her education in a city would necessarily have much valuable knowledge that could not be secured by one educated in seclusion [in the country], supposing their instructors equal," Jeremiah Jeter wrote. Students at the institute would be "rigidly supervised and free from . . . all influences tending to pervert their tastes and habits," thus allowing them to partake of all the advantages of city life without being corrupted by it. Administrators brushed off arguments that the young women would be exposed to fashion and vanity in the city and "become unfit for plain country life."[35]

In spite of the appeal and success of denominational schools like Richmond College and Richmond Female Institute, pastors knew that such institutions would draw only a tiny number of Virginians. These schools were never intended to educate the mass of Virginia's white children. Their high tuition rates assured a discriminating clientele. But pastors' interest in education extended beyond these schools. They set education before all of those in their congregations, rich and poor, as a worthy goal. As men who had an abiding faith in the uplifting and refining properties of education, they saw no reason why even the poorest families could not improve their children. James Taylor himself "loved to see how the Gospel worked up—improving men's circumstances and in every respect elevating their condition as well as their character."[36]

The connection between religion and education was not a specious one; for men like James Taylor it was grounded in their own experience. Many of them had benefited socially from their own education, and of those who had labored at other vocations before the ministry, the vast majority had worked as schoolteachers. Many pastors continued to teach even after they took up preaching. For them, salvation, intellectual refinement, and professional success followed naturally one after the other.

In 1840, the Virginia Baptist Education Society issued a call for the faithful to "tythe of their possessions to Learning and Science, in the hope that they will thereby not only elevate the intellectual, social and moral condition of the present and future generations, but that such elevation will be rendered subservient to the Cross of Christ."[37] The society did more than call Baptists to render to "science" a service usually reserved for God alone. Their call itself suggested that education worked to advance the Gospel by encouraging self-improvement.

The education society was an elite group of pastors and laymen, with a healthy contingent of men from Richmond who had strong financial ties to Richmond College. But other pastors called their congregations to educate in the name of Christ. Even country schools took on a remarkable religious significance, as a scene one summer morning in 1852 suggests. After the daily prayer and Bible reading at Rev. J. B. Tombes's school, a student entreated the pastor and teacher to pray for his salvation. "Soon, I was surrounded," Tombes wrote. "The whole school was in tears." Christian students pressed their peers to flee to Christ and, sensing the futility of proceeding with their usual lessons, Tombes told his students to "put up [their] books and turned the school into a prayer meeting."[38]

Pastors in late antebellum Virginia could hardly distinguish between schools and prayer meetings. Church leaders endowed education and literary culture with an importance that at times rivaled that of Christian conversion itself. In their view, salvation, education, and benevolence were of one piece. In a series of addresses to Virginia Methodist college students in the 1840s, Methodist Pastor David S. Doggett routinely described the pursuit of knowledge in ways that could have applied to Christian salvation itself. Most necessary to an educated man was the cultivation of a "severe taste," the professor and future bishop argued. "Taste may be either pure or depraved. It is the latter by nature; it is the former only by cultivation. A bad taste impairs and depraves the whole character . . . a good taste ennobles, expands, and invigorates the powers." The neglect of taste, he assured his listeners, would result in personal failure; but education could redeem a depraved taste.[39]

Historians have examined the print revolution in antebellum America in a variety of settings—among Northeastern pastors, reform-minded New England women, abolitionists, and temperance enthusiasts. To the extent that it arrived in rural Virginia, pastors brought it there. Virginia pastors, no less than their northern peers, were keenly aware of literature's power to influence tastes and values, as well as to prompt Christian conversion. Southerners outlawed slave literacy precisely because they recognized the power of print. "It is impossible to estimate the power and influence of books in forming the principles and opinion of countries and communities either for good or for evil," a minister wrote in 1852.[40] Virginia pastors were determined that their congregations should read and utterly convinced that such reading would yield both spiritual and social benefits.

Pastors promoted the religious and moral benefits of literary culture at a time when reading, the ownership of books, and the free time in which to read them were largely pastimes of the privileged. Many Virginians scoffed at learning and literature. For them, "education" conjured visions of young gentlemen studying classical subjects in the spare elegance of the College of William and Mary. The much-derided old field schools defined the upper limits of most farmers' sons' formal education. Virginia custom decreed that education was reserved for the gentry.

In the agricultural South, of course, most Baptists and Methodists did not need much learning to make a living, and some did view formal schooling as an unnecessary luxury. But few opposed literacy, and many valued education of any sort. Nearly all viewed education as an inherently moral endeavor that would best be undertaken in a religious context, and in the state that produced Jefferson's Virginia Statute for Religious Freedom, they did not expect public schools to teach religion. Nevertheless, the reading of the Scriptures was at the center of the Protestant life, and some taught their slaves to read the Bible.

Pragmatism defined most Virginians' views of education. Pious families wanted to read the Bible, but they did not need schooling to make a living. The notorious "old field" schools available to common Southerners met irregularly, if at all, and even these were not free. Most were not willing to educate their children at expensive secondary schools, much less colleges. In 1845, a state report estimated that just over 8 percent of white Virginians were illiterate; fifteen years later that figure had fallen a mere 1 percent. Less than one-third of white children attended school regularly in 1860. An overwhelming majority of African Americans were illiterate and barred from formal schooling.[41]

Even so, historians have underestimated interest in reading and education in the nineteenth-century South. They have interpreted low figures for school attendance as a lack of regard for education rather than a lack of opportunity. They have underestimated the number of schools in the region because they have neglected religious periodicals that printed hundreds of notices of schools. They have interpreted opposition to public schools as disgust with taxes rather than a taste for schooling in a religious and moral context. They have viewed the South's characteristic anti-intellectualism as antagonism toward all reading and books rather than a preference for popular literature.

In an agricultural region without public schools, it is literacy, rather than illiteracy, that needs to be explained. Without Horace Mann or public schools, and given their agricultural economy, Southerners learned to read in astonishing numbers. A large majority of white Southerners were literate, and as many as 10 percent of slaves could read. North Carolina had the smallest number of literate white residents in 1860, at 77 percent; Mississippi, Louisiana, and Texas had the highest number, at 90 percent. In 1860, 85 percent of white Virginians could read. This rate is approximately double that of the rate of school attendance for white children, which was about 40 percent in 1860 (see Appendix, Tables 9 and 10). What accounts for this difference? How did Virginians learn to read? And what was their motive for doing so?[42]

Religion provided both the motive and the means to read. Even many of those who never learned to read at all learned to value it because of religion. "The frequent hearing of my mistress reading the Bible aloud," Frederick Douglass remembered of his childhood on Maryland's Eastern Shore, "awakened my curiosity in respect to this mystery of reading, and roused in me the desire to learn." Slave and free learned that religion and reading were bound up together.

This was true not only because of the long association of literacy and piety in the Protestant tradition, but also because education was the chief work of religious benevolence in the antebellum South. In a region with no public schools, churches and ministers shouldered the principle burden of schooling. This work absorbed much of the reform sentiment entertained by Northern churches that had the luxury of schools to teach basic literacy. In the South, churches were schools and church people were schoolmasters and mistresses for a long stretch of the nineteenth century.

In a state that would not see public schools for three decades, few voices preached the virtues of education with the fervor of Virginia pastors and lay leaders. By the 1850s, pastors assumed that church members valued reading, and that if they could afford the tuition or the loss of labor in their fields, they would educate their children. Anyone who read church newspapers or attended a church meeting was assaulted by their enthusiasm. "This is an age of excitement and in some ways, an age of improvement. The cause of education is gaining ground and many are waking up to its importance," Baptist James Gwaltney declared in 1850.[43]

Common Southerners of both races valued reading and books more than they valued formal schooling, and this distinction accounts for much of the disparity between literacy and school attendance. The very rarity of books in their world gave them a peculiar power. The eagerness of emancipated slaves to read had deep roots in the antebellum period. Laws banning slave literacy stand as the most powerful example of how much white slaveholders feared, and revered, books. Southerners feared only books of a certain kind, however. The book of the South was the Bible, and Southerners' obsession with it fostered a popular religious literature of biblical proportions even before the

Civil War. Pastors and colporteurs peddled newspapers, pamphlets, commentaries, lexicons, hymnals, and dictionaries to the remotest corners of the region.

Peddlers of religious books, or colporteurs, sold or gave away thousands of books in rural Virginia from the end of the eighteenth century. One of the best known peddlers of the early national period, the Anglican parson Mason Weems, traversed rural Virginia and the Carolinas selling his wares in the Early National period. Weems's colorful accounts of his travels not only suggest how closely literary and religious culture were intertwined but also reveal the existence of a lively market for books in Virginia.[44]

In the eighteenth and early nineteenth centuries, pastors of all persuasions, high church and low, routinely sold books throughout the Virginia countryside. "Circulate good books," a Methodist elder counseled a young minister in 1824. "Our plan of printing and circulating religious books is admirably calculated to aid the minister in his work." The pastor advised reading religious periodicals to the congregation, as well as reading books before recommending them to laymen and women, so that he "could teach them the necessity and utility of a continual acquisition of Christian knowledge."[45]

The peddling of "Christian knowledge" was particularly significant in the rural South, where reading materials were scarce. Colporteurs provided a critical supply link between urban publishers and printers and readers in the antebellum countryside. And they were successful. One study found that almost three-fourths of the titles owned by Virginians who had fewer than ten books were religious ones. A pastor born in 1831 in a remote mountain area recalled his parents' library of "standard Methodist works, some histories, and a few works of fiction" to which they added regularly from Methodist colporteurs. In addition to forging connections with Virginia printers and bookshops, pastors distributed literature offered by national tract societies. Virginia Baptists, for example, developed an early relationship with the American Tract Society. The Virginia Baptist General Association founded the Virginia Tract Association a few years later.[46]

In part, the use of literature as an important agent of moral persuasion grew out of the traditional Protestant emphasis on study of the Scriptures, but pastors embraced other types of religious literature as well. Colporteurs sold not only Bibles but also biographies, theologies, commentaries, devotional literature, newspapers, and children's literature. They also distributed large numbers of tracts and pamphlets.[47]

The demand for Christian literature opened yet another task to pastors. Publishing, as R. Laurence Moore has argued, was "one of the primary ways to prescribe and contest values during the nineteenth century," and Virginia clergymen did not ignore the opportunity.[48] Publishing not only extended the influence of Christianity but also furthered pastors' professional reputation and provided a source of extra income. Antebellum Virginia clergymen were less susceptible to the whims of the publishing market than those in other places simply because of the scarcity of books in rural areas. In contrast to other parts of the country, the relation between Virginia clergymen, printers, and publishers was particularly close. Religious materials made up a significant number of all works published by Virginia presses, and pastors wielded great influence over the small print market in the state. A number of printers and editors were laymen in city churches. Although these pastors depended on the tastes of readers and the whims of the marketplace for success, publishing a book in antebellum Virginia tended to enhance clerical authority. If preachers still viewed the pulpit as the highest calling of a pastor, they began to give print a prestigious place in the work of religion.[49]

That few pastors published a book underscores the elite connotation books and learning carried in the profession. A search of 173 pastors ordained before 1861 revealed six authors and thirteen titles still extant in major libraries. Pastors published many of these works with New York firms. Of the works published, the majority were either biographies or theological or polemical treatises, which suggests that pastors often wrote for other pastors. They also wrote for a popular audience and published lectures and essays on a wide variety of religious and moral topics. They did not limit themselves to religious subjects. Pastors trained in other professions published specialized works, and one Methodist preacher published an account of his European travels with scarcely a reference to religion. Instead, his purpose in writing it was to both "increase his stores of knowledge and to widen the area of scientific research." In the late 1850s, George B. Taylor, the son of James Taylor, published a series of novels for youths that emphasized the value of reading and education on nearly every page. They presented an idealized world of an educated Southern pastor, who lived in the city and was closely connected with publishers and editors. Their purpose, Taylor wrote, was "not so much to convey direct moral and religious instruction as to have it pervade the very atmosphere of the narrative." As his words suggest, religious novels were a poor vehicle for dogma. Rather, they communicated general religious values and moral principles.[50]

Newspapers provided far easier access to print than books did, and many pastors wrote letters and theological pieces that appeared in the columns of Virginia's Methodist and Baptist weeklies. Both papers reached readers beyond Virginia's borders; the *Religious Herald* was a particularly well-known Baptist organ in the South. Periodicals, too, appeared. The *Virginia Baptist Preacher*, which began publication in the early 1840s, was one of the first publications with an eye toward correcting the deficiencies of the rural church. The editor, a prominent Richmond Baptist layman and printer, argued that his journal was "calculated to diminish the evil" caused by the lack of churches in many areas of the state by providing readers with printed sermons. The journal published "sermons not written on the other side of the Atlantic or a century ago, but among us and now," arguing that "profitable conversation, a well-directed press, salutary laws, popular education, and a general diffusion of good moral principles" would result if Baptists would subscribe. "What do you do all day Sunday—especially when you can't attend meeting? How will you manage to employ long winter nights? Don't you read *politics*?" one writer pleaded for the journal's cause.[51]

The goal of popular education lay at the heart of religious publishing enterprises. Editors used their religious newspapers and periodicals to exhort Virginia congregations to read ever more. Their appeals appeared next to advertisements touting the latest editions of the Bible, theological works, histories, or novels sold by Virginia booksellers and printers. Some Baptists suggested that secular novels were not injurious, so long as they were worthy ones. Sir Walter Scott, for example, fell into the meritorious category; George Sand did not.[52] Advertisements, along with the success of colporteurs, attested to the existence of a lively publishing market in antebellum Virginia.

Antebellum publishers and editors tried desperately to expand this market. Religious newspapers, for example, initially catered to the pastorate but gradually increased subscriptions among laymen and women. By 1850, the Baptist *Religious Herald* reached 2,500 Virginians, fewer than 5 percent of Regular Baptists in the state. Worried editors noted that the competing Virginia Methodist paper had a circulation of almost 4,000, and lamented that "our [Southern] population is not yet so much a reading one as that of the North."[53] Reading, even of religious materials, remained a pastime of relatively few Virginians. And yet these periodicals reached an audience that scorned the exalted tone of Virginia's numerous literary magazines.

By the 1850s, pastors anxious to professionalize the ministry urged that colportage be made a task separate from that of the ordained ministry. Both Baptists and Methodists began to hire full-time colporteurs in large numbers during the 1850s. City dwellers, unlike rural pastors, could refer those who inquired about books to neighborhood bookshops and printers, some of which were owned by Baptist and Methodist laymen. But some Virginians chafed at these new "professional" standards. One Baptist maligned the notion that "has crept into the minds of some people of late that the selling of good religious books and preaching the Gospel are incompatible . . . where is the minister who has not carried books to his appointment and sold them?—and, simple soul, thought he was doing God's service!" Between them, pastors and colporteurs sold books by the thousands during the 1850s. Reports of success poured in from all over the state. In 1852, Baptists alone employed sixty-nine colporteurs who sold 40,000 books and gave away an additional 14,000. These 54,000 volumes alone represented a significant percentage of the entire estimated number of books in the state. By 1856, the number of Baptist colporteurs had increased to nearly a hundred. Many of the materials were printed by the Southern Baptist Publication Society, founded in 1847 to promote "works by Southern men."[54]

Peddling was an institution of rural life in early-nineteenth-century America and, like their peers in the North, Virginia peddlers were generally ambitious and entrepreneurial young men. For colporteurs, like those who sold clocks and other household goods, peddling was a means of social mobility.

Peddlers relished the small but consistent income, their ability to travel, and the contacts they made throughout the state with pastors, congregations, and book publishers. For many it provided a way off the farm and into the pulpit. Colportage was also considered a fine way to train for the ministry "because [a colporteur] sees men as they are and not as they appear to be on Lord's day at church."[55]

Church leaders considered selling books an important missionary task of the church. State denominations paid colporteurs a small annual salary, in return for which they submitted an annual report of their labors. In them, colporteurs reported both success and surprise at the scarcity of books in the Virginia countryside. "I visited a poor family and asked the lady of the house if she had a Bible," Rev. J. C. Clopton wrote of his travels in the Albemarle Association in 1861. She did not, but she had borrowed one from neighbors who could not read and had read it to them in return for the favor. Another man expressed frustration at a visit with a "wealthy" antimissionary Baptist family in the mountains who had no Bible. Yet another related that his sales had touched off a demand for books. "I was told by a merchant this morning that since I sold some books in his neighborhood, he had never heard such an inquiry for books," a colporteur wrote in 1858, noting that he encountered a "great anxiety" for books wherever he traveled.[56]

Like all peddlers, colporteurs were strangers in the communities where they worked, and they often traveled under suspicion. Credentials were important. "The bearer Rev. Hiram Myers is authorized as colporteur of Rockingham District of the Methodist Episcopal Church. . . . I commend the bearer to our people," a letter pinned to the front cover of Myers's account book of 1858–60 read. Such credentials were especially needed because Myers and his peers also collected money for church benevolent work and periodical subscriptions. Impostors abounded. "The Sunday School and Publication Board has *never* had in its employ any one named Brooks," a printed announcement sternly warned in 1861. "In Campbell and Orange Counties we have been censured for the eccentricities of this man who calls himself a 'Baptist colporteur.' "[57]

Colporteurs labored at the frontier of literary culture in antebellum Virginia. Their work provided an important clue to the pattern of religious literary culture in the state, as city pastors and laymen sent colporteurs into the countryside. In literary culture and education, as in other areas of antebellum life, the most profound fault lines lay between Virginia's countryside and her towns and cities. City pastors and editors and their few rural allies tirelessly promoted literary culture and education through colportage, fund-raising campaigns for their schools and colleges, periodical articles, advertisements, and even the pulpit itself. Their work represented one of the most important conduits of city culture into the antebellum Virginia countryside. Through colporteurs, newspapers, and books, rural Virginians who had never visited a city became familiar with urban tastes and customs. "The diffusion of a pure Christian literature is a powerful auxiliary towards building up the Redeemer's Kingdom in the world," a Baptist wrote upon the organization of the Southern

Baptist Publication Society in 1847. "If knowledge is power, the Society proposes to give knowledge to our denomination."[58]

Preaching the virtues of education reached beyond the church. Education was
the foundation of most works of religious benevolence taken up by Virginia
pastors and laity in the prewar period. The mission to the slaves and Sunday
schools were two characteristic venues. Teaching slaves was an integral part
of congregational life in antebellum Virginia. Especially in Baptist churches,
slaves were often a majority of members. In the 1840s, for example, twenty-
one of thirty-nine churches in the Dover Baptist Association had a majority
of free black and slave members, and the Rappahannock Association counted
one hundred more blacks than whites in its membership of almost fifty thousand. Nine all-black Baptist churches, primarily in the cities, had a combined
membership of about six thousand, many of whom were freemen and women.
During the 1850s, Methodist churches across the South and in Virginia saw
an increase in black membership at a rate of nearly 40 percent.[59]

One of the most controversial issues concerning slavery in the antebellum
South, especially after the Turner rebellion of 1831, was whether slaves should
be taught to read the Bible. Southerners' outlawing of slave literacy underscored whites' conviction that reading was an agent of moral and social uplift,
as well as moral subversion. Literate slaves were dangerous, many Virginians
declared. Slaveholding pastors, especially, understood the significance of this
law. For Protestants, ability to read the Word of God was essential to salvation.[60]

White pastors and leading laity were not inclined to credit slaves with any
agency in their salvation. Increasingly during the antebellum period, they took
on the burden of "teaching" slaves and free blacks the doctrines of Christianity, just as they did for common white people. In their view, the spread of
Christianity among illiterate slaves was bound to proceed slowly. Baptists devised oral catechisms for slaves, and many churches held separate meetings
for blacks on Sunday afternoons, after the regular worship service. Small children and slaves, pastors suggested, could learn the Gospel the same way. "Parents may remember that the same methods of conducting their family devo-
tions which suit the servants are also appropriate and necessary for younger
children," John Broadus wrote in 1856.[61]

The most vocal advocates of the mission to the slaves among Virginia
Baptists and Methodists were also some of the most influential advocates of
education. Thornton Stringfellow was one of the foremost apologists for proslavery Christianity in the South and a vocal advocate of Christian education;
Basil Manly Jr. was a prominent Richmond pastor and slaveholder who became first president of the Richmond Female Institute in 1854 and later a
professor at the Southern Baptist Theological Seminary; Robert Ryland was
president of Richmond College and pastor of the First African Baptist Church

in Richmond; William A. Smith was president of Randolph-Macon College and an ardent Methodist defender of proslavery Christianity; Rev. Thomas W. Sydnor was a slaveholder and missionary to slaves and then a county school superintendent in postbellum Virginia; Jeremiah Jeter, although self-taught, was a slaveholder, a prominent member of the Virginia Baptist Educational Society, and one of the most prolific apologists for Baptist education of his generation.[62]

Convinced as they were that reading was an integral part of the Christian life, some of these Baptist and Methodist pastors argued that slaves should be taught to read the Bible. Technically, Virginia law prohibited only teaching slaves to read in large numbers; it did not bar owners or pastors from taking up the task of teaching them individually. "Only teaching [slaves] for pay is made penal," a pastor wrote in 1846. Literacy, another observed, would necessarily increase a slave's value—"sometimes double."[63] Support for slave literacy among pastors gained momentum during the 1850s. By 1852, a group of prominent Richmond Baptists signed a "resolution supporting the education of colored people in Richmond." The signers were the pastors and leading laymen of all three white Baptist churches in the city, including bank directors and officers, insurance company officers, a carriage maker, and a leather dealer. In 1856, the forty-four Baptist churches of the prominent Baptist Dover Association resolved to promote the education of blacks.[64] This position flew in the face of public opinion and even undermined support for the clergy. Leading Richmond Baptist pastors were periodically accused of aiding the escape of slaves and even of abolitionist sympathies.[65]

Antebellum pastors also linked education with works of benevolence among children. Baptists established their own publishing board primarily to produce materials for children. The focus of both Baptist and Methodist publishing for children was the Sunday school. Literature, they believed, would encourage children to exercise self-discipline and self-control, and pastors, laymen, and women taught students basic literacy in Sunday school classes.

Scholars have sharply underestimated the importance of Sunday schools in the antebellum South. Anne Boylan's comprehensive treatment of schools in the nineteenth century cited only those schools that were affiliated with the American Sunday School Union. Southerners were not well represented in the ASSU because they generally disdained the work of ecumenical organizations, preferring instead to cultivate denominational programs.[66]

Many of these schools, primarily those in towns and cities, established a Sunday school library during the 1850s. The influential Baptist Dover Association, which included Richmond churches, was among the first to establish church libraries, arguing that service to God should be "intelligent as well as loving," and characterizing scholars as angels.[67]

Offering books to poor children bolstered the schools' goal of teaching basic literacy. Libraries were important to city churches because Sunday school students generally came from poor families that neither valued reading nor had the money to buy books. Sunday school libraries held geographies, spellers, and other practical texts along with religious works and Bibles. The

Ettrick Sunday School Society of Ettrick Methodist Episcopal Church, South, Chesterfield County, organized in May 1850, made provisions for a school librarian and imposed strict penalties on students who abused the books or their borrowing privileges. Individual members and congregations often donated books, which students could borrow for a specified period. Teachers even gave books to children who did not yet read to take home to their families.[68]

The pastors' unrelenting campaign for education pulled Baptists and Methodists away from their traditional association with simplicity toward the goal of respectability. "The improvement of man, in whatever relations of life involved, wherever born, however nurtured . . . This is ESSENTIAL CHRISTIANITY, progressive and unfailing improvement, based upon fixed and unalterable principles," a Virginia Baptist thundered before a lyceum audience.[69]

Still, many Methodists and Baptists disagreed. In their view, denominational schools such as Richmond Female Institute and Richmond College served the sons and daughters of a small, primarily urban, group of people whose values differed considerably from those of country folk. Their suspicions that these schools undermined their own values were borne out in 1848, when rumors flew across the state that Richmond College students had apparently held a dance in honor of George Washington's birthday. In a published reply to his critics, school president Robert Ryland was on the defensive. Nevertheless, he argued that "a conductor of a *literary institution* is sometimes induced to tolerate things which as a Christian and as a Christian minister he may not cordially approve."[70]

Ryland's comment revealed the changes that education brought not only to the clerical profession but also to church life in the first half of the nineteenth century. College presidents like Ryland could not afford to be purely ministers of the Gospel. Their interests lay not only in religion but also in the administrative and financial issues that crossed their desks daily. Their concerns ranged from the virtue of their students to more worldly issues, such as recruiting enough students to pay the bills.

The college and seminary, then, became the institutional expressions of the pastors' decision to give up alienation for influence in their society. Men like Ryland argued that education was one of the most important social benefits of Christianity, but education also cut against some traditions of Baptist and Methodist life. In antebellum America, education and its advocates cast themselves on the side of progress, and nowhere was this truer than in the South.

Indeed, one of the early signs of education's influence in antebellum religious culture was its erosion of the culture of revivalism, especially among the better educated pastors and church members. Baptists' and Methodists' interest in education began to shift the burden of change from the supernat-

ural conversion experience to the classroom. The chief means of salvation—
the lightning bolt of God's grace experienced in conversion—was gradually
displaced by the more incremental process of education. "Show me a man
who, after intelligent reflection and prayerful consideration, *voluntarily* has
followed the Saviour's commands, and I will show you a pillar of the church,"
a Hanover County Baptist observed in 1852.[71] For those who aspired to gentility, "intelligent reflection" was far more appealing than a tearful confession
in a rude camp meeting. Revivals remained the central ritual of the Christian
community in antebellum Virginia, but the conviction that "intelligent reflection" rather than emotionalism was a fitting means of conversion gained cre-
dence among Virginia pastors. They were attracted to the images of the church
as a school of Christ and of the pastor as schoolmaster. These associations
evoked the tranquility, order, and even domesticity that they wished to set at
the center of their church community. Schoolmasters changed the world, but
through quiet wisdom and example. It was an image far removed from the
unpredictable, even chaotic, atmosphere of early camp meetings, ruled by the
capricious Holy Spirit.

CHAPTER FOUR

Sectionalism and the Rise of Denominations

O n a March day in 1852, the Reverend Noah Baldwin recorded his doubts about a deed he had accomplished the day before.

> Yesterday, (although I have had some scruples in regard to slavery) I purchased a black man named James Martin at 735 dollars. I hope that he will be a good boy, and that neither of us will have cause to regret our relation in this world, nor that which is to come. Had it not been for the desire this man had, that I should purchase him I should not have done it. For this reason, as Slavery is in our midst I was induced to buy him. Pray the Lord to grant, that it may be for mine and his good.[1]

Noah and Nancy McMillan Baldwin were twelve years married and living in the mountains of southwest Virginia when they bought James Martin. At thirty-five, Baldwin had been preaching for the duration of his marriage in a church he described as a "feeble band, numbering at the aggregate 14, most of whom are in the country and all of us in moderate circumstances, so far as *worldly goods* is concerned."[2]

Baldwin's labors in the hard antimission territory of southwest Virginia bore little resemblance to the work of Jeremiah Jeter, fifteen years his senior. In the year Baldwin purchased his first slave, Jeter took the pulpit of well-known Grace Street Baptist Church in Richmond. The son of an overseer, by his own account Jeter grew up determined never to own a slave. In 1828, however, he acquired slaves from his second wife, a planter's daughter from Virginia's Northern Neck. Uncomfortable with what he claimed was the sheer impracticality of manumission, he finally found in a proslavery tract an argument that the Scriptures sanctioned slavery, which put his mind at ease. Fellow Virginia Baptist Thornton Stringfellow first published his "Scriptural and Statistical Views in Favor of Slavery" in the Richmond *Religious Herald* in 1841, and it appeared in tract form in the 1850s. When Jeter read the argument that James Henry Hammond found to be the "best scriptural argument" in defense of slavery, he became an enthusiastic advocate of the mission to the slaves.[3]

The contrast between the lives of these two preachers suggests how slavery entangled Christian belief and practice in both the mountains of the southwest and the parlors of Richmond. As their accounts show, not all Virginia pastors owned slaves for the same reasons. Baldwin reluctantly bought his slave, he said, to redeem a tainted institution; Jeter came to embrace slavery as inherently Christian.

Jeter's approach is more familiar to students of the antebellum South. They have examined many Southerners' conviction that the Bible sanctioned slavery, and the resulting studies explore proslavery Christianity as an ideology that allowed Southerners, Christian or not, to sanctify slavery.

Proslavery Christianity did more than offer an ideological basis for slavery, however. It also marked out a change in the way Southern pastors and many of those in their congregations conceived of religious life and practice. The defense of slavery and the acrimonious disputes and schisms it sparked in the Methodist and Baptist denominations had institutional as well as ideological consequences. The debate over slavery in antebellum America pushed Southern pastors and their churches into a public role unlike any they had taken before. Pastors welcomed this opportunity and used their public stand on slavery to strengthen their denominations. Spurred on by denominational schisms between Northerners and Southerners in the 1840s, denominations grew from small bodies with limited purposes into wealthy and powerful organizations that claimed, and ultimately gained, a vital stake in public culture.

Slavery shaped both the personal and professional lives of Virginia pastors. Historians have debated whether the institution was waning in the state during the 1850s. Lucrative markets for slaves during the cotton boom made many Virginians eager to sell. Yet on the eve of the Civil War, Virginia counted more slaves than any other state, as well as almost 40 percent of the South's free blacks. Half of the counties in the Piedmont and Tidewater regions counted 50 percent or more of their population enslaved. Instead of cotton, the state's field slaves cultivated primarily tobacco and wheat. Others fished, mined, and worked in the iron foundries and manufacturing establishments of Richmond. Regardless of where they lived, Virginians encountered slaves in a variety of settings in the course of a single day's work.[4]

Among pastors, the number of slaveholders exactly matched that among free Virginians generally. In 1850, at least two-thirds of Methodist and Baptist pastors in Virginia owned no slaves. Of the one-third who did, the size of their slaveholdings apparently matched that of free Virginians almost exactly. These pastors, then, fell at every point along the social spectrum of antebellum Virginia. As measured by rates of slaveholding, they were neither privileged nor impoverished. To be sure, the ranks of Baptist and Methodist clergy included

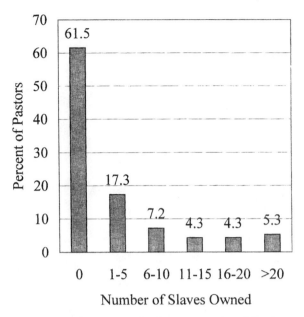

Figure 4.1 Slave ownership by pastors, 1850. Number of slaves = 809, number of pastors = 208. Source: Manuscript slave schedules, Virginia, U.S. Census of 1850.

a few sons of wealthy and influential families, many of whom had gained slaves through inheritance or marriage. But most owned no slaves at all. Those who did were most often like Noah Baldwin, who owned no more than a handful of slaves.[5]

By the 1830s, like other free Virginians, few Methodist or Baptist pastors openly challenged slavery. Virginia had once had intimate ties with Baptist John Leland and Methodist Francis Asbury, leading voices in the antislavery movement of the new republic, but church leaders began to concur publicly after the turn of the century that slaveholding did not contradict the Word of God.[6] Questions about slavery persisted, however. The details of daily life under slavery were not entirely settled, particularly in the community of the saved. Pulpit and pew debated how to treat Christian slaves. They asked whether congregations had the right to hold masters to uniform standards of treatment of their bondsmen and women. Pastors also condemned slave traders, declared the occupation to be incompatible with Christian belief, and sometimes barred them from church membership.[7]

If they agreed on the desirability of a Christian slavery, however, few Virginia pastors viewed slavery, as practiced in their society, to be a Christian institution. They predicated their support for slavery largely on its reform. Though many viewed slavery as potentially more righteous than free labor, pastors saw signs everywhere in the South that all was not well. The abuse of

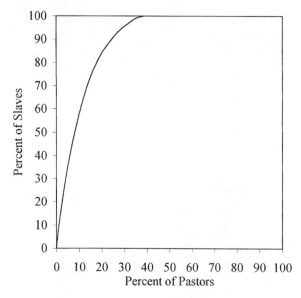

Figure 4.2 Slave Ownership by Pastors, 1850. Source: Manuscript slave schedules, Virginia, U.S. Census of 1850.

the master-slave relationship because of the lack of a Christian slaveholding ethic was the chief flaw in their society, they said, and the only cure was true religion. Master and slave alike, but particularly slaves, needed to be brought into the Christian fold. Thus the proslavery Christian ethic of the Old South, at least as viewed by the Baptist and Methodist pastorate, had at its core a reformist theme. "The Gospel is the only remedy for the evils of slavery," thundered the Methodist Rev. William A. Smith, one of the most articulate published advocates of a Christian slavery.[8]

Growing conflict with Northern churches during the 1840s made Southern pastors more sensitive than ever to the "evils of slavery." From the start, pastors found their own authority bound up with the fortunes of the institution. If they had reconciled themselves and most of those in their congregations to the Christian character of slavery, the increasingly strident tone of their dispute with their Northern brethren did not allow the issue to rest.

Tensions over slavery mounted after abolitionism exploded in the 1830s, and both Baptists and Methodists split over the issue a decade later. Although slavery had caused rising tensions between Northern and Southern Baptists since the early 1830s, the meeting of the American Baptist Antislavery Convention in New York in 1840 accelerated the dispute. Northern and Southern members tried to calm the storm the following year, but tensions heightened after the Northern Baptist press challenged the qualifications of two slaveholding missionaries in Texas, and by 1845 a small group of delegates had gathered in Georgia to determine a separate course for Southern Baptists. The

Methodist dispute erupted over the qualifications of slaveholding bishops. Antislavery Methodists began the exodus from the Methodist Episcopal Church in the early 1840s, and by 1844 the crisis came to a head over the nomination of a slaveholder as bishop. When the conference's membership, weighted toward the North, voted against the bishop from Georgia, the Southern delegation met to draw up its own organization.[9]

By arguing that slaveholders were not fit to be missionaries or bishops, Northern pastors implicitly challenged the right of slaveholders to be ordained at all. The threat to clerical authority was particularly serious in the Methodist church because of the tight hold the denomination exercised over local church affairs. Northern Baptists and Methodists both made it clear that they did not consider slaveholding pastors to be their equals.

Virginians took a leading role both in the denominational schisms over slavery and in the administration of the newly created Southern bodies. Virginia Baptists called the meeting that decided the issue, made up more than 10 percent of the new Southern Baptist Convention delegates, and contributed a vice president and secretary to it. Virginia Methodist leaders played a key role in the decisive General Conference of 1844 as well. William A. Smith, a professor at Randolph- Macon College, was one of the most ardent defenders of Christian slavery and an important influence in Southern Methodism's "declaration of independence" from its Northern connections.[10]

The schisms of the mid-1840s left Southern Baptists and Methodists free to fashion regional denominations to their tastes. Previously, denominations had been small bodies with sharply circumscribed purposes in the South. Advocates of centralized organization had not managed to alter the essentially local character of religious life. Denominational work took a secondary or even minor role in most pastors' lives; the seat of their authority was the local congregation. They spent most of their days preaching and traveling between congregations in the Virginia countryside. Some managed to attend annual denominational meetings, but most did not even do that. Even church leaders, aware of the lack of support from country pastors, emphasized the modest aims of denominational bodies.

The modesty of these aims was especially evident among Baptists. Baptist leaders took care to remind state congregations that the Virginia General Association's purpose, written in its constitution, was to propagate the Gospel— the same task as that of the churches themselves. They purposely left their statewide organization weak and did not pretend to represent the interests of Baptists across the state. Members paid $10 to join, which few individuals could afford and few congregations were willing to pay. When the Virginia General Association met for the first time in 1823, just fifteen men, representing seven of the state's twenty associations, assembled. "The Baptist General Association is nothing more than a Domestic Missionary Society," an appeal for members reassured Baptist readers in 1830. The writer drew a sharp contrast between Baptist assemblies and the annual meetings of the Presbyterians, Episcopalians, and Methodists, which embodied, he said, "the strength of the[ir] denomination[s]."[11]

The small amounts of money these organizations raised underscored their modest purposes. Baptists collected less than $250 from churches across the state in 1823. By 1841, just fourteen of the thirty district associations in the state sent representatives to General Association meeting and monies collected amounted to less than $5,000. Even the Methodists, who were far better organized, raised just $5,000 from more than thirty thousand members for their statewide work by 1845.[12]

The place of pastors in the antebellum temperance movement plainly shows the local basis of clerical authority before the schisms of the 1840s. Pastors failed to maintain control over the movement they had founded. Local temperance societies usually grew out of revivals, and new societies often became auxiliaries to congregations, giving the clergy a prominent role. Congregations and temperance societies were mutually reinforcing bodies. Pastors and laity insisted that renouncing drink was like renouncing sin. The appeal of their message was underscored by the warmth and strength of the community for the "convert" after his decision to abstain. In addition to adopting the language of religion, temperance societies borrowed organizational principles from congregations. In 1833, the interdemoninational Virginia Society for the Promotion of Temperance voted to hold quarterly meetings by district and to employ a "full-time agent to sell temperance literature and solicit funds," all strategies borrowed directly from congregations.

The central issue for clergymen on both sides of the issue ultimately went beyond alcohol consumption to how the Bible should be applied to society. At its heart was the question of whether churches should ban a practice even if the Bible did not prohibit it. The position of abstinence Christians came perilously close to that of abolitionists, who also argued that slavery should be banned without a specific command in Scripture. Abolitionists argued that slavery was contrary to the spirit, if not the letter, of the Scriptures. Abstinence Christians did the same. Many Virginians ardently supported slavery while opposing all liquor, but the comparison between the abstinence position and abolition was not lost on them all. A Baptist editor observed in 1840 that the church could not adopt a temperance oath as a test of membership because antislavery folk used such tests in their churches.[13]

Three years after the Virginia Temperance Society's founding, the state led the South with fifty local temperance societies, and by 1831 Richmond's eight hundred members had the largest local society in the region. Pastors across the state flocked to the movement. But membership peaked after ten years, and by the early 1840s the society was virtually dead in Virginia churches. Why? Historians have attributed the failure of antebellum temperance societies in the South to congregations' otherworldly interests, known as the spiritual doctrine of the church. In their view, congregations were more interested in eternal security than in temporal sobriety. But this theory fails to explain the initial popularity of the movement.[14]

The decline of support for temperance societies among churchgoing people had less to do with the spiritual doctrine of Southern churches than with the workings of clerical authority through the local congregation. By the 1840s, two new societies, the Washingtonian Society and the Sons of Temperance, began to secularize the temperance movement.

The Washingtonians, founded in Baltimore by a group of reformed drinkers, early appealed to the working classes. In Virginia, Washingtonians arrived in 1841 and quickly gained great success among working-class white and black people, especially in cities. By the spring of 1842, African American societies met in Charlottesville, Richmond, and Petersburg. During 1842 and 1843, at the same time that interest in the Virginia Temperance Society was declining, the state was alive with temperance fervor, largely because of the Washingtonians' success.

The Washingtonians, in particular, mixed religious and political imagery, combining the pageantry of partisan celebrations with the powerful emotions and charismatic speakers of revival meetings. Washingtonian orators, who were reformed drinkers themselves, shared their testimonies and then urged the audience to pledge total abstinence. But they also used political symbols. At a Fourth of July celebration in Caroline County, military units paraded with banners that proclaimed, "Freedom from the Tyranny of Great Britain in 1776. Freedom from the Tyranny of Alcohol in 1843."[15]

Some temperate Virginians, affronted by the raw, working-class style of the Washingtonians, organized the more tasteful Sons of Temperance in 1844, modeled on a fraternal society, complete with insurance benefits and elaborate secret regalia. Men were attracted to the organization for social as well as ideological reasons, and they happily indulged in the Sons' practice of passwords, initiation rites, and fraternal mottoes. A few leading clergymen joined as well.[16]

Although the vast majority of pastors who had supported the Virginia Temperance Society became disenchanted with the movement by the early 1840s, the decline of ministerial support for temperance societies did not mean that support for temperance died in Virginia congregations. On the contrary, by the mid-nineteenth century, few congregations admitted drinkers to membership, and virtually none admitted overindulgent ones. In the main, pastors' disenchantment grew out of the secular culture of the new societies. Jeremiah Jeter was one of the founding members of the Virginia Tmperance Society and certainly benefited from the more than twenty years of his association with the movement: it made his name well known in Baptist circles. Descriptions of temperance workers embodied the influence to which leading clergymen aspired. "God has bestowed upon [the temperance worker] a position of power. . . . That power, that duty, involves a responsibility from which as a good man, as a good citizen, he cannot, he must not, shrink." [17]

But all but the most urbane pastors realized that temperance societies competed with congregations for their time and allegiance. "A Christian minister in a Temperance Society, whether secret or open, is out of his sphere and element, and acting out of character," a Methodist wrote in 1850. "We are not prepared to regard Christianity and Temperance as essentially parallel roads."[18] Once temperance meetings moved out of churches and into secular halls, once politics tinged temperance rhetoric, pastors risked weakening their authority in their congregations by supporting such organizations. At a time when their authority was sustained almost entirely by the local congregation, that was a risk that most were not willing to take. Before the schisms of the 1840s, then, pastors exercised a local authority.[19]

The schisms of the 1840s changed this. They opened a new era in the relation of congregations to denominations by providing an unprecedented public platform from which clergy might assert authority beyond the bounds of local churches, and even beyond the bounds of their denominations. The new Southern denominations and their leaders boldly proclaimed that a Christian slavery served not only the Creator but also the nation. It was a short step to a larger point. Christianity served not only the interests of the church but also the interests of society. "I am not aware that . . . the failure to profess Christianity free[s] any one from the duty of being a Christian," Rev. William A. Smith, a well-known Virginia Methodist and college professor, wrote.[20]

Smith made this arresting pronouncement squarely in the context of his defense of a Christian slavery. In his view, slavery would work only if it were Christian. And because the South was committed to slavery, it must also be committed to Christianity. Slavery, then, bound the nation to Christianity in a way that Smith and many other pastors found exhilarating. Where earlier pastors had set up a rigid boundary between the church and the world and built their authority on its defense, late antebellum pastors clambered over this barrier to lecture non-Christians on the universality of Christian values. Such arguments made slavery serve the interests of Christianity. Southern pastors endorsed not a "proslavery Christianity" but a Christian slavery.

Men like Smith used slavery consciously to extend their writings, lectures, and sermons to address non-Christians as well as Christians. Both were bound by the teachings of the Bible, they argued. By setting forth standards of conduct for masters and slaves, preachers like Smith proclaimed not only their interest in the behavior of non-Christians but also their authority over them. A Christian defense of slavery invited pastors to read the Bible as a text of social economy as well as spiritual revelation. As theologian James Henley Thornwell argued, if Southerners "array the Bible against our social economy, then our social economy must fall."[21] Pastors proclaimed the secular benefits of slavery, arguing that the conversion of slaves was not only a spiritual issue but also a civil one. The benefits of their mission to the slaves would accrue to society at large, rather than just to the church.

This transition may be traced in the writings of Thornton Stringfellow, the Virginia Baptist who wrote one of the most influential proslavery tracts of the day. Stringfellow was a native of Culpeper County, in the northern Virginia Piedmont, from a prosperous slaveholding family. His 1841 defense of slavery appeared before the 1845 schism with Northern Baptists. "A Brief Examination of Scripture Testimony on the Institution of Slavery" convinced young Jeremiah Jeter of the Biblical sanction of slavery. It rigorously examines passages that mention slavery in both the Old and New Testaments. Stringfellow followed this piece with the publication of a lesser-known essay in 1860. Instead of an examination only of the Scriptures, the later piece promised an examination of slavery's "Origin, Nature, and History, Its Relations to Society, to Government, and to True Religion, to Human Happiness and Divine Glory Considered in the Light of Bible Teachings, Moral Justice, and Political Wisdom." Whereas in 1841 Stringfellow appealed to the Scriptures alone, twenty years later his appeal broadened to embrace the moral and political expediency of slavery.[22]

The growing emphasis of Stringfellow and other pastors on the social and political utility of Christianity prompted not only theological and political arguments but also institutional arguments. Despite Southern denominations' consensus on slavery, it is notable that they did not organize an interdenominational mission to the slaves. Characteristically, they decided that this work of benevolence, like most others, would remain within the confines of the denomination. After the mid-1840s, the new regional denominations became the institutional expression of pastors' new confidence in society's need for religion and of their own confidence that they were the men for the task. Virginia clergymen tirelessly used the press and the pulpit to appeal for donations of time and money. Denominations organized and linked like-minded people across the state and region. What better and more efficient way could there be, they argued, than organizing to raise money, generate enthusiasm, and spread the spiritual and social benefits of the Christian faith?

Denominations began to take an ever stronger place in the lives of Methodist and Baptist pastors and their congregations after 1845. Denomination building—that is, the bureaucratization of religion in the late antebellum South—was an inherently innovative and forward-looking task. It was, in a word, modern. Like the embrace of elegant new churches and support for denominational colleges, it required passion for institution building and discipline and vision to carry it out.

Southern pastors and lay leaders began to create a modern religious bureaucracy that by 1861 rivaled the efficiency, wealth, and size of that created by their Northern peers. Their devotion to this project altered their understanding of the relation between local church and regional denomination and shaped their standards of clerical professionalism. By the late 1840s, the clerical profession and the denomination were firmly intertwined. In 1860, the most "professional" pastors were those men with the strongest ties to denominational projects.

The rapid growth in denominational fund-raising marked the change. Money for both state-level and regional projects poured into denominational coffers in the 1850s. In Virginia, bulging church coffers reflected the prosperity of the state at large. In a time when many Southerners advocated economic diversification as the key to the region's future, Virginia stood at the head of all Southern states. Although outside the cotton belt, Virginia was the largest, richest, and most populous state in the region. It boasted both the largest slave population and the greatest share of regional manufacturing and urban centers. Encouraged by the construction of hundreds of miles of new railroads in the 1850s, the state economy moved sharply toward manufacturing. Iron production, for example, increased almost 200 percent in that decade. Agriculture, too, became increasingly mechanized. These developments accommodated rather than excluded slave labor, as growing numbers of Virginia slaves worked in urban and manufacturing settings. By 1861, Virginia produced almost one-third of all Southern manufactured goods and contained one-fifth of the region's railroads.[23]

Like the state economy, Baptist and Methodist churches entered a period of surging growth during the 1850s. Membership continued to grow at a rate double that of the population as a whole. The number of Methodist churches increased by more than one-third, and the number of Baptist churches by one-fifth. Gains in church wealth, however, far outstripped the growing membership. Between 1850 and 1860, the value of property held by Virginia Methodists more than doubled, while Baptist property values increased by 80 percent.[24] Although Episcopalians, Presbyterians, Methodists, and Baptists began the decade holding property of roughly the same value, by 1860 Methodists and Baptists combined held more than twice the amount of property of the other two denominations combined. On the eve of the Civil War, Virginia Regular Baptist and Methodist clergymen were the stewards of $2.9 million worth of property. Some of this wealth was in the form of church buildings, but the figure also included growing college and school properties (see Appendix, Table 11).

Paralleling gains in denominational wealth, money raised for denominational works of religious benevolence increased dramatically after 1845. In Virginia alone, Baptists and Methodists increased their annual giving fivefold by the beginning of the war. By 1859, Southern Baptists had raised 62 percent more money for domestic and foreign missions in the thirteen years of their regional organization than they had raised in the 33 years before their separation from Northern Baptists. Total monies raised by the Methodist Virginia Conference grew tenfold between 1845 and 1860.[25]

Although contributions to discrete projects like church buildings and colleges continued to grow, this period also witnessed a growing financial commitment to works of religious benevolence. The 1850s were critical years in the long shift from alienation to influence as a goal of religious benevolence. The denominational impetus toward a proslavery united front encouraged pastors to imagine churches as instruments of social consensus rather than as the outposts of an alienated community.

In addition to providing a vehicle for regional leadership in the defense of slavery, denominations provided a more concrete means by which religion could work in the public interest. Denominations had been created to take up works of religious benevolence that were too large for single congregations to support. During the 1850s, these works gained a new importance in the lives of pastors and their congregations, and after 1845, pastors began to assert that religious benevolence reaped not just eternal benefits, but temporal ones as well.

In its broadest sense, religious benevolence included all work done in the name of Christ, including evangelism, foreign missions, Sunday schools, and denominational academies and colleges.[26] But when antebellum clergymen used the term, it generally meant organized works accomplished by the denomination. In the antebellum period, these were chiefly the mission to the slaves and education, especially Sunday school teaching.

The Southern clergy's approach to religious benevolence differed from that of the Northern clergy. In the North, both the sacred and secular strains of millennialism fed a patently optimistic view of America's place in history and affirmed that human progress would culminate in the end of history. In the North, the energies of republicanism and revivalism intersected in millennial thought, allowing churches to harness republican ideology to the cause of religion and permitting politicians to link religious enthusiasm to political ideology. By contrast, Southern religious benevolence generally ignored millennialism as a motive for good works. Southerners did not routinely counter abolitionists' charges that slavery would delay the Kingdom of God by claiming that slavery would usher in the millennium. Virginia Methodists and Regular Baptists never clearly articulated a position on the millennium. When they talked about the coming of the Kingdom of God, they usually focused on the imprudence of predicting the time of Christ's return.[27]

Southern benevolence, unlike Northern benevolence, remained firmly rooted in a denominational context. Southern pastors encouraged their congregations to work not as Christians, but as Baptists or Methodists. Their aversion to ecumenism grew in part out of its popularity in the North. By the late 1830s, two of the five most prominent national evangelical societies, the American Educational Society and the American Home Missionary Society, were virtually dead in the South, and the limited success of the other three grew out of their adaptation to Southern preferences.[28]

Advocates of a Christian slavery intended to change their world.[29] Proslavery theologians used the Bible as the basis of their vision. "The design of the Gospel ministry is not to build up an earthly empire . . . it is to renovate the world," a Virginia Baptist association exhorted its membership in 1844. "The Pulpit is the grand instrument of civilization. . . . Christianity purifies, enlightens, refines." Another pastor declared that "the Church has the power for reforming mankind[,] which no other institution has or can have[,] and in works of moral reform it should stand foremost."[30] The "hundreds of preachers and clergymen of Virginia . . . have the talents and all the requisite powers to effect any great moral revolution," a Baptist exhorted in 1846.[31]

Growing denominational wealth and visibility impelled leaders to streamline these inefficient and antique organizations, which they began to do as soon as they withdrew from their Northern connections. The departure from earlier practice was especially striking for Baptists. Historically, Baptists had been particularly distrustful of centralized administration, doggedly holding onto the independence of local church congregations. But when they reorganized their Southern convention in 1845, they left more power than ever before in the hands of a few men. They argued that the new power of the Southern Baptist Convention did not fundamentally alter former practice because there were several controls over this new centralized authority. The primary control was financial. Leaders argued that if Southern Baptists believed the convention was wielding too much power, they would simply cut off funding for its projects.[32] But the small group who effected the separation from Northern churches suggested otherwise. Just 293 Baptists attended the Augusta meeting that created the Southern Baptist Convention, and by the last day of the meeting, during which several important issues were decided, only 100 delegates remained. The exclusivity of the convention was not entirely new. Baptists had long organized their conventions on both the national and state level around what they termed the "society method," meaning that only those who represented churches and societies that paid a membership fee attended. The convention was not an organization of Baptist churches, pastors argued, but merely a "gathering of money-giving Baptists" organized to do their benevolent work through a centralized structure.[33]

After 1845, though old controls remained in place, the claims of the convention to represent the South dramatically expanded. State-level leadership echoed changes in the regional convention. In 1852, Virginia Baptists issued a call to raise $10,000 in the next year "for the purpose of enlarging the operations of the Association."[34] Three years later, they reorganized their general association. Formerly a loose coalition of separate and largely autonomous boards, the Virginia General Association centralized under the supervision of a small group of state leaders.

Although Methodist and Baptist leaders viewed their actions on the issue of slavery as public decisions, they showed little interest in the political aspects of the slavery question. The schisms between Northern and Southern churches shook national leaders to the core. Denominations were not political parties, but their pastors "represented" a huge constituency across the South, and it was one that elected officeholders could not afford to ignore.

Political battles, it seemed to Southern pastors, were essentially about "absolute" political truths and thus might destroy civic order.[35] They vehemently denied any interest in politics whatsoever. Virginia Methodists and Baptists had long stressed the incompatibility of religion and partisan politics. They characterized politicians and their "dirty work" as unworthy rivals in a contest for the hearts and minds of the people. "The only inquiry is—not 'what must I do to be saved' but 'who, think you, will be president?' " a Baptist noted with disgust at the height of the 1844 contest between Henry Clay and James K. Polk.[36] In an 1855 letter, Rev. Daniel Witt expressed his loathing of politics. "Have you any religion now amongst your people?" he wrote. "The hurricane of political excitement has blasted everything of the sort in these parts. . . . I do not recollect ever to have seen so much asperity and bitterness, and all manner of ill feeling in the masses of the people." Another Baptist argued in 1852 that "political excitement is detrimental to the interests of religion." Although he denied that politics was "evil per se," he viewed the animosity be-tween parties as increasingly "threatening," presumably to the Republic.[37] The particularly contentious sectarian disputes of antebellum Southern life made partisan politics, and the party prejudices engendered even among some min-isters particularly loathsome.

The Bible did not address politics, the clergy argued, and man, not God, created political parties. They were therefore inherently worldly and unnatural bodies, largely because of the contentious and impious passions they aroused. Ministers who engaged in politics had "come down from a great work to min-gle in the heats of passion and debate," one Baptist argued.[38]

The growth of denominational organization and the vast increases in money and membership had a particularly strong impact on the ministerial profession because of the large numbers of young ministers who entered the pulpit during the 1850s. The ranks of Virginia Methodist pastors increased by 60 percent, more than twice the increase in church membership.[39] These young men stood in church pulpits before the Civil War and into the 1890s. Shaped by insti-tutionalized training and education at colleges, universities, and seminaries, they eagerly embraced the new work of the denominations, and as they ma-tured they placed this work at the center of their professional ideal.

Connections with and participation in the denominational organizations increasingly determined a clergyman's professional fate and pulled pastors' attention away from the local congregation to focus on regional institution building. Senior pastors encouraged the newly ordained to profess unblinking devotion to denominational causes. Professional prestige increasingly flowed from connections with denominational projects, and leadership was no longer based solely on a man's talent in the pulpit.

Historians have argued that slavery privatized religious belief and practice in the South. The spiritual doctrine of the Southern church—the notion that "religion should put people right with God . . . not tamper with society"—has been called the central theme of Southern religious history. But scholars have mistakenly judged Southern pastors' interest in public life on the basis of campaigns for public reform as measured against their Northern peers.

In the South, the defense of slavery resulted in the dramatic growth of denominations during the 1850s. These regional organizations gave Southern pastors a public voice, and the crisis over slavery compelled them to use it. In their proslavery arguments, pastors emphasized the social benefits of reli-gion, sometimes even over its spiritual rewards. As in education, control over denominational affairs remained in the hands of a few city pastors. But their fusion of the interests of religion and society—their prejudices toward orga-nization and denominational work—would be affirmed during the war and would characterize Southern Methodist and Baptist work for the rest of the century.[40]

CHAPTER FIVE

Pastors and Soldiers

I n late January 1861, John Cowper Granbery posted a letter to his fiancée, "Miss Ella" Winston. The thirty-two-year-old pastor wrote from the University of Virginia, where he had served as chaplain for two years. He devoted the first few lines to the issue that weighed most heavily on his mind: war preparations at the university and in Charlottesville. "But I will check myself abruptly and violently," he interjected after several sentences, "so as not to pursue the path of political discussion which everybody travels these days. What have women and preachers to do with sucession [sic] and war?"[1]

Granbery's question rings with irony, for the works and words of both preachers and women played a critical part in the brief life of the Confederacy. It underscored, however, his conviction that warmaking was not an appropriate task for pastors, a sentiment shared by many of his peers in the upper South. As friends and family began to drill in local companies, pastors were uncertain as to how they should help the Confederacy. Was a pastor's participation in war forbidden by the Scriptures? Should a pastor bear arms? "I have never understood the compatibleness [sic] of Christianity with war," Joseph Walker, later a Confederate chaplain, confessed that spring. Like Granbery, many viewed war as an inherently vengeful and political endeavor, and they were confused about their proper role.[2]

Events of that winter and spring did not allow much time for leisurely reflection on the matter. South Carolina seceded on December 20, setting off a cadence of conventions in the other six states of the lower South. By February 4, delegates met in Montgomery to organize a new government. Missouri and Arkansas rejected secession in March, and on April 4, just eight days before Fort Sumter, Virginia rejected secession by a two-to-one margin. Virginians' diaries and letters described that unsettled spring with terms like "excitement," "confusion," and even "panic."[3]

By the end of March, Granbery wrote to Ella that several pastors he knew planned to move to the deep South if their own state did not secede. By May

3, just two weeks after Virginia seceded, Granbery himself drilled daily with the university guard. He still, however, refused to throw himself completely into the effort. "You must not infer that I am carried away with the martial spirit so rife at this time," he wrote to Ella. "I do not approve of ministers quitting their appropriate work to be captains of companies. I am ready to serve my state and the good cause in any honorable and proper way," he continued. "I think preachers ought to stick to their sacred calling which is never more important than now." Nevertheless, he wrote, "I preach to my congregation against vengeful feelings in the war, while of course I inculcate a defence [sic] of our rights at all hazards. . . . We, Miss Ella, can do little for our country now except to commend her cause to the God of peace and the God of battles."[4]

John Granbery eventually set aside his doubts to render exemplary service as a Confederate army chaplain. A member of the 11th Virginia Infantry, he was wounded and taken prisoner during the Peninsula Campaign of 1862. He was soon released, although his wound left him blind in his right eye. The following year, he became a chaplain in the Army of Northern Virginia, a post he held to the end of the war. Like other pastors maimed on the battlefield, his injured eye invoked the war during every sermon he preached for the rest of his life.[5]

The ambivalent and even contradictory sentiments of his letter to his fiancée—drilling in the home guard without participating in "martial spirit"; disapproval of ministers leaving the pulpit, yet willingness to serve his state and its "good cause"; a distaste for vengeance and yet a readiness to defend the South; and his appeal to both the God of peace and the God of war— highlight the problematic path to Confederate service for Southern pastors. If sympathy for the Southern cause came easily enough for Granbery and others, antebellum clerical life hardly provided a precedent for soldier preachers. Even more than other Southerners, pastors had to invent their role in the Confederacy in 1861.

Interpretations of religious life in the Confederacy have focused on Christianity's role in the construction of Confederate nationalism and the maintenance of morale during the war. But Confederates did more than merely bend religion to their advantage during the war. The Confederate experience changed Southern pastors and their congregations in ways that long outlived the Confederacy. The generation of pastors who served as chaplains, officers, and soldiers filled the pulpits in postwar Virginia, and many veterans rose to the highest ranks of the profession (see Appendix, Tables 13 and 14). Granbery himself became a bishop in the Methodist Episcopal Church, South in 1882.[6] Their war experiences shaped church policy to the end of the century.

The Civil War left its most lasting legacy through the opportunity it provided for these pastors to render public service in the name of religion. If proslavery

Christianity had firmly rooted religion in the public sphere by spurring the growth of denominations, wartime tasks involved many more pastors personally in an endeavor that expanded the relevance of their ministry outside church walls. No longer merely representatives of a single denomination, or even of the Christian church, chaplains and soldier-preachers harnessed their faith to their loyalty to their state and region. Preaching and evangelism did not just save souls for eternity; they also influenced the fortunes of the Confederacy, both on the battlefield and off. Without true religion, pastors believed, the South's cause would inevitably fail. War, then, could make pastors' presence and preaching thrillingly relevant to temporal life, and they seized the opportunities they believed that it offered them to expand their earthly influence.

Yet most Methodist and Baptist preachers, like other Virginians, opposed secession in early 1861. Their public and private writings revealed their ambiguity toward war as they sought first to avoid secession and later came to terms with it. Exasperated with politicians whose arguments they believed wielded far too much influence, and who had brought the country to the brink of destruction, pastors pleaded publicly and hoped privately for caution and patience. "If the South is not too *hasty*, and will press their [sic] rights *firmly*, the North will come into proper measures," James A. Riddick, a fifty-one-year-old Methodist pastor, assured a friend in early January 1861.[7] Another, writing to his son, was less optimistic. "I am opposed to secession though I don't see how it is *now* to be avoided," he wrote.[8]

Even in 1861, then, after a decade and a half to settle sectional allegiances and decide their position on slavery, Virginia pastors struggled over whether to support war and secession. They distinguished sharply between support for slavery and support for secession. During the 1850s, when the majority of those who later took up the office of army chaplain were ordained, sectionalism entangled the language of religion, and pastors defined their denominational work in a regional context. They learned to link slavery with religion. In the Methodist Church, whose conference borders did not follow state boundaries, disputes between members of the Baltimore and Virginia conferences were known as the Border War after 1847. Baltimore had remained with the Northern church, but Virginia Methodists retained strong ties with churches in the Baltimore area. Virginians serving in Maryland congregations moved south after 1845, and Virginia churches released pastors so they might move north. Congregations split on unfriendly terms in border towns such as Alexandria, Winchester, and Leesburg, and in several cases they later resorted to civil courts to resolve differences over property rights. Baptists moved as well. Reverend Elias Lyman Magoon, for six years the pastor of the prominent Second Baptist Church in Richmond, resigned because of his sympathy for Northern views.[9]

In contrast to those sectional questions, however, the pressing issue of early 1861—secession and warfare—raised questions about the sovereignty of God, the meaning of American history, and the righteousness of war itself.[10] Virginia pastors faltered at the brink of such a momentous decision, and they betrayed a deep pessimism about the United States, North and South alike. Americans, they declared over and over, were a thankless and rebellious people. "I hope the Great Disposer of events will bring good out of seeming evil— too much prosperity has ruined the country," a Methodist wrote to a friend. Another lamented that "this country is too young and prosperous to be overwhelmed with ruin so soon."[11]

The disease of the country, they argued, was politics. They voiced deep anger at politicians, North and South. The South's enemies, a Baptist editor wrote shortly after war broke out, included not only the "hostile hosts who are invading your land," but also the "PAPERS AND PUBLIC CHARACTERS whose office is to stir up the worse passions of the human heart, and who desire to persecute [sic] the war with a *malicious and vindictive spirit.*" He scoffed at the "oft repeated declarations that all the glory, honor, wealth, prosperity and power of the nation have resulted from the wise measures and discreet policy of such and such parties. If [God] has blessed us with protection in person, property, and pursuit of happiness, we have bestowed all the praise upon the wisdom of our statesmen. . . . We have not recognized the hand of God in it all."[12] Politics alone—those *"political* agencies which have produced the rupture," as a Baptist scornfully described them—did not provide a worthy enough reason for pious men to support secession.[13]

Thus in 1861, pastors embraced "Christian patriotism" as their rationale for supporting secession. This they stripped of partisan interests and endowed with virtual transcendence. "The feelings of true patriotism lie next to the higher sentiments of religion in the heart," a Methodist observed.[14] Virginia pastors had long viewed patriotism as a lofty sentiment, largely apolitical. In a Fourth of July speech in 1856, Methodist Leonidas Rosser asserted that the holiday was a "patriot's day—a day on which all political parties suspend their prejudices and forget their opinions . . . and unite as a nation of freemen." Rosser went on to dissociate himself from any political party, arguing that although he had political convictions, he had no "dogmas or opinions." As long as "the spirit of Christianity exists in our constitution, laws, and institutions . . . and intelligence, patriotism, and religion prevail with the people—I am little concerned who is in power," he said.[15]

Pastors' decisions to support the war were influenced not so much by their confidence in the Confederacy as their assurance of God's sovereign role in history. Their view, simply put, was that if God had allowed secession to occur, it was his will that it be so. Once secession appeared to be inevitable, many who had opposed it changed their views quietly and quickly. The only Baptist pastor who attended the Virginia secession convention in April 1861 went to Richmond firmly opposed to "the horrors of civil war" but voted in favor of secession on April 17.[16] Literally within days of formal secession, many pastors' ambivalence toward the Confederacy turned to firm resolve. Six months after urging cautious action by the South, Rev. James Riddick wrote to a friend, "I think the South will carry the day, and we shall yet enjoy a glorious future."[17] Yet a sober understanding of what lay ahead dampened their hopes for a quick Confederate victory. Resignation to God's will became an important theme of wartime religion. "The troubles of life are from God," a Richmond editor counseled in May. "The Father has ordained our afflictions. When we patiently endure them we yield to His counsel and hand."[18]

Pastors' embrace of a Christian patriotism, however, did not define patriotism as their first duty. Their primary allegiance remained with the cause of God, not that of the Confederacy, and they were careful to guard the interests of religion over and above those of the Confederate leaders and government for which they often prayed. If the firm line between religion and state dissolved later in the war, early on pastors refused to use their Sunday sermons as political treatises. Neither did they aspire to political power. Instead, they remained firm in their conviction that theirs was a higher calling. "Patriotism can be no substitute for piety," Jeremiah Jeter warned his Richmond congregation in 1861. "It is folly to suppose that services rendered to Caesar can absolve from obligation to serve God." A writer in the *Religious Herald* mocked the obsession of the day. "Surely this is a short and easy method to salvation," he wrote. "Just enlist and shed your blood like water in defence of your country, and the work is done." Another simply warned that "our country may be saved and ourselves lost."[19]

Yet other Virginia pastors shared John Granbery's contradictory feelings about the war. Even while they cautioned their congregations against mindless patriotism, they passionately defended the Confederacy's position. In an editorial published just after secession, Baptist William Sands called for humility and repentance. "Neither section regards itself as having done or said aught that was wrong, and consequently, neither seems to recognize that God has any hand in this contest," he wrote. "No matter how atheistical, immoral, and given to mammon worship the North has been that by no means lessens our own guilt." Nevertheless, humility before God was not the same thing as humility before the enemy. "No fault of Virginia brought the calamity upon us. . . . She bore the olive branch until it was stricken from her hand by the sword," he wrote.[20] Convinced that their cause was just, pastors' own Christian humility and even self-doubt coexisted comfortably with patriotism, pride, and self-righteousness. Their preaching and public statements reflected this ambivalence. If pastors' primary object was not the glorification of the Confederacy but the glorification of God, their congregations often heard a message that confused the two. "When we lay all upon the altar of our country, the God of Nations will give us a permanent happy existence," a soldier on the front wrote to his wife in early 1862. "How near akin is patriotism to religion."[21]

The Civil War dramatically expanded pastors' claim to an authoritative voice in Southern society. Even more than in the debates over slavery, religious language informed public rhetoric and government proclamations, as well as worship services and Sunday school meetings. As a Methodist editor observed, the war presented "a remarkable and much to be coveted occasion for the pulpit to assert itself as a power in the land." Pastors cited the successes of religion during the War for Independence. Some viewed the war as an opportunity for religion; others saw it as a liability.[22]

Events, however, did not immediately affirm those who predicted that the church would flourish during the war. As Virginians struggled between themselves to determine their allegiance, the rhythm of congregational life faltered.[23] Church collections shrank, as members became reluctant to hand over money in uncertain times. Attendance at Sunday worship and Sunday schools suffered as families grew restless and began to relocate. Enrollment in denominational colleges fell, as many young men, awaiting the call to arms, did not return to spring classes. In the Richmond offices of the Baptist *Religious Herald* and Methodist *Richmond Christian Advocate*, editors eagerly gave "domestic news" priority in front-page columns, including the full texts of the Confederate constitution and government proclamations.[24]

Declining church attendance and contributions substantiated pastors' fears that people were casting aside their loyalty to God's cause to take up that of the Confederacy. "The times are trying," Jeremiah Jeter warned in 1861. "We are in danger of being led by the excitement of the times to neglect our Christian duties. Religion is our chief interest. No circumstances can justify its neglect."[25] But the breakdown in patterns of congregational life, so dependent on a seasonal schedule of regular meetings, continued throughout the war. These wartime interruptions had serious consequences for pastors and their families. The primary source of clerical authority, especially for rural pastors, remained their headship of the local church. With flocks scattered and churches closed, many pastors "lost" their jobs. Although their ordination ensured that they retained authority within the denomination, in the local community pastors often found themselves with little to do. The disruptions of war thus tended to heighten the dependence of rural pastors on professional connections within the denomination.

Declining church attendance and contributions also left pastors with a difficult financial burden. Although many Virginians suffered from the deprivations of war, pastors were particularly vulnerable. Their salaries depended on the voluntary contributions of church members, and scattered congregations struggling with wartime deprivation no longer gave money to their church. Even those pastors who lived far from the battle lines preached to congregations that had shrunk during wartime. Even the most generous were often unable to spare much for church collections. Some preachers turned to other sources of income for the duration of the war, while others gave up preaching altogether for a time to retire quietly to family farms far from the front.

Once secession was a fait accompli, Virginians' first concern was to defend their state. Although Virginia was the most exposed of the Southern states to Union invasion, "the state's public means of resistance is simply nil," one editor observed, citing only a few serviceable arms and only a small amount of powder stockpiled.[26] Young men left field and college to enlist by the thousands and began drilling and gathering arms and supplies. Many pastors joined them. Abandoning or simply ignoring reservations about war, they enlisted as soldiers and officers, served as chaplains, sold religious literature, preached on national fast days and other civil holidays, and reoriented the denominational press to the army's needs. Virginia's vote for secession set most of them, like Robert E. Lee, firmly on a course for the Confederacy.

Not all Virginia pastors enlisted as chaplains. Some, especially those with family connections that would allow their enlistment as officers, chose instead to become soldiers. Preferring the soldier's work or pay, or both, these men often served as unofficial pastors as well. Others stayed at home, preaching to distracted congregations. Some gave up preaching entirely because their churches were behind enemy lines. Others served as a liaison for local soldiers. "Try and make some arraingement [sic] about funding for my family. I have bin in the army five months and havent recieved anything as yet," a soldier wrote to his preacher in Virginia's Southside late in the war, expecting that the man had some influence with army officials.[27] Pastors routinely set aside regular pastoral work to attend to the more urgent tasks of visiting hospitals and burying the dead. "There were 270 coffins corded in a rick at Hollywood Cemetery," one pastor wrote after the Battle of Seven Pines in June 1862, "and we had to put them in their graves by tens, making one service answer for ten at a time."[28]

Pastors' stature in their communities was underscored by their vulnerability to arrest by Federal troops early in the war. "While walking today near the exchange [in Fredericksburg], I was stopped by Captain Scott of the Federal Army, and informed that by the order of General King I was under arrest," Baptist William F. Broaddus reported of his detention in the summer of 1862.[29] By 1863, however, the Federal War Department declared chaplains to be noncombatants and ordered them to be released immediately if captured.[30]

Although pastors engaged in a variety of tasks during the war, their experience as chaplains left the most important legacy for postbellum church life. The chaplaincy provided an opportunity for pastors to reconcile their aversion to the "martial spirit" of war with their desire to serve the Confederacy. Preaching the gospel in the service of their nation, they upheld religious truth even as they scorned vengeance and partisan loyalty. Chaplains' experiences informed postwar church life, as many became prominent leaders of their denominations. Among the fifty-five army chaplains included in this study were ten future college presidents, eight professors, a Methodist bishop, and five newspaper editors. In addition, fourteen former chaplains later received honorary doctor of divinity degrees, a certain sign of influence among late-nineteenth-century pastors.

An estimated six hundred Southern pastors served as army chaplains during the war. Southern Methodists probably provided about two hundred chaplains over the course of the war, and of these, Virginia contributed at least twenty-two. Some ordained clergymen served as regular officers, performing chaplains' duties when needed. As soldiers or chaplains, pastors customarily served in units from their own communities and thus often preached to young men who had sat in their pews in peacetime or, more likely, whose mothers had.[31] Many Confederate regiments, however, fought throughout the war without a chaplain's services. Even the pious Stonewall Jackson could find chaplains to staff only half of his ninety-one regiments. In early 1863, only two hundred chaplains served the entire Confederate army; by 1864, more than 40 percent of the regiments in the Army of Northern Virginia were without chaplains.[32]

The relatively small number of chaplains highlighted the ambiguous status of the office. A national rhetoric built on Christian imagery did not mean that the government took up the cause of the soldier-preacher.[33] The Confederate government only reluctantly provided for army chaplains and never viewed them as an essential part of army life. The *Regulations for the Army of the Confederate States* never mentioned the office. Some have argued that this reluctance was rooted in strong Southern convictions about the separation of church and state. Yet in the opinion of many government leaders, including Jefferson Davis, chaplains were simply not worthy of government support.[34]

Chaplains suffered throughout the war from poor pay. After prolonged debate, the Confederate government declined to provide chaplains official rank, more than a private's salary, uniforms, or horses. Their wage of $50 to $80 per month was half that received by Union army chaplains, who were granted officers' rank during the second half of the war.[35] Southern churches attempted to ease the financial burden by supplementing low government salaries. Nevertheless, the lack of status and pay angered senior clergymen, in particular, and caused the office to be a transient one. Some estimated that fewer than fifty men served for the duration of the war.[36] This magnified the clergy's poor reputation among officers, who often complained that chaplains' service was inconsistent.[37]

Even after their commission into the army, chaplains routinely encountered opposition from both officers and soldiers. Some officers, particularly those who disparaged a clergyman's views on drinking and gambling, did not shrink from humiliating clergymen in front of the troops. One brigadier general called chaplains "the scourge of the army."[38] Soldiers who scoffed at religion and spent their idle time playing cards were not too proud to exchange the cards for a pocket Bible before battle began. If they were killed, word of their piety would be sent to their mothers.[39] Pastors could hardly imagine that worthy officers defended such practices. Sorely offended by the officers' rebukes, pastors often characterized them as vain, arrogant, and drunken men, much given to swearing.[40]

The troubles that Virginia chaplains experienced among officers and soldiers were especially significant because, as a group, they were older and much better educated than the men to whom they preached. Chaplains were almost twice as likely as other antebellum pastors to have attended college, making them far better educated than the majority of soldiers (see Appendix, Table 15). Their average age of thirty years exceeded by a decade the average age of regular soldiers in the Confederate army. One chaplain enlisted when he was fifty-seven years old. Many chaplains were, or aspired to be, the social peers of officers. But high-ranking Confederate officers, usually members of the gentry, were sharply divided in their attitudes toward these Baptist and Methodist chaplains. Many of them were accustomed to the refinements of the Presbyterian and Episcopal churches. Some, like Thomas "Stonewall" Jackson, graciously welcomed piety of any stripe in their ranks. Jackson's piety became so celebrated after the war in part because his kindness impressed these beleaguered chaplains, and they singled him out for praise in their later accounts of the war.[41]

The experience of chaplains in army camps suggests the formidable opposition to religion that flourished in all ranks of Southern society. Although historians have emphasized the evangelical character of the region, and especially the religious nature of the Confederacy during the Civil War, many Southerners barely tolerated Christian piety and its advocates. Even after the reportedly glorious army revivals, an estimated two-thirds of all Confederate soldiers remained unconverted, a percentage that equaled that of nonchurch members in the South.[42] In camp, as in Southern communities, chaplains were alternately revered, despised, tolerated, or ignored. If the image of a pious, Bible-toting Confederate South is the one that has survived, it is a testimony to the influence of the clergy's interpretations of camp life and war that circulated widely after the war.

The ambivalent status of army chaplains reflected the continuing clash of honor and piety in antebellum Southern culture. Many Southern men viewed the Civil War as a test of manly honor and had difficulty equating masculinity and honor with piety.[43] The lives of some Christian gentleman wove together strands of both honor and piety, but many Southern men continued to view piety as an essentially feminine quality. Their views came close to that of Henry James's view of the nineteenth-century French clergy: "Women, indeed, are not priests, but priests are, more or less, women."[44]

Pastors were especially sensitive to the associations of piety and femininity in wartime. Some worried even before the Civil War about the softening of the clergy. James A. Riddick complained that young men's aid societies would "be instrumental in gathering in a class of soft and effeminate men, unfitted for our work." During the war, as male honor proved itself in battle, Virginia pastors customarily worked with women, staying behind battle lines and in hospitals. The distinction between the soldiers' and the chaplains' tasks was underscored by the masculine environment of the army camps. Preachers accustomed to working in overwhelmingly female congregations found themselves in muddy and uncouth camps surrounded by swearing and drinking soldiers. Some pastors managed to celebrate the clergy's essentially feminine role in such a rude environment. A Methodist bishop exhorted pastors to take the place of a wife's, mother's, or sister's "soft hand" on a soldier's fevered brow. Like these women, he should direct the dying man to Calvary. "How sweet will be the words of kindness from your lips . . . as you kneel beside him and talk sweetly to him of Jesus."[45]

Others, however, were less inclined to shrink from a good fight while battles raged around them. One of the most hotly debated issues of the war within clerical ranks was whether chaplains should bear arms. A meeting of chaplains in 1863 decided that although no absolute rule could be laid down, "ordinarily it is thought wrong for him to take a musket." Generally, they concluded, chaplains should station themselves where ambulances met the litter bearers, "where many die."[46] There was hardly consensus on the matter. Some Southern pastors believed they should never carry arms. Thomas H. Early, son of Methodist Bishop John Early, was granted a certificate of military exemption in March 1864 "by reason of being a Minister in Charge." Baptist Robert Burton pleaded for protection on the flyleaf of his diary: "Please spare the poor preacher, wife and 20 dependents. Especially as he is a friend of North and South, and will submit to the powers that be with Christian cheerfulness."[47]

Nevertheless, those who were unwilling to bear arms suffered repeated humiliations from officers and even regular soldiers. General Jubal Early reportedly once challenged a man he found retreating as battle approached. "I am nothing but a poor preacher, Sir, and am going towards the rear," he replied. "Why, Sir," the general taunted, "I thought you had been praying to get to heaven . . . and now you can go there in fifteen minutes and will not embrace the opportunity?"[48]

Some pastors unwittingly concurred with their critics when they expressed their hopes that war would encourage a more manly piety among their peers. "Among the many evils of war, we should not forget such a benefit as that it corrects the growing tendency to effeminacy," George Taylor wrote. "How desirable, if many of our young preachers in this school shall learn to 'endure hardness.' Then they can preach as the pioneers did, and not be concerned [about] what they shall eat, or where they shall sleep."[49]

Indeed, war gave preachers a brilliant opportunity to masculinize their faith. They often emphasized the physical danger of the office in their accounts of the war and recounted heroic tales of chaplains in battle. In one oft-repeated tale, an Alabama Methodist exhorted his regiment in the heat of battle. "We were under cross fire. Seeing [the men] waiver, I sprang to my feet, took off my hat, waved it over my head and preached them a sermon."[50] Similarly, William Bennett devoted the first pages of his well-known 1877 account of wartime revivals to a detailed description of the Christian convictions of military men in world history. Claiming a heritage in the New Testament's Roman centurion and even Oliver Cromwell, he argued that "every rise of pure faith . . . every genuine revival, has been sustained and helped forward by military men."[51]

If the conflict between honor and piety had a precedent in antebellum life, chaplains encountered in army camps an entirely unfamiliar authority structure. Pastors customarily exercised a strange mixture of autonomy and submission in their regular church work. Baptists, lacking the strong hierarchical structure of the Methodist church, were accustomed to independence in their daily work. As army chaplains, however, pastors placed themselves under the authority of army officers, an unprecedented submission of pastors to a secular authority. Many pastors chafed under the irreverent officers to whom they reported. If not quite civil servants (they never considered their service to the state their primary task), chaplains held an office that even by their own admission had more than a spiritual purpose. Civil authorities tolerated chaplains in large measure because the religious and the irreligious alike agreed that a Christian soldier was more courageous, and certainly better disciplined, than a non-Christian one.

Chaplains also found themselves in a unique relationship to their soldier "congregations." In antebellum churches, they exercised a consensual authority that grew out of members' voluntary submission to their discipline and teaching. In army camps, soldiers neither chose their chaplains nor paid their salaries. The custom of consensual authority was broken, and officers often thwarted chaplains' attempts to enforce a spiritual discipline on soldiers.

The nature of the work chaplains undertook was also new. From the beginning of the war, Southern pastors simply assumed the necessity of evangelizing the army. The huge effort that they eventually undertook represented their first mass evangelistic campaign. The approach mobilized both Southern Baptists and Methodists in a common task that overshadowed all other work during the war years. War pulled their attention away from the local congregation and focused it on the conversion of a national army.[52] The intensity of the experience in battle contrasted sharply with the quiet and even boring life of many congregations behind the lines. Pastors considered congregations useful primarily for their contributions to the more demanding army work. Conversions in camps forcefully illustrated that congregations were not the only places in which Christ might be served. Army camps, like churches themselves, became "schools of Christ."[53]

The massive scale of this effort necessitated an unprecedented reliance on the denomination to organize army work. Here was a huge task of religious benevolence that required coordination far beyond the reach of any congregation. The money and manpower needed to evangelize an army pushed pastors to a renewed appreciation for, and reliance on, denominational bureaucracies. This mass mobilization also lifted some Southern reticence about interdenominational work, although later some pastors would angrily deny that they ever compromised their doctrinal principles in order to evangelize Confederate soldiers.

In fact, printed tracts and Bibles, not army chaplains, were the great evangelists of the war. Although pastors had used religious newspapers, tracts, and books extensively in the antebellum period, preaching had remained their first task. Preaching, not reading, had sparked the powerful revivals of the early nineteenth century. Wartime revivals, however, forced an unprecedented reliance on the press, and its success convinced many that it was the most important evangelistic tool of all. "And this ministry of the printed page may most efficiently work together with that of the pulpit; may even prove, in many cases, the more potent of the two," a Baptist pastor predicted just before the war. In his view, neglecting to read was a sin.[54] Pastors christened the army campaign a "silent revival" because so many young men read their way into heaven. Significantly, they described tracts as "preachers" that preached "silently but powerfully."[55] This experience left an important legacy for the postwar church, as the ranks of army chaplains included five future newspaper editors who witnessed firsthand the success of print. Pastors were so enthusiastic about books and tracts that they sometimes neglected to mention preaching altogether. "In no way can we better aid [the soldiers] in resisting [temptation] than in affording them good books," a Methodist pastor declared. They had supreme confidence in the power of the printed word; pastors even measured the success of their work not in souls converted but in the number of pages they distributed. "I have seen scores of instances in which the reading of tracts has been instrumental in the conversion of souls," Rev. W. M. Young reported.[56] The intensity of interest in reading created a pressing demand for colporteurs to work alongside army chaplains. Chaplains and colporteurs showered troops with tracts, particularly just before battle, with titles such as "Sinner, Are You Ready to Die?" and "The Christian Patriot's Prayer," which included the following stanza.

> Drive back these murderous hosts that come
> To rob us of our land and home
> And let us still in safety sit
> Beneath our fig trees, near thy feet[57]

The focus on reading as a means of conversion led pastors to another familiar task: teaching soldiers how to read. Rev. Joseph E. Martin, working at Chimborazo Hospital in Richmond, wrote of sixteen conversions in its wards through the reading of tracts. "One young man was very anxious to learn to read," he reported. "I procured him a spelling book, and in a few days he learned so rapidly as to be able to read the New Testament. He has since professed religion." Martin reported that another "middle-aged man from Georgia" learned to read while in the army "and has since committed to memory almost all of the New Testament with the Book of Job."[58] Another pastor gave copies of *McGuffey's First Reader* to forty-five illiterate soldiers, after "demanding and obtaining promises that they would try to learn."[59] The First Baptist Church of Richmond even established a school for illiterate soldiers.[60]

Much of the interest in reading grew out of one of the fixtures of camp life: boredom. Waiting for orders to march or to fight was one of the most tedious parts of the soldier's life. Men accustomed to working full days, either in field or factory, office or shop, suddenly found themselves with an unprecedented amount of idle time on their hands. Of the pastimes with which soldiers occupied themselves—playing cards, sleeping, talking, foraging, and reading—pastors encouraged only the last. "Men who scarcely ever read, much less buy, a paper at home are eager to see one in camp," a Tennessee soldier wrote in 1864. Newspapers sold from 5 to 25 cents per copy, but copies of religious papers were usually donated free of charge.[61] "Yesterday morning the mail brought us 100 copies of the *Southern Christian Advocate*," a chaplain of the 55th Georgia wrote, "which gives about 10 to each company . . . walking through the regiment five minutes after this time, you might have seen, in almost every cabin and street, men deeply interested, poring over this silent messenger of intelligence and truth."[62] In addition to newspapers, soldiers read to enhance their military and professional knowledge. Some of the more enterprising even took the time to learn a foreign or ancient language. They also enjoyed comic magazines and novels, both respectable (especially Scott and Cooper) and of the "cheap" variety. Novels in particular provided the opportunity to read for escape—an unprecedented use of reading for many men.[63]

The abundance of reading materials available to soldiers was a luxury. Although an estimated 70 percent of all Confederate free males (and perhaps a higher percentage of soldiers) could read, public libraries were virtually unknown in the antebellum South. Confederate troops, however, had ready access to books. Many units had their own libraries, of which the chaplain usually served as librarian. "This is the collection; take your choice. You get it on the soldier's honor," read a hand-painted sign hanging outside the library tent in a Virginia camp in 1863. Major John Stewart Walker of the 15th Virginia provided a library for his men "during the dreary days spent in winter quarters." Some towns and churches also established "soldiers' libraries." One in Lynchburg held eight hundred volumes. Hospitals also opened reading rooms, and nurses customarily read aloud to patients.[64]

Idle time in camp also provided opportunities for preaching. When battles lulled, some chaplains and lay preachers held as many as five or six revival meetings per day. "I never saw men so anxious to hear preaching," one soldier reported. "They crowd around the preaching place two to three hours before the preacher gets there."[65] Some attributed at least part of the interest in religion to homesickness, as many young soldiers associated worship with family and home, even if they had not professed religious faith. Sometimes a company's chaplain was the same minister who had preached at their home church.[66]

Confederate revivals have received much attention but little systematic study.[67] Scholars have tended to accept uncritically the clergy's descriptions of these revivals, generally published in the 1870s and 1880s, in spite of pastors' obvious self-interest in emphasizing their success.[68] Estimates of soldier converts ran as high as 150,000 over four years. Yet if such estimates were impossible to confirm and some clerical accounts were undoubtedly exaggerated, anecdotal evidence of revivals among Southern troops is too common to discount. Revivals deeply impressed many young soldiers who attended them, not just the clergymen who led them, and contemporary accounts suggest that many who participated in them thought them to be miraculous in their intensity. The successful evangelism of Confederate soldiers stood in sharp relief to the relatively unenthusiastic religious life of most congregations away from the front, and clergymen spent an increasing amount of effort on the army campaign as the war progressed (see Appendix, Table 16).

Many of these themes came together in the experience of William E. Wiatt of Gloucester County. At the age of thirty-five, Wiatt was commissioned as a chaplain for the 26th Virginia Infantry in October 1861, and he was one of the few chaplains who served the full term of the war. An observant and thoughtful diarist, Wiatt suffered the death of his son William, saw his farm destroyed by occupying Union troops, and lost his wife to disease while she was a refugee in Alabama during the war. He remained in the army, however, attending Lee's surrender at Appomattox in April 1865.

Wiatt was born in 1826 to a slaveholding family in Gloucester, on the Chesapeake Bay just north of the York River. As a young man, he taught school and was a committed member and sometime preacher in the local Baptist church. But at twenty-four, he left Gloucester for better prospects in Kentucky, where he settled just across the Ohio River from Cincinnati. "I promised myself never to teach school again if I could help it but I also made another promise to myself that I would not lead an idle life," he wrote to a friend back home in May 1850. Nevertheless, Wiatt soon had to take up teaching to support himself. He marveled that Kentucky was an altogether different country from Tidewater Virginia. Because there were so few slaves in the region, "we all have to wait on ourselves—We clean our own boots get our own water to wash and do every thing of the kind each one for himself. I am rather pleased at that," he admitted. "It does not go hard with me, although I had that done all of it in Virginia."[69]

Wiatt's letters suggested that his avid interest in the Masons, Sons of Temperance, and Odd Fellows was eclipsed only by that in his own Ebenezer Church. Upon hearing of the resignation of one pastor, he doubted the church might replace "so pious and so talented and so justly popular a man. . . . I feel more for Gloucester than for any other place. I try to pray frequently that God would look upon her favorably and make his cause to flourish greatly. I wish you would let me know all about your prospects," he demanded of his friend Tom Montague. "Have your numbers increased any? Whom do you expect to get as your preacher? Has the Church been thoroughly built? Have you received any more money for the payment of it? How much do you now owe &c. What did Bro. Jones do for it? And those Brethren and Sisters in Elizabeth City?"[70]

Wiatt eventually took up preaching himself at Ebenezer after he returned from Kentucky. Ordained in 1854, like many Baptist preachers he did not consider the pulpit a full-time ministry. By 1860, he and his wife, Charlotte, had four children and held property estimated at nearly $10,000, including eleven slaves. By any measure, Wiatt was a slaveholder of substance.[71]

Wiatt's long tenure as a chaplain in the 26th Virginia Infantry took him from Virginia to South Carolina and back again. Because Gloucester was occupied by the Union army from May 1862 until the end of the war, Wiatt sent his family south to relatives in Alabama and eventually sold his slaves and livestock, leaving his farm in ruins. The county suffered great destruction from the Union army, although when Wiatt's own barn burned to the ground in March 1863, he blamed the fire on his own slaves. They were angry, he said, because he had just sold some of his slaves. He promptly arranged for the rest to be sold in Richmond, specifying that they were to be "sold all together. I will not separate a family," he said. He invested most of the profits from their sale (more than $9,000) in 8 percent Confederate bonds.[72]

Wiatt's account of army life suggests the privileged position of a preacher in mid-nineteenth-century Virginia. He bought a small lot of bricks for half price, he said, as "the overseer favored me because I was a preacher." Soldiers and civilians alike entrusted Wiatt as a special courier. He shuttled money from soldiers to their families, carried letters and other documents, and oversaw the regimental fund—money disbursed to soldiers for their purchases. He escorted women traveling alone and was given free railroad passes. On one sad occasion, he carried $50 given to him "in case of misfortune" to the wife of a captured soldier. By the last months of the war, his most precious contraband was pairs of socks.

In early April 1864, Wiatt traveled via train on furlough from South Carolina to see his sick wife in Alabama. "A package of tracts is an excellent means of arresting swearing and blasphemy," he wryly noted of the trip. Indeed, Wiatt found that printed tracts, books, and newspapers encouraged and sustained piety and upheld his own authority as a preacher almost daily. He purchased Bibles to give to soldiers, kept a library for his regiment, read and distributed religious newspapers, and wrote letters home for those who could not write themselves. He was particularly concerned about illiteracy in his regiment. In April 1862, he organized a Bible class and day school for those who could not read, and by June of that year, he reported twenty-five students. In early 1864, his regimental Christian Association appropriated $150 to buy spelling books for those who could not read.

Wiatt also performed the routine duties of his office: visiting the sick and dying in the hospital and on the field, giving spiritual counsel, rebuking deserters, preaching funerals and burying the dead, and sitting up with grieving widows. "I find nearly all of our men, when sick, admit their need of religion and admit that they think about it," he observed early in the war. He preached periodic revivals, generally in summer months, with help from neighboring pastors, and attended "a colored people's meeting" while in South Carolina. "A good many whites were out," he noted, and "the colored people sang several songs delightfully."

The 26th Virginia did not see heavy combat until the siege of Petersburg began in the summer of 1864. There Wiatt and his men lived in the filthy trenches for nine months. "Held a prayer meeting tonight with Capt. Owen's and Sutton's companies, our soldiers seem glad to engage in these prayer meeting exercises. We sing & pray & exhort while bullets are flying thick and fast over our heads," he wrote in October. They would not leave until mid-March.

As Lee fled toward Danville in the spring of 1865, Wiatt carefully noted the Bible passages on which he preached, along with the increasing number of deserters from the Army of Northern Virginia. One Sunday in that grim

March, he turned the soldiers' weary eyes to Revelations, where they shared
John's vision of "a new heaven and a new earth." Finally, on April 8, Lee turned
toward Appomattox Courthouse, where on April 9 he announced his formal
surrender. A hardened veteran of four long years, Wiatt must have seen the
end coming, but he poured out his confused anguish in the pages of his diary
nonetheless.

> The question *has God forsaken us? Is our Confederacy ruined* I, for one, can't
> believe it; God I verily believe, has humbled us to exalt us; I believe He will,
> yet in His good way & time grant unto us deliverance & prosperity & honor;
> His wisdom & power & goodness are the same . . . can all the prayers & faith
> & hope & anxiety, and blood, and sacrifice, in the name of the Lord & of the
> right be in vain? I can't think so; I look for a glorious future to our beloved
> South. Lord, teach us to humble ourselves before Thee, repenting of our sins
> and trusting in Thy son.

Later that afternoon, Wiatt went into the enemy's lines to bring off the
wounded, where he said he was "treated very civilly by the enemy; had conversations with several on the subject of religion." He shed tears, he recorded, twice on that day—once when talking with these Union soldiers and
again when General Lee rode for a final time through the ranks of hundreds
of cheering men. "It has been a sad day for us," Wiatt sighed late that evening before trying to sleep. "May God's grace be sufficient for us; at night,
sang the hymn 'God moves in mysterious ways &c' and had prayer by Lt.
Jones."

Two weeks later, Wiatt had walked back to his farm in Gloucester. Again
that night he poured his anguish into his diary. He returned "to his native
country" with a heavy heart, questioning God's will, God's goodness, the meaning of all the sacrifice that had been made. "I passed my place and my troubles
pressed heavily upon me," he wrote. "Here I lived for several years, happy in
my family relations & much blessed of God; now I look upon my once dear
home with a stricken heart; my home is desolate, my heart is more so." But
in the long passage that he recorded that night, Wiatt began to turn away
from despair. He determined that his sadness was not from a want of faith,
and he resolved to remember that "a Christian is not of the world. . . . O Lord,
make me faithful & useful in my generation; may I be an instrument in Thy
hands to lead many souls to thee!"

Wiatt would become useful again. His property devastated, he would work
in the years after the war as a preacher, teacher, surveyor, and public school
superintendent.[73] But the war had challenged him and changed him. His identity as an army chaplain was strangely dear to him, and as he closed his war
diary, he paused to admit his ambivalence about ending it all.

> Here my journal ends for the present; it may never be resumed by me
> as Chaplain in the Confederate Army . . . may I have some 'crowns of rejoic-
> ing' in the great day as chaplain in the army of my beloved country; this

journal was begun on the 1st day of Jan'y 1862 and has been continued till the present without interruption; I regret the ending of it.

> s/ Wm. E. Wiatt, paroled Chaplain
> 26th Va. Reg't Inf'try
> Brig Gen. Wise's Brigade
> Maj. Gen. B. W. Johnson's Division
> Lt. Gen. R. Anderson's Corps
> Army of N. Va.

William Wiatt's long service as an army chaplain suggests how deeply the Civil War redefined both Southern religious practice and clerical professionalism. Pastors' defense first of slavery and later of the Confederacy pushed religion's relevance into the public sphere and encouraged the growth of denominations as public organizations. As the leaders of regional denominations during the 1850s, pastors understood their influence in the debate over slavery. As chaplains and evangelists of their national army, they were convinced that their work was central to the survival of the Confederacy.

Denominations were the organizational heart of Methodist and Baptist endeavors during the Civil War. The printing and distributing of tracts and the mass evangelization of the army demanded mass appeals, organization, and careful planning. The apparent success of army revivals encouraged great confidence in the organizational strategies and regional vision of the denomination, and pastors eagerly tied their own professional fortunes to that of their denominations in the years after the war. Both the organizational skills pastors acquired during the war and their confidence in such efforts would provide a model for life in New South churches.

Yet pastors' role as chaplains and the lack of esteem shown them by Confederate officials undercut the optimism of this new professionalism. The cool and even hostile reception chaplains received from Confederate officers suggested not only that many derided religion but also that they had little respect for the clergy, professional or no. Their disappointing wartime experience with Southern elites shaped the sensibilities of a generation of clerical leaders, reinforcing their identification with the professional and mercantile classes and leaving them sharply aware of the limits to their social aspirations. In the New South, these pastor-soldiers would denounce both those who lived without refinement and those who lived for it.

The war also slowed the retreat from revivalism that had been increasingly apparent in the public statements of leading Methodist and Baptist pastors of the 1850s, who had dismissed revivalism as an uncouth relic of the past. The generation of army chaplains experienced a renewed respect for revivals. Even as antebellum professional standards had encouraged pastors to tie their authority to the printed word, wartime revivals reemphasized the power of preaching. And that power was made all the more apparent for its ability to make converts among an audience of distracted and honorable men. At the same time, however, the war did encourage the view of revivals as relics of the past. Army revivals were self-conscious affairs, where pastors called forth the power of old-time religion. One pastor described army revivals in 1864 as "resembling so strong the great revival periods of the early pioneer settlements," calling them a "scene for an artist."[74] Such nostalgia would continue in the years after the war, as would pastors' determination to build a social consensus on religion similar to the one they believed they had wrought in the Confederacy.

CHAPTER SIX

Reconstructing Religion

In the summer of 1865, former Confederate chaplain George Taylor wrote to his brother about the meaning of defeat. "For my part, I accept the facts as indicating God's will, and acquiesce with a peace of mind I had not thought possible," he wrote. "Still, I confess that ever and anon the sad facts come over me with fresh power and almost crush and paralyze me. But it is all right, and we must remember that we are chiefly connected with a kingdom which is 'not of this world' . . . because a Christian, I hope to be a good citizen."[1]

For pastors like Taylor, the defeat of the Confederacy did not diminish Christianity's relevance to public life. "Let Southern women exert a patriotism firm, yet feminine," a Baptist woman urged in the fall of 1865. These appeals to Christian citizenship in the immediate postwar period continued the link between religion and the public sphere first forged by slavery and affirmed in the short life of the Confederacy. In their first meeting after the war in early June 1865, Virginia Baptist ministers resolved to be public servants in the name of God. "We deem it our duty as patriots and Christians to accept the order of Providence . . . and we earnestly recommend to our brethren . . . to enter with zeal and activity upon the discharge of the responsibilities devolved on them by their new social and civil relations."[2]

Postwar Virginia pastors did not plead for a private religion; instead, they emerged from the war eager to build a social consensus rooted in religion, particularly in the institutional church and the leadership of Southern pastors. "Society needs to be built up again from its foundation," Virginia Baptist leaders declared in 1866. "The Gospel is that foundation." "Building up" meant lifting up morally, spiritually, and materially; the church would build social consensus by instilling social aspiration in its people. "Order derives its effectual principle from the Gospel," these Baptists continued. "Saving the souls of men, we most potently assist to quicken their despondent energies, repair their shattered fortunes and bring back their temporal prosperity."[3]

The tasks that these pastors took up in the days immediately after the war provide a particularly clear view of their priorities. These priorities had been shaped most immediately by their wartime experience, during which pastors had seized the opportunity to assert their public leadership. Yet their postwar agenda also hearkened back to the antebellum period, which had deeply ingrained in them the necessity of education for self-improvement. Characteristically, they made this the keystone of their postwar agenda. In one area, however, the clergy broke sharply with antebellum patterns: these priorities did not include African Americans. The mission to slaves died with slavery, and any sense of obligation to black brothers and sisters ended abruptly in the rapid segregation of congregations between 1865 and 1870.

This chapter examines both the content and the context of this vision of "Christian citizenship" in postwar Virginia. Christian citizenship was not a political category; rather, it invoked pastors' broad efforts after the war to build a social consensus rooted in religion. Women, although denied the franchise, were heartily welcomed into this effort; indeed, as chapter 8 argues, pastors exhorted women to use their influence in new ways in postwar Virginia.

Pastors' conviction that the Christian life entailed public responsibility was the most lasting legacy of their wartime service as army chaplains, evangelists, and colporteurs. In the wartime church and on the battlefield, they had powerfully experienced the poignant relevance of religion. Surrounded as they were by death, those of pious heart found themselves more than ever suspended between this world and the next, and they found their faith of great use. It reassured dying young men, it justified their struggle, and it gave many the heart to fight on. If not all Confederates were pious, most admitted the advantages of having God on their side, and they recognized that they needed the clergy to show them how to appease him. Even the most staunchly Reformed Southerners found themselves scurrying to win God's favor for their cause by being good and doing good, particularly in the last desperate days of the war. And just as morality had been of critical importance to the Confederate cause, it could be the only foundation of public order in the defeated South. "The best guarantee of public intelligence, the only guarantee of public virtue, is the Gospel," Baptists declared. "The Gospel supplies the true sanction of law."[4]

Pastors urged Christians to take responsibility in social and civil relations outside the church congregation. A defeated and demoralized society needed enlightened leadership and models of good behavior. "It is possible for a high degree of civilization to exist without the Gospel and the Gospel preacher," a Baptist argued in a passionate piece published a year after the war, "but public tranquility, magisterial justice, social happiness, domestic purity, never."[5] "Public tranquility" demanded that pastors address everything from church attendance to personal dress. No aspect of social behavior was beneath their comment. "Every one should try to dress in a way that is suitable to his age and position," an editor scolded. "By neglecting to do this people sometimes make themselves ridiculous."[6]

The war had devastated large parts of Virginia. Church buildings had been used as military headquarters and hospitals. Many had been burned to the ground. William Edwards arrived in the summer of 1865 at Dinwiddie Street Methodist Church in Portsmouth to find "the church in ashes, the congregation scattered, the membership disbanded, and the church register in the custody of a [northern] preacher." Edwards gathered a few souls together and began meeting in a Presbyterian church. Even in 1867, churches in the battle-scarred region of Culpeper remained closed. Edgar Pritchett arrived that year to find five of eight churches on his new circuit destroyed, "the church at Culpeper Courthouse particularly, having been almost literally torn to pieces by the Federal soldiers and used as a stable and for other purposes, so repugnant to a sense of common decency."[7] Congregations two or more generations old were scattered and divided against each other. Federal troops no longer threatened their safety, but Northern missionaries worked to entice Virginians, especially in the Shenandoah Valley and western parts of the state, to join the Northern church. They won converts among the clergy as well as the laity. In his letter of resignation from the Methodist Episcopal Church, South, Rev. T. H. Haynes hinted at the raw feelings in the wake of his own "conversion" by refuting "any accusation published against me unbecoming a Christian gentleman."[8]

Some pastors had contributed liberally to the war effort and were left penniless. Robert Ryland, president of the Richmond College, was left in 1865 with $10 in gold and a good milk cow to his name. To support himself, he sold milk on the streets of Richmond. Another Baptist had "staked all on the Confederacy and lost all. . . . I have eighteen thousand in Confederate bonds drawing eight percent interest . . . and yet I could not have paid for washing a collar when the Confederacy collapsed." He lived in a church basement, sold corn in the city market, and "wrote religious novels for bread and butter."[9] "One of the best preachers in the South plows from nine to ten hours a day—not from choice but from necessity," another reported.[10] Another urged city clergymen "in broadcloth and silk" to remember their poorer country brethren.[11]

Defeat, even of a cause they had so religiously defended, apparently did little to discredit the clergy. J. W. Ryland, a colporteur in King and Queen County, noted in October 1865 the kindness of the people during a recent month-long trip around Virginia. "In sections of the country where I have traveled, they think more of a *preacher* than anybody else."[12] Congregations continued to express their esteem and admiration for pastors as they had before the war with simple gifts, including food and clothing. One church that owed the pastor a year's salary accorded him the dubious honor of paying up the amount in full in Confederate currency. "If that was wrong, how much better is it to pay, as so many churches are doing nothing at all?" chided the editor who reported the fact.[13] Yet among people who were suffering, pastors dependent upon the good will of their churches suffered greatly. They plead in one voice for generosity. "If [a member] can't pay in cash, he may find that a few bushels of meal, a bag of flour, a hog or a shoat or a turkey or a chicken or a piece of cloth may be exceedingly acceptable," a Baptist editor suggested.[14]

Publicly, pastors took the position that defeat, like war, provided an opportunity for religion. They spurned nostalgia and invoked Christian citizenship to turn their congregations toward the future and to mobilize them to meet its challenges. In a society torn by resentment over the Confederacy's failure, the social strains of emancipation, physical devastation, and immense loss of life and property, pastors exhorted and prodded their war-weary congregations to do something in the name of God. Hardened by their wartime experiences, they nevertheless maintained public optimism, condemned those who languished in despair and self-pity in the strongest possible terms, and called for work and for determination. "As soon as the smoke of the final catastrophe blew off, we saw at once the work that had to be done," a Methodist remembered.[15]

As pastors took up the task of "reconstructing religion," as they called it, it soon became apparent that they intended to reconstruct more than religion. They intended to use religion to build order, harmony, and even virtue out of postwar chaos. This, they argued, was possible through the sincere efforts of godly people. In a striking departure from antebellum practice, however, their vision of social harmony did not cross the color line. When whites found their initial paternalistic overtures toward black church members rebuffed, they quickly turned away altogether. Their religion would serve white people; black people could take care of their own.

Perhaps most important for pastors themselves, this focus on the work at hand diverted attention from one of their most difficult tasks, that of interpreting defeat. Pastors had invested heavily in a defeated government, asserting that not only honor but also truth and God himself were on the side that had lost. Every pastor who stepped into a Virginia pulpit faced a congregation that wanted to hear his views on Providence and defeat. There was widespread anxiety that Union victory might have discredited not only their own judgment but also that of their God. Newspaper columns buzzed with questions of whether the South's decision to fight had been a righteous one. One South Carolina Methodist even began publishing a newspaper that advocated Christian pacifism.[16]

Yet Appomattox did not plunge most pastors into a crisis of faith. If it left many sadly confused and even doubtful, they rarely made these concerns public. Indeed, their Bible repeatedly spoke of a God beyond mortal comprehension, whose ways were mysterious; it spoke routinely of defeat and disappointment and encouraged those who suffered to look to God with eyes of faith. If the war brought death and devastation on an unprecedented scale, pastors were no strangers to suffering or to the frailty of human understanding before an all-powerful God. Their faith in God's sovereignty smoothed the transition from war to defeat in 1865 just as it had dissolved opposition to the war in 1861, and they took solace in the mystery of it all. "We should cheerfully admit that the South may have been at fault. . . . This is simply an admission that man is fallible," a Baptist wrote in late 1865. "The truth is, God's ways are too deep, too vast, too complicated for our comprehension. . . . Prosperity is no sure mark of his favor, nor adversity his displeasure."[17]

Defeat did raise thorny theological questions, but not all pastors were partisans of theology. Nor did they all agree on how to interpret the Confederacy's loss. For some, accepting defeat meant admitting that the Confederacy had been wrong. But most simply counseled their congregations, as "followers of Him 'who is meek and lowly of heart' " to patiently endure their present trials. "Harmony is better than discord and love is better than hatred."[18] "Whatever may have been the cause or causes of our defeat and disappointment," Albemarle County Baptists declared, "it becomes us as Christians to yield to what seems to be the will of God concerning our present political relations, and in good faith to carry out our pledges to 'the powers that be.' "[19] As in their decision to support the Confederacy, pastors drew on an understanding of history that simply made defeat, in effect, God's will.

One of the war's most important legacies was the segregation of Southern churches. When the war ended, approximately 50,000 black members were on Virginia Baptist rolls, while just 1,600 remained in Methodist congregations in the Virginia Conference. The speed of their exodus was breathtaking. Just three years after the war, black Virginia Baptists had created three associations with 129 churches and almost 39,000 members. By 1875, just 213 black members remained on white Methodist rolls in the Virginia Conference.[20]

Southerners' turbulent history of sectarianism meant that the segregation of black and white Protestants into separate denominations opened a great gulf between two communities already estranged, a gulf that neither was obligated to try to bridge. No longer would black and white members regularly share the same communion meal or sing and worship together. In the nineteenth-century South, denominational barriers released church members from any real responsibility for or interest in those on the other side, regardless of race.[21]

Few Virginia congregations experienced the exodus of African American members in exactly the same way. Location, size, and denomination all affected the separation process. Rural churches felt the impact of emancipation most sharply, because many city churches had already segregated during the 1840s and 1850s. Even in rural areas, however, few white Protestants agreed on the best policy toward black members. More significantly, their attitudes toward former black members changed, sometimes quickly. Whereas early in 1865 many white pastors and members expected former members to accept their offers of aid, by late 1866 and 1867 their refusals of such help reaped the scorn of many white pastors. White members routinely denied former black members the use of their church buildings for services. By 1868, many concurred with a white Baptist editor who urged African American Christians to organize separate churches, for "there is no law of Christ requiring an opposite course." Violence was not the norm, but black pastors and congregations did suffer attacks against their persons and property. In 1866, the Second African Baptist Church of Richmond burned to the ground in mysterious circumstances.[22]

For white pastors, the departure of thousands of former slaves meant a sharp reduction in the scope of their social authority. Many had led antebellum congregations with a majority of black members. A few white pastors did retain a measure of authority over black church members who continued to seek membership in white churches. Thomas Sydnor, a white Baptist pastor in Southside Virginia, received several such inquiries in the years after the war. "The following naimed negros [five men and three women] request me to give them a certificate so as to become members of your church," A. S. Fitzgerald wrote to Sydnor in 1866. "That I cannot do because I have not bin with them long enough to find out mutch about theire caracter." Sydnor also received a series of requests from blacks who hoped to organize their own congregations. The notes, written in a painfully cramped hand, consisted simply of a list of names. One dated July 24, 1870, listed eight men and ten women, noting "this PePul do Want there Name fore to be ognise in to the church. ex Cuse my bad write fore God do foregive ous."[23]

Nevertheless, most black Protestants quickly freed themselves from obligation to white pastors and began to attend their own services. The appearance of a new "class" of black preachers, primarily former slaves, who claimed authority equal to that of white pastors and freedom from their oversight, was an unprecedented result of segregation. A few black men continued to apply for white permission to preach, but after 1865 white pastors retained only a tenuous authority over black preachers. The dilemma for black preachers, many of whom experienced a calling to the ministry just after emancipation, was to secure spiritual authority for their own ministry. Without ordination, a pastor did not have the authority officially to perform the ordinances of communion and baptism so vital to the Christian community.

In November 1867, Daniel Witt, an elderly Southside Baptist pastor, wrote the first of a long series of letters concerning Henry Fowlkes's desire to be ordained. Witt did not believe that African Americans could meet the "high standards" of ordained white ministers. "We are placed in extraordinary and difficult circumstances," he wrote in frustration. "The colored churches will have negro preachers and the negro preachers will preach." He believed that whites should keep black pastors as much under their influence as possible and argued that the best way to do so was to ordain only those of "good character." Fowlkes was the fifty-five-year-old former slave of P. A. Fowlkes, the sheriff of Nottoway County. He had professed religion nearly thirty years earlier, and Mrs. Fowlkes described him as "a dutiful and faithful servant. . . . I have never known his equal amongst his color." She regularly sought advice and prayers from him for herself and her children. But in spite of the Fowlkeses' good opinion of Henry, as well as Witt's own, protracted indecision in the matter meant that Fowlkes died at age sixty-two without ever being ordained.[24]

White pastors assessed black preachers in categories similar to those by which they judged young white candidates. Black and white pastors submitted to rigorous doctrinal examinations before receiving permission for ordination. But black men were pressed further: they had to meet often capricious standards of "character." Those who "knew their place" and displayed proper respect for white authority usually won favor. The famous black preacher John Jasper of Richmond managed to win some respect from white pastors. Jasper's biographer, Baptist pastor William E. Hatcher, professed his admiration for the man because "emancipation did not turn his head. . . . Freedom did not change him."[25]

Hatcher's biography reveals far more about white pastors' view of themselves than it does about Jasper. In particular, Hatcher's description of Jasper's preaching contrasts sharply with the professional ideals of white pastors. Hatcher described in detail Jasper's lack of education in a chapter called "How Jasper Got His Schooling." In contrast to Hatcher himself and many of his peers, Jasper "missed the help of schools, and never crossed the threshold of worldly science in his pursuit of knowledge," Hatcher wrote. Nevertheless, he "received an aristocratic education" during his service to an old and respected family. Hatcher described the former slave's vocabulary as "poverty itself, his grammar a riot of errors," and his preaching style as "of pictures and theatrical." As for Jasper's famous "Sun Do Move" sermon, Hatcher called it "a scientific absurdity! . . . It never occurred to him that the Bible was not dealing with natural science . . . intelligent people understand this very well."[26]

Hatcher's certainty that John Jasper lacked "taste and dignity" in the pulpit underscored his confidence in the refined and respectable character of white pastors and their churches.[27] In postwar Virginia, black churches became mirrors that confirmed the gentrification of white Methodists and Baptists. In particular, white ministers scorned the emotionalism of black (and lower-class white) worship, which they associated with ignorance and did not believe had a place in polite society. When a Baptist pastor in rural Amelia County preached to a neighboring black church, he sharply rebuked the congregation for moaning loudly while a black member prayed. Those white people who admired the freedom of black religious expression noted that, although it "quickened the pulse and set aglow the heart," white men and women found that their "social position or philosophy made them ashamed to acknowledge its effect."[28]

The denunciations of Jasper and African American religious practices echoed city pastors' criticism of uncouth rural congregations three decades earlier. In their criticism of black pastors, white clergy revealed the distance they wished to maintain not only between black and white religion but also between respectable religion and the excesses of what they would soon label "old-time religion." "Excitement is not piety. . . . Order, stillness and solemnity become the house and worship of God," a Baptist intoned. "Emotional piety, which fizzes and froths and pops today and tomorrow is utterly vapid and lifeless," warned a Methodist.[29]

From the white point of view, the segregation of Southern congregations was a resounding success. Segregation enabled African Americans to gain control over their religious worship and community life, but it also fulfilled the fondest wishes of many Southern white church members: it made African Americans invisible in their congregational life. Urban church members had long learned to deal with a largely invisible black Christian community, as segregated worship had been the norm in many urban congregations for two decades. But the segregation of many rural churches was abrupt, as many congregations had remained integrated for a brief time even after emancipation. The sudden disappearance of black members in rural churches lent even the poorest white congregations a veneer of respectability. If many of these churches segregated because black members simply walked out, white Protestants quickly turned this to their advantage: they argued that segregated churches were not only natural but also desirable. As in the antebellum period, newly segregated white congregations turned the separation into a mark of their social sophistication.

White church leaders continued to call for charity toward African Americans in the New South, but their calls were half-hearted. White members easily ignored them even as they contributed thousands of dollars to benevolence directed toward whites only.[30] Segregation not only sharply diminished white Protestants' public concern for black congregations but also secularized their interest in black Christians. When pastors mentioned African Americans at all, they usually failed to acknowledge their shared Christianity and referred to them almost exclusively in civil terms. As antebellum denominational schisms had prefigured secession, the segregation of Southern churches in the 1860s prefigured Jim Crow. By the time antebellum paternalism had completely dissolved in the caustic environment of the Jim Crow era at the end of the century, white church members had lived for almost four decades with evidence that segregation would, indeed, end the "negro problem."

The war and its results not only segregated Southern churches but also shifted models of piety from the faithful, trusting slave and pious planter to white military heroes. Robert E. Lee and Thomas J. "Stonewall" Jackson became the symbols of Christian citizenship that white Virginia pastors most often invoked in the early years after the war. Confederate military service had encouraged pastors to wed piety to public service and personal honor. Their effusive praise for these generals—secular leaders, regardless of their piety—suggests the war's powerful legacy for religion in the postwar South.[31]

Lee and Jackson stood as white pastors' most prized evidence that the war had been a work of God. If the temporal political cause had failed, ultimate spiritual victory lay in the army revivals and their conversion of thousands, as well as in the raising up of Christian gentlemen such as Jackson and Lee. "Mamma got a letter to-day, and father says there is a great revival in his regiment," a letter to Richmond's Methodist newspaper reported during the war. "What glorious news from the army is this! This is victory—triumph—peace! This is the token of good which the great King gives to cheer his people." God's victory was counted not in battles won, but in souls saved.[32]

Stonewall Jackson was an especially endearing figure to white Virginia Methodists and Baptists. Unlike Lee, Jackson was less an idol than a martyr. In 1866 and 1867, writers invoked his name almost weekly in the state religious newspapers. "It is not of Jackson the military genius or heroic commander, but of Jackson the humble, fervent, uncompromising Christian I write," wrote a Baptist editor in early 1866. "His piety was . . . demonstrative, aggressive and more effective" than that of Lee or Davis because he was, the writer concluded, a man of prayer.[33] "He has exalted religion, and so blent goodness and greatness, we can hardly discern one from the other," a Richmond Methodist wrote in 1867. At the dedication of the Jackson Memorial, unveiled several years later, Methodist Bishop David Doggett prayed that the memorial would remind people of God himself by teaching "the youth of this land . . . that the foundation of true greatness is fidelity to thee." Methodists later adopted a hymn based on Jackson's last words.[34]

The Southern clergy's successful elevation of Jackson, Lee, and a handful of others as representative Confederate heroes, notable for combining piety, military prowess, and manly honor, persuaded pastors that they would be heard on other matters as well. Forgotten was the wartime opposition of irreligious officers and the taunts of irreverent card-playing troops.

Lee and Jackson embodied the kind of public piety that white Virginia clergymen intended to make the foundation of the New South. Baptist and Methodist pastors worshiped neither of these men, nor did they encourage their congregations to worship the cause they had fought for. Instead, they boldly set forth these heroes as fitting symbols of Christian service in the new social order. In this way, they used the Confederacy not to invoke nostalgia, but to encourage change. Even Jackson's military strategy could become a metaphor for innovation. In 1867, a Methodist editor cited Jackson's unorthodox military maneuvers against McClellan at Chickahominy as a model for new methods of evangelism in the church.[35]

These heroes helped to create the broadly Christian public culture of the South, first hinted at in the controversies over slavery and then in Confederate nationalist sentiment. Robert E. Lee was a devout Episcopalian; Jackson was a Presbyterian. Yet even in a region riven by sectarian controversy, Baptists and Methodists eagerly embraced these men as their own, suggesting the South's broadly Christian identity in the war years and after.

Reverence for Lee and Jackson leveled social differences as well as doctrinal ones. Both were widely revered as Christian gentlemen, while Lee was Virginia nobility. In postwar Virginia, Christian gentility needed a new guise.

The quintessential Christian gentleman, the pious planter, was a relic of a dead era. In Lee and Jackson, Virginia clergymen found a new model, fit for the New South. Particularly those who had served in the Confederate army found themselves powerfully drawn to this model of Christian gentility.[36] These men became especially potent symbols for Christian leadership in the wake of the segregation of Southern churches. If the time for military leadership had passed, pastors fancied themselves as generals of a white civilian army, mobilizing their congregations to face the challenges of postwar life. In this, they claimed some of Lee's gentility for themselves.

Pastors were eager to distance their public-minded piety from politics, particularly during the chaotic days before the end of Union occupation in 1870. "It may soothe the feelings of a Christian to remember that Jesus, of his own free will, became a citizen of a subjugated province," a Baptist editor wrote in an editorial entitled "Jesus Christ—Citizen."[37] By focusing on Confederate heroes' Christian character, pastors made both Lee and Jackson apolitical figures and elevated them above the partisan fray. As servants of God in the public interest, they never stooped to petty political means. Religion, unlike politics, they argued, worked in the public interest. "The Legislature has done much to aid in building up waste places of the state. But . . . it can't command the clouds and sun so as to unite their genial influence on our crops. It can't bless the Labor of the land, so as to prosper the various professions of the day," a Methodist wrote. "In the Bible we have the very legislation we want. It brings to all who embrace it the things that they need," another pastor argued.[38]

Accounts of postwar religious life have equated such denunciations of politics with the clergy's eagerness to disengage religion from public life following the war. Yet pastors were deeply interested in modeling a civil and moral leadership in the years after the war. Sometimes, as in their reverence of Confederate heroes, they demonstrated their interest in public leadership through the traditional stance of a preacher: by preaching ideals and models worthy of imitation. But often they demonstrated their concern for the health of public culture in more tangible ways. "This is a propitious time to inquire what reforms should be introduced among us," a Baptist editor insisted in early 1866. "We need personal, social, and religious reforms."[39]

In January 1866, a pastor in Manchester, just across the James River from Richmond, began a public campaign to accomplish all three. William E. Hatcher, pastor of the town's "best" Baptist congregation, Bainbridge Street Baptist, published a series of letters in the Richmond *Dispatch*. Written over the pseudonym of "Struggle," a young female factory worker, the letters needled town leaders for failing to fix the streets, ridiculed property owners for the sad appearance of the town, and demanded that mill owners shorten the workday. Not least, the letters demonstrated an intimate knowledge of conditions in the mills and set before readers Hatcher's view of the poor.[40]

Manchester was a poor cousin to the capital city just across the James. By the time Hatcher arrived in the 1850s, the town already counted several cotton mills. By 1865, clusters of houses with names like Morgan's Row and

Sizer's Corner stood haphazardly between dusty fields and smoky mills powered by the falls of the James and coal from nearby mines in Chesterfield County. The year after Struggle's letters appeared, the town had two paper mills, several cotton and woolen mills, a flour mill, a corn mill, foundries, machine shops, a tannery, and a tobacco factory.[41]

Hatcher's understanding of conditions in the mills grew out of his pastoral work, which, like that of many urban Baptists, touched residents of widely varying social status. His own congregation met in a solid and staid edifice, raised in the 1850s, suggesting a well-heeled congregation, or at least one that aspired to be. President of Manchester's fledgling Philologian Debating Society, Hatcher was also master of a singing school attended by children of mill families. In short, he was an ambitious middle-class pastor who well knew the world of the working poor in his town.

The story that Hatcher gave to Struggle reflects both his sympathy for and romanticized ideals of what he called "the deserving poor." Her place in the factory was most likely the result of her father's death in the war, he wrote. In former years her family had lived at "Chestnut Lawn," a vaguely blissful plantation. Fatherless and poor, the family lost their old home in the war and ended in the mill. Struggle and her family were "worthy of any circle of society." They were poor in circumstance but refined in character. "I do not ask that all social distinctions be abolished and everybody put on equality," she wrote. "There are certain standards by which society must and always will be graduated." But in the postwar South, Hatcher argued through Struggle, these standards could not be determined by appearance: misfortune did not discriminate between the worthy poor and those who "deserved" their fate because of sloth. Hatcher intended Struggle's letters as a rebuke to those upper classes who neglected to notice Struggle's hope of a "higher life" and her fight "to attain a better sphere." Some poor people, Struggle explained, were ignorant and coarse-mannered; others, she insisted, were beautiful, modest, and sensible people who stood in grave danger of being degraded by their circumstances.[42]

That the worthy poor were even physically beautiful people in Struggle's view suggests just how tightly, in Hatcher's view, spiritual and material progress were bound up together. His letters focused on attaining a higher earthly life, not a spiritual one. Good works mattered a great deal in Hatcher's world, even if they did not gain one eternal security; he was no social Calvinist, powerless to change the status quo. Instead, he argued, pious people should clean up squalor and beautify their towns because degrading conditions themselves degraded people. Struggle railed against the poor conditions in Manchester. She skewered ineffective city officials who failed to repair the streets. She complained to landowners in the city about their poorly painted buildings. She literally equated paint with progress.

One of her most protracted fights, however, was over an issue that carried far more social and political weight than paint: she clashed with mill owners over working hours. Struggle's arguments for shorter working hours reveal the links in Hatcher's own thinking between circumstance and social status.

Twelve-hour shifts and night work in the hot mills not only harmed the health of mill workers, Struggle wrote, but also left workers too exhausted to pursue self-improvement. Struggle and her little brother longed to attend night school, but work on the night shift made this impossible. It also severely limited their opportunities for social interaction, which she believed would "soften our manners, enlarge our view, and quicken our virtuous pride."[43]

Struggle engaged her most passionate voice on this issue. "Ah well, if we die few weep," she wrote. "Stockholders smile at growing dividends and pause not to ask whose life was taken to make them rich, and our places are soon filled." Hatcher's letters exhibited an intimate knowledge of daily life among mill workers. "Many factory people think that heaven consists in getting out of the factory by marrying," Struggle wrote. "I know a few girls who were doing well enough before they married; some of them have now to support their husbands and then furnish them their whiskey besides." Another letter denounced the "windblowers," idle men who taunted young women from street corners as they walked to and from the mills. In late February 1866, Struggle demanded that townspeople engage in reform and benevolence, specifically that they end night work and open schools in the town. But she was careful to distinguish between false sympathy for reform and the real thing. She raged against what she termed "the unsubstantial froth of artificial benevolence." In the end, the mill owners did suspend night work in March of 1866. Dutifully, Struggle reported a few days later how glad she was to have the extra time so that she might spend her evenings teaching her little brother and reading historical novels.[44]

Whether Struggle's letters influenced the mill owners' decision to shorten the twelve-hour shifts (at least for a time) cannot be known. Her influence on the results of Manchester city elections held in April 1866, however, is more probable. Struggle waged a sharp rhetorical campaign against town leaders and urged readers of the *Dispatch* to vote on a reform ticket for the city's board of trustees in the April election. In the end, voters obliged. "Happily for the cause of progress and civilization our old Board of Trustees have gone to the grave," Struggle crowed. But she immediately turned to attack another of the town's ills: gamblers and the stinking soap factory. No doubt Hatcher was pleased with the new board's agenda. At their first meeting, they announced their intent to clean up the city's finances, open public schools, and establish a Board of Health.[45]

Struggle continued her letter campaign for several months before Hatcher left early in 1867 to lead a large Baltimore congregation. It was a dramatic illustration of a pastor's determination to exert direct influence on public life during Reconstruction. As the paid correspondent of the *Dispatch*, Hatcher cleverly used the columns of a secular newspaper not only to reform his town but also to publicize the work of his own church and that of others. And he earned some money for his trouble.

Hatcher's campaign was unique in its boldness, but many pastors shared his social concerns. Throughout the nineteenth century, ambitious town pastors uniquely bridged the experience of middle- and working-class Virginians.

As James Taylor had taught his church members, newly arrived from the countryside to early nineteenth-century Richmond, to read and to aspire to improve
themselves, so, too, did Hatcher reach out to the working class in postwar
Manchester. They and many others like them persuaded Virginia's working
classes, urban and rural alike, that they were, indeed, a "worthy poor" who
deserved better. And because their message was embedded in the uniquely
powerful context of eternal salvation, they won many converts to their temporal causes as well. Spiritual and material progress were one, in their view.

Hatcher's middle-class appropriation of an innocent young working girl's
voice for his Manchester campaign also suggested the complexities of the
clergy's stance toward partisan politics in the explosive political climate after
the war. Pastors like Hatcher saw themselves as advocates of the public interest, innocent of partisan intent, and with pure motives, much like their
beloved Confederate heroes. Confident of a solid constituency of churchgoing
people, they contrasted themselves to self-serving politicians who had cobbled
together false support through their corruption. In sharp contrast to the dirty
deeds of politicians, the work of a minister was "a mighty engine of moral
power," in the words of one Baptist writer.[46] Yet Hatcher's use of Struggle's
voice also underscored his tentative stance toward public affairs. Clearly,
Hatcher's impression was that Virginians would best tolerate a pastor's meddling in public affairs through indirect, even unconventional, means.

The works that Virginia pastors took up immediately after the war reveal their
priorities in a particularly clear way. More characteristic than William
Hatcher's campaign against politicians in Manchester was organization of
charitable education. If education had been a favorite tool of influence in the
antebellum years, the clergy's almost blind devotion to it immediately after
the war underscored their conviction that physical relief was not, and should
not be, the first responsibility of their churches. To be sure, pastors did not
discourage charity, but nearly all of the charitable work that was taken up by
churches was directed toward white people. Some congregations raised funds
for artificial limbs for disabled veterans, churchwomen funded a Richmond
orphanage for the children of veterans, and clergymen appealed for aid in
interdenominational charitable work in Richmond. Pastors also briefly exhibited some concern with charity for war widows and orphans. Their concern
for the families of soldiers focused their attention exclusively on white Virginians.

Confederate soldiers across the South generally received no government
support until at least the end of Reconstruction, and Virginia did not establish
a veterans' pension until 1888. The Federal government began a pension program for Union veterans in 1861 that would consume 40 percent of the federal
budget by 1893. Federal pensions constituted a significant financial resource
for Northern veterans' families well into the twentieth century.[47]

Southern churches declared in 1865 that it was their own responsibility to care for veterans' families, suggesting how deeply their involvement in the war effort had extended their sense of responsibility to those beyond the church. As in the antebellum period, however, pastors did not intend these needs to become the primary focus of religious benevolence. Instead, they expected individual Christians to take responsibility for feeding and clothing those in need.[48] Even when pastors did consider charity, they often tied their concerns to denominational interests. "How are we to meet the appeals coming to us daily from the widows who were once in positions of comfort?" a Methodist layman wrote in 1866, noting that he had recently heard of three families who sent their children "to Episcopal and Baptist schools because these denominations clothed them . . . must those who love our dear old church be forced into other denominations through their poverty?"[49]

Instead of physical relief, pastors channeled their interest in aiding postwar Virginia into education. They were far more eager to educate Virginians than to offer outright charity. Leading Baptist and Methodist pastors had themselves benefited from education in unprecedented numbers before the war. Moreover, their experience in army camps had convinced them more than ever of the evils of illiteracy and ignorance. Pastors also found education attractive because it provided a nonmaterialistic focus for the church. Their shrill denunciation of materialism in postwar Virginia continued a long trend begun during the war. William Wiatt was among many pastors who spluttered in rage about wartime greed, denouncing in 1864 "the love of money which is cursing the land and making us a nation of thieves and robbers." In 1866, things were no different. "An avidity to repair broken fortunes and to make money at all hazards is becoming the habit of the times," a Baptist worried in early 1866.[50] By contrast, education meshed perfectly with pastors' convictions about the need for self-discipline and self-control in the Christian life. The way to work oneself up in society, pastors argued, was not to earn money but to improve one's character, and the best way to do this was through education.

Although pastors couched their commitment to education in religious language, they focused primarily on its utility for rebuilding a devastated region rather than just churches. Moral and religious education, in their view, would bring social order and stability. Indeed, their educational charity focused on those outside their own congregations. Pastors initially wanted to educate freedmen and women, although their interest in this quickly died after the segregation of churches. More significant was their interest in veterans' orphans and veterans, whether they were church members or not. They also recruited children for Sunday schools, regardless of whether their families belonged to the church.

Denominations were the chief agency for this educational benevolence. The visibility and usefulness of denominations in evangelizing the Confederate army encouraged pastors to organize postwar church life in a similar manner. Their fever to organize infused church work with an exciting sense of innovation. They even regularly punctuated their pleas for action with references to technology. "The power of steam never sent the ponderous train across the plain without a mind to plan and execute it," read an article recruiting workers for Sunday schools in 1865.[51]

Baptists had discussed educating soldiers' children even before the end of the war. By June 1865, the General Association had appointed a committee to oversee the work headed by a Charlottesville pastor. They received some funds from the North and sent pastors to raise aid in other Southern states, although this effort proved less than successful. "The state was almost *flooded* with [fund-raising] agents and wherever I went 2 or 3 had just preceded me," a Virginia pastor reported after several months' work in Kentucky in 1866.[52] By that year, however, Baptists were aiding four hundred children, and four years later that number reached a thousand. They enrolled the children primarily in existing schools and persuaded some teachers to work for $1 per month. This short experiment highlighted pastors' conviction that church-based education served the public interest. But the project consistently suffered financial problems, including difficulty in procuring books. By 1870, the effort was limping along in debt. "Hear the cry of the soldier's orphan, 'I AM ALONE IN THE WORLD, and hearing, send help to our cause,' " pleaded a circular distributed across the state. The program's director viewed the establishment of state public schools in 1870 as a sign that the project should end. "The 'Free School' system breaks down our work. I can promise nothing more than to struggle to pay for bills already on hand," he wrote to a donor.[53] A few months later, apparently predicated on the opening of public schools, pastors abruptly abandoned this work, though their payment on the program's debts lingered on for several years.

Pastors also intended to educate thousands of returned soldiers. Reports from all over the South recounted tales of a restless and idle population of young veterans. "A demoralization has succeeded the disbanding of the army which manifests itself in drinking and dancing, and which has drawn within its restless vortex many a young Christian," a rural Virginia pastor worried.[54] Pastors especially felt the need for moral influence over these young men. In a time when civil authority was tenuous, many communities maintained a fragile sense of order, and Virginians feared that an unruly population of disturbed and idle young veterans would roam the state.[55] Editors filled religious newspaper columns with advice to young men about how best to secure work. In 1866, one advised young men to abandon their hopes for clerkships or other occupations "in conformity with former notions of respectability" and to band together to obtain agricultural jobs. Moral issues, especially temperance, took a prominent place in their public discussions throughout the late 1860s.[56] At "A Meeting for the Moral and Religious Improvement of Young Men" in September 1865 in King and Queen County, Baptists tried to instill a sense of direction in neighborhood veterans. "Young men must give a right tone and moral direction to the country," J. H. C. Jones, Esq., told the gathering. "This is your greatest responsibility. . . . We are poor, and shall continue so, without industry, economy, and enterprise."[57] They formed Young Men's Associations and missionary societies across the state. At a Methodist church in Richmond, young men spent their evenings debating such issues as whether capital punishment was forbidden in the Bible and whether God used evil for his own purposes.[58]

In their appeals to establish young men's societies, ministers first cited the state's economic and social interests, and religious benefits fell to a distant third. This impulse ran through many church endeavors in these years. Northern Neck Baptists held a "convention" a year after the war ended and passed a number of resolutions concerning postwar church life. The first called for discipline of church members who attended parties, and the following three concerned temperance. Other goals included urging industry upon the young and opening Sabbath schools. Last, the group resolved to hold regular prayer meetings. Congregations as much as pastors viewed religion as a tool for social order during Reconstruction.[59]

Pastors also continued their longstanding practice of offering educational charity to prospective ministers. Baptists and Methodists provided free or cut-rate tuition and loans at state denominational colleges. The Education Board of the Virginia Baptist General Association proposed to "assist all young brethren, unable to defray their own expenses, who are properly recommended by their churches." The board accepted applications from young men from all states. A committee interviewed each candidate and read testimonials from his congregation, as well as a statement of his conversion experience, calling to the ministry, and doctrinal position. The college endowment paid in full the $170 tuition; the board paid just over $80 per student for rooms. The board considered the payment a loan, however, and argued that students benefited by the program were not "charity students." To meet the rest of the boarding expenses, students in the early years after the war organized the Clerical Club of Richmond College, appointing one member as commissary to purchase provisions.[60]

Although pastors depended on denominations for these educational programs, these bureaucracies, which had been their crowning achievement before the war, were in tatters. Pastors appealed for money at every turn. "One of the many ways in which ladies do good is by encouraging young brethren to enter the ministry and helping them to gain preparatory education," a Baptist editor wrote in 1866. Methodists, meanwhile, established a "Children's Preachers' Education Society," the sole object of which was to raise money for young ministers-to-be from children. By 1869, it had more than a thousand members, and a year later it had tripled that number.[61] White pastors voiced support for the education of black ministers, but gave little else.[62]

In spite of such enthusiastic endorsements, educational charity for ministers was not wholly successful. Of the twenty-nine students who entered Richmond College in the fall of 1868, just five, all army veterans, later became Virginia preachers. Charles James converted to Christianity in the trenches around Petersburg in 1864, and the Women's Aid Society of John Newbill's congregation in Middlesex County paid his expenses. Newbill and James both later served as school administrators, suggesting that their own education made a deep impression on them.[63] The number of ministers who numbered among the graduates of Richmond College in the postwar years declined sharply. Between 1849 and 1861, almost one-half of the college's graduates had been ordained; between 1867 and 1879, this number had plummetted to one-fifth.[64]

The small number of young men who took advantage of Richmond College's offer also suggests that the success of wartime revivals fell far short of what the chaplains who had directed them, and later interpreted their history, claimed. Although the effects of the revivals on postwar church membership is impossible to measure, the number of young white men entering the ministry declined or stayed constant in both Virginia Methodist and Baptist churches in spite of rising membership. Scattered accounts suggest that some Virginia congregations did receive a number of new members in the immediate postwar years, but the success of these revivals did not appear to be widespread.[65]

The longest-lived project of postwar educational charity was the Sunday school. Sunday schools emerged as the first signs of the rebuilding of the denominational bureaucracy in the postwar era. The first Sunday School Board of the Southern Baptist Convention appeared in 1863, with its supporters arguing that the "Sunday school is the nursery of the church, the camp of instruction for her young soldiers." Virginia had no public school system before 1870, and charitable education through Sunday schools continued to be an important benevolent work of the church immediately after the war. Members of wealthier city congregations exhibited the keenest interest in these schools. "The Sabbath school is the great lever by the proper use of which we may move and control the masses of society," a Baptist editor bluntly observed in 1867.[66]

And Sunday schools continued as works of charity for poor and orphaned children. Many children received some physical aid in Sunday school, if for no other reason than that they should be decently clothed to attend church. Across the state, Methodist women began Dorcas Societies, which raised funds to clothe impoverished Sunday school students. But the poor were not necessarily heathen; Christian families were poor as well, these women recognized. Mrs. S. G. Hughes, a Richmond Baptist, appealed for assistance for the Baptist Sunday School Relief Society for two neighborhoods in her city by assuring readers that the project was not for the "vile and abandoned, but children of Christian families" such as soldiers' orphans.[67]

Less successful than schools for white children were those organized by white churches for African American children. These schools represented one of the first faltering steps that white churches took toward blacks in the months after the war, but their efforts were short-lived. As in their work with veterans, white Protestants set moral purity above religious conversion in their goals. "I know of no power equal to the Sunday school in bringing about a reformation—first of *morals*, then in leading the young into the church," wrote a young Sunday school teacher. In arguing for white support for these schools, Baptists and Methodists took a characteristically secular perspective. White Virginians needed the good will, votes, and labor of African Americans, they argued, and the stability of society depended on black education. If white people did not take the initiative, the ignorance of the freedman would have a "baneful effect on social and political life." The spiritual state of black Virginians was noticeably absent from their list of concerns.[68] Church membership among freedmen and women was heavily Baptist, and attendance in white Baptist "colored Sunday schools" reached a height in 1871, when 150 schools involved eight thousand teachers and students.

In the Sunday school campaign, as in other works of educational benevolence, pastors relied on denominational networks and connections. Interdenominational efforts were usually short-lived. Pastors focused on rousing Baptists and Methodists across the state by holding state Sunday school conventions and publicizing the need for such work through the state's religious newspapers. In August 1867, Virginia Methodists held their first statewide Sunday school convention in Richmond, and Baptists followed with their own convention the following March. The Baptist convention covered such topics as organization, superintendency, and teaching, as well as a special session on "country Sunday schools," suggesting the urban bias of the convention's leaders.[69] State conventions inspired numerous smaller meetings at the county level. In 1869, Albemarle County Methodists sponsored an interdenominational meeting presided over by Professor J. B. Minor of the University of Virginia and attended "by some of the most prominent and influential citizens of the county."[70] By 1873, Methodists in the Virginia Conference claimed more than five hundred Sunday schools with 35,000 scholars and teachers, more than any other Methodist conference in the South.[71]

Part of the impulse to organize these schools through statewide denominational organizations rather than local congregations grew out of the need for books. "Our Sunday school is getting on far beyond our most sanguine expectations," a Baptist wrote in 1866, noting that it had been operating for three weeks and had already fifty students. But, he added, "our great need is books."[72] These schools used not only Bibles but also Sunday school readers, Bible dictionaries, catechisms, and secular readers, spellers, and dictionaries. Baptists and Methodists launched campaigns to collect books and raise money to buy them. One Baptist pastor in an eastern Virginia congregation "destitute of money" asked every child in his Sunday school to bring an egg. Nine dozen were collected and exchanged for books in Richmond.[73] In many cases, efforts to find books were unsuccessful, and some pastors advocated using materials published in the North. Others, however, angrily denounced any sectional bias, even Southern, in the literature. "Now, we do not want to see any books dedicated to Lincoln, Grant, Jeff Davis or General Lee in any Baptist Sunday school of the South," the author of an 1866 Baptist editorial insisted.[74]

The answer was to use their own press. One of the cheapest means to distribute a standard curriculum across the state and region was in the pages of religious newspapers. By the early 1870s, both Baptist and Methodist papers published weekly lessons in their pages. Laymen and women and pastors alike hailed the uniform curriculum as a fine innovation in Sunday school teaching. "I hope you will continue to publish 'Notes for Sunday School Teachers,' " W. M. Mason of Caroline County wrote to the Baptist editor. "I think they are the best I have seen."[75] A Methodist pastor on the rural West Point Circuit was even more enthusiastic. "That International System [published weekly in the *Richmond Christian Advocate*] is the thing we have needed. A school without a system is a poor affair."[76] Thus, within a few years after the war, Baptists and Methodists embraced the uniform curriculum. In this, they were far ahead of rural Virginia public schools.[77]

White interest in black religious education, like interest in the education of veterans' children, faded quickly after the establishment of a state public school system in 1870. A more "civilized" black citizen could be produced by a state secular system, they decided. White Sunday schools, however, thrived. By the end of the century, almost every congregation in the state, even the most isolated, had some sort of class. Sunday schools involved countless men and women in the work of the church, giving them significant responsibility for teaching for the first time. By the 1870s, a Methodist writer noted that the Great Shepherd called Sunday school workers to "Feed my Lambs."[78] Significantly, he did not mention pastors. By that time, however, the Sunday schools' purpose had shifted. They were intended to train the children of church members in Christian doctrine rather than teach poor children to read and write. By 1879, a Richmond congregation noted with pleasure that "the good [the Sunday school] is accomplishing is simply beyond calculation. To it we have to look mainly for reinforcements to the membership of our church."[79]

The tasks that pastors took up in the first years after the Civil War revealed their priorities in a particularly clear way. Education lay at the heart of their vision of what religion should contribute to the shattered South. Their campaigns for educational benevolence continued to invoke Christian citizenship, and to favor the public role of religion. At every turn, they emphasized the importance of denominational organizations in sponsoring religious benevolence. Their works of benevolence also carried with them an unmistakable sense that the social context of church life had changed dramatically from the early antebellum period. That pastors and their congregations were so busily involved in works of charity underscored their sense that they were in a position to uplift those beneath them. Religion could help the lower classes of their society in the same way that it had helped them, they insisted, clearly setting themselves somewhere above those whom they were helping.

These pastors and church members seized Reconstruction as an opportunity to look forward. Among those things they left behind was their obligation to African Americans. Some nostalgia for the antebellum period endured, but in the main Virginia pastors and their congregations made plans to build their denominations and repair their churches, and educate and better themselves. Their dependence on denominational structures to accomplish this benevolence characterized church life long after the last Federal troops withdrew across the state line in 1870.

CHAPTER SEVEN

The Ministerial Profession

In 1870, Rev. Daniel Witt wrote to a friend about two congregations that he had pastored for forty years. Aging and in poor health, Witt had recently retired from full-time work and had passed his churches over to the care of his correspondent, Thomas Sydnor. Baptist prospects in his county were good, he reported, because "almost every body has been brought into the church." "But," he added, "we are mighty poor!" Witt's practiced eye found his congregations wanting. "There are many things to discourage in the desertion of the church of their fathers by the young & fashionable religionists of the day," he wrote.[1]

Witt was himself one of the fathers of the Virginia Baptist tradition. Converted alongside Jeremiah Jeter almost fifty years earlier, Witt had traveled the state with him as the first missionary for the Virginia Baptist General Association. But while Jeter made his career in city pulpits, Witt followed a relatively undistinguished career in the remote Southside. Jeter "has occupied an eminent position & has been eminently useful," Witt wrote of his friend. "I have moved in an humbler sphere & occupied a position no doubt, suited to the gifts which the Lord has conferred upon me." He thought that his own labors among the "common people" of the Southside followed in the tradition of Christ and the apostles, who sought the company of plain and uneducated people. "If the fastidious & fashionable people will not be Baptists, I cannot help it," he concluded. "God will see to his own cause."[2]

Daniel Witt's critique of fashionable religion and its followers recurred throughout the postwar years in the public and private writings of Virginia pastors. His sense that the new generation was more concerned with fashion than with doctrine was shared by many of his peers. All over the state, church-going people seemed to be newly aware of the social benefits—and costs—of church membership. "Some people won't be saved, unless they can be saved by and in, a church that, in their view, will at the same time it saves them, lift them up socially," W. W. Bennett, editor of the Methodist *Richmond Chris-*

tian Advocate, wrote in 1871. His view of the situation, however, was frankly pragmatic. "We don't object," he wrote. "We want them to go to heaven, even if they must be handed up in kid gloves . . . we don't object to trying to save the rich."[3] Baptist William Landrum concurred. In a speech to his peers in 1883, Landrum chafed at Baptists' identification with the lower classes, which did not do credit to his own aspirations. "Why should the Baptist be looked upon as only an uneducated gawk when he has passed through the University with highest honors?" he asked in frustration. He told of his meeting an accomplished Baptist lady, "who possessed both wealth and piety in large measure," who asked him whether he had ever considered that rich people had souls. "She knew that I had been tramping for several days in the slums of the city to dig up mud-sills and prepare them by the appliances of the Gospel for a polished position in the Temple of God." The woman's question shamed him, Landrum admitted. Under the influence of Baptists' "democratic ideal," he had "despised the rich" and foolishly believed that "my mission required me to pass by culture, wealth and refinement."[4]

But others sharply disagreed about the virtues of a cultured and refined church. Instead of refinement, Rev. Oscar Flippo saw only empty pretension in "the average wealthy fashionable city congregation" in 1883. It was

> represented by a costly edifice, towering spire—tapering to the smallness of nothing like the devotion of the audience—cushioned pews, interior decorations of tinseled splendor, a worldly fashionable choir, with operatic music at one end of the building, and a polished clergyman preaching polished essays at the other end; pews filled with the world's children of pride and fashion, saying nothing, doing nothing that has in it a single element of true worship— simply enjoying an entertainment! There is no *heart*, no *life*.

Such congregations elevated form at the expense of content, Flippo charged. His pen also tarnished the "polished clergyman," whose "polished essays" were full of intellectual pretension, but empty of spiritual power.[5]

The clerical profession was itself badly torn between those who valued refinement and those who scorned it as mere fashion. As in Southern society generally, distinctions in the postwar ministry fell most sharply between town and country, and a running quarrel between rural and city pastors shaped postbellum religious life. "What a deplorable spectacle if a ministerial aristocracy should develop," a Methodist warned in 1871. "This is no agrarianism— it is not the cry of fanatical nonsense. . . . Who will leave a 'fashionable' church for the glory of God?" he implored.[6]

Rural pastors, however, knew that a "ministerial aristocracy" was already in place. They read about the city clergymen in their newspapers and saw them across the room at their annual meetings. But they heard little else from their leaders, and they thought they knew why. "We would be glad to have some of your city preachers with us [at a special minister's meeting]," a Chesterfield pastor chided in 1872. "I do not remember to ever have seen a Richmond minister at Skinquarter. The name does not impress favorably. . . . If we are poor, you will be sure to get something to eat and somewhere to stop."

Figure 7.1 Delegation of the Virginia Conference, Methodist Episcopal Church, South to the General Conference of 1890. Virginia Conference Collection, Page-McGraw Library, Randolph-Macon College.

Another Methodist assured his peers in 1881 that "Old Henry Circuit [near Martinsville] is no longer to be despised. . . . We are to have a railroad by Christmas; so you city preachers will have no excuse for not coming up."[7]

Rural Methodists drew on an especially rich image in their criticism of city-"stationed" preachers: that of the cold and weary itinerant preacher. Those who still rode the circuits fumed at the distinctions between their own feet, accustomed to "frozen stirrups at daylight," and those of their urban peers, which they imagined as being "toasted in satin slippers." In former days, self-sacrifice had been revered and even rewarded. In the New South, the satin-slippered city pastors, it seemed, received not just more material rewards but more respect as well. "The line between station preachers and circuit preachers is almost as deeply and distinctly drawn as if they belonged to separate conferences," one writer charged in 1885.[8]

This rural scorn was rooted in more than envy. It reflected the existence of at least two distinct classes of ministers and congregations in postwar Virginia. An elite, comprising one-fifth of all ministers, held the pulpits of wealthy city and town congregations. They were paid up to twenty times the salaries of their rural peers, whose pay sometimes matched sharecroppers' wages. They preached in churches designed by architects, and they lived in finely furnished parsonages. Although they led their denominations and their profession, these men had little contact with their rural peers. They lived an increasingly insulated life, associating but little with a rural way of life that they had little patience for and even less interest in. The rural majority's discontent, then, was compounded by the urban bias of the profession itself.[9]

Pastoral salaries reflected the wide range of congregations in postbellum Virginia. In 1880, about half of all pastors earned $500 or more per year. Pastors in the leading city churches, who earned salaries in the top 10 percent, made more than three times that amount. The salaries of urban congregations did vary, however. Pastors of churches in poorer sections of the city or in newly founded "mission" churches earned salaries far less than the average rural pastor. Urban salaries in 1880 year ranged from a low of $67 in Richmond's Nicholson Street Church, a humble congregation of 103 souls, to well over $1,000. Nicholson was exceptional, however. The next lowest salary, $425, went to the pastor of Wesley Methodist in Petersburg. The highest salaries of that year were earned by the pastors of Richmond's Centenary Church, Lynchburg's Court Street, and Petersburg's Market Street, all of whom paid their pastors $1,800. In all, eighteen of the twenty-five city pastors in 1880 earned more than $1,000.

Salaries depended on more than simply a rural or urban location, however. In general, there was keen competition between leading urban churches to keep their salaries high. Salaries depended on the size of the congregation, as well as its wealth. Members of churches that paid their pastors relatively modest salaries sometimes contributed more money to religious benevolence than churches that paid their pastors more. Wesley Methodist in Petersburg, with 202 members, raised $10.65 per member in 1880. Clay Street Church in Richmond, with 490 members, raised only $5.84 per member, but it paid its pastor $1,400, more than three times what the pastor of Wesley earned.

The very upward mobility that the ministry held out to young Virginians aggravated the tensions between the two classes of preachers. Many men did better themselves in the pulpit. The pastorate encouraged farmers' sons to seek an education, and the salaries of even the humblest ministers rose significantly over the course of their careers. Some defended distinctions between pastors as only natural. "It is deplorable to hear [the] cries against the salaries of leading officials of the Church," a rural pastor calling himself "Content" wrote in 1881. "One work is worth more than another—One man more than another." Leading city pastors deserved more, he said, because they catered to "a higher standard of moral and social culture."[10] If very few earned the high salaries of leading city men, enough succeeded for them to view the ministry as a means of social improvement. "The pastor may be of very humble extraction . . . but everywhere he is received as a social equal," a Baptist minister wrote in 1884, probably with his own experience in mind. "And the pathway to preferment and worldly renown, of the best and most enduring sort, is open to him."[11]

Samuel A. Steel's experience bore out such assessments. He arrived in Richmond in September 1875 to take the pulpit at Broad Street Methodist

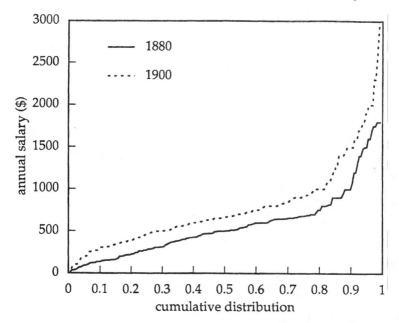

Figure 7.2 Salaries of Virginia Methodist pastors, 1880 and 1900. Sample of 100 pastors, *Minutes*, Virginia Annual Conference, Methodist Episcopal Church, South, 1880 and 1990.

Church. The twenty-five-year-old pastor came from Charlottesville, where he had served as chaplain at the University of Virginia. "The Lord has led me in a wonderful way," he reflected after the move to Richmond. He immodestly declared that there was "already enough romance in my life to make a thrilling tale. . . . It has not been but five years since I was a regular field hand, plowing and sweating in the hot cornfields of Mississippi." From an "awkward, rough woodsman," he had become "pastor of the largest and finest of our city churches . . . in a far distant state and city, with my life, my associations, my tastes, my all, completely changed."[12]

The son of a Methodist farmer and pastor, Steel claimed no conversion experience but vividly recalled hearing the call to preach while hoeing cotton in his father's field at the age of twenty. After a short time at a small college in Mississippi, he moved north briefly to attend college in southwest Virginia and then to take the chaplaincy at the University of Virginia. Why the young man was called to a prestigious Richmond church is difficult to explain, although experience at the university was considered to be a great recommendation for a young pastor.

Steel realized the dreams of many young men who entered the ministry in postwar Virginia. His diary reveals him as an intensely pious young man who nevertheless was keenly aware of the social benefits of the pastorate. His acknowledgment that good fortune came through God's grace did not prevent

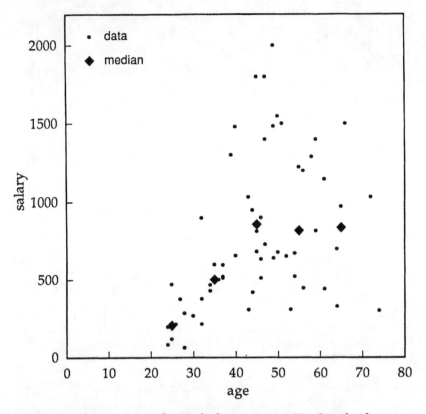

Figure 7.3 Salary versus age for Methodist pastors in 1880. Sample of 100 pastors, *Minutes*, Virginia Annual Conference, Methodist Episcopal Church, South, 1880.

his determination "to *pray*, to *persevere*, to *push* with all my powers of body, mind and soul." Steel's resolve to better himself ranked with that of many young Americans of the day, who expected that piety and social elevation could both be won by those who pursued them.[13]

The most tangible sign of Steel's success in Richmond was his generous salary. As chaplain in Charlottesville, financial worries had plagued him. A "spell of anxiety about my temporal affairs. . . . Poor pay, high living, some debt and the demand I cannot meet to buy new books" left him particularly low-spirited in early 1875. The young man's social life among the university professors left him yearning for the means to meet his tastes. He frequented soirees at their homes, and marveled at their tastes in food and furniture. His experiences in Charlottesville gave Steel tastes that far exceeded his means and created a genuine tension in his life.[14]

Steel accepted the call to Broad Street Church in Richmond with a deep sense of relief. A pastor favored enough to win a prestigious city pulpit in postwar Virginia was assured a steady, generous salary for the duration of his stay. During his four years at Broad Street, Steel's congregation paid him $2,400 annually, a top salary for his day. The amount compared favorably to that of other city pastors, in spite of his youth. Steel's salary, like that of other urban pastors, reflected the professional status of the ministry in Virginia cities. Steel's salary reflected his congregation's esteem, and was intended to afford him a lifestyle worthy of their own aspirations.

His new salary, however, did not end Steel's financial concerns. When a doctor who was nursing his invalid wife refused to be paid for his services, Steel expressed relief at the "very gracious Providence of God for my purse is low and it is going to require great management to square my account with my salary this year." Moving to the city meant not only a higher salary but also more expenses.[15]

The other benefits of Steel's appointment sometimes pushed his financial worries into the background. As the leader of one of Richmond's best congregations, he mingled with state politicians, city officials, and railroad presidents. One of his members even gave him a holiday trip to New England. The limits of his upward mobility, however, clearly came into view when he attended the wedding of a friend in Alexandria. There, the farmer's son from Mississippi encountered old Virginia Episcopalian society in full flower. His friend's fiancée was the daughter of a U.S. Senator, and the ceremony took place in the Episcopal Church of Alexandria. At the reception, when the dancing began, the blushing Methodist felt obliged to excuse himself. "I fear great offense was given," he wrote.[16]

Steel's experience highlighted both the opportunities and limitations of the ministry in postwar Virginia. His fine Richmond pulpit contrasted starkly with the experience of his father, also a Methodist pastor, who hoed cotton in Mississippi. Like Jeremiah Jeter's success in Richmond half a century earlier, Steel's career did represent a significant advance from his family's humble life. Yet social distinctions were far more complex in the New South than Steel's own rather straightforward success had prepared him for. His position as a Methodist pastor from one of the best city pulpits in the state did not carry much weight in the Episcopal social circles of old Alexandria.

The speed and degree of Samuel Steel's success made his experience exceptional, but his move to the city followed the pattern of life in the New South. The weight of professionalization had always bent pastors toward the city, but in the postwar South this pressure increased. The growth of city population, as well as church membership, added weight to urban pastors' influence in church affairs. Between 1880 and 1900, while state population increased by 23 percent, urban population increased by 80 percent. Growth of city membership among Baptists and Methodists doubled membership growth at large during the same period. Methodist and Baptist church membership grew by 70 percent, whereas church membership in cities grew by 146 percent. City church members also grew as a percentage of all members. In 1880, urban Baptists made up 11 percent, and urban Methodists 15 percent, of all members; by 1900, they had grown to 17 percent and 21 percent, respectively (see Appendix, Table 17).

As Virginians moved to town in ever larger numbers, their search for good fortune came at the expense of the communities they left behind. Rural churches, particularly, felt the effects of the change. Virginia's diversified agricultural economy fared better than that of other former Confederate states, but country pastors were left to fend for themselves in an increasingly isolated and impoverished rural landscape. They lost the benefits of hospitality and financial support that wealthy farmers and planters had provided before the war. To add insult to injury, city people turned their backs on the rural majority and labeled their way of life provincial and backward.

In 1876, a Baptist traveled to the countryside for several weeks to spend Christmas with some of his relations. His opinions, published in the *Religious Herald* as soon as he returned, suggested how deeply city dwellers, even in the 1870s, disdained the country life. Although he praised the quiet and "calm beauty" of the country ("I feel that I could be a better Christian here than in the city," he wrote), country habits irritated him to no end. His hosts thwarted his plan to read during his holiday. "It is talk, talk, talk all the day long and until bedtime at night. And such small talk!" Gossip prevented the reading of books, magazines, and newspapers, which he considered "*a necessity in every well-regulated family.*" His uncle and his friends apparently did more than just gossip. "The farmers I have met complain greatly of the hard times," the visitor wrote. His uncle, in particular, had harsh words for commission merchants, telling his nephew that they had "put down the price so that I shall get no more for a large crop than I realized last year from a small one."

The main object of the visitor's derision, however, was the country church and its pastor. "There is such a slip-shod way of doing things in the country churches," he moaned. When he "complained of the church floors, almost covered with tobacco juice and dirt and of the old stove, pouring its smoke into my eyes, they call me 'citified.' " While his city church took up two or three collections every Sunday, he noted that the country church never took one in five weeks. And although the congregation paid their field hands every Saturday night, they owed their pastor for his work from the year before. But the country pastor, too, was at fault. He did not "know how to put his members to work." After preaching the sermon, he went to "one of two families at which he always gets his meals" and then rode away, not to return until the next meeting. "If he only knew how to develop his church," the city man sighed. "He is in the old ruts, and like many others, he will die in them."[17]

The rural South suffered a constant shortage of pastors. Pulpits remained empty for years at a time, contributing to the breakdown of community life. Even inexperienced ministers were willing to spurn humble rural appointments in the postwar era. One ambitious young man turned down more than a dozen offers from churches in rural Virginia, West Virginia, Alabama, and Georgia in 1868 before accepting the pulpit of First Baptist Church in Alexandria, with an annual salary of $1,200. His shrewdness proved him to be a good student, for his inclination to "*demand* a specified salary—if it's not enough, *decline* it," followed exactly the instructions in his seminary lecture notes of several years earlier.[18]

Meanwhile, rural congregations often waited in vain for a preacher. "A working, pushing preacher is all needed in our county. Where can he be gotten and where is the money to pay him are the questions," a Baptist layman in a Southside county lamented in 1873. A. J. Sadler described three villages in Chesterfield County in 1870 with two "feeble churches without pastors and without preaching, and with a population of about 2,000," all of whom were poor. "Whiskey shops have sprung up in our villages, and we are in a sad condition."

The problem did not ease with the passage of time. A decade later, "in almost every county in Eastern Virginia you can find Baptist churches without pastors." And after the turn of the century, at least 75 Baptist congregations statewide remained without pastors. In 1884, A. Bagby of Stevensville, in the Tidewater, noted that within a forty-mile radius of the town there were 14 churches without pastors. Even in 1896, a Baptist in Farnham, Virginia, estimated that there were 120 pastorless churches in the state and 200 ordained ministers without churches. In 1905, a Baptist committee reported that "it is worthy to note that of the seventy-seven Churches that failed to contribute any thing [to denominational work], nearly all of them are without pastors." Low pay was undoubtedly one of the reasons for this. At the end of the century, Baptists reported at least 37 churches in the state with an average "promised" salary of less than $150 annually. Educated young men were simply not willing to work for such meager pay.[19]

Even a decent salary could not offset the other disadvantages of country life. "I have been here, this will be my fourth year," D. A. Woodson wrote from Modest Town on the Eastern Shore. His circuit comprised four congregations and paid $875, yet Woodson thought the money hardly worth the trouble. "I have to preach twice every Sabbath & travel 10 miles from morning to evening appointment. The labor is too much I cannot stand it. . . . They are very kind to me but it is an *isolated, unhealthy* country & I do not feel that I can stay in it much longer."[20] An elder on a poor Methodist circuit noted sadly that one preacher's "wife would hardly be willing to go there. Besides, there is not a school for his girls to go to and it would hardly support him."[21]

Those who fled the countryside left behind others who either would not or could not leave. Thomas W. Sydnor, a senior pastor and farmer in Virginia's Southside, found himself badly off after the war. Sydnor's extensive training at college and a Northeastern seminary, as well as his inherited wealth and slaves, had made him a distinguished resident of Nottoway County when he settled there with his wife Blanche in 1847.[22] He remained in Nottoway during the war, where he learned of the death of his soldier son and endured raids by Federal troops. By the end of the war, most of his slaves had fled. In his midforties, he was reluctant to leave his longtime home, and he continued farming by signing sharecropping agreements with some of his former slaves. But the farms of Sydnor's Southside languished. The soil was exhausted from long cultivation for tobacco, even as tobacco prices and farm values plummeted. Sydnor simply could not make ends meet.[23]

The priority Sydnor and his wife placed on educating their children put a considerable financial burden on the family.[24] They paid their daughter's school tuition, generously discounted because he was a pastor, in part with bacon and butter.[25] Their son, enrolled at Richmond College, did chores for the president's family in exchange for room and board.[26] Sydnor received offers from small congregations desperate for a preacher, but their salaries were apparently too low for him to consider.[27]

After a short stint as an agent for a Northern missionary society, Sydnor offered himself for the job of county school superintendent.[28] In his letter of application, he explained his reluctance to take appointments of civil or secular character for fear they would interfere with his preaching. But "in this case, the duties of the office in question come in so well with my regular ministerial duties [that] if it shall be found that the people of the county generally desire me to serve them [as superintendent] I must not hesitate to do it." He cited as his chief qualifications his long experience with the county black population and his acquaintance with Northeastern benefactors. Although he had few political connections—he was "acquainted with but few members of the Legislature—with none of them personally that I can now think of except our own county representative"—he was widely known among the "old citizens" of Richmond.[29]

State officials were initially skeptical that pastors could balance the duties of superintendent with that of the pulpit. J. William Jones, former chaplain to R. E. Lee, a leading Lost Cause figure, and fellow Baptist with high political connections, assured Sydnor in June 1870 that he had put in a good word for him to [State Superintendent] Ruffner. Ruffner apparently believed that ministers applied to become superintendents because they did not think it to be a full-time job. For his part, Jones believed that the position would "afford a fine opportunity for evangelistic labors." Sydnor received the appointment, which he held with only one brief interruption until his death in 1890.[30] Prospective teachers soon filled his mail with requests for appointments. "I am on the lookout for a place to teach school at," Joseph Giles wrote in late summer 1871. "Please let me know how soon you will commence your school term and what price you would be willing to give me." A year earlier, Lucie A. Hamilton had pleaded to be hired "*now,* as we can never be in more needy circumstances. Last year was so dry we did not make anything and had nearly every hog stolen."[31]

At least seven Virginia counties had pastor-superintendents in 1871.[32] Like pastoral appointments, the gap between salaries for rural and urban superintendents yawned wide. In 1871, Sydnor earned about $500 for his trouble. Some rural superintendents earned less than $200 per year, while those in Richmond and Lynchburg received between $1,000 and $2,000 annually. Even these small incomes were attractive to men like Robert Burton, who wrote to Sydnor late in the year of the 1873 Panic in near despair over his financial affairs. "You will excuse me for telling you that I am anxiously exercised as to how I am to support my family & keep out of debt," the fifty-five-year-old pastor wrote. "I would like to do regular & full pastoral work, but I fear I cannot . . . the uncertainty is too great for me to hold and work out my appointment much longer." He apparently had several plans in mind to make some money. Like Sydnor, Burton was a college graduate and had been a pastor for more than twenty-five years. Yet he was unable to support his family of nine children on a country pastor's salary. He asked for Sydnor's recommendation for a job as a county school superintendent. "I understand," he wrote, "that [State Superintendent] Dr. Ruffner is much pleased with the *Baptist ministers* he has appointed." Burton offered to relocate to Charlotte County, and suggested that he would "like the business, & am vain enough to think that I would make a good superintendent."[33]

Pastors did make good superintendents. Their service demonstrates that if some religious people opposed *public* education, nearly all recognized the social benefits of education. Promoting education had been part of the pastor's duty since before the war. Moreover, the office of superintendent demanded the persuasion and tact required of pastors. Especially in the early years, public schools depended heavily on the good will generated by community leaders for their success. Pastors were accustomed to working to build consensus for change in their congregations.[34] No doubt, Sydnor's good reputation in his county helped the cause of public education there, but the battle for the public mind was a difficult one. Four years after Sydnor took the superintendent's post, he reported that two-thirds of county residents were either indifferent to or opposed to public schools. Such opposition highlighted the difficulties, as well as the success, of the clergy's own decades-long campaign for religious education.

"I know there are very few churches able to support a pastor alone," a Baptist observed of a congregation in Southside Virginia in 1872, "but it might be able to pay a man for half of his time and by connecting with another good church would pay a living salary."[35] A "living salary" meant different things in late-nineteenth-century Virginia, depending on a person's upbringing and location. Samuel Steel had one expectation of how he should live, and Thomas Sydnor had quite another. In general, however, pastors across the state wanted to live respectably. They wished to furnish a modest home, dress their wives and daughters for trips to town, and educate their children. "I don't want you to go until you get a new dress and bonnet and some other things," George Wright wrote to his wife Josie about a proposed trip to Petersburg, "for I want you to look your best as my best and nicest friends are there."[36]

Modest though these expectations were, they suggested that the clergy's view of their salaries had changed over the course of the nineteenth century. The calling had become a profession. For a professional, a salary's meaning went far beyond its dollar amount. It implied authority, respect, and trust.[37] Pastors' expectation of a steady and secure income had replaced a willingness to make do with whatever the Lord provided.

Salary had long been a sensitive subject for pastors. In the early part of the century, they argued that the money they were paid did not represent a fee for services rendered. As a calling, the pastorate differed from other professions. After the war, however, money became a more critical point of contention within the profession. The number of pastors who took city churches grew, but they remained a tiny part of the profession as a whole, as they had in the antebellum era. The reason for the discontent lay elsewhere.

For postwar pastors, the meaning of salary had changed. As preaching became a profession, members of the pastorate were less willing to put up with distinctions between their peers. They were convinced that all pastors should live comfortably, with money enough to pay for things like schooling for their children and to ensure that they would not be left destitute if they could no longer work. As professionals, pastors considered money the measure of a man.

The willingness of many to forgo a rural appointment and wait for a more secure one in a town or city measured the difference between antebellum and postbellum practice. In the antebellum period, a man who had felt strongly called by God to preach often took the first pulpit that presented itself. Leaving a congregation without a shepherd for the sake of personal comfort would have been unthinkable. But in the postwar period, such a decision appeared eminently reasonable. "The fact remains that some men in the ministry do not succeed. . . . Why then, should they continue in the work for which they are not qualified?" a critic wrote in 1891. The sense of calling among pastors had dulled so much that by the end of the century, clergymen even debated whether "unsuccessful" pastors should leave the pulpit for another profession.[38]

The expectation that a minister should lead a comfortable life reflected the reality of clerical salaries of the late nineteenth century. By the 1870s and 1880s, most Virginia pastors earned a respectable amount of money, and most could expect their salaries to rise significantly over the course of their careers.

Nathan Bangs Foushee served his entire half-century career in undistinguished and remote Methodist churches. Born a farmer's son in Culpeper County in 1848, Foushee was educated by his father, a schoolteacher. After experiencing conversion at the age of twenty, he remained at home to help his father, who was broken financially by the war. He took a job as a colporteur for the American Tract Society during the early 1870s. As a book peddler, he read many of the books that he sold. But his desire to preach soon caught up with him. He preached his first sermon in 1874, and the following year began his tenure as a junior preacher on the Rappahannock Circuit. In 1876, the Virginia Conference accepted him as a preacher in "full connection."

His first year, Foushee was assigned to the Berlin Circuit on the remote Eastern Shore, where he received a salary of $298. He traveled as an old-fashioned itinerant, with a horse and saddlebags full of religious books, and he stayed at members' homes. His later appointments included circuits in Campbell, Henrico, and Princess Anne counties. For the first ten years of his career, when he served four different circuits, he received an average salary of $350 per year. In 1881, the year he married Lelia Anne Robertson, his congregations paid him $220. Although rural parsonages were becoming increasingly common, Nathan and Lelia Foushee often found themselves on circuits without one, forcing them to rent their own house.

Foushee's salary gradually rose, although his appointments, by the profession's standards, were not distinguished. The second decade of his career earned him an average salary of $635, the third, $770. By the late 1880s and early 1890s, he earned about $700 per year. Even this modest salary allowed him to send two of his four daughters to a private academy. He and his wife boarded a ministerial student and a young woman who later became a missionary to China. By the turn of the century, Foushee earned $800 annually from a circuit near Portsmouth. Weary Southern farmers sweating in their fields to stave off falling commodity prices could hardly dream of what Foushee accomplished: he more than doubled his salary during his working years to maintain a modest but relatively secure middle-class lifestyle, even while he and his wife struggled to keep the wolf from the door.[39]

Aspirations rather than needs took on a larger and larger role in defining the minimum salaries that most pastors would accept. "Methodist preachers, as the world goes, are a peculiar people," a sympathetic observer wrote in 1885. "They get about the pay of colored porters in our Richmond stores. Out of that meagre salary they must dress like professional men and educate their children."[40] Ministerial salaries had begun to reflect not the standards of the local community, but those of the profession. Regardless of how little he actually earned, a preacher was expected to lead a certain lifestyle. A pastor judged his own possessions and style of life not by those of his neighbors, but by a clergyman friend living several counties away, or in town. Nathan Foushee, Thomas Sydnor, and many others sacrificed to send their children to private academies not only because they valued education but also because they were expected to do so.

New South pastors not only demanded, and received, the means for a higher standard of living in the postwar years. They also required a new measure of financial security. Illness or retirement left destitute those who had not prudently saved money, and such risk was increasingly unacceptable to professional clergymen. With the help of the laity, pastors set in place an unprecedented series of measures designed to make the pastorate more financially secure. "If I break down in health I have not the means of support," an elderly Methodist of modest means worried in 1884. "But will not the Lord provide?"[41]

The Lord provided through relatively novel means in postwar Virginia: insurance policies. Insurance drew many clerical customers—and some clerical salesmen—in the New South. Pastors bought life and home insurance for themselves and fire insurance for their churches and parsonages. Rev. John E. Edwards, a prominent Virginia Methodist and president of an insurance company, unashamedly promoted policies from his own firm among his peers. In 1867, he persuaded a committee of laymen to publish a letter arguing that all pastors should purchase life insurance policies, preferably from Edwards's company. Not only would these policies provide for their families but also they would develop "the resources of the South." Edwards's company and others even offered to insure pastors free of charge, no doubt in hopes of luring customers from their congregations. Some pastors, discouraged by their struggles to wring even the poorest of salaries from their beleaguered congregations, gave up the pulpit to sell insurance full-time, apparently believing that selling temporary security was next best to preaching about the eternal kind. Congregations also began to purchase insurance policies for their church buildings. "Insure Your Churches," the headline of a story about a church fire in 1873 warned. Many congregations took the editor's advice. By the end of the century, Virginia Methodists held policies worth almost $800,000 on their $2.3 million worth of churches and parsonages.[42]

Pastors also gained financial security through the widespread construction of parsonages after the war. Parsonages had been rare before the Civil War. But interest in providing a "decent" life for financially pressed pastors grew in the postwar period, particularly among women. Methodist pastors were especially hampered in their efforts to provide a respectable and stable lifestyle for their families because they generally moved every four years. Accordingly, Methodist women's home missions societies, created in 1886, took as one of their first tasks the provision of permanent and comfortable housing for pastors. They succeeded wildly. In the first eight years of their campaign, they built 985 parsonages across the South—half as many as were built in the entire century before. In 1875, Virginia Methodist pastors had access to 51 parsonages. Twenty-five years later, Methodists had invested more than $200,000 to build more than 100 additional parsonages. By 1900, more than two-thirds of the 225 churches and circuits had parsonages, with an average value of $1,800.[43]

Pastors also sought security for retirement. Those who labored for a lifetime in small rural churches usually could not afford to retire, and many continued working long after their health had failed. "My health is far from good," sixty-seven-year-old Edward Wilson wrote, as he agonized over whether to retire. "I am deaf in one ear and I often mistake what people say . . . this is very embarrassing to me." Surely one of Wilson's gravest concerns was money. Pastors, once retired, often suffered from severe want if they had no immediate family to care for them. The elderly Baptist William Pedigo and his wife lived in a boxcar in Pittsylvania County before their plight came to the attention of the Preachers' Aid Society in the late 1880s. The chief purpose of these societies, or brotherhoods, was to insure families after pastors died. A twenty-five-cent initial fee and a $3 beneficiary fee, when invested, yielded between $500 and $600 to a bereaved family by the mid-1890s.[44]

The new reliance on insurance policies, parsonages, and retirement funds underscored pastors' expectations that their profession would bring them security and social respectability in postwar Virginia. Their motives for purchasing insurance policies and joining aid societies differed little from those of secular professionals. Yet this new emphasis on comfort and security represented a sharp departure from earlier assumptions about the ministry. If New South pastors lionized their itinerant and preacher-farmer forebears, they certainly did not emulate their lifestyle. Risk seemed far less tolerable and less noble than it had in antebellum years, and reliance on God's providence no longer precluded shrewd financial planning and self-reliance.

Like Thomas Sydnor, many New South pastors sought financial security in work outside the pulpit. Their attitudes toward that work, as well as the types of tasks they took up, had changed from that of their predecessors. The constraints of professionalism had rendered work unrelated to the ministry—such as farming—less desirable than in the antebellum years, and they were increasingly obliged to "spiritualize" all of the work in which they engaged. Sydnor submitted his name for school superintendent only because, he said, "the duties of the office in question come in so well with my regular ministerial duties."[45]

At the same time that they limited the categories of appropriate work, however, pastors began to endow the work they did deem appropriate with a peculiar sense of Christian mission. More took up work sanctioned by the profession, to which preaching served as not the central but as a secondary focus. These pursuits became "sacred vocations" in the sense that for many pastors, they became a source of self-definition and self-esteem. All of these activities, whether in country or city, took the pastor out of the pulpit and away from the usual pastoral duties of a regular minister.[46]

As in other matters, city pastors held an advantage over their rural peers in finding work outside the pulpit. They profited from the urban location of most enterprises: colleges, denominational agencies, and newspapers. Pastors became editors, principals of secondary schools, college and seminary professors, and heads of denominational agencies and presses. These positions were often full-time, and in most cases their pay equaled that of the best city pulpits in the state. The growing church bureaucracy provided a large number of jobs. Denominations created a variety of paid positions that pastors could take up without feeling that they were abandoning the often financially precarious work of full-time ministry. College professors, full-time agents who collected money for church causes, newspaper editors, colporteurs, and heads of denominational boards often earned handsome salaries and were still considered clergymen.

Country pastors had to forgo the more distinguished and profitable positions in the church bureaucracy. Many already preached at more than one congregation, farmed, or taught school. The superintendency of public schools was one of the few jobs open to them, but those posts were rare. Instead, rural pastors profited from an entrepreneurial spirit. They made small incomes by writing, opening small schools, or lecturing.

After the Civil War, pastors devoted an increasing amount of time and energy to the printed word. Mark Twain's observation in 1871 that Americans had learned the Gospel story through plays and novels rather than from the "drowsy pulpit" aptly described the state of affairs in Virginia. "At this day the influence of the press is so enormous and omnipresent that not only every Christian but every man ought to seek to elevate to purify to enlist it in the cause of virtue and religion," a Baptist wrote in 1872.[47] During the Civil War, the dramatic success of tracts, books, and pamphlets in the largest mass evangelism campaign ever conducted made many pastors enthusiastic advocates of the press. Alfred Dickinson, a graduate of Richmond College, directed Baptist colportage among troops in Virginia and later edited the Baptist *Religious Herald* until his death. "What agencies are at work for the spread of truth?" demanded the tiny *Methodist Recorder*, published in Farmville in Virginia's Southside. "They are the pulpit and the press."[48]

New South pastors believed that the printed word was as powerful and effective as any sermon delivered from the pulpit. Many of them published newspaper and periodical articles, novels, theological treatises, sermons, travel accounts, and Sunday school materials. They were also famous biographers of themselves and each other.[49] Their own intellectual and spiritual lives were profoundly affected by what they read, and they expected that their congregations had much the same experience. They read a great deal, and their eyes often strayed from the pages of the Bible to secular newspaper reports and academic journals. The news they found there about sensational crimes, declining morality, and religious sentiment, as well as broad advances in secular scholarship, colored many of their sermons and public writings. As a consequence of their familiarity through print with the wider culture, pastors began to preach broadly against that culture rather than specifically to the concerns of those in their pews.

These publications insistently pushed the pulpit away from the center of church life. In the New South, pamphlets, tracts, Sunday school books, newspapers, professional journals, and even the YMCA "preached" as effectively as—sometimes, their proponents argued, more effectively than—preachers themselves. "Feed My Sheep" was no longer just the call of Christ to pastors but embraced editors and Sunday school teachers as well. The ubiquitous publications of the religious press ended the pulpit's exclusive claim to teach and preach the Gospel. If antebellum pastors had made their reputations in revival meetings, postbellum pastors increasingly turned to writing as a source of professional prestige. In stepping out of the pulpit, pastors suggested that God needed popular literary culture to spread his Gospel in the New South.[50]

Religious publications had a new task after the Civil War, when even pious readers expected to be entertained as well as informed. Editors devoted fewer and fewer columns of their papers to doctrinal material and sermons and more to current issues and entertainment. "I read all the articles in the juvenile department to my children and at the conclusion of each piece, [they say] 'First rate! First rate! Pa, is there any more of them?'" a reader in Taylorsville wrote to the editor of the *Richmond Christian Advocate* in 1865.[51]

Entertainment, although a controversial topic in church circles, became an integral part of religious life in the New South. As more and more Virginians worked at jobs with limited hours, they looked for ways to entertain themselves during their time off. The pursuits they chose became an important index of tastes, values, and social class. Whether one had leisure time at all and how one spent it became important marks of social status.

Churchgoing people, no less than other Virginians, wanted to be entertained. From advertisements for baseball and lawn tennis equipment in religious newspapers, to sports clubs at denominational colleges, to fairs, feasts, and Sunday school outings, churchgoing people displayed an earnest interest in having fun. "Charlie is very busy making preparations for an excursion to Ocean View with his singing class . . . the proceeds of which will go towards getting a pipe organ," Rev. George Wright wrote to his wife, Josie, from Portsmouth in 1884. "Excursions are all the go. Every day they come from some place and pass through on their way to Ocean View or Virginia Beach. I never saw anything like it."[52]

Pastors, too, admitted that they enjoyed being amused. In a striking departure, they began during the 1880s to hold their clerical meetings at hotels. Antebellum meetings had convened in churches, with participants housed in private homes. They were occasions of great solemnity and importance in the community as well as the church. All church members and pastors in the city, not just those of the denomination convening there, took part, as churches all over the city opened their pulpits to visiting pastors. After the Civil War, pastors began to discuss moving these assemblies to private hotels. In 1879, a Virginia Methodist editor urged that the state ministerial assembly be held at the posh Greenbrier resort, noting that "the cost would be but a trifle" and that ministers could bring their wives.[53] Such hotels sprang up all over the South as towns discovered the tourist industry. By the end of the century, these hotels made money from clergymen as well. Methodists even appointed a committee charged with the responsibility for "conference entertainment." In 1897, the committee paid out more than $1,100 for the ten-day conference, including room and board for twenty-eight ministers at local hotels. "You see where I am," Methodist John Granbery wrote to his daughter from a hotel on the North Carolina coast in 1889. "Does it not make you think of the Hygeia Hotel at Old Point [Va.]? This is the biggest hotel in the state. . . . We have at the table fish, soft crabs and scallops." After the afternoon session, Granbery wrote, "I am promised a sail on the ocean. Of course, a ride in a boat is no more a violation of the Sabbath than a ride in a buggy would be."[54]

But as Granbery suggested, the kinds of entertainment in which Christians might indulge were sharply circumscribed. "While we may and should rejoice in the innocent pleasures and amusements of life, we should live and act in constant reference to that day when we must give account," a pastor wrote in 1873.[55] Even as the godly embraced "innocent pleasures," they shunned many kinds of amusements. Christians had a particularly difficult time accepting professional entertainments, which began to make a tentative appearance in Southern towns and cities in the late nineteenth century. They disliked public spectacles, as they called them, especially theater and the circus. Other targets included tobacco, dancing, card playing, and, of course, drinking.[56]

On entertainment, as in other matters, church people rarely agreed. City people were more lax than those from the country, but country people were not entirely immune to its appeal. "Even in the rural districts, away from 'society circles' in the cities there are Methodists who mingle in the german waltz and in other forms of round dance, at balls and parties," Rev. John Edwards charged in 1889.[57]

By the end of the century, Christians had reconciled their unease over such matters by developing a wide variety of morally acceptable "popular entertainments." Rather than public spectacles, churchfolk considered them tasteful gatherings which afforded opportunity for self-improvement. They held their own fairs and feasts and more vaguely termed "entertainments" in the church building itself. Cearsley's Methodist Church, on the Surry Circuit, planned a "grand festival" at the church, including a "sumptuous dinner and side-tables with confectionaries, all of which are to be sold" to raise money to pay for their new building in the summer of 1880.[58] Still, many did not approve. "Strange that we should have to appeal to [members'] stomachs to move them to acknowledge Christian duty," one pastor wrote to his wife. Entertainments such as fetes and carnivals, a Methodist complained, "obscure the true motives which should prompt us to give to the Lord's cause."[59]

Pastors found they could use their skills as public speakers, teachers, and writers to create "legitimate" entertainment for churchgoers. Learning often passed for entertainment on these occasions, and the public lecture was a popular forum. Pastors delivered lectures in churches, libraries, and other public buildings. Lectures, like publishing, were important for the income they brought to pastors; lecturers sometimes earned as much as $50 for one evening's work. Rev. Oscar F. Flippo mounted a widespread publicity campaign for himself in 1871. His broadside boldly claimed his success in several large cities on the Eastern Seaboard. "These lectures . . . are full of stirring truths and amusing facts, delivered in an animated, thrilling and pathetic style. Hundreds of Ministers and many of the Officials of Societies and Lodges have engaged Rev. Mr. Flippo." The lectures themselves, although they undoubtedly included religious themes, were primarily intended as morally appropriate entertainment. Flippo listed six titles, including "Ice in the Pulpit and Who Put It There," "The Defeat of Old Fogyism," and "Friendship, True and False."[60] Other pastors offered more explicitly biblical amusement. William Fitcher, who had trouble feeding his family of sixteen after the war, developed an illustrated lecture series using a stereopticon machine. Entitled "Palestine, the Holy Land and Egypt," the series brought to life the contemporary scenes and customs of the lands the audience had encountered so often in their Bible reading.[61]

"It is believed," wrote a Petersburg librarian inviting a Methodist pastor to lecture at his library in 1868, "that our lectures have very materially aided— at least in the more intelligent circles—to prevent the establishment of a theater in our city."[62] The popular religious culture that pastors created in the New South provided a variety of benefits to religion. It extended the clergy's popularity and influence, heightened the visibility of religious ideas, spread the moral influence of religion, brought in extra income, and provided one line of defense against the perception that the authority of the pulpit was on the decline in the New South.

But as the librarian suggested, all such endeavors—lectures, newspapers, books—found an audience among, as he delicately put it, "the more intelligent circles." Through the forms of popular entertainment religion assumed after the Civil War, religion reached a "mass" audience, but it was one composed of a relatively narrow segment of society: the middle classes and those who aspired to join them.

Pastors plied their wares to an audience that looked much like them, people who revered education, yearned for social uplift, and imposed strict standards of moral decency. They incorporated all of these characteristics into the popular cultural forms they created. Like the sermon, these popular "preachers" were prescriptive. Unlike the sermon, their lectures did not usually focus on theology or detailed analysis of the Bible. Fiction was a poor vehicle for dogma, but it taught general moral and religious principles very well. Although each denomination had its own press, publications tended to give wide berth to doctrinal issues and to focus on general principles of Christian belief and morality. Printed sermons, which at one time had filled the pages of religious newspapers, appeared only rarely in print by the end of the century.

These publications and other forms of entertainment also schooled their readers in social refinement. Sometimes unwittingly, at other times quite consciously, authors and speakers laid out ideals of piety side by side with ideals of material life. Texts were full of images that defined good taste in matters of personal style. One tract written by a Methodist woman promoting foreign missions ended with a quote from Goethe. By the end of the century, such references mattered a great deal to reader and author alike. Taste had become, quite literally, a spiritual affair. As a Baptist argued in 1892, worshiping in an ugly church made people "vulgar and coarse-mannered." God, he added, was "the author and lover of beauty."[63]

The infusion of religion into popular cultural forms also deeply affected clerical authority in Southern society. When religion entered the marketplace, pastors stepped out of the pulpit and into the street to hawk their wares. The audience, not the author, ultimately determined what sold. Jeremiah Jeter may have stubbornly argued that public opinion would not shape his newspaper's content, but the advertisements that appeared on the same page with his editorial suggested otherwise. If Jeter and most of his peers did not seek an earthly fortune from their writing, the financial realities of publishing determined to a great degree what they wrote.

Popular religious culture bound Southern Methodists and Baptists together, reinforcing regional identity, albeit usually within denominational boundaries. Pastors and laity standardized much of the teaching in their churches by publishing Sunday school and Bible lessons in their newspapers and by distributing their own publications. Methodist children in Portsmouth learned the same lessons as those in Nashville and Atlanta, and adults read the same books and tracts. But religious entertainment also underscored the social and cultural distance between city and country, rich and poor. Where rural church members might attend the odd lecture in a nearby church, Richmond men amused themselves by organizing the Baptist Social Union. The group cultivated an image that rivaled that of any country club and sought a reputation as the city's smart set with a difference. They met in first-class hotels and restaurants to hear national figures speak on topics such as "How to Make the Most Out of Life" and "The Natural History of Religion."[64]

Ultimately, however, popular religious culture did unite churchgoing people more than it divided them. It helped Baptists and Methodists to define who they were and what they stood for. Through newspapers and novels, people learned the minds of their pastors and fellow laymen and women. They learned to be loyal to their denomination. Most of all, this popular culture reinforced and broadened a task long assumed by the denomination: that of serving as a conduit between urban and rural society in nineteenth-century Virginia. Just as city churches had dominated this exchange in the antebellum period, they continued to do so in the New South. Rural churchgoers learned about Methodists and Baptists far beyond their own neighborhoods and even outside their state. They learned what it meant to be members of a regional denomination even as they learned how city people lived and what they aspired to. By the end of the century, these publications and other forms of entertainment also revealed who had won in the long struggle between the advocates and opponents of refinement. When Daniel Witt wrote to Thomas Sydnor in 1870, he had asserted that the "fastidious and fashionable" people would not be Baptists. But two decades later, they were joining the church in droves.

CHAPTER EIGHT

A Call to Order

B y the end of the nineteenth century, denominational agencies cast so long a shadow over religious life that some pastors felt obliged to defend the very existence of the local church. "I believe in the local church with all my heart," Dr. B. C. Henning wrote, "but [for a] church to fence herself in and seek all for her separate ends is the surest way to spiritual death."[1] These "simple agencies of the New Testament" had lost their "primitive power" and appeared almost obsolete. They seemed spiritually dead, provincial, and outmoded. "What is the special aim of the local organization called the church?" a Baptist woman asked scornfully in 1888. "To preach the Gospel to the ends of the earth. Does it fulfill its mission? No," she argued. "It gives to build up *itself* in nine cases out of ten. Horrible spectacle! A selfish church of Christ!"[2]

The congregation's loss of respect corresponded to a rise in the fortunes of denominational agencies. Denominational growth, which had begun in earnest during the 1850s, had by the late nineteenth century become a fixture of Methodist and Baptist life. Even those who opposed the sprawling agencies conceded their ubiquity by the very fervor of their opposition. Denominational agencies, rather than congregations, took up most works of religious benevolence, and there was a growing sense that congregations existed primarily to support an ever growing list of Sunday schools, domestic missions, young men's and women's clubs, children's mission societies, and clerical education societies. The woman who criticized the church as selfish was a fierce partisan of foreign missions and believed that congregations' chief task was to support missionaries.

Agency work, its supporters argued, embodied a progressive and efficient approach to religion that the times demanded. Unlike congregations, agencies compelled bold vision and detailed planning. By its very nature, agency work demanded mass appeals and a regional perspective on social and religious problems. Its bureaucratic ethos entailed extraordinary optimism, and it argued fervently that another committee or a few more dollars raised could make all the difference. Those swayed by such optimism viewed congregations, with their tiny membership and cramped financial base, as stumbling blocks to the larger and more important work of denominational agencies. In their view, devotion to society work could, in fact, rekindle the spirit of dead local churches. "Need I say anything of the importance of organization into [Woman's Missionary] Societies?" Jennie Hatcher, president of the Virginia Baptist women's organization, wrote to her peers in 1888. "You know that there is strength in union; that enthusiasm is engendered by contact with kindred spirits. A 'live' Society helps to make a 'live' church."[3]

Religious societies afforded an opportunity to "get out of one's narrow environments" and "provincial limitations," and they encouraged "greater tolerance and charity, a wider outlook, and deeper and juster conceptions of humanity," a Virginia Baptist wrote in 1894.[4] The ability to transcend "narrow environments" and "provincial limitations" was attractive to many in the New South, but it was especially treasured by women. The Baptist woman who so passionately defended foreign missions as the lifeblood of the church wrote her appeal in 1888, the same year that the Southern Baptist Convention officially incorporated the Woman's Missionary Union (WMU) as part of the convention. This transformation of women's missionary work from a cluster of local societies into an official arm of the denomination marked a startling gain in public leadership for religious women. Because these agencies operated beyond the bounds of the local congregation, they afforded women an escape from the traditional limits on church leadership, which, with few exceptions, was exclusively male.

Women, then, were the chief beneficiaries of a broad movement to extend lay authority in postwar Southern Methodist and Baptist congregations. In the Methodist church, this movement began officially just after the Civil War, when leaders voted to allow lay representation in 1866. In the Baptist Church, the change happened more gradually and somewhat less officially. Over the course of the nineteenth century, however, the laity took up a greater part of church work in both denominations. By the end of the century, both the Southern Baptist Convention and the Methodist Episcopal Church, South, were minutely organized bureaucracies that stitched together the interests of laity across the region. The localism that had long characterized church life eroded as these societies took a larger role in church life.

The emergence of a strong lay movement in both denominations fundamentally changed the work of pastors. "I have no objection to 'societies' of a proper kind within the church," wrote a critic in 1888, "provided that they owe no allegiance to anything outside of the church and are under the guidance and advice of a pastor."[5] In fact, these societies were often not "under the guidance and advice of a pastor" but of laymen or women. Although pastors had initially encouraged the creation of these societies as the best way to build a Christian consensus in the lean years just after the war, the laity's enthusiastic embrace of them brought some unexpected results. Tensions arose between laity and pastors, not least on the issue of women's leadership. Pastors found themselves drawing back, relying on their penchant for professionalism and increasingly defining themselves as administrators and fund-raisers for these societies.

Women were always the majority of church members in Virginia, and some congregations were overwhelmingly female. The deaths of thousands of young men made the imbalance even more obvious for a time after the war. Gordonsville, a village of five or six hundred inhabitants in the Piedmont, was reported to have not more than five men who professed religion in 1865.[6] Overwhelming numbers of women did not alter traditional limits on their authority, however. Women did not exercise full voting privileges in churches and were generally barred from any position of public leadership.[7] The traditions of exclusively male authority were anchored in both tradition and interpretation of Bible passages, particularly the teachings of Paul.

Nevertheless, women were critical to congregational life, and pastors knew that they relied on women more than most were willing to publicly acknowledge. Pastors particularly relied on women's money. Women not only gave generously but also proved to be able fund-raisers.[8] Often pastors leaned on the sympathies of pious women to persuade tight-fisted congregations to hand over their salaries. Women often developed warm attachments to their pastors, and this often translated into financial support. "An excellent sister," living near Bland Courthouse in 1876, offered to support a young ministerial student for the summer, as the closest Baptist preacher was in Wytheville, thirty miles away. She was willing to make her own pastor.[9]

Pastors regularly exchanged letters with women and held their advice in high regard. Rev. D. G. C. Butts remembered Lizzie Walton as a woman of exceptional good sense and Christian spirit. "Her piety was known throughout the [Caroline Circuit]," he recalled. "The leading Stewards at that point were Jennette Carneal and Robert Oliver, earnest and faithful men; but the inspiration of every onward movement at Wright's [Chapel] was Miss Walton."[10] Martha Fowlkes revealed her familiarity with her pastor when she requested that he preach from a particular text during a controversy in 1871—"We have erred and strayed like lost sheep. . . . I do not know where abouts in the Bible it is but of course you can find it," she told him.[11]

Mary R. Walker Hilliard revealed her lifelong devotion to Methodist Bishop John Early in a poignant letter written in 1874. Upon hearing news of his death, she asked his son to send her a lock of his hair and a copy of his autograph. Her father and Early had been cousins. When her father died, Early had comforted the grief-stricken eight-year-old Mary by assuring her that God was her father instead. "He was ever our most loved guest," Mrs. Hilliard wrote. "He was to me the embodiment of *joyous hopes*, of religion made tangeable [sic] to man kind; by his grand ideas his firm faith his godly conversation . . . and the comforting influence of his life. . . . I really first learned to feel that *his* God was *my* Father, a present help." After moving to

Louisiana, she had his portrait painted by a Richmond artist. Early later visited her in New Iberia to give a special blessing to her eldest son, a Confederate captain, who was later killed in battle.[12]

In a time when friendships between men and women were rare, such affections could be easily misconstrued. Pastors themselves often distrusted women and felt themselves burdened by their duties to them. "Ministers, of all men, should be most particular in the bestowment of flattering remarks upon others, especially upon *young ladies*," Rev. George Beale warned himself in his notebook in 1867. "*Foolish women* repeat what a preacher says as though they were not weak & blind like other men."[13]

Some, however, did more than bestow flattering remarks. Charges of sexual misconduct sometimes sullied pastors' reputations. Although the arbitrary nature of the records that have survived make it impossible to estimate how frequently such charges occurred, they made up the single largest category of disciplinary charges brought against pastors in Methodist records examined for this study. Such offenses were apparently considered church business. None of these men was subject to a criminal trial, suggesting the power of church courts and their leaders. P. W. Archer was charged with fathering an illegitimate child in 1863. Wilbur F. Robins was acquitted in 1877 of charges that he was "guilty of indelicate and unchaste conduct towards Miss Bettie Thomas" while she was alone with him in his office.[14]

M. L. Bishop faced charges in 1874 of taking improper liberties with Mary Stone, a thirteen-year-old new convert. Bishop, a recent widower, was acquitted in spite of the testimony of the girl's father, who said that "those in his house decided not to hear him preach again" after Mary told them that Stone had detained her at the well for half an hour in the snow. Bishop was acquitted, barely. "We beg leave to report that in our judgment, the testimony does not sustain the report, nevertheless, we think grave indiscretion attaches to his conduct," a committee of three pastors concluded. In this regard, his case was typical: pastors were often rebuked for their conduct, but committees declined to defrock the offenders, except in rare cases.[15]

The case of C. D. Crawley was particularly difficult, combining as it did charges of sexual misconduct with the explosive issue of race. In the end, Crawley, a Methodist of the West Brunswick Circuit, refuted charges that he had seduced a young black woman, Martha Jones, by presenting witnesses who indicted the characters of both Mrs. Jones and her husband, James. Fearing that her encounter with Crawley would further damage her already troubled marriage, Martha Jones approached a local justice of the peace in the summer of 1878 and swore an affidavit. On the way to milk Crawley's cow, she said, "she turned aside from the main path and went to some cherry trees" when she saw Crawley standing in the door of a privy. "He told her to come there and she went. He told her what he wanted. She told him she could not do that for it was wrong; she was standing near the door, he caught her by the hand and pulled her in and did what he wanted to do."

Twenty-three pages of testimony recounted the incident in excruciating detail, including the number of yards from the notorious privy to the nearest house. In the end, a committee of four senior pastors dismissed Jones's charge after learning that she had a troubled marriage and was pregnant, to be "confined in three months." The deciding testimony came not from Martha Jones or her husband, but from a white Methodist deacon who had employed James Jones for two years. When asked about Jones's character, the deacon asserted, "I would not believe him on his oath." The committee then unanimously declared "that there is no ground whatever for the reports which have been circulated against the moral character of Rev. C. D. Crawley."[16]

The practice of sustaining charges against ordained ministers without imposing penalty was apparently common. Records of disciplinary trials between 1861 and 1890 show a majority of the charges were not sustained. Such a verdict indicated only that the investigating committee did not deem the charges serious enough to defrock the pastor. Nevertheless, a formal trial, even with an acquittal, could have serious consequences for a minister whose unstained reputation was probably his most valuable professional asset. William Rowzie reported that a "tedious trial" during the Virginia Conference of 1855 was "very much to the injury of Dr. Smith. . . . I am sorry to say too—that I fear he has sustained some injury, his acquittal to the contrary notwithstanding."[17]

Pastors' extensive contact with women also provided opportunities for courtship and marriage. Preachers' wives considered their position to be a vocation in its own right, a conviction that strengthened over the course of the century. "He should be the shepherd, I the shepherdess of the flock. . . . Let us then awake to the duties of our high calling," a Methodist pastor's wife urged her peers in 1873.[18] Published manuals described in detail the qualifications, duties, trials, and rewards of marrying into the ministry. Like the pastorate itself, the position had both singular rewards and hardships. As the titular head of a majority of the congregation, a pastor's wife gave spiritual counsel, served on committees, ran the kitchen for church festivals, nursed the sick, comforted the dying, and delivered babies. They were often left with precious little time for their own families, much less themselves. "The wives of preachers get so worn out that their highest conception of heaven is a clean apron and a rocking chair," a Tennessee woman wrote in 1893.[19]

After the Civil War, churchwomen and many pastors argued that women should exert greater influence in society. "Shall we, the women of the South, the descendants of noble Christian matrons, sink in listless despondency or waste our years in vain lamentations?" a Baptist woman asked in 1865.[20] Even the Southern past did not escape criticism. "Here this great Southern empire, with all its social elevation and boasted chivalry, has failed. Woman has never been fully prepared for her mission," a Baptist editor wrote in 1866. "The present is a momentous crisis in the history of our state; we cannot judge what is to come by the past; the future looms up in new and uncertain aspects—now is your time to begin a new life, to receive into your minds new ideas."[21]

The new idea he and many others had in mind was women's education. Of course, education for women was not an entirely new idea among Baptists and Methodists. They had long supported schools for women, but they gave the subject a fresh urgency after the war. They also shifted its focus. Where antebellum Baptists and Methodists had educated young women primarily with social aspirations in mind—to make them ladies—those in the New South thought of women's education, much like men's, as fitting them to be useful. Southern society desperately needed the firm moral influence of Christian women. The traditional avenue of this influence—the family—was closed to many young women after the war because high rates of war casualties left many without prospects for marriage.[22]

What better way, then, to disseminate influence than in the classroom? In 1867, a Baptist woman declared in a column entitled "Woman's Rights and Duties in the Family, the Church and the State" that "I never could and never will believe God intended the intellect of woman to be cramped or unexpanded. On the contrary I think that many parents who have neglected their daughter's education will be called to account." Female teachers began to appear in droves, and much of women's education was directed to the goal of producing more. "Every lady now seems to be disposed to be a teacher while before the war they were too proud to do so," a friend wrote to Bettie Sydnor in 1866. "Give your daughters an education," an editor pleaded, "if to do so you must for years live on bread and water."[23]

The new more assertive churchwoman received mixed reviews from the clergy. Even as some pastors supported women's quest for a new usefulness in church life, others tried to shoo them back into more traditional roles and ways of thinking. Clergymen launched a scornful indictment of women's frivolous preoccupation with fashion as one of the worst examples of postwar materialism, and Baptists debated whether women should pray in public.[24] Pastors were especially sensitive to women's criticism of their preaching. One story, probably apocryphal, told of a woman who had long prayed for the salvation of her husband. After church services, she launched a harsh critique of it, only to look over and see her husband in tears. She was ridiculing the very sermon that had saved him.[25]

Yet postwar pastors, whether they admitted it or not, were dependent to an unprecedented degree on women in their congregations. Women's schools provided a stable source of income for some pastors, and, even more important, women proved themselves able fund-raisers in the postwar years.

Virginia women had a number of schools and academies from which to choose if they could pay for them. Many were loosely affiliated with a denomination by virtue of the headmaster's or headmistress's own preference; others were headed by pastors. Many pastors and laity, pressed to make a living in the lean postwar years, opened small academies. Women conducted many of these schools in their homes. Larger schools included Roanoke Female College, Church Hill Female Seminary of Richmond, Albemarle Female Institute,

Richmond Female Institute, Wesleyan Female College of Murfreesboro, North
Carolina, Hollins Institute, Winchester Female Academy, Farmville College,
Southern Female College, Bowling Green Female Seminary, Suffolk Female
Institute, Blackstone Female College, and Norfolk College for Young Ladies.

Churchgoing people and especially clergymen eagerly patronized and publicized these schools. Clergy and laymen served as trustees, teachers, and administrators. They enrolled their daughters and invited their administrators to
clerical assemblies. The religious press took up the cause of education with
fervor. School administrators advertised weekly in denominational papers, and
editors reciprocated by devoting hundreds of column inches to recommending
education in general and some schools in particular. "With a Faculty probably
unsurpassed by that of any similar institution in the South, with an accessible
and healthy location, with commodius [sic] buildings may we not confidently
expect a liberal patronage?" a typically immodest appeal for Roanoke Female
College of Danville asked in 1866.[26] Together, laywomen, the clergy and press
demanded that women be educated. As early as 1874, a minister's wife could
assert that "the time has past [sic] for the importance of female education to
need an argument for its support. That question is settled."[27]

Women's education was intended to make them better mothers, to encourage voluntary work in the church, and to polish their tastes. In addition
to subjects such as drawing, penmanship, elocution, French, and music, students chose from courses such as etymology, history, physiology, algebra,
geometry, chemistry, and astronomy.[28] The limits of women's intellectual development seemed clear, however. "I shall not speak of what is called scholarship," Methodist Bishop J. C. Granbery told the graduating class at Wesleyan Female College in 1884. "I shall not urge you to pursue classical or
mathematical studies." Instead, speaking on the theme of "the opportunities
of mental culture which lie open to lady-graduates," Granbery urged the graduates to read for personal improvement, practice the fine art of conversation,
teach, and write. "The hustings, forum, senate, platform, pulpit, belong to
stronger, bolder man," he advised them, "but woman's hand, small and frail,
soft and smooth, in the seclusion of home . . . can grasp the pen, wonder-
working wand of the magician."[29]

Because of the zeal with which Baptists and Methodists supported both
men's and women's education in the postbellum years, comparisons between
the quality of the two were inevitable. Some women chafed at the limited
subjects offered by their institutions, as well as the limited purposes of their
schooling, as compared with those of young men. As early as 1880, many
Methodists and Baptists argued that the rigor of women's education should
match that offered to men. Even those who articulated clear limits on both
women's education and vocational choices sometimes advocated that a more
serious curriculum should be offered to women, one equivalent to that of the
better men's schools.[30]

Writers in the religious press argued that women, too, should have access
to a state-supported public university. The headmaster of the Albemarle Female Institute, Alexander Eubank, argued in the pages of the *Religious Herald*

in 1882 that education in Virginia would never gain the status it deserved until "arrangements are made for the girls as grand and far-reaching as Jefferson made for the boys." In 1892, the Board of Visitors of the University of Virginia apparently agreed to pursue the question of women's education in some form, but two years later a Virginia Baptist woman decried "man's inhumanity to woman" by pointing out that nothing had been done on the matter.[31] Among both Baptists and Methodists were those who lamented that many of their peers "had not yet arrived at a full recognition of the fact that a woman is a person, not a thing; an end in herself, not a mere means to an end."[32] By the 1890s, they adopted rigorous curriculums in their women's colleges, heralding them as the equal of those in elite men's schools. Baptists changed the name of the Richmond Female Institute, first opened in the 1850s, to Richmond Woman's College, and in 1892, Methodists opened Randolph-Macon Woman's College with much fanfare.[33]

Tuition at even the most modest of these schools, however, remained far too expensive for most Virginia families. Only a few hundred young women enrolled across the state. The most expensive schools, such as Richmond Woman's College, charged up to $400 per year for tuition, fees, and board. More modest schools generally cost about $200 per year. But there were other costs as well. "And now, I have to ask you for something which I do not want to ask for at all," Ella Granbery, daughter of the Methodist bishop, wrote to her mother from Wesleyan Female College in 1884, "—that is, some money. Will you please send me $5.00?" She needed the money to pay for a new dress she had worn at the school's recent "exhibition." Although she got "very much frightened" in her short speech, Ella later assured her mother that the dress was splendid.[34]

The small numbers of young Virginia women who could aspire to a place in Ella Granbery's world could not curtail the power of the ideal, however. In a time when public education was hardly a priority in Virginia, Baptists and Methodists ran a non-stop publicity campaign for both the virtues and social benefits of education. In doing so, they defined the highest educational ambitions of many aspiring middle-class Virginians. Education was the clearest path to a better life in the New South, clergymen and schoolmasters argued, regardless of status. Even as tax revenues for public schools nearly dried up, Baptists boldly launched a campaign in the depression year of 1873 to raise $300,000 for Richmond College. The reason, they said, was that the "educated mind, controlled by Christian principles, is the mightiest conceivable influence for good."[35]

Women proved their deep interest in education through their keen commitment to giving money for the cause. The furious pace of postwar denominational growth moved women—with their long-standing financial weight—into a position of larger influence. Women often answered before anyone else the appeals for money that dominated public religious discourse, and a favorite cause was education for both men and women. Women were particularly eager to give money to educate pastors. [36]

In the mid-1870s, Baptists launched a new campaign, the second of the decade, to raise an endowment for Richmond College. They called it the dollar roll because they appealed to every Virginia Baptist to contribute one dollar. Women responded enthusiastically. "Please tell me *what* to do, and *how* to do it," wrote Fannie Rumsey of southwest Virginia in 1876. "I saw the advertisement in the *Herald* and am greatly interested in the cause." Betty Brockman sent $14 and had "nearly as much promised. You may rest assured I am working for the Dollar Roll with my whole heart."[37] Another told her pastor, "I have long been anxious to get something to do for God. Please appoint me collector." Pastors did not fail to notice such enthusiasm. "The best work yet done for the Dollar Roll in this State has been done by our consecrated women. Brethren, if you are timid, please step out of the way," Charles Ryland wrote in January 1876. "We want the help of all—but *women* preferred." Methodists, too, found women the most receptive to their calls for money, and they even urged men to stay out of the matter except to give generously. "Please send me *immediately* the names of such persons as you would think will work for us," W. W. Bennett, president of Randolph-Macon College, wrote in 1877. "*Ladies preferred.*"[38]

Even as pastors defended women's schools and urged their congregations to make educating their daughters a priority, most were oblivious to the changes that educated women would bring to church life. Women's desire to enter into church work in a more public and organized way during the late 1870s and 1880s was the fruit of their experiences in school. Education sharpened young women's minds, offered a wealth of social networks, and honed their ambitions.

Accordingly, during the 1870s and 1880s, churchwomen began to organize a new type of missionary society, one that sought to become an official denominational agency. Women had met together in missionary societies for decades, but they had done so in voluntary societies attached to a local congregation, not as an agency of the denomination. Thus, although they raised significant amounts of money, their status remained semiofficial. They did not handle the money they raised, and they did not appoint missionaries. After the war, women began to campaign for official status for their benevolent work. They desired both wider recognition and greater efficiency. Like laymen, women in the New South embraced organization to advance the cause of Christ.

Encouraged by their success in fund-raising for clerical education and flattered by the attention they won for their efforts, churchwomen looked for a cause to make their own. They found it in foreign missions. "Never were women recognized, as now, as an indispensable agency for the abolishing of idols," a Baptist woman declared in 1870 in her "Address to Southern Women."

Figure 8.1 Virginia School, Hochow, China, n.d. Built by the Women of the Virginia Missionary Societies of the Methodist Episcopal Church, South. Virginia Conference Collection, Page-McGraw Library, Randolph-Macon College.

Many men agreed. "There is a far more general and profound conviction that pious women are to act an important part in the evangelization of mankind than there was a few years since," an editor wrote in a call for female missionaries in 1872.[39] Methodist women began organizing for this purpose in the late 1870s. Virginia Methodist women founded their foreign missions society in 1878, and within the year fourteen societies met with more than 450 members. Within five years, these numbers had grown to sixty societies with more than 1,500 members.[40] The Baptist Woman's Missionary Union (WMU) became an official auxiliary to the Southern Baptist Convention a decade later. Its organization was marked by compromise. The union centralized fundraising for home, state, and foreign missions but did not directly handle the money. Neither did it officially appoint its own missionaries. Both of those tasks remained in the hands of the Southern Baptist Foreign Missions Board. The union did, however, work furiously to raise support for women missionaries to preach the Gospel to "heathen women." One of the best known and earliest of these was Charlotte "Lottie" Moon of Albemarle County, who went to China in 1873.[41]

Their success in foreign missions unleashed a veritable flood of women's societies to support a wide variety of charitable work. Women visited prisons, opened homes for aged women, raised money for Virginia orphans and victims of famine in India, organized Sunday school picnics and parsonage societies, and supervised children's missionary meetings. All of these causes demanded forming committees, electing officers, scheduling regular meetings, taking in collections, and keeping minutes. In short, women were at least as eager and efficient as men in their determination to bureaucratize religious benevolence.

Of primary concern for women, as for men, was money. From the beginning, women assumed that money for their causes would be raised primarily from within their own ranks. "Not many women in the South have an income of their own," a Baptist woman pointed out at the organization of the WMU. "Most of us will be compelled to save or make the money we give, will have to practice self-denial . . . plainer dressing, plainer living will make our treasury overflow." Others raised funds by planting a "mission patch" or a few rows of cotton, or by raising a "missionary hen." Women also used "mite boxes" to collect their family's spare change.[42] A popular means of fund-raising was sewing circles. A group of nearly twenty Methodist women in Goochland County organized in 1879. They paid ten cents to join the circle and met monthly to work on sewing projects with materials bought by the circle. In five years, they earned more than $250, with all profits donated to church causes. "We paid the carpenters' bill for the church ($65), bought a nice organ, communion service and other things, sent Rev. Armistead $10, gave our next preacher $10, the parsonage $5, some to the Sunday school and helped the poor in the neighborhood," a member reported. "I believe the Lord has given each of us a talent and I see no reason for not improving it."[43]

Such "connectional work" dominated the daily lives and thoughts of middle-class Virginia women from Tidewater cities to crossroads villages. Rosalie Whitter Anderson, a Richmond Methodist, let nary a day pass during 1881–82 when she was not engaged in some charitable or church-related work. A partial list of the duties she took up that year included: was delegate to the Women's Temperance Society in Washington, D.C.; raised funds for Methodist home missions, the YMCA, and the Methodist District Parsonage Society; visited the sick, the bereaved, new converts, the city poor house, and the state penitentiary; attended monthly citywide Sunday school meetings; organized Willing Workers, a society to relieve the aged poor; served as lady manager of the Eye, Ear, and Throat Infirmary; and was a member of the Ladies' Industrial Society.[44] These responsibilities came in addition to running a household and attending church on Sundays and several nights each week. The motives for keeping such a schedule varied. Some frankly admitted that church activities filled their need for companionship. "I'm afraid," one woman wrote of the missionary society, "they all joined for the fun of meeting their friends rather than for the love of their sisters in far away China and Korea." Rosalie Anderson, meanwhile, hinted in her diary of her unusually warm feelings towards her pastor, Rev. John Hannon.[45]

Mary Pollard Clarke, a Richmond merchant's wife, was the daughter of a prominent Virginia Baptist minister and the sister of future governor John Garland Pollard. An intelligent and energetic woman, she divided her days between rearing four children, literary clubs, church activities, and, after the turn of the century, suffrage meetings. The press of her responsibilities, private and public, often wearied her. "Never before have my duties so crowded upon me," she wrote in her diary in 1898. "I try to be housekeeper, dress-maker, school-teacher, companion for husband and children, at the same time not forgetting I owe something to myself in way of cultivation, and something to the outside world in giving my interest and consideration to some of its good causes. It seems to me that I accomplish nothing to my entire satisfaction."[46]

Clarke shared with Anderson a pressing sense of obligation to the world beyond her threshold that she channeled into church society work. Neither woman was able to rest assured that she had done enough. Their lives suggest how the growth of church bureaucracies, and women's increasing participation in them, complicated women's understandings of public and private life in the late nineteenth century. Largely through the efforts of women like Anderson and Clarke, churches took an increasing interest in tasks that were formerly the province of private domestic life, moving them into the "public" space of church life.

The popularity of Sunday schools provides an important example of this trend. The number of Virginians, children and laity, involved in Methodist and Baptist Sunday schools doubled between the mid-1870s and the end of the century. Founded as benevolent societies to teach poor children to read in the antebellum period, these schools turned to the Christian education of church members' children after the 1870s. Hence, Sunday school classes—many of which were taught by women—adopted a task formerly reserved for mothers, that of engendering piety in children. Church societies such as the Sunday school encouraged women to work out their faith through public works of religious benevolence rather than in a private, domestic setting (see Appendix, Table 18).

Societies also expanded the "provincial environments" of Virginia women. At their missionary meetings, they heard reports from women who worked in faraway lands. The impact of these firsthand reports was heightened by women church members' own participation in the work. They passed around photographs of schools built with the money from their own mite box or missionary hen. They handled strange objects or admired a child dressed in the costume of her adopted home. Members of a Methodist society in Danville heard a report about India in the 1890s from a local woman whose daughter was a missionary there. After instructing them on the beliefs of the "Hindoos," the woman passed a toy around the group. Even the simple object fired their imagination, prompting one woman to imagine looking "upward to mountain piled upon mountain, or [peer] down into Himalayan gorges wrapped in perpetual twilight gloom."[47]

One of the best indications of women's new prominence was their appearance in print. In the antebellum period, pastors wrote and published almost all religious literature; women appeared only rarely in print. After the Civil War, however, a chorus of voices from the pew joined pastors in print. One after another, publications dedicated to a specific cause or group appeared. They took such names as *The Organizer, Baptist Orphanage News,* and *Baptist Young People's Union Quarterly.* By the turn of the century, even congregations printed newspapers. First Baptist Church of Richmond had *The Times*; a church across town had the *Tabernacle Tidings.*

Women, too, began their own publications, especially for missions, with such names as *Missionary Talk.* Their access to print underscored their new role in church life. Women wrote in an authoritative and confident tone, consciously copying the sermons they had heard all their lives. They supported their arguments with Scripture and exhorted their readers to repent of their lack of enthusiasm for the cause of religion and to act boldly. "A Midsummer Sermon, by a Woman," a headline on page one of a state newspaper proclaimed in 1888. "We asked a well-known Baptist sister to preach a little sermon to our *Religious Herald* people," the editor explained in a short preface. "It is all right. The apostle Paul said a good many things, but he never said a word against a woman's speaking to *Herald* readers."[48]

But many Baptists and Methodists did not think women's new assertiveness was "all right." The premise of women's new work was generally the support of other women, both aged and infirm in their own city or non-Christian in a far land. "Woman's Work for Women!" was their cry.[49] But the boldness of the new endeavors seemed dangerous to many men and some women. The specter of women conducting their own public meetings was shocking to those who debated whether women should even pray in public. They feared that women's new independence and leadership would eventually lead them to the pulpit. Bold women "prepared a soil in which the seed of female preaching will readily sprout."[50] Opponents cited the harmful influences of Northern societies, especially the hated Women's Christian Temperance Union. Some women fiercely denounced the agitation that the missionary society question caused. "I feel that we lose time in giving place to these questions," a Mississippi woman complained, arguing that women should be given even more work to do, "so much that they will find no time for anything but work."[51]

Virginia Baptist leaders' opposition to women's leadership sparked great contention within Baptist ranks. In 1887, the year before Southern Baptist women organized their missionary union, the Virginia General Association appointed a committee "to distribute an address to women urging them to cooperate with the churches in missionary work and cautioning them against a separate organization." The association did not oppose all women's organization, only a separate organization, they reported.[52] Even after women were formally recognized by the Southern Baptist Convention in 1888, some Virginia pastors continued to object. At the general association meeting that year in Bristol, a special committee read a "Report against Female Missionary Societies." The committee took "strong ground" against women in separate societies. "Undue multiplication of societies is a serious source of evil," they argued, saying that women should remain under the superintendence of the church.[53] Other Baptists, too, were "horrified" at the prospect of women meeting in public, and progress was uneven. The Woman's Missionary Union of the Albemarle Baptist Association did not hold a separate meeting for women until 1901. At a meeting that year at Mooreland Church, the men "grudgingly let the women have the church for one hour." When the rains came up, however, they went back inside, insisting that the women continue their proceedings. Not until 1921 did the association allow a woman officer of the union to read its report at their meeting.[54]

The debate, it turns out, was over far more than just missionary societies. The impassioned tone of the relatively few pieces on the subject that made it into print suggests the intensity of the dispute. Throughout the 1880s, the pages of the religious weeklies buzzed with opinions, and women found some fierce advocates in the ranks of both editors and pastors. Not only did editors publish women's letters and essays (albeit inconsistently) but also many published editorials that supported laywomen. In 1874, a Baptist editor protested man's treatment of "woman as if she was a sort of plaything to which we might come down, in ideal moments, to amuse ourselves. We regard woman as not only more devoted, disinterested and constant in her affections, but his equal in mind."[55] The Virginia Methodist editor, J. J. Lafferty, was equally blunt. "Almost every day we read or hear of unfavorable criticisms of our women in the grand work they are trying to do," he wrote. "This thing is humiliating. It is a reproach to our men; it is a grievous wrong to our women."[56] Lafferty, who suggested that women be ordained deaconesses, granted women their own column called "Women's Work," beginning in 1883. "We are sometimes asked if our women have turned preachers, etc.," a North Carolina woman wrote in the column that year. "We answer the covert sneer with 'Yes, we are preachers every day of our lives.' " By 1890, however, the column had disappeared, and it was difficult to learn anything of women's activities from the pages of his paper.[57]

Other editors were apparently less accommodating. "Do you not know that it has been whispered to us by some of your own sex, that we must not appear so often in print?" a North Carolina Methodist wrote in 1883 to an editor who chose, nonetheless, to publish her letter. She asserted that nothing would hinder her from writing, "however often you close the door against us; or in other words, throw our communication in the waste-paper basket."[58]

But neither side of the debate would be silenced. Newspapers crackled with charges from both sides. " 'A few tattling women are at the bottom of all our troubles,' said a pastor to us," an editor wrote in 1884. "Where there are two or three ambitious women in a church, each of whom is trying to boss the concern, there will be no end of trouble."[59] "I make haste to record," Jennie Hatcher, president of the state Baptist women, wrote indignantly, "that never before have a people been more harshly judged or badly treated by their friends, their Christian brethren."[60] When Baptist leaders argued that foreign mission societies would hurt the local church, a Middle Tennessee woman shrewdly pointed out that this argument perfectly mirrored that of Hardshell Baptists. She wondered "why it would result in so much harm for women to form mission societies when no such harm had been found to grow out of missionary societies directed by men."[61]

Money lay at the heart of disputes over women's leadership, as it did in so many postbellum church matters. Women understood that church leaders wanted control over the vast sums of money that women raised for foreign missions. Churchwomen's "hearty and refreshing aversion to debt" also aroused the public ire of some clergymen. Churches and denominations had been mired in debt since the antebellum period, particularly for new buildings. Women apparently departed from this long-standing practice, preferring to run their societies in the black. Even as the Methodist Episcopal Church, South, struggled with a long-standing debt in 1891, the Woman's Missionary Society fund was reported to hold $104,000 in a Nashville bank. Pastors were outraged, arguing that women, too, should operate on an annual basis. "There has been no little reproach and misapprehension in regard to a surplus, so called," Mrs. E. C. Dowdell reported in 1893. "In money matters, the best women are more particular and exact than men," another woman explained. "They pay their debts, they lay stress on punctuality." Or, as Mrs. Dowdell quoted St. Paul, " 'owe no man anything' is a safe rule and orthodox."[62]

The terms of the debate over women's proper place in church work had changed by the end of the century. Whereas in the late 1860s pastors had objected to "women speaking in public," they generally narrowed their objection by the 1890s to "women speaking in mixed assemblies." The changes came, in the end, in the small things. "The most amazing development has been in the attendance in our Annual Meetings," Mrs. C. H. Hall recalled on the twentieth anniversary of the Methodist Women's Foreign Missionary Society of Virginia, founded in 1879. At that time, Virginia women responded with consternation to organizers' invitation to attend a board meeting in Louisville. "To attend a public meeting! Impossible!" was the universal cry in 1879. Even after the Society was founded, board members "urged and besought and wrestled with the Auxiliaries to send delegates, and felt encouraged if half a dozen answered. . . . Now, looking upon such an assemblage, I am filled with amazement at the change that a few years have wrought in the prejudices of our Virginia women."[63]

The determined involvement of women across the South in missionary and other benevolent agencies during the last two decades of the nineteenth century marked the triumph of organization in the Christian life. Denominational priorities and activities shaped religious life to the smallest detail by the end of the century. From missionary hens to mite boxes, Sunday school picnics to clerical conferences, church events and activities bound together Virginians across the state. Organization, as a woman explained, created "a line of communication between women in all parts of the church, showing them what is doing and what needs to be done by our sex to build up, strengthen, and aid the church."[64] Significantly, the "church" to which she referred was neither the local congregation nor the worldwide body of Christians, but the denomination.

Virginia pastors and laity confidently considered the growth of the denomination and its "connectional work" to be one of the great achievements of the nineteenth century. It showcased Christianity as successful, efficient, and decidedly progressive. In raising money, in enrolling students, in accomplishing benevolence, denominational agencies were vastly superior to congregations. Only the efficiency of mass appeals and campaigns could meet religion's growing responsibilities. Although the eggs from one missionary hen raised a paltry sum, the eggs from one thousand hens could raise an elegant brick school building in China. In the antebellum period, Baptist churches stood alone, but, as a Baptist observed in 1882, their united works of late had effected "great and grand results."[65] A Methodist saw the change in a much shorter time. He described church life of just fifteen years earlier, in 1874, as "almost congregational" and lacking in "esprit de corps."[66] Church membership had once entailed little more than attending Sunday services and perhaps a midweek prayer meeting. In the New South, by contrast, church membership meant having "something to do."[67]

The huge amounts of money Baptists and Methodists raised for denominational causes in the postbellum period made the good sense of this approach self-evident to many. Throughout the nineteenth century, rates of growth in church membership outdistanced growth of the population at large, but giving increased even faster than church membership. In a region noted for its reluctance to raise public revenues and its hearty aversion to taxes, Methodists and Baptists raised millions of dollars, all voluntarily, for their educational and benevolent work.

Many Virginians contributed liberally without even being asked, of course. Ideally, contributions to the church were "freewill offerings of loving hearts to a blessed redeemer."[68] But church leadership usually took a dimmer view of their congregations' generosity. To belong to a church, or even just to attend one in the New South, meant hearing a continual call for money. New church buildings and schools, the dying non-Christians in faraway lands, or the poor on the other side of town all competed for church members' generosity.

Systematizing church giving became central to these campaigns. The need for hundreds of thousands of dollars annually to support denominational enterprises demanded a serious, systematic approach to raising money if there was any hope of meeting growing financial obligations. All giving remained voluntary, but church leaders set into place as many incentives, as well as structured means of collection, as they could. The use of pew rents declined, and churches adopted "financial plans" instead. They distributed dated envelopes in which to place weekly offerings and kept receipts from each member. Both Methodists and the somewhat less methodical Baptists set an expected annual contribution for individual churches for denominational work. One printed "remittance form" for the WMU of Virginia listed twenty-one separate funds to which the zealous might contribute.[69]

Their campaigns succeeded overwhelmingly, despite calls from pastors that congregations should do more. Proof of success came not only in the sheer amounts of money raised, which continued to rise, but also in the pattern of giving. These church campaigns, although they promoted causes generally conceived of and organized in cities, successfully persuaded thousands of rural church members to give generously to denominational work. Although urban members gave consistently more than their rural counterparts, urban and rural giving increased at approximately the same rate. During the depression of the early 1890s, even as urban Methodist giving plummeted, rural Methodists' contributions remained steady. Baptists across the state, meanwhile, continued to increase their contributions even in the midst of depression (see Appendix, Table 19).

Throughout the late nineteenth century, both denominations published a virtual sea of figures on church finances. Curious members could compare expected giving with the actual amounts contributed, identify the wealthiest churches and the poorest, and peer into the private finances of their pastors. Church leaders expected that the publication of these figures would encourage competition, both between congregations and between denominations. One city church kept a book, open to public inspection, listing all the enrolled members with the amounts they contributed. "The effect of this is readily realized," the pastor observed.[70]

Churches tried to systematize giving through a variety of methods. One of the most popular was printing dated envelopes. An 1873 envelope from Richmond's Second Baptist church even advertised its printer. "The Church asks you to give something, however small the sum, every Sunday," it read. "Enclose it in this envelope, endorse your name on it, and drop it in the basket. When you cannot be present, send your gift. If you find this in your possession after the above date, it will remind you that you have neglected your duty." The envelope was printed with the phrase "Sold By Starke & Ryland, 915 Main Street, Richmond, Va."[71]

These campaigns measured the distance Virginia congregations had traveled from the rougher and less efficient habits of their forebears. The obsession with measuring, calculating, and publishing statistics, with appeals for giving, committee meetings, and fund-raising goals, contrasted sharply to early antebellum interest in the mysterious, random, and even arbitrary work of the Holy Spirit. "The great business of the Convention," a Baptist wrote in 1866, "is to report the money collected and disbursed."[72]

Religion was systematic and rational in the New South, and pastors and laity attempted to measure spirituality with statistics. "When I was a boy, and for a long time afterward, piety was the standard of religion," a Methodist layman complained in 1893. To him and many others, that seemed no longer the case. Pastors were judged by the number of people who joined their churches, the quality of their buildings, and the amount of money they collected. Descriptions of congregations frequently focused entirely on financial considerations. B. F. Ball wrote proudly to the Methodist newspaper in 1877 about the achievements of his congregation. "A plucky people, this little squad of Waynesboro Methodists," he wrote, describing how they had replaced their log-house parsonage with a proper and "commodious" one and had stopped meeting in a fifty-year-old barn upon completion of a large and handsome

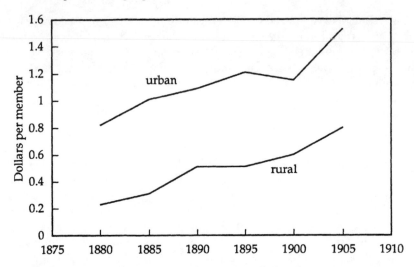

Figure 8.2 Giving per Baptist in urban and rural churches. *Minutes*, Baptist General Association of Virginia, 1880–1905.

brick church. Their goals, he concluded, were to cancel their indebtedness for these buildings, as well as to complete an "audience room" for the church.[73]

Methodists particularly were known for their interest in quantifying almost every aspect of church life, although in 1899 a Methodist pastor protested what he called the "statistical illusions" that such practices invited. While acknowledging the time, labor, and money spent in keeping and publishing statistics, he charged that the figures themselves were often either inaccurate or subject to misinterpretation. Membership figures often included members "long since dead" or "utterly lost sight of," simply because falling membership figures would damage a minister's reputation. Above all, statistics did not account for human experience. "At the end of [my] first year on Gloucester Point Circuit," he wrote, "the whole assessment for ministerial support was reported paid. At the end of the second year there was a deficit of $170. This was occasioned by the almost unparalleled failure in the oyster trade and the consequent destitution among our people."[74] Another critic protested the "modern method" of raising money, which he described as "to turn loose upon an inoffensive community with exasperating regularity a horde of little children, with tickets to this or that . . . thus robbing the community of its peace and the children of their modesty."[75]

This campaign for organization changed people as much as it altered the institutional church. Many men and women warmly welcomed the growing religious bureaucracy. It gave them a heady sense of participation and a feeling of belonging to something larger than themselves and their communities. Like political parties, these societies provided a satisfying opportunity to indulge in the late nineteenth century's propensity for boosterism and public display.

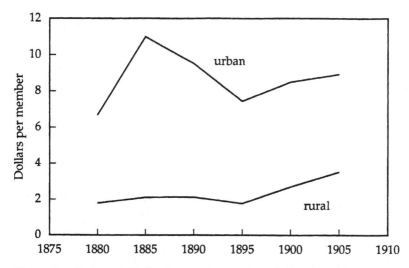

Figure 8.3 Giving per Methodist in urban and rural churches. *Minutes,* Virginia Annual Conference, Methodist Episcopal Church, South, 1880–1905.

Unlike political parties, however, denominations presented Virginians with a cause in which they felt they could express nearly complete confidence, one unsullied by partisan rivalries and corruption.

The laity's success in winning a place in the denominational bureaucracy did not displace pastors, but it did sharply shift their responsibilities. Pastors had to refit the ministry to accommodate the new influence of the laity. They were caught between contradicting assessments of lay authority. The sharp opposition to women's work in foreign missions suggested the unease that many felt about the laity's new prominence. Yet most continued to trumpet the need for denominational expansion at every turn, entrenching themselves in agency work.

The Virginia Baptist Layman's Union, organized in 1888, measured the new activism of postbellum laity. Charles L. Cocke of the Hollins Institute led this group. The first meeting addressed the necessity of organization, how Christian men should vote, how to retain a religious sense in one's business day, and "How Can We Hold Our Young Preachers in Virginia." One of their primary grievances was their lack of representation in the Virginia General Association. Throughout the nineteenth century, churches and individuals were admitted to the association only after the payment of a fee. Many churches were thus not represented at all, and the interests of wealthier churches were represented by several delegates.[76]

The triumph of the organization in religious life also changed the day-to-day lives of Virginia pastors, even those who lived far from the cities and towns that served as the headquarters for these programs. Pastors administered an ever increasing amount of wealth and property, as well as boards, agencies, and church committees. Some pointed proudly to the new similarities between the pastorate and business, hoping that the ministry would gain new respect from the growing class of businessmen in the state.

Fund-raising, or as one Methodist put it, squeezing the money "out with many rebuffs, as if milking a kicking cow," became a central task.[77] Pastors not only took the lead in giving their own money but also appealed to their members. The need for money grew relentlessly throughout the last half of the century, and fund-raising threatened to overwhelm pastoral work altogether. "If I were to respond to all of these urgent appeals for worthy and deserving objects," Methodist John Edwards complained in 1889, "I would have to take at least two or three collections every Sunday and literally do nothing else but go round and beg and collect."[78] "The pastors have truly come to be the financial pack horses of the church," sighed Rev. J. E. DeShazo in 1893.[79]

Much of the momentum behind denominational growth grew out of its participants' sense of a formidable opposition to their principles and goals. Not all Virginians agreed that organization was the key to expanding the influence of Christianity and elevating society. Some resented the imposition of plans and organizational principles on their churches by a faceless committee in a faraway city. A number of Baptist congregations simply ignored the Virginia General Association's call for money entirely. To rectify this situation, Baptist leaders appointed a committee in 1881 expressly to promote a "more active cooperation between churches." They showered the state with printed circulars, exhorting church leaders to begin plans of "systematic beneficence." Their reports indicated less than full success. Some churches had no systematic plans at all, others implemented such plans in vain. At one church, collections "depended upon the pastor . . . but they come slow and far between"; another reported they had no plan and were "asleep and doing almost nothing."[80] Others failed to report what they did collect. Although the number of noncontributing churches declined, pastors and layleaders continued a steady plea for more cooperation. Clearly on the defensive, they let it be known that they were not "a set of interlopers or autocrats determined to rule the women of the state."[81]

Denominational success also came at the expense of the church's role in the local community. A growing enthusiasm for regional denominations eroded the localism that had long characterized church life. The sharp decline in church disciplinary trials by the end of the century is evidence of this shift of attention to matters outside the local congregation. Congregations grew larger and dissolved into cliques; many people on church rolls did not know one another, which made discipline increasingly difficult. Congregations became so engrossed in raising money that their pastoral commitment to their own members weakened, even as agency work strengthened their ties with others across the state.[82]

Congregations traditionally took responsibility for the welfare of their own members, especially those who were destitute. By the end of the century, however, this was no longer the case, and some church members were forced to rely on the small, if growing, charitable agencies of the state. A Danville Methodist noted in 1899 that a local church member's funeral was held at the state-supported almshouse. "This occurred in a church whose membership is worth many hundreds of thousands of dollars," he wrote. And although he commended their desire to worship in "comfortable and even elegant" houses of worship, he did feel that "some provision should be made to keep our members from being accounted a pauper."[83]

Few church leaders noticed. Convinced of the wisdom of organization, they hurried ahead, working to make this corporate ethic the central feature of church life in the New South. Where early antebellum revivals had focused on the conversion of individuals, postbellum denominations emphasized reaching the largest number of people in the most efficient way. Concern with conversion was subtly, yet insistently, pushed away from the center of church life to make way for interest in the moral health of society at large. Historians have not investigated the links between the bureaucratization of church life and the methods cf Progressives after the turn of the century, yet there were clear connections between the educational method advocated by Methodists and Baptists and the Progressives' interest in educating people out of ignorance and poverty. Schooled as they were in the benefits of bureaucracy through their denominational work, evangelicals became some of the most enthusiastic advocates of bureaucratic reform in the New South.[84]

Ironically, the growth of denominations in the late nineteenth century diminished pastors' influence in the community outside the church. Denominational growth ensured that pastors had an ever larger and wealthier bureaucracy to oversee. But even as their empire expanded, the world that pastors administered was an increasingly insular one. Methodists and Baptists had their own schools and colleges, presses, benevolent agencies, buildings, retreat centers, young men's and women's groups, and social clubs. Those outside the church viewed denominational interests and sectarian disputes as narrow and irrelevant.[85] Populists, in particular, resented clergymen who promoted the interests of the denomination above liberty and economic justice; they denounced those "who loved denomination or sect more than [they] loved the liberties of the people."[86] Throughout the first half of the century, the secular press had published the proceedings of clerical meetings, sometimes in full, because their editors viewed them as matters of public concern. By the end of the century, this practice had long since ended, underscoring that those outside the church had little at stake in what the clergy might decide to do.

By knitting together the interests of church members across the region, denominations created a regional community of their own. But they also isolated their people, and particularly the pastors that led them, from those outside the denomination. By 1900, even pastors of large city congregations had to rely on other connections—social, family, and business—to maintain recognition and influence outside denominational circles.

Women's increasing participation in denominational affairs wrought irony of its own: it came at a time when denominations themselves, although growing in size, were losing relevance in larger society. Women, then, won leadership in religious institutions that were becoming in a sense themselves "privatized" in the late nineteenth century; they gained in an institution that was losing widespread public influence. If they themselves noticed this, they did not say so, and many appeared to be contented with their new place of prominence in church affairs. Yet the language they used strained against the boundaries that set church affairs apart from those of the world. Clearly, religious men and women still intended religious benevolence to change their world.

Yet intended or not, the influence of religious women and their pastors did not, in practice, reach beyond denominational boundaries. In this sense, then, religion had become a smaller concern, one that was markedly less relevant to public life in the late nineteenth century than it had been in earlier times. The very denominational growth that many thought held the key to religion's future ended in limiting its influence. Most pastors and lay leaders, however, did not see this. They read the rise of "secularism" as the failure of the church and worked even harder to build denominations to change the world. During the 1880s, many turned to causes such as temperance to bolster religion's influence outside the church.

CHAPTER NINE

The Divided Mind of New South Pastors

In 1870 the editor of the *Religious Herald* gave his readers a history lesson. "Let us form just opinions of our fathers," he wrote. "We hold them in highest veneration . . . but it would be absurd for us to regard them as infallible religious guides. We are, in one aspect, the fathers and they are the children." Baptists, he noted in triumph, "have been borne along by the current of the age. The increase of general intelligence, the multiplication of books and periodicals" and the advantages of "wider intellectual culture have . . . added much to the good taste and dignity of pulpit exhibitions."[1]

Among pastors who wrestled with history in the New South, a place and a time when interpreting the past mattered a great deal, Jeremiah Jeter's voice was particularly audacious. His editorial appeared in the same year that a group of Virginians were organizing to celebrate the heroes of the dead Confederacy. Caught in the currents of social, economic, and political change that enveloped the postwar South, former Confederate leaders and their families chose to revere the past. Jeter and many of his peers in the ministry, however, allied themselves squarely with change.[2]

The narrative of social progress pastors began writing in the antebellum period was far from finished, and it did not leave much room for nostalgia. Of course, they continued to celebrate the heroism of their Baptist and Methodist founding fathers and did not entirely reject their past. But they paused to revere them only briefly before pulling back toward the shining progress of their own day. While partisans of the Lost Cause sketched their romantic plantation legends and sought to relive the past, Virginia pastors celebrated the simplicity and boldness of their forebears but found their inspiration in the present.

Like other Americans, these Virginians were preoccupied with progress in the late nineteenth century, and in writing and telling their histories, they measured progress against the foil of an old-fashioned, bygone era. They defined progress in terms of the growth of intellectual culture, good taste, and dignity, and they were quite certain that they themselves and their churches were steadily advancing in each category. At the same time, pastors viewed life in the New South generally as a study in both progress and decline. They were not blind to the darker side of progress—state and local governments groaning under a windfall of liquor revenues, industrialists building huge mansions on the edge of town, Sunday trains, corrupt political machines—developments that troubled them deeply.

Men like Jeter also told their story of social and institutional progress against the story of black churches and their preachers. In contrast to their own ascending narrative, white pastors told the history of African American churches, and particularly of black preachers, as a tale of sharp decline. Their views on slavery ranged across the spectrum of opinions embraced by other Southerners; they saw it as everything from a positive good to a necessary evil to a questionable relation that in hindsight they realized God had wisely allowed to be destroyed. But white preachers relentlessly romanticized slave religion and black submission to white spiritual authority, and thus slavery itself, in a manner worthy of the staunchest partisans of the Lost Cause. It was here that their own views of the Southern past intersected most broadly with what C. Vann Woodward called the region's "archaic romanticism." African Americans could succeed neither socially nor spiritually without enlightened white spiritual leadership, they believed. Black people's potential for success had peaked in slavery. White pastors refused to grant to a new class of black preachers a status at all comparable to their own. Instead, white Baptist and Methodist pastors scorned black ministers for a "nouveau riche" attitude and social pretensions, just as wealthy white Virginians often accused "lessers" of their own race.[3]

All of this suggested the long legacy of slave religion for the white church in the New South. White pastors simply could not imagine a free black church. Their vision of a free church was founded on notions of social, spiritual, and material progress, and African Americans of all classes were outside this vision. Their long experience of segregated congregations allowed them to see segregation as progress long before Jim Crow broke over the South. Although most white pastors never publicly condoned violence against blacks in the New South, they often lacked the will to intervene in the face of it. More commonly, their language itself did violence by stripping blacks of their identity as brethren and sisters in the Lord and reducing them to a "civic problem" that might be addressed only through legislation. If they pinned all their hopes on progressive religion, it was a progressive religion for whites only.

Pastors' disdain for the aspirations of black preachers highlighted the tenuous hold they themselves had on social progress. They were divided in their own minds and within their own ranks about the security of clerical authority, their place in society, and the health of that society. Pastors in the New South were less quick to praise what was old, more open to change, and far more inclined toward self-criticism than scholars have been willing to grant. Their passionate debates about the history and future of their profession set older pastors against younger ones and city residents against those in the countryside. Likewise, their raucous public feuds over temperance split the church. But these conflicts also allowed pastors to work out the place of their churches in the New South.

By the 1870s, the generation of pastors who had come of age in the 1830s and 1840s keenly felt their age. "The old brethren, with whom I used to work, and who were pillars in the church, are gone," Daniel Witt wrote to his friend Thomas Sydnor after the war.[4] These older ministers interpreted changes in postwar church life as decline and yearned for a return to the manners and customs of the fabled days of their youth. "Our churches are declining in that old-fashioned practical piety that was so common in other days," a Baptist lamented.[5] "The laity have departed from the old landmarks of Methodism," one of the oldest pastors in the Virginia Conference told his peers at their annual meeting in 1868. "Let us come back to the old paths."[6]

Nostalgia did not entirely cloud the vision of Witt's generation. The leadership of the denominations they had nurtured did shift after the Civil War. The change was particularly striking for Southern Methodists, who replaced three of five antebellum bishops at their first general meeting after the war in 1866. The meeting itself foreshadowed the generational tensions of postwar church life, as bitter disputes broke out between pastors who supported old ways and younger advocates of "progress." Virginian John Granbery, later a bishop himself, attended the New Orleans meeting and reported a "personal and offensive discussion" concerning changes in the church.[7] The controversy involved the new and relatively radical changes instituted by the conference: the removal of the six-month probationary period for church membership, lengthening of the pastoral term from two to four years, and the admission of lay representation to all church conferences, (see Appendix, Tables 20–23).

But if denominational leadership changed, young pastors with new ideas did not take over the rank and file of Virginia pulpits during the 1870s. In spite of claims that the army revivals made scores of young ministers, the number of pastors ordained in Methodist and Baptist churches through the 1870s did not suddenly increase. Instead, the number of Baptists ordained remained fairly constant, and the number of Methodist pastors actually declined throughout the 1870s.[8]

Pastors ordained after the war were anxious to embrace the opportunities, limited though they appeared to be, of their youth. Forty percent were army veterans, compared with less than one-third of an older generation of pastors ordained in the 1850s. More had been born outside the state, and a slightly higher number were from rural families than the earlier generation. Although raised in the country, fewer were farmers' sons and more were the sons of preachers. Like those ordained in the 1850s, more than two-thirds of these pastors received some college education. About a fifth reported little or no formal education. Virginia Baptists attended their theological seminary, moved to Louisville, Kentucky, from South Carolina after the war, in ever higher numbers. Almost a quarter of all Baptist pastors included here who were ordained after the war attended seminary. Those who held other positions before or while they preached were overwhelmingly teachers. This marked the greatest change between pastors ordained in the 1850s and those ordained in the 1860s and 1870s: whereas fewer than half of those ordained before the war had taught school, after the war almost two-thirds had done so before they entered the pulpit.

Older pastors' impressions that things had changed, then, were both right and wrong, but the sense of change was heightened by the trick of memory in the postwar South. The war became a fixture in Southerners' memories that cracked their lives into two pieces. "Before the war" was irrevocably estranged from their own day. Antebellum pastors had held to a peculiarly truncated view of their sacred history and had evidenced little need to place themselves squarely in the Christian lineage. The war changed this. For the first time, pastors were compelled to link themselves to the Baptist and Methodist "founding fathers," as they called them, of the late eighteenth and early nineteenth centuries.[9]

To this end, they became deeply interested in writing and reading clerical biographies, as well as histories of their denominations. Virginia Baptists founded their denominational historical society in 1876. Members collected documents, generally from the eighteenth century, and presented and published papers in their own journal and denominational newspapers. The process of culling their own memories and examining the historical record confirmed to them that there was much to admire in the old days. They spoke admiringly in print and from pulpits of the days when preachers of the Gospel "had a strong faith in the doctrines which they preached, and felt them to be true, awfully true."[10]

In their reading of the past, pastors sought a model for the ministry of their own day. Southern pastors, like those throughout the Christian era, turned to biographies of their forebears to anchor themselves and to provide role models. "Christian biography is the repository of the names and character of the honored servants of God," Methodist Bishop David Doggett of Virginia wrote in 1880. "It performs the grateful task of rescuing their record from oblivion . . . and of transmitting to others the treasure of their usefulness."[11] In the years after the Civil War, Southern pastors prized biography even more than other Americans did. They adopted clerical biographies as textbooks in their seminaries two decades before their Northern peers took up the practice.[12] The men they studied seemed to them to embody all of the qualities that their own generation lacked. "Oh, for a revival of the apostolic spirit which distinguished our Fathers, when they went everywhere, preaching the word with power and success," a Baptist writer lamented just after the war.[13] Methodists remembered heroic figures who resembled the Old Testament patriarchs. They "were men of prayer. And they communed with God . . . they were bold . . . they had the faces of lions . . . they feared no man."[14]

Interest in the Confederate past also emphasized the heroic and manly character of the clergy. Methodist William Wallace Bennett's *A Narrative of the Great Revival Which Prevailed in the Southern Armies*, the first and most comprehensive account of the army revivals, was published in 1877 after it appeared in serial form in a Virginia newspaper.[15] Bennett, editor of the newspaper and an ordained Methodist, made his account cheap and available to a wide audience. In his hands, the war became a moral tale that celebrated army chaplains. Bennett was irritated by the direction of the memorial movement in Virginia during the 1870s. Contrary to what those former Confederate officials and officers claimed, Bennett argued that "the great moral phenomenon of the war was the influence and power of religion among the Southern soldiers."[16] The clergy's place in the war eclipsed that of military leaders; the generals had lost their temporal battles, but the clergy had won their spiritual ones.

Bennett's interpretation eventually became one of the most influential readings of the war. The rank-and-file pastors of the 1870s and 1880s, however, did not share his interest in the war. Although some leaders of the Lost Cause were ordained, they were not regular pastors. Most working pastors never deeply involved themselves in the Lost Cause, and denominational publications rarely mentioned the war after 1870. Neither did private papers or church documents reveal much interest in the war or the Lost Cause.[17] Confederate veterans held many pulpits in postwar Virginia, but they had other business to attend to. Some even viewed the war as a hindrance to their work. "One of the things I had to do in nearly all the places I visited was to put away the war," a Methodist wrote in the late 1860s. "[People] very naturally supposed I would like to talk of the war scenes. I felt strongly that we should give it a Christian burial."[18]

If the past provided a model, however, it could also be a source of great embarrassment. Pastors struggled to reconcile their reverence for their forebears' piety with their disdain for their ignorance and provincialism. While older pastors longed for the old days, younger men scoffed that the past held few charms. The present was superior, they argued, materially, intellectually, and spiritually. The fathers became the children. Ministers and churches had progressed to a level of refinement in the New South that their forebears had never dreamed possible. Richmonder A. E. Dickinson spoke for many when he described a "plain old preacher" in 1882: "His style of speech and dress is antiquated and uncouth" and "his thoughts smack of the olden days. We are not enthusiasts about plain old preachers."[19]

Neither were Dickinson and his peers enthusiasts of black preachers. The reasons for their distaste bore striking similarities to their views of plain old preachers. As in the antebellum period, refined white preachers scorned uneducated and emotional religion among both blacks and whites. Alongside their own story of white progress, pastors laid the story of black decline, and they used this myth to affirm their own sense of success.

Virginia Baptists counted in their ranks one of the most famous black preachers of the nineteenth-century South, John Jasper of Sixth Mount Zion

Church in Richmond. Jasper, who began preaching as a slave, attracted huge crowds after the war. He was best known for his sermon "The Sun Do Move," in which he claimed that the Old Testament proved that the earth did not revolve around the sun. His preaching drew thousands, black and white alike, ranging from true believers to curious skeptics. Whites went to hear Jasper primarily for entertainment; he became a tourist attraction for white visitors, who delighted in him as an eccentric curiosity.

Yet Jasper was also renowned as a preacher of the Gospel. His powerful and energetic preaching convicted black and white hearts alike. It was to celebrate Jasper's Gospel preaching that William Hatcher sat down, in about 1907, to draw together his impressions of the man, gathered over more than thirty years of observations. One of the best known Virginia Baptists of his generation, Hatcher and his wife, Jennie, were known for their progressive views, particularly for their vocal advocacy of churchwomen's leadership. Hatcher wrote about Jasper secure in the knowledge of Baptist social and material progress and even political power. A. J. Montague, who had just left the governor's office, was a staunch reform Democrat and active layman, a gentleman of deepest Baptist conviction. [20]

Hatcher had apparently been fascinated with Jasper for decades. He attended his preaching at least as early as the 1870s. But his fascination honored Jasper less than he suspected. Hatcher approached this black man convinced of his utter simplicity. He wrote confidently, expecting that he completely understood Jasper, and set out to capture the man's life in a few colorful phrases. But the man he captured in his book remained a slave. What Hatcher intended as an appreciation of Jasper for a white audience disinclined to consider the virtues of a black man ended as an apology for slavery and a celebration of slave religion.

Jasper died in 1901, the very year in which Virginia delegates were writing a new state constitution that tore away from black men nearly all hope of exercising the franchise. Hatcher's book embodied the Jim Crow era; he wrote for a segregated audience. "The man in question was a negro, and if you cannot appreciate greatness in a black skin you would do well to turn your thoughts into some other channel," Hatcher commented in the introduction. "But do not be afraid that you are to be fooled into the fanatical camp. This story comes from the pen of a Virginian who claims no exemption from Southern prejudices and feels no call to sound the praises of the negro race." [21]

Yet if his condescension was predictable, Hatcher's appreciation of Jasper's spirituality was genuine, and this ambiguity suggests the complexity of race and religion even in the caustic atmosphere of Jim Crow. Hatcher's comprehension of Jasper's faith was rooted in his conviction, shared by many whites, that white authority properly mediated black faith. A legacy of slavery, this view left them unable to conceive of a free black church and closed their minds to the possibilities of a free black religion in the New South.

Nostalgia for white spiritual authority over slaves so colored Hatcher's account of Jasper's antebellum conversion that he made Jasper's pious white boss, rather than Jesus, the central figure of his conversion. Moved to tears on hearing of Jasper's profession of faith one morning while he was stemming tobacco, Sam Hargrove called Jasper to him, extended "the right hand of fellowship" to the slave, and gave him the rest of the day off. Jasper's response, Hatcher wrote, was to "shout," the customary practice in African American worship. Significantly, Hatcher even made Jasper's decision to preach a matter of submission to Hargrove: it was the white man's idea that Jasper do so at all. By deciding to preach, then, Jasper obeyed not the call of Jesus, but that of his white master, who had discerned the call for him. "Oft'n as I preach I feel that I'm doin' what my ol' marster tol' me to do," Jasper says in Hatcher's account. And when he and Hargrove would meet "in that heavenly city," Jasper would tell him in triumph, "Mars Sam, I did what you tol' me."[22]

Hatcher's biography of Jasper starkly revealed white Southerners' bent and static understanding of black spirituality. Even four decades after emancipation, whites clung to a model of black faith rooted in slavery, predicated on the mission to the slaves, and deeply influenced by proslavery Christianity. Black people could not be depended on to deal with God without white people's mediation. Of course, slaves' spirituality had often challenged and enriched that of antebellum white folk, and some had recognized the dignity and independence of slave religion. But in Hatcher's clouded memory, all black spirituality sprang from a white source. Stripped of white mediation, Christianity did not have power to uplift black people the way it did whites. Without white guidance, black people were bound to decline. Uncharacteristically, then, Hatcher's consideration of this dead former slave turned him away from his beloved narrative of social progress and religion. The lesson of slavery for him was that Christianity could not be the same for black and white, and his perception of this "natural" spiritual segregation proved to be a powerful rationale for what had already become the status quo in the Jim Crow South.

The chief fixture in the religious landscape of the old days imagined by New South pastors was the revival. Revivals, like the "founding fathers," were a source of embarrassment as well as pride and nostalgia. Pastors found much to dislike about old-time revivals, and as time passed, their criticisms grew sharper. A few pastors had disparaged them even before the Civil War, but their views were not widespread. Postbellum pastors, however, were quick to express their reservations. In 1866, even as church leaders called for revivals to build up their languishing congregations, and hundreds were reported saved in them, Baptist leaders cautioned that they tended "to nourish a spasmodic and intermittent, rather than a steady and healthy piety and to lower the standard of knowledge."[23]

Pastors reserved their harshest criticism for revivals led by independent evangelists. By the 1880s, these had gained a large following throughout the country. Regular pastors did not approve. "One of the pests of the day is the brazen, self-appointed and self-sufficient evangelist," a Methodist editor complained in 1889. Unlike the "devout and scholarly gentlemen" among the regular clergy, these "coarse fellows" and "illiterate humbugs" paraded their "trade like a fertilizing factory."[24] Pastors found themselves competing for the attention of their congregations with those who plied their own craft. This threat came at a time when regular clergymen felt their own hold over their congregations was weakening. They condemned the crass techniques of these "tramps ecclesiastic" and accused them of staying in town just long enough to collect the financial rewards of revival enthusiasm.[25] "Don't have a professed revivalist," a Baptist seminary student wrote in his notes during a lecture. "They will take the entire management of the meeting and this the pastor should never submit to."[26]

In criticizing these evangelists, pastors set forth a sweeping reinterpretation of their own history of preaching. Preachers in the South had always been gentlemen of taste, they argued. Methodists suggested that the itinerants of the eighteenth century were neither narrow nor unpolished, but "some of the best scholars of the age."[27] Their revisionism extended as far back as the apostolic age. A Baptist writer scorned "the loose popular notion that the most successful preachers that the world had ever seen were illiterate Galilean peasants," arguing that the twelve apostles wrote and spoke some "two or three languages."[28]

To distance themselves from "vulgar" evangelists, pastors identified themselves as scholars. This had several advantages. For one thing, it wed pastors to the specialized knowledge that bestowed professional status. "There is a much larger amount of scholarship and exclusive devotion to study in our ministry than at any former time," a Baptist declared in 1882.[29] Their increasing partiality to Doctor of Divinity degrees also reflected their interest in professionalism. At one time a source of controversy among pastors, these degrees became virtually obligatory for prominent pastors in the New South. At the General Conference of the Methodist Episcopal Church, South, held in Richmond in 1886, clergymen comprised just over half of the 243 delegates. Of them, 40 percent held divinity doctorates, nearly all of them honorary degrees. The popularity of these credentials suggested pastors' interest in building their authority from sources outside the local congregation.[30] Their identity as scholars also set pastors apart from the largely business-affiliated laymen who headed church committees and, most critically, from the women who were gaining lay leadership.[31]

The pursuit of scholarship bolstered what pastors almost universally agreed was a badly slipping reputation, both in churches and in society at large. "Is the Pulpit Losing Its Power?" and "Cramps on the Modern Pulpit" headlined stories in the religious press. "The old respect with which the preacher was invested has largely disappeared," lamented a writer in 1894.[32] The primary cause, most agreed, was a general "elevation of mental culture" among their congregations. Where pastors at one time had been better educated than their congregations, by the late nineteenth century, their congregations had caught up with them. The modern ministry demanded ever more time spent in study. "The age demands an educated ministry," Albemarle County Baptists declared.[33]

Scholarship was a manly pursuit in the New South. For their flagship schools, Methodists had Vanderbilt and Trinity College (later Duke University), and Baptists had Columbian College (later George Washington University) and Southern Baptist Theological Seminary. Virginians had the Methodist Randolph-Macon College and the Baptist Richmond College. Both denominations had a handful of other institutions as well. Pastors lavished ever more money and attention on these schools and looked nervously over their shoulders at the advances of secular scholarship. In the dispute over the role of churchwomen, some pastors had suggested that support of education was men's work, as missions was that of women.

This single-minded focus on education and pastors' increasing attention to the intellectual defense of Christianity in part blinded them to religion's success on other fronts. Clerical jeremiads in the latter part of the century focused rather lopsidedly on the church's loosening grip on the academy, rather than on its success in foreign missions and other endeavors buoyed by the support of women.

Pastors' criticism of independent evangelists underscored the propriety and dignity they cultivated in their own worship services. "There should be neither singing nor praying in a congregation without stillness and attention," a Baptist rebuked another who had recommended enthusiastic worship. "Order, stillness and solemnity become the house and worship of God and every minister should so conduct religious meetings as to avoid noise and confusion." No one, he argued, could "furnish evidence of conversion by bawling, jumping and other extravagances."[34] Whereas only wealthy city congregations could afford organs and paid choirs in the antebellum era, even the smallest churches spent precious funds on new organs and pianos in the postwar years, pursuing godly taste in their worship services. "We failed to interpret in melody the sentiment of the poet," one pastor lamented after a service in 1881, "and sing the beautiful hymns of Watts in plaintive funereal dirge from beginning to end."[35] Pastors also wanted dignity in the pulpit, and they admonished one another to cultivate a careful oratory. Even preaching became a careful science. "The average sentence should have 26 words," one proclaimed in 1881. "At the climax of an argument, you may extend the length to 100," he continued. "In the fresh morning air, stand erect, close your lips and draw air through the nostrils. . . . Hold twenty to thirty seconds. Repeat this nine to ten times."[36]

However carefully they tried to distinguish their religious culture and professional ethos from that of itinerant evangelists, however, pastors could not ignore the evangelists' immense popularity. Both Dwight Moody and Sam Jones came to Virginia several times during the 1880s and 1890s, leaving in their wake a wave of popular support and a weakened self-confidence among the state's pastors. Moody preached for one week in Richmond in January 1885 to a crowd of between two and three thousand and left the city a genuine celebrity. "In good truth," the city's Methodist editor growled, "Moody is the type of the race of primitive itinerants that turn the world upside down."[37]

His visit sparked months of soul searching by state pastors. Painfully aware that hundreds were saved by the preaching of one man when Richmond was home to forty preachers, writers suggested a variety of cures for regular pastoral work. Moody's success questioned the very practices and attitudes that the clergy had set at the heart of their professional ethos. At a time when Virginia pastors were shunning polemics and embellishing their sermons with theological and literary references, Moody and Jones preached with a plain style and bluntly denounced social privilege and sin.

The popularity of Sam Jones's roughshod preaching, in particular, deeply troubled Virginia pastors. At the height of his popularity, he was one of best known figures in the country. Few were bold enough publicly to indict Jones's sincerity, but they were convinced that he hurt the cause of religion more than he helped. Jones's religion was neither denominational nor organized, neither restrained nor respectable. Virginia pastors bristled at his condemnations of citified religion with its committee meetings and educated sensibilities. They denounced his "inelegant and coarse" language and his merciless criticism of pastors. They scorned his lack of professionalism. But, in spite of themselves, they marveled at his power over his listeners. The popularity of plain-speaking itinerants even convinced some pastors that they were on the wrong track. Emboldened by men such as Jones, some began openly to denounce wealth and privilege.[38] One minister advised his peers to shun "theological terms, metaphysical lore, scientific surmises and stilled rhetoric" and urged them to preach in a conversational manner. Another taunted pastors for using "ivory-handled pen-knives" in the pulpit, "where the gospel axe should have been wielded. Much of this merely smooth, nice, pretty, fine preaching is the curse of the church and the bane of society."[39]

The crowds revered Jones as a preacher. In an age when the collective noise and influence of the national and local press grew unchallenged, many pastors were haunted by a sense that the Sunday sermon had been drained of its power. "The preacher once received all reverence. . . . Contrast that with the state of things now," a Methodist journal noted in 1888. "The daily paper, not the pulpit, makes public opinion on morals and social questions. Thus it is, from being an acknowledged dictator in morals, the pulpit has become simply one among many factors in determining moral questions." After a sermon, the writer complained, the congregation was heard to remark, "that is his opinion, I think differently."[40] But where regular pastors were plagued by doubt, Jones seemed to have none. His success affirmed that preachers could still be prophets. Unfortunately, his brand of prophecy was one that many Virginia pastors had long since dismissed. As educated men, they could hardly have adopted Jones's coarse style even if some wanted to. There was no retreating from their doctorates in divinity.

Pastors' criticism of independent evangelists inevitably tarnished the reputation of revivals themselves. Many Baptist and Methodist pastors considered revivals that were not led by regular pastors to be merely tasteless entertainments. People flocked to them, they argued, because they wanted to be entertained, not because they were serious about religion. Evangelists were celebrities, not men of God. They even persuaded themselves that revivals were declining in popularity. "I doubt if we shall ever have an old-fashioned revival again," a young pastor observed at the turn of the century. "If we have any it will be an ethical revival."[41]

Visions of tents crammed with ethicists scattered across the Southland, however, were premature. Revivals survived as a potent symbol of spirituality in the New South, albeit in a different form. In them, Southerners could change while "seeming to remain the same." Churches continued to hold annual revivals, usually in late summer. Although they had traditionally supplied the churches with new converts and members, by the late nineteenth century, revivals allowed members to reaffirm an earlier religious commitment, to resolve to lead a new life. Instead of in the woods, they were often held in church sanctuaries. Those that continued to meet in the woods did so with a powerful sense of nostalgia for days gone by. Nevertheless, many camp meetings grew to resemble vacation resorts more than the rough camps of their forebears.[42]

Baptists and Methodists also appointed their own evangelists. These men, considered to be particularly gifted preachers, traveled across the South and reported good results for their work. Virginian Leonidas Rosser preached to small Methodist congregations outside Virginia. He was a negative image of Sam Jones, the type of man at whom Jones scoffed. He had attended a Northeastern university and held an honorary doctorate in divinity. As an evangelist, his first identity was that of a regular pastor, and he built his reputation on his position within the denomination rather than on his ability to draw a crowd.[43]

A deep loyalty to revivals persisted, but its self-consciousness measured the distance between old-time revivals and new "old-time" revivals. A Methodist gauged the gap between old and new in 1877 by praising the people on the Eastern Shore of Virginia, who held "genuine camp meetings—none of your social woods gatherings of well-to-do city people, but the real sort where godly folks are not afraid to shout when they feel happy."[44] Throughout the last three decades of the nineteenth century, Virginia Methodists and Baptists gathered for both "genuine camp meetings" and "social woods gatherings." The small clapboard churches of the Eastern Shore were a world away from the fine brick churches in Richmond and Norfolk, as were the lives and lifestyles of those who preached to them.

The weight of change did not convince all pastors that old-fashioned simplicity should be discarded for progress. At the end of the century, both Methodists and Baptists managed to combine the two. An editorial published in 1883 admirably illustrated how the two styles, plain and refined, coexisted. "Churches ought to be our best and most agreeable public buildings," the Methodist writer argued, noting that the current demand for "comfortable and tasteful houses of worship" was "exceedingly proper." Yet, he cautioned against display for display's sake. There was a need for all churches, no matter how

Figure 9.1 Dedication of the Hopewell Church, Methodist Episcopal Church, South, Hopewell, Virginia, about 1915–1917. Virginia Conference Collection, Page-McGraw Library, Randolph-Macon College.

wealthy, to maintain a sense of decorum and lack of pretension, because "if [the church] be costly, showy, or extravagant, it loses all true spiritual significance." Instead, churches should adopt a "simple and economic beauty, elegance without gaudiness." Here was the perfect middle class compromise: simplicity was elegant.

A preacher, too, could be too showy and extravagant in the New South. "Educated people have a right to an educated preacher," the editor wrote. But instead of preaching a "simple, fervent, scriptural" message, a pastor could be too "learned, literary, or sensational. . . . A great deal may be said about Christ, the Christ of history and philanthropy, and not much of the Christ of sinners." Such preaching fell into "ways tainted by the world." Tasteful simplicity, in preaching as well as in church decoration, he concluded, was not a compromise with the world.[45]

At the end of the nineteenth century, Methodists and Baptists attempted to strike a careful balance between Sam Jones's coarse style and intellectual affectation in their preaching. In their houses of worship, too, they wanted something between a plain wooden church and a soaring cathedral. Old-fashioned simplicity continued to exercise a powerful influence over both churches and preachers of the late nineteenth century, lending a character-

Figure 9.2 Dedication of the Hopewell Church, Methodist Episcopal Church, South, Hopewell, Virginia, about 1915–1917. Virginia Conference Collection, Page-McGraw Library, Randolph-Macon College.

istically modest tone to their worship, to their social gatherings, and to their leaders. This identification with their past, the tension between old-fashioned religion and progress, pulled Methodists and Baptists back from the excesses of their Gilded Age. As in the antebellum period, their religious style reflected their aspirations, and by the end of the century those aspirations were resolutely middle class. Notions of modesty and simplicity, style and taste, changed with the community; they meant one thing on the Eastern Shore and quite another in a wealthy district of Norfolk. It was this flexibility, however, that allowed the church to remain as vibrant in Virginia at the end of the century as it had in the beginning. Regardless of the huge success of the denominational bureaucracy, religious life retained local variations. Overarching these variations was a denominational identity that celebrated a simple, yet tasteful, middle class religion.

Liquor muddied the waters of religion considerably during the 1880s, stirring up controversy among church members and between congregations and politicians. The temperance campaign of the 1880s was about more than drinking, however. Temperance advocates viewed liquor sellers and manufacturers as the dark side of the postwar economy. As such, pastors' stand against liquor represented a sharp critique of the New South.

Pastors' interest in temperance had faded in the years before the Civil War. Although neither Methodists nor Baptists had adopted strict rules on alcohol for church membership, in practice nearly all church members abstained from drinking from midcentury onward. The antebellum crusade had failed in its attempt to formally regulate liquor but had succeeded wildly in making drinking disreputable. Reconstruction, however, saw the liberalization of state liquor laws, including the easing of licensing restrictions on barrooms and decreased local control over liquor sales. These measures raised a flurry of interest in temperance among churchpeople, not least because of the violence associated with drinking. "Soon after I left Petersburg near the depot a terrible tragedy occurred," Methodist Edward Wilson noted in his diary in 1881. Two men died, one shot and the other's throat cut, within a few minutes of each other. "Liquor was at the bottom of it—O intemperance—what a fearful scourge."[46]

Across the state, Virginians rallied behind the cause. The Friends of Temperance was an early society favored by Robert E. Lee that firmly opposed a political solution to the problem. By 1878, Virginia women had organized a branch of the Women's Christian Temperance Union. The Good Templars were more radical in their object. A Northern society, the Templars early embraced the notion of a Prohibition Party, and in Virginia they were linked to Republican sentiment. Eventually successful in Virginia, the Templars also founded an organization exclusively for black members in 1874. Like these organizations, pastors directed their temperance campaigns against those who manufactured, sold, and drank liquor, whether they were members of their own congregations or not.

By the late 1870s, antiliquor forces had gained enough support to persuade state legislators to begin granting petitions for communities to prohibit liquor sales. Significantly, the towns that first petitioned for this right were college towns. By 1881, the pressure had grown strong enough to persuade members of the Virginia House to pass a local option bill. The State Senate ignored the measure then and again in 1883, but pressure continued to grow. In 1884, Virginia Baptists formally endorsed local option. Virginia Methodists also passed a resolution, albeit a weak one, that opposed saloons. By 1885, with temperance advocates threatening to throw their support to the Prohibition Party, Virginia Republicans and Democrats agreed to put local option in their party platforms. Support for the Prohibition Party in Virginia grew tenfold during the 1880s, and nervous legislators passed the Virginia Local Option Bill in February 1886 by a two-to-one margin.[47]

Those who supported local option hardly savored their victory before they were again agitating to organize. There were to be fights in almost every county and city across the state. "To your tents O Israel!" urged a Baptist in early

March. "We must organize at once—the liquor dealers in Richmond have already taken steps to organize what they are pleased to call a 'Personal Liberty Association.' " Two months later, delegates from the Templars, Sons of Temperance, Council of Friends of Temperance, Local Option Alliance, state churches, and WCTU met in Lynchburg to plan their attack. By May, a local option section had replaced the political section in the *Religious Herald*'s secular news column. Such publicity and enthusiasm carried the drys to victory in many elections held later that year. By the end of 1886, nine counties, four towns, and eighteen magisterial districts were dry.[48]

Postwar drinking presented pastors and their congregations with a quandary: should they rely on piety or law to end it? Should they evangelize the state through mass revivals to make more temperate Christians, or should they commit the church to a public campaign for local option? The answers were not self-evident. Before they could throw their support behind local option, pastors had to resolve the larger issue of how the church should work in the world. Disagreements on the issue raged throughout the 1870s and 1880s.

Changing people, and hence society, by converting them to Christianity was, of course, the traditional position of the church. Even in the 1880s, with liquor's hostile presence at the door of their communities, many church members were convinced of the futility of legislation against liquor. Not only did they fear that liquor would politicize the church but also they were convinced that using laws to restrain sinful behavior implied that the Gospel was not powerful enough to change people's behavior. Drinking was an individual's decision, and only an individual could decide to stop by the grace of God, they argued. "Civil government is powerless to change the heart," a Baptist implored, while another argued that "the Gospel was the only hope of the South."[49] The agency for changing the world lay squarely with the Gospel. "The country can never become better until men individually become better. The work of reform must begin with us," a Methodist advised in 1877.[50] Much like conversion to Christianity, reform could come about only one person at a time. "I never had any use for local option," an Orange County woman wrote in 1888. "Every man should carry it in his heart. God gave us the Ten Commandments. They will never make those stop drinking that will drink."[51]

Supporters of local option phrased the problem differently. They were still certain that religious conversion could make sober citizens of the kingdom of heaven as well as of Virginia. But the conversion of individual sinners could not suppress human greed, particularly greed as manifested in the liquor business. Revival meetings seemed to them a feeble and even naïve response to the powerful interests of money and politics marshaled by the liquor dealers. The stakes were high. As a Methodist bishop declared, "The Whiskey power must be put under, or it will put us under."[52] Supporters of local option held that corporate reform, backed by the muscle of the state, was the only chance to stem the tide of liquor. They frankly conceded the limits of Christianity to regulate the liquor business. At the very least, the urgency of the problem blurred the line between politics and religion. "Local option, in spite of the efforts of its friends, will be made, in some districts, a party measure," a Baptist wrote in 1882. "Shall we be thereby stopped from advocating temperance?"[53]

The conflict between these two views reflected a tension in the lives of pastors in Virginia, throughout the South, and across the country. It reflected more than a difference of opinion about liquor; it pointed toward fundamentally differing views of the role of the church in society.

In spite of the strong sentiment against liquor dealers in their ranks, pastors had close ties to the business community of the New South. Pastors ordained after 1880 had a far greater likelihood of previous training and experience in business than those ordained in earlier years. As in previous generations, these young men turned to pursuits other than those of their fathers: pastors' sons continued to make up about half of all pastors ordained, and the rest rejected the farming and trade pursuits of their fathers. Merchants, clerks, and salesmen turned to the ministry in numbers four times greater than those in the previous generation, while the number of teachers ordained after 1880 fell by half (see Appendix, Tables 24 and 25).

This shift from teaching to business experience among pastors reflected changes in the postwar economy. The New South saw the proliferation of small stores and other businesses, even in rural areas, and such enterprises provided an increasing number of young men an alternative to agricultural work. Planters fled the countryside for the towns and cities, and unprecedented opportunities arose for those with capital or perseverance or both to make their fortunes in business and manufacturing. In 1875, one observer declared that within "twenty years the manufacturers will be the aristocrats in Virginia." By 1880, Virginia had the highest per capita wealth in the South, and twenty years later led the South in the value of its manufactured goods.[54]

Because of its relative prosperity among Southern states, Virginia was a study in extremes. Even as the countryside languished, the size of land holdings there shrinking along with farm profits, the towns and cities overflowed with prospering merchants and professionals. The 1880s marked a particularly heady time for business, and cities across Virginia flourished. Richmond taxes brought in enough for the city to inaugurate a new electric streetcar system in 1887, the first in the nation. That city, along with Petersburg, Norfolk, and Portsmouth, experienced an unprecedented real estate boom. During the 1880s, Norfolk's trade more than doubled in value to $91 million, and the new port of Hampton Roads swelled from fewer than 2,500 people to 20,000 between 1880 and 1900. Even southwest Virginia felt the boom. Roanoke became a railroad center during the 1880s, with its population growing from 3,000 to 15,000 during that decade. West of Roanoke, towns sprang up to service the growing mining industry.[55]

Pastors were among the most ardent advocates of business and untiring boosters of their communities, large and small. They devised economic schemes for underpopulated and poor counties and reported regularly on the business growth of their towns. W. W. Bennett, editor of the *Richmond Christian Advocate*, announced in January 1873 his plans to publish the *Prospectus of the Journal of Industry*, "having full faith in the future, rapid growth and prosperity of Richmond as one of the most important railroad centres of the country." Subscriptions would be $1 per year. Later, the *Advocate* also published *Our Business Directory*, which listed firms and services recommended to readers. One Methodist writer from languishing Brunswick County urged its residents in 1871 to "try any plan to get the country filled up."[56] Others held out hope that the South's new wealth would spur generosity among the rich, arguing that the great philanthropists were "the apostles of a new political and social dispensation." Their optimism was sometimes absurd. Editor John J. Lafferty of the *Richmond Christian Advocate* hailed a proposal to flood the Sahara Desert in 1879 as a fine way to Christianize the continent of Africa. "Eminent engineers and capitalists" were making the plans, and it surely heralded the partnership of Christianity and commerce. "The missionary blazes the way for the trader," he enthused.[57]

To Lafferty and his readers, of course, "business" meant commerce and industry, not farming. Religious newspapers and other publications were unapologetically biased toward towns and cities. Their silence on the troubles of farmers and the problems of country life was deafening. Almost nothing appeared in them about agriculture, even during the era of the Farmers' Alliance and Populism. By the end of the century, editors had even dropped their agricultural columns, apparently assuming that their readers would find them irrelevant.

The clergy's interest in business was not mere boosterism. It was a value that they taught to their children and around which they built their lives and churches. "You must form regular business habits," Rev. William Christian wrote to his son Willie in 1878. "The only way to succeed is to practice systematic regularity in your business . . . your main fortune depends on your own business habits—especially upon your moral character."[58] Business habits and moral character could go hand in hand because moneymaking and religion were not necessarily incompatible. "The fact is brother, the best way to keep from materializing our spiritual work is to spiritualize our material work," a Methodist wrote in 1883. Baptists concurred with this view, and went even further. "Let us make 'business' of the Lord's work, applying to our religious duties the principles and methods which we deem indispensable in our secular affairs," an editor wrote in 1880. Those principles included the classic middle class virtues of industry, perseverance, forethought, and self-restraint. In the New South, the world became, for some, the model for the church.[59]

The business experience that many pastors brought to the pulpit was useful in their day-to-day work. The expansion of denominational bureaucracies meant that pastors worked as administrators and fund-raisers as well as preachers. This was especially true of pastors of large urban congregations. Church officials routinely invested donated monies in private stock and municipal bonds. One-third of all money donated to the Virginia Baptist Ministers Relief Fund, begun in 1871, was invested in an "endowment." In 1879, the endowment of $2,610 was distributed among Richmond city bonds, bank stock, and railroad stock. Later, Virginia Baptists even invested in Atlanta city bonds.

By 1890, the endowment of the fund totaled more than $18,000.[60] Denomi-national officials also enthusiastically compiled reams of figures on every as-pect of church life. Their publications resembled business ledgers, with col-umn after column of numbers quantifying everything from membership to the donations to children's missionary societies, from the value of church property to the number of periodicals sold. Pastors encouraged one another to apply principles of business management to their churches. "Business in our Reli-gion is good," a Methodist wrote in 1880. "Religion in Our Business is still better . . . but Religion is Our Business is the best of all."[61]

It was not business per se that worried most Virginia pastors, then. They welcomed the higher standard of living and growing church coffers that New South prosperity brought. It was not hard for them to see how life in a pros-perous town was preferable to gray days on an isolated farm. Instead, they attacked the wrong kind of business—like liquor—that profited at the expense of other people, and especially business that violated what they called moral law. A blistering Methodist editorial of 1887 charged that "the boasted New South is a rising tide of worldliness." Money had become the great goal, and the accumulation of wealth in the hands of a few persons was causing social decay.[62] "Perhaps at this present writing there is greater jostling, and crowding, and pulling, and pushing and squeezing, elbowing, scraping, and grinding to obtain wealth than at any time," a Virginia Methodist despaired in 1875.[63]

Pastors singled out debt as a particularly telling sign of social decay. Busi-nesses, individuals, politicians, and even churches wore debt as a badge of honor. "Look around you and see how many men rush into debt with no reasonable possibility of their being able to pay," a Methodist wrote of a bank-ruptcy law passed in 1869. "I am no enemy to the insolvent debtors' act. It is well in this grasping, griping world to have some source of relief. But when men use it only to keep dishonestly their ill-gotten gains . . . it is a great curse." Another writer, aptly named Jabez Blunt, in 1873 criticized church members for professing religion and refusing to pay their debts at the same time.[64] Greed drove liquor traffickers and Sabbath breakers alike. "The rushing, screaming locomotives annoy the quiet country congregation," complained one opponent of Sunday trains.[65]

Concern over greed and dishonesty in business underlay pastors' support for the conservatives' battle with Readjusters in state politics during the 1870s. A genuine desire to clean up state politics and business, rather than just nos-talgia for honor, motivated their criticism of the Readjusters' desire to "read-just" the state debt. Pastors felt so strongly about the issue that they broke their tacit silence on political issues. "The obligation to pay debts, private and public, is a subject that comes fairly within the purview of our religious edi-torship," a Baptist argued, calling repudiation "unfair, dishonest and shame-ful."[66] Likewise, church editors and pastors spoke out against proposals for a state lottery, horse racing, and other enterprises tainted by gambling.[67]

Again and again, pastors asserted that the problems of late-nineteenth-century America—the "struggles of the laboring classes and the increasing impoverishment of the people in moderate circumstances"—were rooted in greed, and therefore were fundamentally problems of religion and morality rather than of politics or public policy. J. J. Lafferty, editor of the *Richmond Christian Advocate*, decried the unequal distribution of wealth across the country in 1883. "This is no question of party politics, no question of North and South, no question of Republicans and Democrats, but a question vital and profound of morals and religion," he wrote. "Government is man's institution as to form and shape. Government is God's ordinance as to its principles, objects and ends."[68] Trusts, the accumulation of wealth in the hands of a few, and the problems of the laboring people all resulted from violations of moral law, W. F. Tillett argued in 1893. Moral law was that thing "most needed in the great battle being waged between capital and labor," he declared. "Moral law, which must have consideration for the poor, would say the trust combination is wrong," he wrote. He advocated any governmental plan to weaken those schemes that made the rich richer and the poor poorer. His primary concern, however, was the burden of the church in the matter. "If Christianity is ever to save the world, it must permeate society, and moral law dominate the industrial and business world."[69]

For such men as Tillett, the question was not whether the church should involve itself in politics; they agreed that it should not. Instead, the debate centered on defining what was political. Those who wanted the church to take up local option did not consider the issue a matter of politics but of public policy and moral law. They considered public policy—or the "science of government, the enactment and administration of laws"—entirely separate from politics.[70] Throughout the postbellum period, even as they published editorial after editorial concerning a particular bill, or against political corruption, or urging their readers to vote, pastor-editors continued to argue that they were not engaging in partisan debate. They were not merely being hypocritical; they did not consider the issues they took up to be primarily of political interest, but of public interest. In this, they continued the tradition of the church since the days of proslavery Christianity in defining public affairs as the proper province of Christian concern. If, as Tillett urged, Christianity was to save the world, it would have to "permeate society" through the law.

The decision by many pastors to rely on the state rather than on the church, on law rather than on piety, to rein in the liquor interests marked both a break with past practice and the continuation of a long tradition of interest in public issues. Those who supported local option argued that social issues should not displace the conversion of individuals but could accompany it. A few antebellum pastors had called for laws to change drinking habits, but most had agreed that individual "conversion" from drinking was the most that could be hoped for. By contrast, postbellum pastors focused on corporate reform of drinking in society as a whole. Instead of relying on piety, they argued that Virginians should pass laws to restrain sinful behavior. Instead of being reluctant to work outside of the local church, they eagerly sought public influence, and they stressed the civic undesirability of drinking rather than just the spiritual consequences of sin. Mirroring their appeals for Christian support of slavery during the 1850s, pastors argued that the Bible was a reasonable guide that set out a moral law for all people, not just for professing Christians.

Advocates of local option faced opposition both from within their churches and from politicians. They were sensitive to charges by some of their members and other clergy that a public campaign for local option meant compromise. "It is not for the Christian church to compromise with the world. . . . She is antagonistic to it—aggressively and unchangeably so—in spirit, principles, methods and aims. She is in the world for the express purpose of transforming it." Neither did the campaign signal their entry into politics. "It is not fair to fight the Local Option movement by stigmatizing it as a political organization," declared the Local Option Alliance in 1882. "It attempts to use politicians as a means to an end."[71] Of this the politicians themselves were well aware, and many urged the church to stay out of the matter. Across the South, politicians joined church members in arguing for a "spiritual" church that would leave politics to them. "The politician says Hands off; keep in your place; care for your unseen kingdom," a Baptist wrote scornfully, "leave us to manage our own matters."[72]

But, pondered the Rev. A. J. Kern, "how can you preach the Gospel and let immorality alone?"[73] Those who agreed with him found themselves rather abruptly locked in a partisan battle during the 1880s and 1890s. Before the war, the clergy's support of slavery had aligned them with those who held political power. During the 1880s, their support for temperance pitted them against those in power, and they found themselves scrambling for influence. They publicly denounced politicians and parties, explaining that they wanted to make government itself more moral and force it to uphold what Rev. Tillett had called "moral law." An immoral government could hardly write, much less enforce, moral laws. Pastors boldly denounced political corruption and politics itself, echoing the arguments of the burgeoning agrarian movement. The pages of their newspapers crackled with calls for the people to take power away from demagogues who "looked to the State as their cow, all of whose teats are for their milking." "The time is ripe for revolt against the reign of the dirty dynasty," a Methodist declared in 1880. "Patriotism, Decency and Religion cry out against the present plan."[74] Politicians had sullied themselves and their causes through connections with liquor. Clergymen fumed about the power of the liquor lobby. "If the rum shops were shut for two years, half of the lower house of the Legislature would never see Richmond again," spat a Methodist editor in 1881.[75]

The primary way a responsible Christian man might fight the corrupt "present plan" was through the ballot box. Voting was to be done "in the fear of the Lord, and by the use of legitimate means, by fair, open, manly Christian action."[76] Church leaders were well aware that many voters were churchgoers, or were married to one, and they threatened state political leaders that such men would not just switch parties but, worse, boycott the election altogether.

"Gentlemen of the nominating conventions, give us candidates of at least av-erage morality, or we may be forced to stay away from the polls," a Baptist layman warned in 1888.[77] Pastors were adamant that politicians should do their part to uphold moral law. "We should blush for any Christian legislator who would not rightly use his power to conform every enactment of civil law to the dictates of an enlightened Christian conscience," a Baptist editor wrote.[78] "Wise and beneficent legislation cannot but be helpful, and is, therefore, to be sought."[79]

Those who pledged to support legal prohibition did seek wise legislation in communities across the state during 1886 and in years following. In the end, Virginia pastors took a large hand in shaping the political geography of temperance, but their success was limited. The pattern of wet and dry locales in Virginia was a negative image of the churches' strength. Although city pas-tors led their denominations and more city residents were church members, temperance failed in almost every instance in Virginia cities. By the end of 1886, Charlottesville, Lynchburg, Richmond, Manchester, and Fredericksburg had voted in favor of liquor. By the end of the century, rural Virginia was overwhelmingly dry, but the cities remained wet. Even those few cities that had voted dry by that time, including Harrisonburg, Roanoke, and Norfolk, declined to enforce the law. In those rural areas where the drys prevailed, speakeasies often replaced legal saloons, and the number of saloons in the state increased overall. By 1902, one-third of state's counties had few or no licensed barrooms, and three-fourths of the magisterial districts were dry. But of state cities and towns, only the small towns of Buena Vista and Williams-burg had no saloons. The southwest was the driest area, with fifteen of twenty-two counties dry. In the valley, four of nine counties were dry. In the east, however, just fifteen of sixty-nine counties were dry.[80]

The failure of temperance in nearly all of the state's cities highlighted the political influence pastors wielded at century's end. The leading advocates of temperance among both Baptists and Methodists were city men (see Appendix, Table 26). In spite of denominational growth, professionalization, elegant and expensive church buildings, and a host of social and benevolent church-based agencies, these city men found their influence outside their churches sharply circumscribed. The pastor of First Baptist Church in Richmond, an advocate of temperance, was forced publicly to ignore his convictions because several of his church members opposed him. Although rural pastors were able to maintain some status in their small communities—the success of drys in rural areas undoubtedly owed much to their efforts—few city pastors were able to muster that kind of influence. Even those urban residents who opposed liquor sometimes considered pastors to be advocates of special interests, not the public interest.

An exception was the Rev. John R. Moffett of North Danville, a milltown on Virginia's Southside. His daring opposition to liquor dealers, as well as to local Democrats, raised his profile well above the crowd in that city and even-tually cost him his life. Although his campaign against liquor was exceptional, Moffett in many ways represented his generation. Born in 1858 in Culpeper

County, he spent the war on his family's farm, virtually a battlefield.[81] His mother nursed wounded soldiers, and young Moffett learned to revere General Lee. Converted at the age of fourteen, he attended local schools before being licensed to preach in 1881. He graduated from Southern Baptist Theological Seminary in 1884 and moved to North Danville, his second church, in 1887.

Moffett's new community was filled with day laborers from local mills. Few were well off, even by his own fairly modest standards. Moffett was hardly put off, however. He increased church membership from 30 members to 163 in his first year and began taking collections to build a new church. Moffett had boundless energy and enthusiasm for organizing and systematizing, especially on financial matters. He distributed cards that urged that every member to contribute something weekly. "We are making an effort to enable EVERY MEMBER of our church to do something systematically [to have the Gospel preached to all the world]," one read. He kept strict records of giving, and to those who did not contribute, he sent notices chiding them for their neglect. "Of course you forgot it, dear friend. Of course you intended doing it," one read. Apparently, his strategies worked, as giving per member in the church was well above the Baptist average.[82]

Moffett also had a long-standing interest in temperance. He traveled throughout the state as a grand lecturer for the Good Templars and urged the Virginia Baptist General Association to take a firm stand against liquor. By 1890, Moffett began publishing *Anti-Liquor* in Danville and announced his support for the Prohibition Party. For his fervor, he was condemned from both within the church and without. A local Democrat, J. T. Clark, took personal offense at one of Moffett's editorials, and their public squabble turned ugly. Clark shot Moffett four times on November 11, 1892, in the middle of the day on the street. The pastor died two days later from the wounds. Clark was later found guilty of voluntary manslaughter and sentenced to five years in prison.

The reserved reaction of Moffett's peers to his death suggested their disapproval of his political activism. Hearing of his death during their annual meeting, Virginia Baptist pastors adjourned to attend his funeral. Their public comments about the violent means of his death were strangely subdued, however, suggesting both the commonplace of violence in their society and their view that his activism was unseemly. Moffett was a particularly fine example of how uncouth, how unprofessional, such activities inevitably became, some argued. He should have known that he was playing with fire.[83] Outside the ranks of the ministry, many were appalled and angered that a minister would undertake such a blatantly political stand. A witness reportedly testified at Clark's trial that Christ himself would have applauded the murder of John Moffett.[84]

Moffett's violent death vindicated the views of those who believed that preachers had no business mixing religion and politics. But if they disagreed with Moffett's methods, at least in hindsight, they had long agreed with his assessment of what was wrong. Two years before his death, Moffett wrote to the *Religious Herald* denouncing the lack of activism in the church. "Many Baptists fail to understand the difference between the organic union of the church and state and legitimate contact and influence," he wrote. He described the state as a snake, arguing that the church had been so fearful of union with the state that it was about to be swallowed whole.[85] A Methodist editorial published a year earlier had made exactly the same point.[86]

But by the early 1890s, many church members disdained politics in any form. Mounting corruption and incomplete success in local option had disillusioned them. As far as most voters could see, voting could dislodge neither political machines nor corrupt leaders, and many Virginians were ready to wash their hands of the entire affair. Even the united efforts of Christian people in their communities could not prevail against the more powerful forces of liquor and business. "A Christian cannot be a partisan . . . a chronic politician, without destroying his character and sinning against Christ," a Baptist editor warned bluntly in 1880.[87] By the late 1880s, more and more Virginians agreed. They stayed away from the polls altogether, and voter turnout began to plunge.[88] Moffett's goal was a good one, they felt, but he was both naïve and wrongheaded: naïve because nothing could break political corruption by the 1890s, and wrong because, by attempting change, Christians would make politics into an idol. Godly men, many argued, should simply leave politics alone.[89] "Legislation against crime of any sort serves as a wall of protection only. It reforms no one," W. L. Richardson wrote to the *Richmond Christian Advocate* in 1891. "Prohibition cannot save men from sin, and in no sense must it be looked upon as a forceful gospel."[90]

The campaign for local option gauged the distance that postwar congregations and ministers had traveled over the course of the nineteenth century. Public worship and the life of the Christian community had in some respects changed very little from the antebellum period. Congregations still held revival meetings in the hot days of August, they still met for church suppers and picnics, and gathered for worship in their Sunday best. Many of the hymns they sang were those their grandparents knew. To see their children accept Christ was still one of their dearest wishes, and the sight of a weeping sinner kneeling at the front of the church still brought tears to many eyes.

Yet in the antebellum period, pastors had marked out the differences between the church and the world with pride. The Gospel changed people. Sinners were saved, drunks became sober, and cheats became honest. By the 1890s, however, the distinction between world and church measured the church's failure. Sinners were still saved for a glorious eternity, of that fact Christians were quite certain. But the great advances in religion that had occurred in their century—the refinement and education of ministers and their people, elegant new churches, a host of agencies for religious benevolence, church coffers overflowing, denominational publishing houses that turned out reams of religious literature—had not seemed to help the cause of Christ in this world. Newspapers arrived daily full of news about the most lurid and horrible sins. Even in their own communities, men beat their wives, speakeasies thrived, slick politicians won again and again, and whole sections of town seemed to scoff at decency. In many places, not even all Christian people could agree to condemn liquor. Such things suggested to many that America was on the wrong track and probably too far gone to turn back. By these measures, the outlook for progress was dim, and the wildly optimistic tone of pastors' public rhetoric became more subdued during the 1890s.

Postwar ministers and their people did indeed live in a world quite different from that of their antebellum forebears. But just as surely, they looked at it from a different perspective and with different expectations. They expected more—more of their pastors, their churches, their communities, and themselves. What they saw as a decline in religiosity and in clerical authority was really just a matter of asking a different question. Instead of asking how they should save people, postwar ministers were more interested in whether their society reflected the values of Christianity.

This perspective had been developing for more than half a century in Virginia churches and in itself reflected the startling success of religion on many levels. Pastors' early interest in self-improvement and education had filled Baptist and Methodist churches with educated men and women, or at the least with those who aspired to be. Less provincial and more literate, they looked outward more than they had before, noting things in which their forebears had exhibited little interest. The rise of the denominations and their place in Virginia during the debates over slavery, the Civil War, and Reconstruction pushed the church's interests, and its pastors, into a public role.

As such, it was hard for pastors to be entirely pessimistic about the state of things at the end of the century. There were still signs that progress—tangible progress—had been made. Denominational work did not suffer too much even from the depression of the early 1890s. Money still poured, much as new members did, into their churches. Their clerical meetings gave them great pleasure, as they surveyed the "culture and gentlemanly bearing" of their peers. "What a fine social and intellectual influence must be exerted upon people by sending out into the country places, as well as the cities, these hundred and seventy-five men," a Methodist observed. "There must be a wonderfully refining power, to say nothing of the religious influence."[91] By the end of the century, even the most remote areas had a measure of refinement. "The preachers were in good heart," a Methodist reported of a pastors' meeting in southwest Virginia. "The Hard Shell Baptists are the chief adversaries, but the new railroads, public schools and local option will soon put an end to these people," he wrote. This battle, and many others in his view, would be won not by pulpit-pounding Bible preaching and the repentance of sinners, but by steam power, education, and temperance.[92]

Epilogue

Religion and Progress in the
Nineteenth-Century South

Religious institutions, and the minds that built them, were far more important to the story of Protestants in the South than historians have allowed. Southern churches were not immune to the bureaucratization of religion that coincided with, reflected, but at times thwarted, what Nathan Hatch called the "democratization of American Christianity" in the nineteenth century. Accounts that stress the importance of revivalism and individual piety in the South have neglected the institutional context in which these revivals and conversions took place.

Antebellum Southern pastors were better bureaucrats than their Northern peers. They built thriving institutions devoted to education, printing and distributing literature, and foreign and domestic missions in a slave society. Unquestionably, clergy and laity built these institutions because they believed that they would spread the Gospel. But denominational bodies also institutionalized their conviction that the Gospel "worked up." They embodied pastors' ambition to improve themselves, legitimate their calling, and expand the authority of religion. By the mid-1840s, pastors found that an institutional base lent weight to their defense of slavery. During the 1850s, their zealous sectionalism and talent for fund-raising tapped growing Southern wealth to produce unprecedented denominational growth.

The Civil War did not arrest this institutional growth; instead, like slavery, it spurred it. Pastors viewed their chief wartime task as the conversion of the army, in itself an astonishing departure from earlier practice. Evangelizing an army required an institutional base far beyond that of the local church, or even of statewide denominations. Defeat ended neither Southern pastors' dreams of organization nor their resolve to maintain a broadly public role for religion. Pastors and laymen persisted in their fund-raising and organizational expansion through Reconstruction and recession, begging financially savvy women to join them. By the end of the century, pastors controlled millions of dollars' worth of property and a vast network of agencies devoted both to religious benevolence and to raising the money required to sustain it.

The story of institutional religion in the nineteenth-century South is rich in irony. The minds that built these institutions were born in the slave South and deeply committed to slavery; indeed, slavery provided both the incentive and the means for their growth, particularly during the 1850s. In the end, pastors succeeded too well. By 1900, the institutions they had designed to expand their authority only contained it. For reasons they never fully understood, religion seemed to matter less, and their social authority had not grown along with their denominations. Some continued their search for social authority in Progressive reforms, such as Prohibition, to try to make religion matter as it had in the already legendary days of old-time religion.

But old-time religion had never been very old-time at all. Instead of looking back, nineteenth-century religion looked forward. To be sure, it embraced nostalgia—such a pure strain of nostalgia that historians have mistaken it for the real thing. Nineteenth-century pastors deceived themselves with such talk and have persuaded historians to neglect the vast record of their institution building. But the shrewdest innovators always clothe their projects in nostalgia, particularly in the South. The impassioned reaction to the vision of religious progress—first in the Primitive Baptist and Christian movements of the 1830s, later in the Landmark Baptist, Holiness, and Pentecostal movements— laid bare the self-deception in this nostalgia. These fierce attempts to recover the pristine ideals of the early church from the sullied hands of denominational bureaucrats—and the counterreformations they sparked—give the lie to formulations of a monolithic "Southern evangelicalism."

The question remains as to what drove clergy and laity in the South to embrace this vision of religious progress. Their vision was not rooted in postmillennial dreams, like that of Northern Republicans. The pastors in this book had an abiding aversion to millennial speculation of any kind. Such speculation did not fire their dreams of a better world. Instead, the cold social fact of slavery weighed them down, mocking any millennial hopes of a perfected society. The growth of religious institutions did not end Southerners' long fascination with revivals and emotional religion. Even the most devoted bureaucrats were forced to turn inward, toward the possibility of their own revival, in a society in which the best-laid plans of organized religion could not usher in the Kingdom.

Appendix

A Note on Sources and Methods

At the heart of this study are 400 Methodist and 400 Baptist pastors who preached in Virginia between approximately 1830 and 1900. I found these men in two series of books. John James Lafferty, editor of the Methodist *Richmond Christian Advocate*, published three volumes of his *Sketches and Portraits of the Virginia Conference* in 1880, 1890, and 1901. These books contain 673 biographical sketches of almost all of the full-time pastors in the Virginia Conference of the Methodist Episcopal Church, South, at the time of their publication. Lafferty obtained his information chiefly from his subjects themselves. I supplemented this self-reported information by reading these pastors' obituaries, published in the Virginia Annual Conference Minutes between 1873 and 1941.

The Baptists are drawn from a series of similar volumes on the Baptist General Association of Virginia, the third through sixth series of *Virginia Baptist Ministers*, edited by George Braxton Taylor, and published in 1912, 1913, 1915, and 1935. Unlike Lafferty, Taylor compiled his information from published obituaries of his subjects and arranged them chronologically according to date of death. Taylor's books were not comprehensive—they were probably biased towards full-time pastors.

From these sketches, I compiled data on birth, family, education, and career path. I divided the pastors into three generations according to their date of ordination. Generation I was ordained between 1830 and 1849, Generation II between 1850 and 1879, and Generation III in 1880 and after. In some cases, I divided Generation II into two groups: those ordained before the war, 1850–61, and those during and after, 1862–79.

The data are weakest for the antebellum period. In 1850, the men in my study represented 11 percent of all pastors in the state, 38 percent of all Southern Methodists in Virginia, and 19 percent of all Regular Baptists. For Methodists, my sample accounted for 38 percent of all Methodist pastors in 1850, 53 percent of all in 1860, and 99 percent of all in 1880.

Figures on slaveholding for antebellum pastors (see chapter 4) were compiled from microfilmed copies of the manuscript slave schedules for Virginia from the 1850 U.S. census held at the Library of Virginia. For 283 pastors working in antebellum Virginia, the resident counties for 60 were not found, and 16 were known to have resided out of state in 1850. I searched for 207 names in the slave schedules, and identified 79, or 38 percent, as slaveholders. Of these, 10 percent owned half of all the slaves in this sample.

Data on postwar salaries for Virginia Methodist pastors (see chapter 7) were compiled for one hundred men, chosen at random from my postwar group, from annual figures published between 1873 and 1900 in the *Minutes* of the Virginia Conference of the Methodist Episcopal Church, South.

Table 1 Church Members by Denomination and Region in Virginia, 1850

	East†		Valley		West		Total	
	Count	%	Count	%	Count	%	Count	%
Reg Bapt	77350	61	3679	9	8776	27	89805	42
Meth	40496	32	31363	74	20781	63	92640	43
Episc	4397	3	735	2	212	1	5344	3
Presby O.S.	4172	3	5729	13	2980	9	12881	6
Presby N.S.	1356	1	875	2	25	0	2256	1
Total	127,771	100	42,381	100	32,774	100	215,626*	100

† Eastern Virginia probably means the region east of the Blue Ridge Mountains.

* Includes 12,700 Methodist Protestants, which were not included in the other regional compilations.

Source: *A Map of the Baptist Churches of Virginia, 1850.*

Table 2 Population and Church Membership in Virginia

	1810	1860
Virginia population	878,000	1,220,000
Virginia Baptists#	35,164	108,888
Virginia Methodists*	25,432	47,726

First figure is from 1814.

* First figure is from 1812. Methodist figures are for the Virginia Conference, which included part of northeastern North Carolina, but excluded the Shenandoah Valley and southwest Virginia.

Sources: *Historical Statistics of the United States,* Part I; Sweet, *Virginia Methodism; Minutes,* Virginia Conference, 1873.

Table 3 Pastors' Age of Conversion

Age	Generation I		Generation II		Generation III	
	Count	Percent	Count	Percent	Count	Percent
<10	1	2	3	1	8	5
10–14	13	19	72	30	69	39
15–19	28	41	103	43	68	38
20–24	18	27	47	20	20	11
25–29	7	10	9	4	7	4
>29	1	2	6	3	6	3
Total	68	101*	240	101*	178	100
N =	123		382		290	
<24	60	89	225	94	165	93

Row N indicates total number of pastors from each generation; the age of conversion is not available for all pastors.

Row <24 indicates the composite of those converted at age 24 and younger.

* Percentages may not add to 100 owing to rounding off.

Table 4 Father's Profession

	Generation I		Generation II		Generation III	
	Count	Percent	Count	Percent	Count	Percent
Pastor	9	35	51	47	45	49
Pastor/Doctor	—	—	1	1	—	—
Pastor/Teach/Farm	—	—	1	1	—	—
Pastor/Teach/Insurance Agent	—	—	1	1	—	—
Pastor/Editor	—	—	1	1	—	—
Farmer	8	31	22	20	26	29
Farmer/Merchant	—	—	1	1	—	—
Teacher	—	—	1	1	2	2
Teacher/Surveyor	—	—	1	1	—	—
Teacher/Farmer	—	—	1	1	—	—
Teacher/Editor	—	—	1	1	—	—
Doctor	3	12	5	5	8	9
Merchant	1	4	4	4	1	1
Owner Cotton Warehouse	—	—	1	1	—	—
County Clerk	—	—	1	1	—	—
County Judge	—	—	—	—	2	1
Commonwealth Attorney	—	—	—	—	1	1
Sheriff	—	—	1	1	—	—
Lawyer	—	—	3	3	1	1
State Assembly	—	—	3	3	—	—
Administrator, Poor House	—	—	1	1	—	—
Currier	1	4	—	—	—	—
Furniture Maker	1	4	—	—	—	—
Tanner	—	—	1	1	—	—
Overseer	—	—	1	1	—	—
Lumberman	—	—	—	—	1	1

Table 4 **Father's Profession (Continued)**

	Generation I		Generation II		Generation III	
	Count	Percent	Count	Percent	Count	Percent
Fisherman	—	—	1	1	1	1
Plumber	—	—	—	—	1	1
Architect	—	—	1	1	—	—
Ship Captain	—	—	—	—	1	1
Railroad Engineer	—	—	—	—	1	1
Musician	1	4	2	2	—	—
Toll Keeper	—	—	1	1	—	—
"Wealthy"	2	8	—	—	—	—
Total identified	26	102*	108	102*	91	98*
Number of pastors in sample	123		382		289	

* Percentages may not add to 100 owing to rounding off.

Table 5 **Previous Professions of Antebellum Pastors**

	Generation I		Generation II (prewar)	
	Count	Percent	Count	Percent
Teacher	18	37	33	45
Teacher/Lawyer	1	2	—	—
Teacher/Clerk	2	4	—	—
Teacher/"Business"	1	2	—	—
Teacher/Editor	1	2	—	—
Singing Teacher	1	2	—	—
School Superintendent	1	2	—	—
Teacher/Doctor	—	—	1	1
Doctor/Dentist	3	6	5	7
Doctor/Farmer	1	2	1	1
Druggist	—	—	1	1
Farmer	6	12	5	7
Farmer/Miller	—	—	2	3
"Business"	1	2	5	7
Clerk	2	4	2	3
Merchant	1	2	1	1
Lawyer	1	2	10	14
Apprentice/Trades	4	8	1	1
Sawmill Owner	1	2	—	—
Miller	1	2	1	1
Surveyor	—	—	1	1
Editor	4	8	1	1
Printer	—	—	1	1
Colporteur	—	—	3	4
Total Identified	50	101*	74	99*
Total Teachers	25	51	34	46
N =	123		76	

* Percentages may not add to 100 owing to rounding off.

Generation I: ordained between 1830 and 1849.

Generation II (prewar): ordained between 1850 and 1861.

Table 6 Highest Educational level,
Generation I (Ordained 1830–49)

Education	Percent
Self-educated	7
Local academy	17
Denominational college	17
Other college	5
University of Virginia	5
Theological seminary	4
Unknown	45
All college	31
Sample size	123

Table 7 Lay and Ordained
Pastors in Virginia Conference,
M.E. Church, South

Year	Lay	Ordained
1850	189	124
1855	186	156
1860	174	198

Source: *Minutes,* Virginia Annual Conference, 1875.

Table 8 Highest Educational Levels of Antebellum Pastors

	Generation I		Generation II (prewar)	
	Count	Percent	Count	Percent
Self-educated	9	7	7	5
Academy	21	17	20	13
Denominational college	21	17	49	33
Other college or seminary	11	9	31	21
University of Virginia	6	5	15	10
Unknown	55	45	28	19
Total	123	100	150	101*
Total college	38	31	95	63

Generation I, ordained about 1830–49; Generation II (prewar), ordained 1850–61.

* Percentages may not add to 100 owing to rounding off.

Table 9 Percentage of White Children Enrolled in School, 1860

State	Whites in School	White Children†	Percent
Kentucky	182,450	459,742	40
Tennessee	162,970	413,361	39
Mississippi	66,522	176,949	38
Alabama	98,090	263,135	37
N. Carolina	116,434	314,971	37
S. Carolina	46,225	145,650	32
Texas	63,614	210,445	30
Virginia	154,922	523,649	30
Louisiana	47,748	178,728	27
Arkansas	42,721	162,071	26
Florida	8,494	38,873	22
Georgia	44,128	295,775	15
Connecticut	88,558	225,752	39
New York	799,856	1,915,795	42
Maryland	78,320	257,959	30
Ohio	599,985	1,151,404	52
Kansas	13,318	53,195	25

† Estimated at half of the total white population.

Source: U.S. Census, 1860.

Table 10 Percentage of White Population Illiterate, 1860

State	Total Whites	Illiterate	Percent
N. Carolina	629,942	68,128	11
Tennessee	826,722	70,359	9
Georgia	591,550	43,684	7
Kentucky	919,484	67,577	7
Arkansas	324,143	23,642	7
Virginia	1,047,299	74,055	7
Alabama	526,271	37,605	7
Florida	77,746	5,341	7
S. Carolina	291,300	14,792	5
Louisiana	357,456	17,808	5
Mississippi	353,899	15,526	4
Texas	420,891	18,414	4
Connecticut	451,504	8,488	2
New York	3,831,590	115,965	3
Maryland	515,918	15,819	3
Ohio	2,302,808	58,642	3
Kansas	106,390	3,044	3

Source: U.S. Census, 1860.

Table 11 Churches in Virginia, 1850*–1860

	Baptist	Methodist	Episcopal	Presbyterian
No. Churches, 1850	649	1025	173	244
No. Churches, 1860	787	1403	188	290
Percent Increase	21%	37%	9%	22%
Accommodations,† 1850	247,589	323,708	79,648	103,625
Accommodations,† 1860	298,024	438,244	68,498	117,304
Percent Increase	20%	35%	−15%	13%
Property Value, 1850	$688,518	$725,003	$529,450	$571,165
Property Value, 1860	$1,243,505	$1,619,010	$873,120	$901,020
Percent Increase	80%	123%	65%	58%

* Does not specify Regular or Antimission Baptist, Methodist Episcopal South or North, or Old or New School Presbyterian.

† Number of seats in all churches

Source: U.S. Census, 1850 and 1860.

Table 12 Average Values and Seats per Church in Virginia, 1850–1860 by Denomination

Denomination	Average Church Values			Average Seats Per Church		
	1850	1860	Increase	1850	1860	Increase
Baptist	$1,061	$1,580	49%	300	380	27%
Methodist	$707	$1,154	63%	310	310	0%
Episciscopal	$3,060	$4,644	52%	460	360	−22%
Presbyterian	$2,380	$3,107	31%	431	404	−6%

Source: U.S. Census, 1850 and 1860.

Table 13 Clergy with Confederate Service

	No. of Pastors	No. in Service	Percent
Generation I	123	18	15
Generation II 1850–61	150	52	35
Generation II 1862–79	232	96	41
Generation II total	382	148	39
Generation III	289	5	2
Total, Generations I, II, and III	794	171	22

Table 14 Pastors of Military Age with Army Service

Denomination	Number	Veterans	Percent
Baptists	221	93	42
Methodists	137	63	46
Total	358	156	44
With 18% mortality		184	51

Table 15 Confederate Chaplains (Methodist and Baptist)

Level of Education	Count	Percent
Self-educated	1	2
Academy	6	10
College	34	59
Theological seminary	8	14
Education unknown	9	15
Total	58	100

Percent of college-educated pastors from generation I & II prewar = 37%.

Percent of college-educated army chaplains = 59%.

Table 16 Veterans Ordained 1866–70

Date of Conversion	Count	Percent
Before war	13	33
During war	6	15
After war	7	18
Unknown	14	35
Total	40*	

* 17 Methodist, 23 Baptist.

Table 17 Virginia Population and Church Membership, 1880–1900

	1880	1900	% Growth
State population	1,513,000	1,854,000	23
White population	881,000	1,020,000	16
Urban population	189,000	340,000	80
Methodist/Baptist membership	125,105	212,935	70
Methodist/Baptist urban membership	16,099	39,598	146

Sources: U.S. Census, 1880 and 1900; *Minutes,* Baptist General Association of Virginia; *Minutes,* Virginia Annual Conference.

Table 18 Sunday Schools in Virginia

Year	Schools	Teachers and Students
Regular Baptist		
1876	411	34,041
1900	870	76,137
Methodist, South		
1873	537	35,678
1900	769	70,926

Sources: *Minutes,* Virginia General Baptist Association; *Minutes,* Virginia Annual Conference.

Table 19 Baptist versus Methodist Giving per Member, 1880 and 1900

	Urban	Total
Baptist, 1880	$.82	$.29
Baptist, 1900	$1.15	$.69
Methodist, 1880	$10.63	$4.24
Methodist, 1900	$11.75	$5.88

Sources: *Minutes,* Virginia Annual Conference; *Minutes,* Virginia Baptist General Association.

Table 20 Father's Profession

	Generation II Prewar* (%); N=40	Generation II Postwar* (%); N=69
Preacher	43	55
Farmer	25	19
Doctor	8	3
Lawyer	3	3
Merchant	5	4
Public Official	8	4
Musician	3	1
Teacher	3	4
Architect	3	0
Overseer	3	0
Fisherman	0	1
Owner Cotton Warehouse	0	1
Toll Keeper	0	1
Tanner	0	1

* Generation II prewar: ordained 1850–61.

† Generation II postwar: ordained 1862–79.

Table 21 Education

	Generation II Prewar (%); N=150	Generation II Postwar (%); N=232
Self-educated	5	4
Academy	13	10
Denominational College	33	33
Other College	23	20
Theological Seminary	8	15
All College	63	68
Unknown	19	19

Table 22 Previous Profession

	Generation II Prewar (%); N=74	Generation II Postwar (%); N=90
Teacher	45	62
Lawyer	14	6
Business	11	8
Farmer	9	7
Doctor	9	4
Printer/Editor	3	7
Colporteur	4	4
Surveyor	1	0
Miller	1	0
Shoemaker	1	0
Druggist	1	0
Bookkeeper	0	2

Table 23 Education

	Generation II Postwar (%)	Generation III (%)
No Secondary Education	18	17
Self-educated	4	3
Academy	10	10
State Denominational College	33	37
Other College	20	6
Theological Seminary	15	26
Total	100	100
Percent with College or Seminary Education	68	70

Table 24 Previous Profession

	Generation II Postwar (%)	Generation III (%)
Teacher	62	31
Farmer	7	5
Business	8	31
Lawyer	6	10
Doctor	4	0
Editor	7	4
Pharmacist	0	1
Accountant	2	1
Engineer	0	1
Cavalry	0	1
Colporteur	4	1
Missionary	0	2
Telegraph	0	1
Railroad	0	2
Coalminer	0	1
Carpenter	0	2
Worker	0	3
Iron Worker	0	4

Table 25 Father's Profession

	Generation II Postwar (%)	Generation III (%)
Preacher	55	49
Farmer	19	29
Doctor	3	9
Teacher	4	2
County Judge	0	2
Lumber	0	1
Law	3	1
Merchant	4	1
Ship Captain	0	1
Commonwealth Attorney	0	1
Railroad Engineer	0	1
Plumber	0	1
Fisherman	1	1
Public Official	4	0
Musician	1	0
Architect	1	0
Cotton Warehouse Owner	1	0
Toll Keeper	1	0
Tanner	1	0

Table 26 Clerical Temperance Leaders, 1870s–1880s

	School*	Profession	Principal Residence
John E. Massey Baptist, b. 1819	UR	Law	Albemarle
William W. Bennett Methodist, b. 1821	UVA	College president, editor	Richmond
Austin E. Owen Baptist, b. 1837	UR	Colporteur	Portsmouth
William E. Hatcher Baptist, b. 1834	UR	—	Richmond
William W. Jones Baptist, b. 1836	SBTS	Author	Richmond, Charlottesville
George W. Beale Baptist, b. ?	SBTS	General, politician	—
John Pollard Baptist, b. 1839	Columbian	Professor	Richmond
W.F. Dunaway Baptist, b. ?	No college	Lawyer, politican	—
Francis M. Edwards Methodist, b. 1826	No college	Teacher	Farmville, Danville, Portsmouth
W.W. Smith Methodist, b. 1845	UVA, R-M	Professor	Richmond
John Hannon Methodist, b. 1845	R-M	Bookkeeper	Richmond, Lynchburg
William W. Lear Methodist, b. 1844	R-M	Teacher	Rural, Petersburg
John R. Moffett Baptist, b. 1858	SBTS	Editor	Danville
James Cannon Jr. Methodist, b. 1864	Princeton	Teacher	Farmville, Portsmouth

UR, University of Richmond; UVA, University of Virginia; SBTS, Southern Baptist Theological Seminary; Columbian, Columbian College (Washington, D.C.); R-M, Randolph-Macon College; Princeton, Princeton University.

Notes

Abbreviations Used in the Notes

UVa   Alderman Library, University of Virginia
VBHS   Virginia Baptist Historical Society, University of Richmond
R-M   Virginia Conference Collection, McGraw-Page Library, Randolph- Macon College
LOV   Library of Virginia
VHS   Virginia Historical Society

Introduction

1. Jeter, *Recollections of a Long Life*; Hatcher, *Life of J. B. Jeter*; Loveland, *Southern Evangelicals and the Social Order*, pp. 1–7. For comment to his wife, see Hatcher, *Life of J. B. Jeter*, p. 213. On the country, see Jeter, "Let All Things Be Done Decently and in Order," *Religious Herald*, 18 September 1845, p. 3.

2. Steel diary, 18 September 1875, 5 October 1876, UVa.

3. Scholars ranging from C. Vann Woodward to Sydney E. Ahlstrom to George Marsden have described Southern theology and churches as antimodern. A growing body of history explores the meaning of progress among white Southerners in the nineteenth century, but it has not considered religion. Woodward, *Origins of the New South*, pp. 451–52; Ahlstrom, *A Religious History of the American People*, Vol. 2, p. 170; Marsden, *Fundamentalism and American Culture*, p. 103. On "progressive" Southerners, see Genovese, *The Slaveholders' Dilemma*; O'Brien, "Modernization and the Nineteenth-Century South," in O'Brien, ed., *Rethinking the South*, and "W. J. Cash, Hegel, and the South"; Thornton, *Power and Politics in a Slave Society*; Crofts, *Old Southampton*; Howe, "The Evangelical Movement and Political Culture in the North during the Second Party System."

4. Twentieth-century scholars now view fundamentalism, evangelicalism, and Pentecostalism as a response to modernity, as "modernity itself creates certain circumstances that evoke the bold reassertion of religious meanings" (James Hunter, *American Evangelicalism*, p. 134). This is an immense and rapidly growing body of work. For the

basics, see Max Weber, "The Social Psychology of World Religions," in Gerth and Mills, eds., *From Max Weber*; John Wilson, "Modernity."

5. For this insight, I am indebted to Donald Mathews.

6. For a summary of the literature on professions, industrialization, and modernization, see Haber, *The Quest for Authority and Honor in the American Professions*, pp. ix–xiv.

7. The extent to which the captivity thesis has discouraged creative and subtle analysis of the white church is thrown into sharp relief when its history is compared to the rich literature on African American churches. See, for example, Raboteau, *Slave Religion*; Genovese, *Roll, Jordan, Roll*, pp. 159–284; Levine, *Black Culture and Black Consciousness*, chapters 1 and 3; Orlando Patterson, *Slavery and Social Death*, pp. 66–76; Sobel, *Trabelin' On*; Higginbotham, *Righteous Discontent*; Dvorak, *African-American Exodus*.

8. The cultural captivity thesis bears the stamp of Wilbur J. Cash's 1941 classic, *The Mind of the South*, which stressed continuity and unity in Southern history. Like Cash, the captivity thesis is concerned primarily with white Southerners. A new generation of scholarship is beginning to challenge captivity, but it remains the prevailing interpretation in studies of the region. On captivity, see S. Hill, *Southern Churches in Crisis*; Eighmy, *Churches in Cultural Captivity*. Challenges to the captivity thesis have come from Harvey, *Redeeming the South*; Owen, *Sacred Flame of Love*; Wills, *Democratic Religion*; and Stowell, *Rebuilding Zion*.

9. Donald Mathews has pointed out how evangelicals' proslavery stand has made them particularly distasteful to historians (*Religion in the Old South*, pp. xv–xvi).

10. Taylor, *Life and Times of James Boardman Taylor*, p. 53.

11. Isaac, *Transformation of Virginia*.

12. Hatch, *Democratization of American Christianity*, p. 195.

13. The phrase is Donald Mathews', *Religion in the Old South*, p. 1.

14. A student of Southern women noted that every journal and diary by antebellum slaveholding women mentions the church; few of them fail to "comment on the texts of sermons, the quality of preaching, or even points of theology." Fox-Genovese, *Within the Plantation Household*, p. 44 n. 13.

15. The lack of attention to the nineteenth-century clergy contrasts sharply with studies of the seventeenth and eighteenth century, especially in New England. An exception is Haber, *Quest for Authority and Honor in the American Professions*. See also Scott, *From Office to Profession*; and Bledstein, *The Culture of Professionalism*. Nearly every study of the American South has noted Protestantism's critical role in the region. For the antebellum period, see Mathews, *Religion in the Old South*; Loveland, *Southern Evangelicals and the Social Order*; Holifield, *Gentlemen Theologians*; Boles, *Great Revival*; Sparks, *On Jordan's Stormy Banks*; and Heyrman, *Southern Cross*. The clergy have most often been studied in the context of secession and Civil War: Faust, *Creation of Confederate Nationalism*; Snay, *Gospel of Disunion*; Silver, *Confederate Morale and Church Propaganda*; and Beringer, et al., *Why the South Lost the Civil War*. A good older study of postwar Methodists is Farish, *Circuit Rider Dismounts*. Other helpful studies include Ownby, *Subduing Satan*; and C. Wilson, *Baptized in Blood*. Most helpful for the 1890s is Bode, *Protestantism and the New South*. Sociologist Liston Pope's analysis of the background of the Gastonia strikes, *Millhands and Preachers: A Study of Gastonia*, remains one of the best studies of the Southern clergy. See also K. Bailey, *Southern White Protestantism in the Twentieth Century*.

16. After 1830, the percentage fell below 30 percent. For the entire period, 513

ministers left Virginia. D. Bailey, *Shadow on the Church*, pp. 27, 62, 132, 198; Sweet, *Virginia Methodism*, pp. 171–77.

17. Faust, *The Creation of Confederate Nationalism*, p. 81.

Chapter 1

1. Baldwin diary, introduction, VBHS.

2. Baldwin diary, 2 December 1894, VBHS.

3. "Daniel Gray Taylor, 1821–1890," Taylor, *Virginia Baptist Ministers*, Fourth Series, 1913, p. 65; obituary, William A. Crocker (1825–1901), *Minutes*, Virginia Conference, 1901, p. 39; "Jacob Manning, 1816–1898," *Minutes*, Virginia Conference, 1898, p. 34; "Davis P. Wills, 1816–1895," *Minutes*, Virginia Conference, 1895, p. 39.

4. Virginia Catherine Harwood, "Rev. Noah Carlton Baldwin," *Addresses delivered before the Historical Society of Washington County, Virginia*. (Abingdon, Va.: Washington County Historical Society, 1945).

5. Bruce, *Virginia Iron Manufacture in the Slave Era*, chapters 7 and 8; Beeman, *Evolution of the Southern Backcountry*; Lewis, *The Pursuit of Happiness*; Lebsock, *Free Women of Petersburg*; Goldfield, *Urban Growth in the Age of Sectionalism*; Andrews, *Virginia: The Old Dominion*; Davis, *Intellectual Life in Jefferson's Virginia*; Schlotterbeck, "The 'Social Economy' of an Upper South Community"; Mitchell, *Hollywood Cemetery*, chapter 3; Ayers and Willis, eds. *The Edge of the South*.

6. In these 34 towns and cities, 82,111 whites, 10,494 free blacks, and 32,030 slaves resided, for a total of 124,635 people; U.S. census of 1850, Table II, Population of Cities and Towns, p. 258.

7. Gray, *Writing the South*, pp. 18–30.

8. Methodist membership grew by 3.6 percent between 1845 and 1850, while state population grew less than 1 percent for the decade after 1840. For quote, Richey, *Early American Methodism*, p. 49; on membership, *Minutes*, Virginia Annual Conference, 1875, Appendix I, n.p.; Sweet, *Virginia Methodism*, pp. 142, 187.

9. Virginia Baptist membership grew at an annual rate of 3.9 percent between 1814 and 1845; Virginia population grew at 0.88 percent annually. Baker, *Southern Baptist Convention*, pp. 105–26.

10. On O'Kelly, see Wigger, *Taking Heaven by Storm*, pp. 39–42.

11. Goss, *Statistical History of the First Century of American Methodism*; Hatch, *Democratization of American Christianity*, p. 3; Ahlstrom, *Religious History of the American People*, Vol. 1, p. 537.

12. "To Our Readers," *Religious Herald*, 4 January 1844, p. 2.

13. Mathews, "The Second Great Awakening as an Organizing Process."

14. McCurry, *Masters of Small Worlds*; Heyrman, *Southern Cross*; Mathews, *Religion in the Old South*, pp. 37–38; and Schneider, "The Ritual of Happy Dying." On the diverse constituency of antebellum revivals, see Owsley, *Plain Folk of the Old South*, pp. 98–102; Friedman, *Enclosed Garden*, pp. 3–4; Oakes, *Ruling Race*, pp. 97–98.

15. Interview with Armaci Adams of Hampton, Virginia, in Perdue, et al., eds., *Weevils in the Wheat*, p. 1.

16. Interview with Horace Tonsler of Charlottesville, Virginia, in ibid., p. 286.

17. Jeter, *Recollections of a Long Life*, p. 19; Olmsted, *Journey in the Seaboard Slave States*, p. 74.

18. Rhys Isaac (*Transformation of Virginia*) has noted the importance of simplicity

for eighteenth-century Virginia Baptists. For a contemporary view, see Hundley, *Social Relations in Our Southern States*, pp. 55–57.

19. Taylor, *Virginia Baptist Ministers*, Fifth Series, pp. 249–50; Taylor, *Virginia Baptist Ministers*, Third Series, pp. 61–62.

20. For William Harris, see Taylor, *Virginia Baptist Ministers*, Third Series, pp. 61–62; and Jeter, *Recollections of a Long Life*, pp. 57, 87–88.

21. Hymn by James Newton, noted for use "After Baptism," *The Baptist Psalmody*, p. 554.

22. Charles Alexander Gregory to Herbert Tyree Bacon, 4 October 1845, and Lucy Frances Gregory to Herbert Tyree Bacon, 11 October 1845, Gregory Family Papers, Section Eight, VHS; Thomas Early to "My dear Fannie," 9 March 1859, Early Family Papers, R-M.

23. Walter Sawyer and Stonewall Jackson Brown in Lafferty, *Virginia Sketches* (1890), pp. 185, 220; R. R. Burton Diary, 20 October 1855, VBHS. On women and religion, Kierner, "Women's Piety within Patriarchy"; Fox-Genovese, *Within the Plantation Household*; Friedman, *Enclosed Garden*; Heyrman, *Southern Cross*.

24. Mead, "Rise of the Evangelical Conception of the Ministry," p. 231. Quotation is from Jeremiah B. Jeter, "Ordination," *Religious Herald*, 16 July 1840, p. 1.

25. *Religious Herald*, 30 April and 7 May 1840, p. 3. See also notes on "Pastoral Theology" in C. H. Ryland's Notebook, 1859–1860, Southern Baptist Theological Seminary, Greenville, S.C., VBHS; Robert Ryland to "My Dear Willie," 31 August 1854, VBHS.

26. Wills, *Democratic Religion*, pp. 50-66; Daniel, "Bedford Baptists, 1840–1860."

27. *Sketches of History of the Baptist Churches within the Limits of the Rappahannock Association*. On the number of women, Mathews, *Religion in the Old South*, pp. 47–48; Friedman, *Enclosed Garden*, p. 4; Ownby, *Subduing Satan*, p. 129.

28. Lucy Frances Gregory to Herbert Tyree Bacon, 11 October 1845, Gregory Family Papers, VHS; "R. N. Sledd, 1833–1899," *Minutes*, Virginia Annual Conference, 1899, p. 41; Wyatt-Brown, *Southern Honor*, p. 125.

29. Wyatt-Brown notes that "not many whites below the high gentility were in a position to gain status or livelihood by entering some occupation outside agricultural enterprise" and that "in the South, the ministry lacked social standing unless it was coupled with plantation ownership" (*Southern Honor*, pp., 176, 187).

30. Methodist Thomas J. Wray (1858–1906) was converted by his preacher brother at his father's fireside (*Minutes*, Virginia Annual Conference, 1906, p. 48). Also Potts, "Potts Family of Preachers," pp. 3–4, R-M; Robert Ryland to "My dear Willie," 31 August 1854, VBHS; Ryland to "To My Dear Preacher," 21 September 1860, VBHS.

31. On preaching and teaching, see Owsley, *Plain Folk of the Old South*, p. 145. For career patterns in the antebellum North, see Brown, *Knowledge Is Power*, chapter 9. Wyatt-Brown (*Southern Honor*, pp. 186–87) has argued that teaching had low status in the antebellum South. This may explain why many young men left the classroom for the pulpit.

32. Pritchett in Lafferty, *Virginia Sketches* (1880), p. 116; Tennille in Lafferty, *Virginia Sketches* (1880), pp. 146–47.

33. Reed was the father of Dr. Walter Reed. Lemuel Sutton Reed, "An Itinerant's Meditations," *The Methodist Recorder* (Farmville), 1 October 1894, pp. 5–6.

34. On speculation about pastoral appointments, see W. R. D. Moncure to Edward Garlick Gwathmey, 30 August 1859, Gwathmey Family Papers, VHS. On conflicts between pastors, see Thomas Early to Mary Early Brown, 23 May 1858, Early Family Papers, R-M.

35. Baldwin Diary, 29 April 1855, VBHS.

36. Eaton, *The Itinerant's Wife*, p. 8; Rev. Thomas White Sydnor to Miss Sarah L. M. Chapin, May(?) 1838, Thomas W. Sydnor Papers, UVa. See also Baldwin Diary, 1 April 1855, VBHS; Edward Portlock Wilson Diary, entries for the year 1846, R-M; and Mathews, *Religion in the Old South*, pp. 239–40.

37. R. R. Burton Diary, 15 March 1857, VBHS.

38. Ibid., August 25 1849, VBHS; Elizabeth Rice Lacy Hoge to Samuel Davies Hoge, quoted in Hoge, *Moses Drury Hoge: Life and Letters*, p. 25.

39. In the early part of the century, some pastors earned less than $100 per year. Sweet, *Virginia Methodism*, p. 44. Parsonages were rare until after the Civil War. "John Gallatin Rowe," *Minutes*, Virginia Annual Conference, 1891, p. 41. Methodist preacher James A. Riddick bartered a modest education and a start as a mercantile clerk into a comfortable fortune in land and slaves by midlife. James Andrew Riddick to William Gray, 30 December 1858, William Gray Papers, VHS; "Rev. James Andrew Riddick," in Lafferty, *Virginia Sketches* (1890), pp. 4–5.

40. William F. Broaddus (1801–1876), quoted in Moore, ed., "A Nineteenth-Century Minister's Problems."

41. First quotation, R. R. Burton Diary, 21 November 1852, VBHS; second quotation, "A Query," *Religious Herald*, 14 November 1850.

42. Courtney performed more than 1,600 weddings between 1816 and 1865, not counting slave couples. He also served as the teacher of the Richmond Lancasterian School. See Courtney, Marriage Register, 1816–1865, LOV; Ernst, "Urban Leaders and Social Change." Rural Methodist Robert Wilkins Berryman recorded $26 in fees from 13 weddings in 1851. Berryman Marriage Register, 1844–1890, LOV.

43. Wilson Diary, undated entry, R-M. On public debates on doctrine, see Baldwin Diary, 30 July 1852, VBHS.

44. "Cornelius Tyree, 1814–1891" in Taylor, *Virginia Baptist Ministers*, Fourth Series, pp. 130–131; Eli Ball, "Minister's Library," *Religious Herald*, 11 January 1844.

45. Helsabeck Diary, 13 January 1856, Southern Historical Collection, University of North Carolina at Chapel Hill, (SHC).

46. Baldwin Diary, 29 May 1851; 15 July 1852, VBHS.

47. Wilson Diary, R-M; Steel Diary, UVa.

48. Taylor, *George Boardman Taylor*, pp. 53–54.

49. Richard Andrew Fox, sermon on Ezekiel 33:8, 1878, VHS; Baldwin Diary, 4 June 1851, VBHS.

50. "Friends are kind, giving warm fires and good beds," one weary man wrote in 1856 (Helsabeck diary, SHC, 29 January 1856). For Wilson, *Minutes*, Virginia Conference, 1895, p. 43; Thomas Clarke Goggin, 1815–1895, in Taylor, *Virginia Baptist Ministers*, Fourth Series, p. 278; for Harrison, *Richmond Christian Advocate*, 7 July 1881, p. 1; George Holman Snead in Taylor, *Virginia Baptist Ministers*, Fifth Series, p. 309.

51. "Canal Reminiscences" in *Miscellaneous Writings of Dr. George W. Bagby*, pp. 125–26.

52. Cf. T. Hall, *Contested Boundaries*.

53. The incident probably occurred during the 1850s. Joseph Henry Amiss (b. 1834) in Lafferty, *Virginia Sketches* (1880), p. 90.

54. John O. Turpin, 1810–1884, in Taylor, *Virginia Baptist Ministers*, Third Series, p. 368; Byrne, *No Foot of Land*, p. 84.

55. Beverly Jones (b. 1848), quoted in Perdue, et al., eds. *Weevils in the Wheat*, pp. 184–85.

56. Letter of Thornton Stringfellow, *Religious Herald*, 27 January 1842, p. 3.

57. Baldwin's Democratic congregation charged him with being a Know Nothing because he had criticized Roman Catholics. Baldwin Diary, 1 July 1855, 12 July 1858, 11 November 1860, VBHS.

58. Littlebury W. Allen, 1803–1872, in Taylor, *Virginia Baptist Preachers*, Third Series, p. 174; S. T. Moorman to *Richmond Christian Advocate*, 15 April 1847, quoted in Sweet, *Virginia Methodists*, p. 248.

59. This consensual, or fraternal, style of authority was typical of other relations in Southern society. Sociologist Steven Lukes does not view consensual authority as a strict exercise of power. Cash, *Mind of the South*, p. 115; Wyatt-Brown, *Southern Honor*, p. 69; Lukes, *Power: A Radical View*, pp. 26–33.

60. E. Hatcher, *William E. Hatcher*, p. 37; Broaddus in J. Moore, ed., "A Nineteenth-Century Minister's Problems."

61. Baptist congregations "called" a pastor; Methodist bishops appointed pastors. William Brooking Rowzie to William Gray, 6 November 1849, William Gray Papers, VHS.

62. Stewards Book, Centenary Methodist Church, Richmond, 1843–57, 2 December 1844, and Leaders' Book, Centenary Methodist Church, Richmond, 27 October 1851, LOV.

63. Wyatt-Brown (*Southern Honor*, p. xviii) has argued that church discipline was not a serious deterrent in Southern communities. Gregory A. Wills, by contrast, suggests that it was a serious threat that prevented many from seeking formal church membership (*Democratic Religion*, pp. 14–15). See also Ayers, *Vengeance and Justice*, pp. 120-23; Kenzer, *Kinship and Neighborhood in a Southern Community*, pp. 11–12.

64. Congregations "examined" the character of all members at each congregational meeting, and those who had a complaint against the behavior of a member were required to make their charge publicly, usually in the presence of the accused. Members could "withdraw" from a church without implication of wrongdoing, but were "excluded" or excommunicated only after they were found guilty of sin and refused to repent. See Wills, *Democratic Religion*. For discipline concerning economic behavior, see Baldwin Diary, 21 August 1852, VBHS; and Ford, *Origins of Southern Radicalism*, pp. 34–35. Also, "Rights and Powers of the Church," C. H. Ryland notebook, Southern Baptist Theological Seminary, Greenville, S.C., 1859–60, VBHS. Sometimes, churches reversed their decisions. In 1862, Centenary Church granted an appeal for a woman from the African Mission across town who had been expelled for "indulgence in improper words" because her pastor had neither privately reproved her nor given her the opportunity to repent, which she was willing to do. Stewards' Book, Centenary Methodist Church, Richmond, 1857–1867, 4 August 1862, LOV.

65. E. Hatcher, *William E. Hatcher*, p. 39; Affidavit of James Jones, n.d., Trial of Rev. C. D. Crawley, West Brunswick Circuit, August 1878, Virginia Conference Collection, R-M.

66. Burton Diary, 4 September 1853, VBHS.

67. E. Hatcher, *William E. Hatcher*, p. 39.

68. Letter to High Hills Baptist Church, 14 August 1829, *Minute Book*, pp. 39–43, quoted in Rosenburg, "John Davis Williams." On Mitchell, see Bogger, *Free Blacks in Norfolk*, pp. 145–50. Bogger suggests that black leaders used Mitchell as a "cover" in an era when black churches needed white leadership by law.

69. Stewards' Book, Centenary Methodist Church, Richmond, 1843–1857, LOV. See also scattered records of disciplinary trials, R-M.

70. "Pastoral Visits at Night," *Religious Herald*, 14 March 1861, p. 2; Robert Ryland to "My Dear Preacher," 21 January 1859, VBHS; *Religious Herald*, 28 March 1861, p. 2.

71. Wilson Diary, 30 December, year unknown [1840s?]; 13 May 1846, R-M.

72. Wilson in Lafferty, *Virginia Sketches* (1890).

Chapter 2

1. Holifield, *Gentlemen Theologians*, p. 6.

2. Jeter, *Recollections of a Long Life*; Hatcher, *Life of J. B. Jeter*; Loveland, *Southern Evangelicals and the Social Order*, pp. 1–4.

3. In the 1820s, only white freeholders could vote in Virginia. Although westerners agitated for liberalization of the franchise in the constitutional convention of 1829, Virginia did not practice universal white manhood suffrage until 1851. Freehling, *The Virginia Slavery Debate of 1831–32*, pp. 17–35.

4. Hatcher, *Life of J. B. Jeter*, p. 179.

5. Ibid., p. 213; Jeremiah B. Jeter, "Let All Things Be Done Decently and in Order," *Religious Herald*, 18 September 1845, p. 3.

6. Jeter, *The Life of Rev. Daniel Witt*, pp. 148–50; Daniel Witt to Thomas W. Sydnor, 20 September 1870, Sydnor Papers, UVa.

7. Witt, "Autobiography," in Jeter, *Life of Rev. Daniel Witt*, p. 64.

8. Haltunnen, *Confidence Men and Painted Women*, chapter 1; for letter of introduction, see Benjamin Wilkes to James Thomas, Jr., 4 January 1858, quoted in Kimball, "Place and Perception," p. 64; Kett, *Rites of Passage*, p. 94.

9. Cf. Kirby, Richey, and Rowe, *The Methodists*, pp. 261–65; Hatch, *Democratization of American Christianity*, pp. 210–16; Farmer, *Metaphysical Confederacy*.

10. Bender, *Toward an Urban Vision*, pp. 9–10.

11. Ibid.

12. Goldfield, *Urban Growth in the Age of Sectionalism* and "Communities and Regions." See also Kimball, "Place and Perception;" Lebsock, *Free Women of Petersburg*; Beeman, *Evolution of the Southern Backcountry*.

13. The best history of antebellum Richmond is Kimball, "Place and Perception." See also Goldfield, *Urban Growth in an Age of Sectionalism*; Tyler-McGraw, *At the Falls*; Tyler-McGraw and Kimball, *In Bondage and Freedom*.

14. Dickens, *American Notes and Pictures from Italy*, p. 136; Tocqueville, *Democracy in America*, p. 382.

15. Rates of church membership among black residents of cities far exceeded those for whites. In Richmond, for example, 25 percent of the black population were members of Baptist churches, and in Norfolk, 19 percent of the black population were Baptists. See *A Map of the Baptist Churches of Virginia*.

16. Joseph Martin, "New and Comprehensive Gazetteer of Virginia", Charlottesville, 1835, pp. 194–95, quoted in Bruce, *Virginia Iron Manufacture*, p. 260.

17. Bushman, *Refinement of America*, pp. 169–80. Richmonders were often keen critics of church architecture. See comments of Bessie Lacy, for example, quoted in Kimball, "Place and Perception," p. 83; also Loveland, *Southern Evangelicals and the Social Order*, pp. 43–44.

18. "The type of religion, the spiritual progress and needs, the Kingdom outlook of any company of people have, therefore, revealed themselves in the types of buildings produced." See Brunner, *The New Country Church Building*, p. 13; Sydnor, *First Baptist Church of Richmond*.

19. Baldwin Diary, 30 November 1860, VBHS.

20. The Methodist church in Portsmouth was also enlarged in 1841. *Minute Book*, Monumental Church Board of Trustees, Portsmouth, LOV.

21. Sydnor, *First Baptist Church of Richmond*, pp. 55–60.

22. George Braxton Taylor's Staunton church cost $9,250, of which the congregation could pay only $6,750. "Our Meeting House in Staunton," *Religious Herald*, 14 January, 1858, p. 2; untitled article, *Religious Herald*, 24 January 1856, p. 3; editorial, "Nickellsville, Church, Scott County, Virginia," *Religious Herald*, 1 May 1856, p. 2.

23. The pews were sold on 31 May 1843. Trustees Book 1839–1863, Centenary Methodist Church, Richmond, LOV; Stewards Book, 1843–1857, Centenary Methodist Church, Richmond, LOV. See also Bennett, *Methodist Church on Shockoe Hill*, pp. 29–37.

24. Bennett, *Methodist Church on Shockoe Hill*, pp. 42, 117. Reference to the controversy appeared in January 1879 editions of the *Richmond Christian Advocate*. See "Methodism in Richmond in 1846 and 1878," *Richmond Christian Advocate*, 16 January and 23 January 1879, p. 2.

25. James L. Powell, "Dedicating Meeting Houses," *Religious Herald*, 29 July 1852, p. 1.

26. Anonymous ["A Baptist"], "Choir Singing," *Religious Herald*, 18 March, 1858, p. 1. Interest in church interiors probably indicated the growing participation of women in church affairs. See Turner, "Women's Culture and Community."

27. "Elegant Churches and Rented Pews," *Religious Herald*, 11 February 1858, p. 1.; "A Little More Progress," *Religious Herald*, 25 February 1858, p. 1; "Elegant Churches and Rented Pews," *Religious Herald*, 4 March 1858, p. 1; "Rebuttal to Progress," *Religious Herald*, 18 March 1858, p. 1.

28. Alfred Wiles to Hon. John Young Mason, 21 May 1851, VHS. On Mason, see Virginius Cornick Hall Jr., *Portraits in the Collection of the Virginia Historical Society* (Charlottesville: University Press of Virginia, 1981), pp. 163–64; and *Dictionary of American Biography*, Vol. 12 (New York: Charles Scribner's Sons, 1937), pp. 369–70.

29. Robert Ryland, Jeremiah Jeter, and James Boardman Taylor, "To the Baptist Churches of Virginia," *Religious Herald*, 6 January 1842, p. 1; Henry Keeling, "Our Rising Ministry," *Religious Herald*, 8 June 1848, p. 3.

30. Holifield, *Gentlemen Theologians*, p. 16.

31. Historians have most often viewed denominational lines as contiguous with those of social status. Most Baptists and Methodists were less wealthy than most Episcopalians and Presbyterians, but by the 1840s, this was not always the case, particularly in town. See for example, Boles, ed., *Masters and Slaves in the House of the Lord*, p. 9.

32. Chester Raymond Young, "Primitive Baptists," in Samuel S. Hill, ed., *Encyclopedia of Religion in the South* (Macon, Ga.: Mercer University Press, 1985), pp. 37–38; 612–13. Cf. Wyatt-Brown, "The Antimission Movement in the Jacksonian South"; Ryland, *The Baptists of Virginia*, pp. 243–62. Historians have been reluctant to apply the ideas of "progress" or "reform" to Southern congregations, but nineteenth-century Southern Protestants themselves used the terms.

33. Baldwin Diary, 23 March and 5 April 1852, VBHS.

34. "A war is now commencing," a Pittsylvania County Baptist wrote on the eve of the Civil War in reference to the doctrinal dispute. "One more battle and the land is ours." See B. Hardwick, "Can Mission and Anti-Mission Churches Unite Consistently?" *Religious Herald*, 4 March 1858, p. 1. The answer, obviously, was no.

35. Wyatt-Brown, "Antimission Movement."

36. Carwardine, *Transatlantic Revivalism*, pp. 18–26; Doyle, *The Social Order of a Frontier Community*.

37. Differences between North and South were far less pronounced in cities. Lebsock, *Free Women of Petersburg*, p. 2. Daniel Walker Howe has argued that evangelical religion was prevented from being an agent of modernization in the antebellum South not only because of slavery but because of the region's "relative absence of cities," suggesting that, in Southern cities, evangelical churches functioned somewhat like their Northern counterparts ("The Evangelical Movement and Political Culture in the North during the Second Party System"). For another view, see Haber, *Quest for Authority and Honor in the American Professions*, and Pease and Pease, *The Web of Progress*.

38. Woolsey, *The Supernumerary; or Lights and Shadows of Itinerancy* (New York, 1852), quoted in Donald Edward Byrne Jr., "Methodist Itinerant Folklore of the Nineteenth Century with Particular Reference to Autobiography and Biography," Ph.D. diss., Duke University, 1972, p. 41; *Richmond Christian Advocate*, 30 June 1881, p. 1.

39. See Bruce, *Virginia Iron Manufacture*, chapter 7, for antagonism between planters and city residents. For salary, see Bennett, *Methodist Church on Shockoe Hill*, pp. 28, 41, 50.

40. Holifield, "The Penurious Preacher? Nineteenth-Century Clerical Wealth."

41. James Andrew Riddick to William Gray, 30 December 1858, William Gray Papers, VHS.

42. "The Estate of Reverend Bishop John Early in Account with Thomas H. Early His Executor," Early Family Papers, R-M.

43. Quoted in Holifield, *Gentlemen Theologians*, p. 22.

44. Seventy-nine percent of pastors ordained before 1850 were born in rural areas, whereas 83 percent of those ordained between 1850 and 1861 were rural born. On contrasts between rural and city spirituality, see "The Privileges of Rural Christians," *Religious Herald*, 17 August 1848, p. 1. For quote, Anonymous, "Communications," *Religious Herald*, 25 April 1844, p. 1. On the dullness of town life, see Taylor, *Rev. George Boardman Taylor*, pp. 52–53.

45. The Gillfield Baptist Church, for example, segregated when the congregation moved from just outside of Petersburg into town at the beginning of the nineteenth century. See Raboteau, *Slave Religion*, p. 142.

46. "The Colored Population of Virginia," *Religious Herald*, 25 May 1848, p. 3.

47. Raboteau, *Slave Religion*, p. 137; Phillips, *American Negro Slavery*, quoted in Larry M. James, "Biracial Fellowship in Antebellum Baptist Churches," in Boles, ed., *Masters and Slaves in the House of the Lord*; letter of James C. Clopton, *Religious Herald*, 8 August 1844, p. 3. Clopton notes that because of rapid increases in black membership in Lynchburg, it had become "utterly impossible" for whites and blacks to worship together.

48. On black preachers, Raboteau, *Slave Religion*, p. 136. Minutes of Second Baptist Church of Richmond, August 3, 1843, quoted in J. O'Brien, "Factory, Church, and Community: Blacks in Antebellum Richmond," p. 524.

49. Jeter, *Recollections of a Long Life*, p. 209. See also John A. Broadus, "Report of the Religious Instruction of the Colored People—Albemarle Association," *Religious Herald*, 23 October 1856, p. 1; and "Report of the Committee on the Colored Population Presented in the Rappahannock Association," *Religious Herald*, 3 September 1846, p. 2.

50. Jeter, *Recollections of a Long Life*, pp. 19–23; C. H. Ryland Notebook, Southern Baptist Theological Seminary, Greenville, S.C., 1859–60, VBHS.

51. Cornelius Tyree, 1814–1891, in Taylor, *Virginia Baptist Ministers*, Fourth Series, p. 130–131.

52. Mathews (*Religion in the Old South*, p. 183) called the instance of a Baptist pastor forced out of his South Carolina congregation in 1863 because he was too educated a "classic case in class conflict."

53. Nathan Hatch (*Democratization of American Christianity*, p. 205) has suggested that this divide was, in the long run, more significant than the divide between Northern and Southern branches of these denominations.

Chapter 3

1. G. Taylor, *The Life and Times of James B. Taylor* and *The Life and Letters of George Boardman Taylor*.

2. *Religious Herald*, 28 February, 1856, p. 3.

3. For a comparison of Northern and Southern views on education, see Pease and Pease, *The Web of Progress*, pp. 108–14.

4. Wyatt-Brown, *Southern Honor*, p. 99.

5. John Cralle Long (1833–1894) in Taylor, *Virginia Baptist Ministers*, Fourth Series, p. 209.

6. "When given a polite education, [the middle classes] usually prefer the company of gentlemen" (Hundley, *Social Relations in Our Southern States*, p. 95). See also Wyatt-Brown, *Southern Honor*, chapter 7.

7. Hundley, *Social Relations in Our Southern States*, chapter 2. On the North, see Brown, *Knowledge Is Power*, chapter 8.

8. On education reform, see Shade, *Democratizing the Old Dominion*, pp. 184–86. For Alabama, see Thornton, *Politics and Power in a Slave Society*, pp. 293–94, 300–2.

9. "S. S. S.," "A Hint to Politicians," *Religious Herald*, 13 February 1845, p. 3.

10. "Education," *Religious Herald*, 4 September 1845, p. 2; "Education," *Religious Herald*, 25 September 1845, p. 4; "To the Clergy of Virginia," *Religious Herald*, 2 October 1845, p. 4; "Education Convention," *Religious Herald*, 18 December 1845, p. 2; "Popular Education," *Religious Herald*, 12 September 1850, p. 2; Phipps, "Legislation Affecting Secondary Education in Virginia, chapter 14; Boitnott, "Secondary Education in Virginia," Moger, *Virginia: Bourbonism to Byrd*, p 2.

11. Letter of "Old-Fashioned Preacher," *Religious Herald*, 5 May 1852, p. 1. See also editorial, *Religious Herald*, 21 March 1850, p. 2.

12. "Circular Letter of Beulah Baptist Association," *Religious Herald*, 8 February 1844, p. 1.

13. Ministerial candidates were examined on "Divinity, History, English grammar, and Geography" ("Report of the Committee to Examine the Candidates for Admission," Raleigh, N.C., February 1828, John Early, Chairman, Virginia Conference Collection, R-M); "Course of Study for Local Preachers," undated clipping, *Richmond Christian Advocate*, John C. Granbery Scrapbook, R-M.

14. James A. Riddick to William Gray, 5 January 1858, William Gray Papers, VHS.

15. James Dryborough Lumsden, 1811–1887, and Joseph Henry Amiss, 1834–1916, in Lafferty, *Sketches of the Virginia Conference* (1880), pp. 25, 90.

16. C. H. Ryland Notebooks, Southern Baptist Theological Seminary, 1859–1860, VBHS.

17. See, for example, Hartwell Hobbs Gary, b. 1811, ordained in the 1840s, in Lafferty, *Sketches of the Virginia Conference* (1880), p. 28.

18. *Minutes*, Virginia Baptist Education Society, 1851, p. 47.

19. *The George Washington University, 1821–1966* (Washington, D.C.: Office of the University Historian, 1966); Alley, *History of the University of Richmond, 1830–1971*, pp. 2–22; Ryland, *The Baptists of Virginia*, chapter 12.

20. Scanlon, *Randolph-Macon*, chapters 1 and 2.

21. Mathews, *Religion in the Old South*, pp. 88–97.

22. Robert Ryland, President of Richmond College, for example, opposed the opening of a theological seminary for Southern Baptists in 1849. See Hatch, *Democratization of American Christianity*, p. 163; William Wright Barnes, *The Southern Baptist Convention, 1845-1953*, (Nashville:Broadman Press, 1954), p. 120.

23. "Richmond College," *Religious Herald*, 25 April 1861, p. 2; 2 May 1861, p. 1.

24. Lebsock, *Free Women of Petersburg*, pp. 174–75.

25. Sweet, *Virginia Methodism*, p. 310.

26. Doggett, *The Responsibility of Talent*, p. 14.

27. Crane, *Literary Discourses*, p. 28; Scanlon, *Randolph-Macon*, pp. 55–57; letter of Robert Ryland, quoted in Alley, *University of Richmond*, p. 16.

28. Thirty-eight Baptist and Methodist pastors ordained between 1830 and 1849 attended college. In 1845, approximately 403 Baptist and Methodist pastors preached in Virginia.

29. *Minutes*, Virginia Baptist Education Society, 1851, p. 47.

30. Crane, *Literary Discourses*, p. 32.

31. Two-thirds of the male colleges and more than half of all the female colleges operated by the Methodist Episcopal Church, South, in 1882 were founded in the antebellum period. Peterson, *Hand-Book of Southern Methodism*, pp. 97–99. On congregational schools, see "Reedy Spring Academy, 1840–1875, Spout Spring, Appomattox County, Virginia" typescript by Harriet A. Chilton, 1976, 1980 rev., VBHS. Antebellum enrollment at Richmond College peaked in 1856. For the school as the center of intellectual life, see Robert Ryland, "Richmond College," *Religious Herald*, 1 February 1844, p. 3. For the college, see Daniel, "The Genesis of Richmond College," pp. 131–49; and Ryland, *The Baptists of Virginia*, p. 289. Sweet, *Virginia Methodism*, pp. 322–23.

32. "Maternal Association," *Religious Herald*, 15 September 1842, p. 2; Kierner, "Woman's Piety within Patriarchy, pp. 79–98; Hall and Scott, "Women in the South."

33. Address delivered before Mr. Robert F. Stubbs' Female School, Little Plymouth, King & Queen County, 28 July 1842 by John R. Wright, printed in *Religious Herald*, 1 September 1842, p. 1. Jeremiah B. Jeter, "Female Education," *Religious Herald*, 19 August 1858, p. 1.

34. Jeter, "Female Education," *Religious Herald*, 2 September 1858, p. 1.

35. "Mrs. Thomas Sydnor proposes to open a school for young ladies in Farmville," *Religious Herald*, 8 December 1842; "Valley Union Seminary," *Religious Herald*, 5 May 1852, p. 3; copy of Committee Letter to the Churches of Goshen Association," *Religious Herald*, 4 February 1858, p. 2; Records of the Richmond Female Institute–Woman's College of Richmond, Vol. 1, VBHS; "Richmond Female Institute–Woman's College of Richmond, 1854–1916–A Brief History," unpublished term paper, Anne Park, December 1969, VBHS. Jeter, "Female Education," *Religious Herald*, 26 August 1858, p. 1; 9 September 1858, p. 1. Men took a larger role in women's education in the 1850s. Lebsock, *Free Women of Petersburg*, pp. 172–76.

36. G. Taylor, *Life and Times of James Boardman Taylor*, p. 53.

37. *Minutes*, Tenth Annual Meeting of the Virginia Baptist Education Society, 1840, p. 19.

38. Letter of J. B. Tombes, *Religious Herald*, 1 July 1852, p. 2.

39. Doggett, *The Destiny of Educated Young Men*, p. 16.

40. R. Moore, "Religion, Secularization, and the Shaping of the Culture Industry in Antebellum America," pp. 216–42. Quote is from letter of Joseph Baker of Winchester, *Religious Herald*, 30 September 1852, p. 2.

41. These figures probably represent white males only. Calvin H. Phipps, "Legislation Affecting Secondary Education," pp. 568–69, 588.

42. Percent of white children enrolled in school represents the percentage of the population aged 5 to 20 years of age and is likely a conservative estimate. *Population of the United States in 1860* (Washington, D.C.: Government Printing Office, 1864). On slave literacy, see Cornelius, *When I Can Read My Title Clear*, p. 9.

43. James L. Gwaltney, "Education," *Religious Herald*, 26 December 1850, p. 1; "Desultory Thoughts—No. 2" by "Aquila," *Religious Herald*, 8 January 1852, p. 1.

44. Kett and McClung, "Book Culture in Post-Revolutionary Virginia," pp. 97–147; R. Moore, "Religion, Secularization, and the Shaping of the Culture Industry in Antebellum America."

45. "E.," "Letter to a Junior Preacher," originally published in *Methodist Magazine* in 1824, reprinted in *Theological and Homiletic Monthly* 1 (July 1879): 361–366.

46. Richardson, *From Sunrise to Sunset*, p. 15; Kett and McClung, "Book Culture in Post-Revolutionary Virginia," pp. 97–147. On Baptists' relation with the American Tract Society, see letter of J. Cross, *Religious Herald*, 19 October 1848, p. 3.

47. Stroupe, *The Religious Press in the South Atlantic States*, pp. 3–37.

48. Moore, "Religion, Secularization, and the Shaping of the Culture Industry in Antebellum America."

49. D. Hall, *Worlds of Wonder*, quote on p. 31; Hatch, *Democratization of American Christianity*, chapter 5; R. Moore, "Religion, Secularization and the Shaping of the Culture Industry in Antebellum America." On the small numbers in journalism and printing, see Wyatt-Brown, *Southern Honor*, pp. 176–77.

50. G. Taylor, *Kenny, Cousin Guy*, and *Claiborne*; Sands, *Recreations of a Southern Barrister*. Edwards, *Random Sketches and Notes*, p. 456.

51. "The Virginia Baptist Preacher," *Religious Herald*, 27 January 1842, p. 3. On the beginning of the Virginia Baptist Sunday School and Publication Society, see "Our Publication Society," *Religious Herald*, 5 October 1848, p. 3. On the Southern Baptist Publication Society, see *Religious Herald*, 1 June 1848, p. 2. For last quote, see letter of "Matthew" of Fork Union, *Religious Herald*, 12 February 1852, p. 2.

52. According to Wyatt-Brown, Scott's novels figured prominently in Southern readers' libraries, a point Kett and McClung's research substantiates. Wyatt-Brown, *Southern Honor*, p. 37; Kett and McClung, "Book Culture in Post-Revolutionary Virginia," pp. 123–24; editorial, *Religious Herald*, 31 January 1856, p. 2.

53. On circulation, see *Religious Herald*, 31 January 1850, p. 2, and 1 January 1852, p. 2; "Three Reasons for Largely Increasing the Circulation of the Religious Herald," *Religious Herald*, 23 December 1858, p. 3. Both papers reached readers outside Virginia. Methodist circulation numbered about 15 percent of all members of the Virginia Conference, which had 26,500 members in 1845.

54. "Query," *Religious Herald*, 14 November 1850, p. 2; "Southern Baptist Publication Society," 1 June 1849, *Religious Herald*, p. 2; "Libraries, Colleges, Public Schools, Academies, and Other Schools," U.S. Census, 1860, p. 505; "Abstract," *Religious Herald*, 22 April 1852, p. 3.

55. On books and peddling in the North, see Jaffee, "Peddlers of Progress," pp. 511–35. For quote, see "X.," "A Good Theological School in Virginia," *Religious Herald*, 11 February 1858, p. 3.

56. "News from Colporters," *Religious Herald*, 28 March 1861, p. 1; "News from the Colporters, *Religious Herald*, 11 April 1861, p. 2; "News from the Colporters—Extracts from Reports of December and January," *Religious Herald*, 25 February 1858, p. 2.

57. Account book of Hiram Myers, 1858–1860, Colporteur for the Methodist Episcopal Church in Augusta, Rockingham, and Shenandoah Counties, Virginia, VHS; notice of Alfred E. Dickinson, General Superintendent, *Religious Herald*, 9 May 1861, p. 3.

58. "Southern Baptist Publication Society," *Religious Herald*, 1 June 1848, p. 2.

59. Black membership in the Virginia Conference of the Methodist Episcopal Church, South, grew from 4,949 in 1844 to 6,861 members in 1859. Sweet, *Virginia Methodism*, p. 245. "Dover Baptist Association," *Religious Herald*, 14 November 1844, p. 2; "Report of the Committee on the Colored Population Presented in the Rappahannock Association," *Religious Herald*, 3 September 1846, p. 2. On number of black Baptist churches in Virginia, see *Religious Herald*, 30 May 1844, p. 2. Also, see Boles, ed., *Masters and Slaves in the House of the Lord*.

60. Cornelius, *When I Can Read My Title Clear*; Raboteau, *Slave Religion*, pp. 239–42; Genovese, *Roll, Jordan, Roll*, pp. 561–66.

61. John A. Broadus, "Report of the Religious Instruction of the Colored People," Albemarle Association, *Religious Herald*, 23 October 1856, p. 1.

62. On Stringfellow, see Faust, "Evangelicalism and the Meaning of the Proslavery Argument." On Manly, see Mathews, *Religion in the Old South*, pp. 182–83, and records of the Richmond Female Institute, VBHS. On Ryland, see Ryland Papers, VBHS. On Smith, see Sweet, *Virginia Methodism*, p. 321; "William A. Smith," *Dictionary of American Biography* (New York: Scribner's Sons, 1928–58), 17: 361–62; and Dabney, *Virginia: The New Dominion*, p. 288. On Sydnor, see Thomas White Sydnor Papers, UVa; on Jeter, see Jeter, *Recollections of a Long Life*, and Hatcher, *Life of Jeremiah B. Jeter*.

63. "W.," "Instruction to Slaves," *Religious Herald*, 15 January 1846, p. 3.

64. "Resolution Concerning Education of Colored People," *Religious Herald*, 11 November 1852, p. 3; "Dover Baptist Association," *Religious Herald*, 27 November 1856, p. 2; *Ellyson's Business Directory and Almanac* (Richmond: H.K. Ellyson, 1845).

65. Letter of J. B. Jeter in support of Robert Ryland, *Religious Herald*, 14 September 1848, p. 2; "Religious Instruction of Colored People," *Religious Herald*, 11 November 1852, p. 3.

66. Boylan, *Sunday School*. For a letter voicing support for the work of the ASSU, see "American Sunday School Union," by "A Parent," *Religious Herald*, 2 May 1850, p. 3. Anne Loveland (*Southern Evangelicals and the Social Order*, pp. 33–34) noted that the ASSU organized Sunday schools primarily in urban areas.

67. Boylan, *Sunday School*, pp. 36–38; quote on scholarly angels is from "Church Libraries," *Religious Herald*, 11 December 1850, p. 2.

68. Records of Ettrick Methodist Church, 1874–1891, microfilm, LOV; Sunday School Record Book, Acquinton Methodist Church, King William County, "List of Books in Library Session 1872," R-M; "Hints on the Formation and Management of Sunday Schools in the Country," *Religious Herald*, 28 March 1844, p. 2; *Minute Book*, 1870–1876, Dorcas Society of Court Street Methodist Church, Lynchburg, LOV; report of a Sunday school parade of 1,500 in Richmond in the *Religious Herald*, 8 September 1852, p. 2.

222 Notes to Pages 74–82

69. Crane, *Literary Discourses*, p. 9.

70. Letter of Ryland, *Religious Herald*, 23 March 1848, p. 2.

71. Letter from "Alpha" of Hanover County, *Religious Herald*, 2 September 1852, p. 1. See also letter from "Cypselus," "Protracted Meetings," *Religious Herald*, 1 April 1858, p. 1.

Chapter 4

1. Baldwin Diary, 9 March 1852, 25 August 1865, VBHS.

2. Baldwin Diary, 28 October 1853, VBHS; Taylor, *Virginia Baptist Ministers*, Fifth Series, pp. 46–48.

3. Faust, "Evangelicalism and the Meaning of the Proslavery Argument"; Jeter, *Recollections of a Long Life*; Hatcher, *Life of J. B. Jeter*; Stringfellow, *A Brief Examination of the Scripture Testimony on the Institution of Slavery*.

4. During the 1840s and 1850s, Virginia's slave population grew at a rate of about 4 percent. By 1860, Virginia had about 500,000 slaves. See census of 1850. See Carter, *When the War Was Over*, p. 149; Gregg L. Michel, "From Slavery to Freedom: Hickory Hill, 1850–80," and John C. Willis, "From the Dictates of Pride to the Paths of Righteousness: Slave Honor and Christianity in Antebellum Virginia," in Ayers and Willis, eds., *The Edge of the South*.

5. These data were culled from manuscript slave schedules for Virginia from the 1850 U.S. census. From 283 antebellum pastors in my total sample of 800 nineteenth-century pastors, the resident counties for 60 were not found, and 16 were known to have resided out of state. I searched for 207 names in the 1850 slave schedules and identified 79, or 38 percent, as slaveholders. This is probably a conservative figure. Older studies suggested that, by 1843, about 1,200 Methodist pastors and local church leaders owned almost 12,000 slaves throughout the South. See Sweet, *Virginia Methodism*, p. 245; Ahlstrom, *Religious History of the American People*, Vol. 2, p. 107.

6. Mathews, *Slavery and Methodism* and *Religion in the Old South*; Loveland, *Southern Evangelicals and the Social Order*.

7. *Religious Herald*, 23 July 1846, p. 2. Also in the *Religious Herald*, "Instruction to Slaves," 15 January 1846, p. 3; letter of Jeremiah B. Jeter, 14 September 1848, p. 2; "Religious Instruction of Colored People," 11 November 1852, p. 3.

8. Mathews, *Religion in the Old South*, chapter 4; and "Charles Colcock Jones and the Southern Evangelical Crusade to Form a Biracial Community"; Freehling, "James Henley Thornwell's Mysterious Antislavery Moment." Quote is from Smith, *Lectures on the Philosophy and Practice of Slavery*, p. v.

9. Baker, *Southern Baptist Convention*; Barnes, *Southern Baptist Convention, 1845–1953* (Nashville: Broadman Press, 1954); Ryland, *Baptists of Virginia*. On Methodists, see Ahlstrom, *Religious History of the American People*, Vol. 2, pp. 106–9; and Sweet, *Virginia Methodism*, chapters 9 and 10.

10. Sweet, *Virginia Methodism*, p. 244.

11. "General Association," *Religious Herald*, 4 June 1830.

12. On Baptist giving, see Ryland, *Baptists of Virginia*, chapters 11 and 15. For Methodists, see *Minutes*, Virginia Annual Conference, 1875, Appendix 1.

13. Founded by a Virginia Baptist minister, the society had 81 members on its first anniversary, 29 of whom were ministers, 27 of those Baptists. Letter of "P.," *Religious Herald*, 1 January 1846, p. 1; *Religious Herald*, 9 July 1840, p. 2.

14. Schultz, "Temperance Reform in the Antebellum South."

15. Tyrell, *Sobering Up*, pp. 162–83; Shultz, "Temperance Reform in the Antebellum South."

16. When one writer attacked ministerial memberships in the Sons, a pastor argued that ministers should freely join "charitable and beneficial" societies. Reply to "Enquirer," *Religious Herald*, 26 September 1844, p. 1.

17. Shultz, "Temperance Reform in the Antebellum South," p. 334.

18. Thornton Stringfellow, the author of the important tract defending slavery, opposed ministerial membership in both temperance societies and secret societies such as the Masons. See the series of letters in the *Religious Herald*, for example, of 24 January 1850, denouncing the Sons. Quote is from "W. S. G.," "The Church and Temperance Societies—Thoughts on a Mooted Question," *Quarterly Review of the Methodist Episcopal Church, South* 4 (April 1850): 205–29.

19. Clement Read, pastor and chair of Hampden-Sydney College, in "Reasons for Not Joining the Temperance Society," 1836, quoted in Pearson and Hendricks, *Liquor and Antiliquor in Virginia*, p. 71.

20. Smith, *Lectures on the Philosophy and Practice of Slavery*, pp. 320–21.

21. Thornwell, "Religious Instruction of the Black Population," *Southern Presbyterian Review*, (January 1852): 380–94, quoted in Freehling, "James Henley Thornwell's Mysterious Antislavery Moment"; Smith, *Lectures on the Philosophy and Practice of Slavery*.

22. Stringfellow, *A Brief Examination of Scripture Testimony on the Institution of Slavery*, and *Slavery: Its Origin, Nature and History*.

23. Bruce, *Virginia Iron Manufacture*, chapter 8; McPherson, *Battle Cry of Freedom*, pp. 91–103; Robertson, *Civil War Virginia*, pp. 15–16.

24. Presbyterian churches increased by 58 percent, Episcopal churches by 65 percent.

25. Southern Baptists raised an annual contribution after their separation from the North seven times that of their contribution before schism. Baker, *Southern Baptist Convention*, p. 202. Between 1845 and 1860, giving for foreign missions increased from $4,300 to $20,338 in the Methodist Virginia Conference. Conference collections increased from $851 to $8,033 for the same period. Baptist giving for the General Association increased five times from $3,120 in 1851 to $15,607 in 1860. *Minutes*, Virginia Annual Conference, 1875, Appendix 1, n.p.; *Minutes*, Proceedings of the Annual Meeting of the General Association of Virginia, 1851 and 1860.

26. Mathews, *Slavery and Methodism*, p. 67.

27. Jack Maddex has found evidence of proslavery millennialism among Southern Presbyterians and has argued that this "idea transcended denominational boundaries" ("Proslavery Millennialism: Social Eschatology in Antebellum Southern Calvinism"). See Loveland, *Southern Evangelicals and the Social Order*, p. 162. For examples of Virginia clergy's thoughts on the millennium, see Edward Baptist, "A Sermon on the Millennium" [premillennial], *Religious Herald*, 1 May 1844, p. 1; "A Sermon Preached before the Strawberry Association at Its Last Session" ["Thy Kingdom Come," Matt. 7:10, amillennial], *Religious Herald*, 31 January and 7 February 1856, p. 1. On millennialism in the antebellum North, see Moorehead, *American Apocalypse*, pp. 1–22; Tuveson, *Redeemer Nation*.

28. The American Sunday School Union, American Tract Society, and American Bible Society all relied on colportage and individual contacts for the Southern work after about 1840. Involvement with all three of these organizations depended largely on the Southern need for published materials. After the schisms with Northern de-

nominations, Southerners viewed these agencies as superior sources to those of the northern branches of their denominations. Kuykendall, *"Southern Enterprize,"* pp. 66–99. On Protestant ecumenicism in the antebellum North, see Howe, "The Evangelical Movement and Political Culture in the North."

29. Ronald G. Walters, among others, has pointed to the Christian utopian impulse shared by Northern abolitionists and Southern proslavery theologians (*The Antislavery Appeal*, p. 148). See also Howe, "The Evangelical Movement and Political Culture in the North."

30. Anonymous, "The Power and Responsibilities," *Religious Herald*, 18 August 1842, p. 1; "Circular Letter of the Beulah Baptist Association," *Religious Herald*, 1 February 1844, p. 1.

31. Untitled article by "Philo-Gulielmus," *Religious Herald*, 7 May 1846, p. 1.

32. Baker, *Southern Baptist Convention*, pp. 174–75.

33. Ibid., p. 175.

34. "Ten Thousand Dollars," *Religious Herald*, 15 July 1852, p. 2.

35. The state constitution barred ministers from the state legislature, and convention decreed that state charters were banned from religious schools. *Religious Herald*, 2 March 1848, p. 3. For "party prejudice," see James A. Riddick to William Gray, 5 January 1858, William Gray Papers, VHS; "The Fundamental Elements of Church Government," *Quarterly Review of the Methodist Episcopal Church, South* 7 (January 1853): 15–30; Stewards' Book, Centenary Methodist Church, Richmond, 18 October 1852, LOV; letter of 1851 to John Early, quoted in "Remarks of J. Rives Childs on the Occasion of the Presentation of the Papers of Bishop John Early to Randolph-Macon College," 23 October 1930, R-M.

36. "Politics against Godliness," *Religious Herald*, 26 September 1844, p. 1.

37. Daniel Witt to R. Gwathmey, Esq., 4 July 1855, quoted in Jeter, *Life of Rev. Daniel Witt*, p. 198; letter of "R. McD.," *Religious Herald*, 4 November 1852, p. 1.

38. "Impropriety of Ministers Meddling with Politics," *Religious Herald*, 23 July 1840, p. 1.

39. In 1850, the Methodist Virginia Conference counted 124 traveling ministers. By 1860, there were 198. The large numbers of new pastors meant that the average congregation's size dropped from 302 members in 1850 to 241 in 1860. *Minutes*, Virginia Annual Conference of 1875, Appendix 1.

40. Loveland, *Southern Evangelicals and the Social Order*, pp. 158–85; Faust, "The Peculiar South Revisited," in Boles and Nolen, eds., *Interpreting Southern History*, p. 92; Mathews, *Religion in the Old South*, p. 77; Lewis, *The Pursuit of Happiness*, pp. 54–55; and S. Hill, *Southern Churches in Crisis* and *Religion and the Solid South*. Quote is from Ayers, *Vengeance and Justice*, p. 57.

Chapter 5

1. John Cowper Granbery to Ella Fayette Winston, 26 January 1861, Granbery Papers, UVa.

2. Taylor, *Virginia Baptist Ministers*, Fourth Series, p. 270. Quote from Joseph Walker of Richmond, "Christian Patriotism," *Religious Herald*, 9 May 1861, p. 2. On soldiers' struggles to reconcile warfare with their faith, see McPherson, *For Cause and Comrades*, pp. 71–74.

3. John L. Pascoe of Alexandria to Rev. Leonidas Rosser, 12 November 1850, R-M; Rev. James A. Riddick to William Gray, correspondence of 1859 and 1860, William

Gray Papers, VHS; Report of the State Missions Board, H. K. Ellyson, Corresponding Secretary, *Religious Herald*, 14 March 1861, p. 2.

4. John Cowper Granbery to Ella Winston, 3 May 1861, Granbery Papers, UVa.

5. At Frayser's Farm, or Glendale, Confederate troops lost 3,500 men killed or wounded, twice the number of Union casualties. The circumstances of Granbery's injury are unknown. See Lafferty, *Sketches of the Virginia Conference* (1880), pp. 59–60; McPherson, *Battle Cry of Freedom*, p. 469. James Clayton Reed (b. 1842), a Methodist pastor, lost a hand on the field of Sharpsburg. See Lafferty, *Sketches of the Virginia Conference* (1880), p. 157.

6. J. William Jones also stressed the success of veterans in postwar religious life. He estimated that four-fifths of all college students (implying most prospective pastors were in college) in 1867 were veterans and that the "leading pulpits" of the South were all filled with vets. Jones, *Christ in the Camp*, p. 462.

Like many other young men of his generation, Granbery experienced the war as a turning point in his life. Ordained in 1848, his early career had been marked by undistinguished appointments and illness. But by the late 1850s, he had served in several good posts, including the University of Virginia and a congregation in Washington, D.C. After the war, he preached to three of the most prominent Methodist congregations in Virginia. He moved to Nashville to teach practical theology and moral philosophy at the new Vanderbilt University and was appointed bishop seven years later.

7. Rev. James A. Riddick to William Gray, 8 January 1861, William Gray Papers, VHS.

8. Robert Ryland to "My dear Willie," 23 November 1860, VBHS.

9. The Southern allegiance of members of the Baltimore Conference later proved too great; it joined the Methodist Episcopal Church, South after the war. The rift between Baptists in border states and the Southern Baptist Convention was so serious that many believed the convention would split into Upper and Lower South conventions. See "Elias Lyman Magoon, D.D." in *Baptist Encyclopedia* (Philadelphia: Louis H. Everts, 1881), vol. 2, pp. 738–39; Sweet, *Virginia Methodism*, pp. 247–50; "Southern Baptist Convention," *Religious Herald*, 28 March 1861, p. 2. For other examples of clergy who moved north or south, see Silver, *Confederate Morale and Church Propaganda*, pp. 22–23.

10. Bellah, "Civil Religion in America."

11. James A. Riddick to William Gray, 8 January 1861, William Gray Papers, VHS; "Southern Baptist Convention," *Religious Herald*, 28 March 1861, p. 2.

12. "Volunteers for War," *Religious Herald*, 23 May, 1861, p. 1.

13. Jeremiah B. Jeter, "Loyalty and Piety," 1861 sermonbook, VBHS; "Volunteers for War," *Religious Herald*, 23 May 1861, p. 1.

14. Bennett, *Narrative of the Great Revival*, p. 17.

15. "The True American Spirit and Its Destiny—An Oration Delivered before the Scientific and Literary Institute in the City of Norfolk, 4th of July, 1856," Leonidas Rosser Papers, R-M.

16. "Resignation," *Religious Herald*, 9 May 1861. See also "Volunteers for War," *Religious Herald*, 23 May 1861, p. 1. The Rev. Addison Hall represented Albemarle County at the secession convention in Richmond. Daniel, *Virginia Baptists*, p. 3.

17. Rev. James A. Riddick to William Gray, Esq., 1 July 1861, William Gray Papers, VHS.

18. Rev. James A. Riddick to William Gray, Esq. 22 January 1861, William Gray Papers, VHS; Robert Ryland to "My Dear Willie," 23 November 1860, VBHS.

19. Sermon on Matthew 22:21, "Render unto Caesar," Sermonbook, Jeremiah Bell Jeter, 1861, VBHS; "Patriotism is not religion . . . ," *Religious Herald*, 3 October 1861, p. 1, quoted in Miller, "A Religious Press in Time of War"; Bennett, *Great Revival*, p. 95.

20. William Sands, "Volunteers for War," *Religious Herald*, 23 May 1861, p. 1.

21. Soldier to "Precious Wife," 19 February 1862, quoted in Silver, *Confederate Morale and Church Propaganda*, p. 13.

22. *Southern Christian Advocate*, 2 April 1863, quoted in Faust, *The Creation of Confederate Nationalism*, p. 22; "The Crisis," *Religious Herald*, 14 March 1861, p. 3; "The Crisis," *Religious Herald*, 25 April 1861, p. 2.

23. One-half of the Virginia officers in the U.S. Army chose to fight for the North. Robertson, *Civil War Virginia*, p. 18.

24. "To the Churches of the Valley Association," *Religious Herald*, 25 April 1861, p. 2; Stewards' Book 1857–1867, Centenary Methodist Church (Richmond), 25 March 1861, p. 90, LOV. For government announcements, see *Religious Herald*, 25 April, 2 May, and 9 May, 1861.

25. Jeremiah Jeter, preface to sermonbook, 1861, VBHS.

26. John M. Daniel, quoted in Dabney, *Virginia: The New Dominion*, p. 300.

27. A. Johnson to "Mr. Sidner," 18 March 1864, Sydnor Papers, UVa.

28. "Joseph Walker," Taylor, *Virginia Baptist Ministers*, Fourth Series, p. 270.

29. Broaddus was released two months later. Reuben Ford, imprisoned for not taking the oath to the Federal government during the occupation of Nashville, died soon after his release. William F. Broaddus diary, VBHS, and "Diary of the Late W. F. Broaddus While in Prison during the War," *Religious Herald*, 3 January 1878, p. 1; "Reuben Ford," in Taylor, *Virginia Baptist Ministers*, Third Series, p. 55. See also account of Alexander H. Spilman in John K. Gott, "Carter's Run," *Virginia Baptist Register* 2 (1963): 93.

30. Shattuck, *A Shield and a Hiding Place*, p. 57.

31. Ahlstrom, *Religious History of the American People*, Vol. 2, p. 122; Sweet, *Virginia Methodists*, p. 275.

32. Daniel, "Chaplains in the Army of Northern Virginia"; Jones, *Christ in the Camp*, p. 233; Shattuck, *A Shield and a Hiding Place*, p. 66.

33. "Christian Patriotism" and "The Confederate Constitution," *Religious Herald*, 9 May 1861, p. 2. The editors urged readers to examine the Confederate constitution, printed in full on the front page, "as patriots and as Christians." On Walker, see "Joseph Walker," Taylor, *Virginia Baptist Ministers*, Fourth Series, p. 270. Faust, *Creation of Confederate Nationalism*, p. 22.

34. Some Baptists argued that the government should not appoint and pay chaplains, saying it was a clear case of the state supporting a church. Daniel, "An Aspect of Church and State Relations in the Confederacy." See also Haber, *Quest for Authority and Honor in the American Professions*, p. 137; Shattuck, *A Shield and a Hiding Place*, p. 64.

35. Federal army chaplains received $1,200 annually, which increased to $1,400 by the end of the war. Romero, *Religion in the Rebel Ranks*, pp. 12–13; Shattuck, *A Shield and a Hiding Place*, pp. 53, 65; Daniel, "An Aspect of Church and State Relations in the Confederacy," p. 48.

36. Southern Baptists petitioned to pay their own chaplains' salaries, and Methodists moved to supplement their chaplains' salaries by as much as $1,800 annually if they were married. Daniel, "An Aspect of Church-State Relations in the Confederacy," p. 51.

37. Romero, *Religion in the Rebel Ranks*, p. 17.

38. Bennett, *Narrative of the Great Revival*, p. 31.

39. Kaser, *Books and Libraries in Camp and Battle*, p. 49.

40. George B. Taylor, chaplain of the 25th Virginia Regiment, noted that soldiers generally wanted chaplains but that opposition from some officers was well-known. Bennett, *Narrative of the Great Revival*, pp. 31, 212–13.

41. For pastors' interpretations of their wartime experiences with officers such as Jackson, see Chapter 5 below.

42. Jones, *Christ in the Camp*, p. 390.

43. Wyatt-Brown has described the Civil War as a simple test of manhood for many Southerners (*Southern Honor*, p. 35).

44. James quoted in Leon Edel, "Introduction," in Henry James, *A Little Tour in France* (New York: Farrar, Strauss and Giroux, 1983; London: Penguin Books, 1985), p. xiv.

45. Riddick to William Gray, 5 January 1858, William Gray Papers, VHS; letter of Bishop Andrew, Methodist Episcopal Church, South, quoted in Bennett, *Narrative of the Great Revival*, p. 98.

46. *Minutes*, Chaplains' Association, 29 April 1863, reprinted in Jones, *Christ in the Camp*, Appendix, p. 522.

47. Early Family Papers, R-M; Burton Diary, VBHS; Bennett, *Narrative of the Great Revival*, p. 213. See also Shattuck, *A Shield and a Hiding Place*, p. 67.

48. Romero, *Religion in the Rebel Ranks*, p. 40.

49. Chaplain George B. Taylor, letter from camp in Charles City, 9 July 1862, quoted in Jones, *Christ in the Camp*, p. 228.

50. *Richmond Christian Advocate*, 14 May 1874, p. 1.

51. Bennett, *Narrative of the Great Revival*, pp. 10–11.

52. Faust, "Christian Soldiers," p. 66.

53. Bennett, *Narrative of the Great Revival*, p. 73.

54. "Pastoral and Church Colportage," *Religious Herald*, 17 January 1861, p. 2.

55. Jones, *Christ in the Camp*, p. 155. The two standard accounts of wartime revivals, Jones's *Christ in the Camp* and Bennett's *Narrative of the Great Revival*, devote several chapters each to the effects of literature on soldiers. "So important was the work of colportage in promoting religion among the soldiers, that we feel constrained to devote to it a separate chapter," Bennett wrote (*Narrative of the Great Revival*, pp. 72, 345, 84, 77).

56. Bennett, *Narrative of the Great Revival*, p. 77.

57. Silver, *Confederate Morale and Church Propaganda*, pp. 94–95; "The Christian Patriot's Prayer," based on Psalm 53, in Keeling, *The Colporteur's Commission*.

58. Bennett, *Narrative of the Great Revival*, p. 80.

59. Rev. Robert Ryland reported this during the Peninsula Campaign. Bennett, *Narrative of the Great Revival*, p. 152.

60. Kaser, *Books and Libraries*, p. 110.

61. Ibid., pp. 34, 29.

62. Rev. A. M. Jones, quoted in Bennett, *Narrative of the Great Revival*, p. 269.

63. Kaser, *Books and Libraries*, pp. 3–30.

64. Ibid., pp. 3, 10–11, 52–60; Bennett, *Narrative of the Great Revival*, p. 166.

65. Bennett, *Narrative of the Great Revival*, p. 268.

66. "It was home-like to meet for the worship of God," one pastor observed. Ibid., p. 20.

67. An exception is Faust, "Christian Soldiers."

68. Bennett, *A Narrative of the Great Revival*; Jones, *Christ in the Camp*.

69. Wiatt to "My dear friend & brother," 31 May 1850, Robins Family Papers, Section 65, VHS. On Gloucester County, see Spottswood Hunnicutt Jones, *The World of Ware Parish in Gloucester County, Virginia* (Richmond: Dietz, 1991), pp. 130–41; and Ludwell Lee Montague, *Gloucester County in the Civil War* (Gloucester, Va.: DeHardit Press, 1965), pp. 1–2.

70. Wiatt to "My dear friend & brother," 31 May 1850, Robins Family Papers, Secion 65, VHS.

71. Personal property tax rolls, Gloucester County, Virginia, 1859, 1860, microfilm, LOV; U.S. Census, manuscript population schedules for 1860, Gloucester County, Virginia, p. 757, microfilm, LOV.

72. This account of his war years is from William E. Wiatt Diary, October 1 1862–December 1865, photostat, LOV.

73. Wiatt's estimated worth of more than $9,000 in 1860 was reduced to an estimated $1,100 in 1870. U.S. census, Manuscript Population Schedules for Gloucester County, Virginia, 1870, p. 303. Wiatt was an active member of the United Confederate Veterans during the 1890s. Records, 1890–1915, Page-Puller Camp No. 512, United Confederate Veterans, Gloucester County, Virginia, VHS.

74. Bennett, *Narrative of the Great Revival*, p. 412.

Chapter 6

1. "George Boardman Taylor" in Taylor, *Virginia Baptist Ministers*, Fifth Series, p. 194.

2. "Women," *Religious Herald*, 19 October 1865, p. 4; *Minutes*, Baptist General Association of Virginia, 5 June 1865, p. 21. Such appeals anticipated those of Robert E. Lee, who later emphasized "active citizenship" as a way to heal dissension after the war. Moger, *Virginia: Bourbonism to Byrd*, p. 6.

3. Report of the State Mission Board, *Minutes*, Baptist General Association of Virginia, 1866, p. 31.

4. Ibid.

5. "Aral of Lunenberg," "The Importance of the Gospel Ministry," *Religious Herald*, 24 May 1866, p. 1.

6. *Religious Herald*, 23 November 1865, p. 4.

7. William Emory Edwards, in Lafferty, *Sketches of the Virginia Conference* (1880), p. 140; Edgar Herndon Pritchett in Lafferty, *Sketches of the Virginia Conference* (1880), p. 117.

8. Letter of T. H. Haynes (Richmond) to Virginia Annual Conference, 20 November 1866, R-M.

9. On Ryland, see untitled typescript, n.d., Robert Ryland file, VBHS; Taylor, *Virginia Baptist Ministers*, Fourth Series, p. 269. On preachers' financial hardship, see Farish, *Circuit Rider Dismounts*, p. 32; *The Baptist* (Memphis), "Hard Times," 1 February 1867, p. 5.

10. *The Baptist* (Memphis), 1 June 1867, p. 3.

11. J. B. McFerrin, Secretary, Board of Domestic Missions, Virginia Conference, *Richmond Christian Advocate*, 18 November 1869.

12. J.W. Ryland, "A Colporteur's Report," *Religious Herald*, 30 November 1865, p. 1.

13. *Religious Herald*, 18 January 1866, p. 2. For gifts of food and clothing, see *Religious Herald*, 11 January 1866, p. 1; and *Religious Herald*, 8 March 1866, p. 2.

14. "Hard Times," *The Baptist* (Memphis), 1 February 1867, p. 5.

15. "Cheering Signs," *Richmond Christian Advocate*, 13 June 1867, p. 2.

16. The pacifist Methodist was Rev. Sidi H. Brown of South Carolina. *Richmond Christian Advocate*, 8 August 1867.

17. "The Skepticism Engendered by the War," *Religious Herald*, 21 December 1865, p. 2. For the war's effects on denominational structures, see Stowell, *Rebuilding Zion*. For theology and views of history, see Beringer, et al., *Why the South Lost the Civil War*, especially pp. 82–107 and 336–67. For interpretations that stress the disillusionment of defeat and a subsequent "crisis of faith," see Maddex, "Proslavery Millennialism"; Foster, *Ghosts of the Confederacy*, pp. 13–14.

18. Editorial, *Religious Herald*, 19 October 1865, p. 2.

19. *Minutes*, Albemarle Baptist Association, 15–17 August 1865, p. 17.

20. Black Methodist membership had plunged from almost 7,000 in 1861. Baker, *Southern Baptist Convention*, p. 232; Daniel, *Virginia Baptists*, p. 76; *Minutes*, Virginia Annual Conference 1875, Appendix 1.

21. Dvorak has emphasized the unity and egalitarianism in antebellum biracial congregations. Dvorak, *African-American Exodus*, pp. 12–20.

22. Ibid., chapter 3; on sympathy for African American members, see *Minutes*, Baptist General Association of Virginia, 1865, pp. 18–19; *Religious Herald*, "Our Relations to the Freedmen," 29 October 1865, p. 2; "To the Private Members of the Baptist Churches of Virginia," 26 July 1866, p. 1; "A Query," 28 June 1866, p. 2; "Religious Instruction of the Colored People," 16 January 1868, p. 3. Examples of less sympathetic views may be seen in *Minutes*, Baptist General Association of Virginia, 1866, p. 26; "Sixtieth Anniversary of the Chowan Association," *Religious Herald*, 12 July 1866, p. 2; Minute Book, Shiloh Baptist Church, Charlotte County, 24 June 1866, p. 179, LOV; "Queries," *Religious Herald*, 19 March 1868, p. 2; *Religious Herald*, 5 April 1866, p. 2.

23. A. S. Fitzgerald to Thomas White Sydnor, 5 May 1866, Sydnor Papers, UVa. Requests to organize churches, 21 July 1870, 24 July 1870, and undated, Sydnor Papers, UVa.

24. Daniel Witt to Rev. Thomas W. Sydnor, 20 November 1867 and 7 June 1868, Sydnor Papers, UVa.

25. Isaac Lane, a freedman ordained in the Methodist Episcopal Church, South, during the Civil War, recalled his exam as consisting of "many questions bearing upon almost every phase of the doctrines of Christ and the Church" (Lane, "From Slave to Preacher among the Freedmen," in Sernett, ed. *Afro-American Religious History: A Documentary Witness*, pp. 229–33). See Hatcher, *John Jasper, The Unmatched Negro Philosopher*, pp. 17, 94.

26. Hatcher, *John Jasper*, pp. 10–11, 32–35.

27. Levine, *Black Culture and Black Consciousness*, p. 141.

28. John Mason Brown, 1868, in ibid., p. 28. Members implicitly rebuked him in their response: "We was mourning, sir!" J. H. Harrison of Amelia County, Virginia, "A Newsy Letter," *Religious Herald*, 5 January 1888, p. 1. On Northern teachers' criticism of black religious practice, see Levine, *Black Culture and Black Consciousness*, pp. 141–42.

29. "Baptist Progress," *Religious Herald*, 3 January 1878, p. 1; and *Richmond Christian Advocate*, 23 January 1873, p. 2. On other protests against religious excitement before 1880, see *Religious Herald*, "Protracted Meetings," 8 March 1866, p. 2; "Protracted Meetings, Revivals, &c," 20 January 1870, p. 2; and *Richmond Christian Advocate*, "Protracted Meetings," 23 January 1879, p. 1; and 23 October 1879, p. 2.

30. Daniel, *Virginia Baptists*, chapter 5.

31. The significance of Confederate heroes as religious role models has been eclipsed by the focus on their use in the Lost Cause. Of the two detailed studies of the Lost Cause, Charles Wilson's *Baptized in Blood* focuses on the significance of these heroes in what he describes as the South's civil religion. He does not, however, demonstrate a strong tie between the institutional church and the Lost Cause. Gaines Foster has also noted that Lee, Jackson, and Davis received "extensive and ecstatic adoration." *Ghosts of Confederacy*, pp. 120–21.

32. Bennett, *Narrative of The Great Revival*, p. 325.

33. "The Moral Influence of Representative Men," *Religious Herald*, 1 March 1866, p. 2.

34. *Richmond Christian Advocate*, 28 April 1867, p. 1; Wilson, *Baptized in Blood*, pp. 18–36.

35. Untitled editorial, *Richmond Christian Advocate*, 11 July 1867, p. 2.

36. Cyrus Fry, a Baptist colporteur, treasured for the rest of his life a pass written by General Jackson. Cyrus Franklin Fry (1824–92) was from the Shenandoah Valley of Virginia. Taylor, *Virginia Baptist Ministers*, Fourth Series, p. 153.

37. "Jesus Christ-Citizen," *Religious Herald*, 28 June 1866, p. 1.

38. *Richmond Christian Advocate*, 18 April 1867, p. 1.

39. "A Time for Reformation," *Religious Herald*, 1 February 1866, p. 2.

40. He began the series in response to a request from the newspaper's editor, a Baptist layman who wanted to increase the circulation of the *Dispatch* in Manchester. See E. Hatcher, *William E. Hatcher*, p. 52.

41. Weisiger, *Old Manchester and Its Environs*, pp. 17, 69.

42. Struggle letters, *Richmond Dispatch*, 31 January 1866, p. 1; 15 February 1866, p. 1. An account of the Struggle letters appears in E. Hatcher's biography, *William E. Hatcher*, pp. 52–69.

43. Struggle letter, *Richmond Dispatch*, 6 February 1866, p. 1.

44. Struggle letter, *Richmond Dispatch*, 15 February 1866, p. 1; "Manchester Affairs," 5 March 1866, p. 1; Struggle letter, 17 March 1866, p. 1.

45. *Richmond Dispatch*, 24 April 1866, p. 1; 28 April 1866, p. 1; Struggle letter, 12 May 1866, p. 1.

46. "The Importance of the Gospel Ministry," by "Aral of Lunenburg," *Religious Herald*, 24 May 1866, p. 1.

47. Maris A. Vinovskis, "Have Social Historians Lost the Civil War? Some Preliminary Demographic Speculations," and Amy E. Holmes, " 'Such is the Price We Pay': American Widows and the Civil War Pension System," in Vinovskis, ed., *Toward a Social History of the American Civil War*; Bremner, *The Public Good*, pp. 144–50; Porter, *County Government in Virginia*.

48. "Resolutions," *Religious Herald*, 19 October 1865; "An Urgent Appeal," *Religious Herald*, 25 January 1866, p. 2.

49. Asa Snyder to William Gray, 23 April 1866, William Gray Papers, VHS.

50. William E. Wiatt Diary, 29 March 1864, LOV; "A Little Sermon for Whom It May Concern," *Religious Herald*, 15 March 1866, p. 1.

51. "Sunday Schools," *Religious Herald*, 30 November 1865, p. 2.

52. George F. Bagby, Agent of the Orphans' Committee, "Education of Soldiers' Children," *Religious Herald*, 18 January 1866, p. 1.

53. Daniel, *Virginia Baptists*, pp. 141–42; *Minutes*, Baptist General Association of Virginia, 1866, pp. 43–45, 1867, pp. 46–47; "Work for Virginia Baptists," *Religious Herald*, 27 January 1870, p. 2; "Education of Soldiers' Children," circular, 1870, Sydnor Papers, UVa; W. F. Broaddus to "Brother Powell," 21 May 1870, Sydnor Papers, UVa.

54. Letter from James Walker of Keysville, Va., in *The Baptist* (Memphis), 27 April 1867, p. 5.

55. On violence by returned soldiers, see Rable, *But There Was No Peace*, pp. 12–13.

56. "Labor," *Religious Herald*, 22 February 1866, p. 2. On temperance, see *Minutes*, Albemarle Baptist Association, 17 August 1865, p. 12; in *Religious Herald*, 23 November 1865, p. 2; Abner Clopton, "Temperance," 14 December 1865, p. 1; and 15 February 1866, p. 1; and in *Richmond Christian Advocate*, "The Whiskey and Wine Question," 6 May 1869, p. 2; and "Christian Morals," 19 August 1869, p. 2.

57. J. H. C. Jones, Esq., in *Religious Herald*, 19 October, 1865, p. 2.

58. Minutes, Young Men's Association, Trinity Church, R-M. On young men's missionary societies, see "Report of Young Men's Missionary Society, Second Baptist Church, Richmond," *Religious Herald*, 19 April 1866, p. 2 and 24 May 1866, p. 2.

59. "An Important Baptist Convention in the Northern Neck of Virginia," *Religious Herald*, 14 June 1866, p. 1.

60. The arrangement was not a prudent financial decision for colleges that depended on student tuition to help them remain solvent. Education Board of the Virginia Baptist General Association, located at Richmond, 1868.

61. On the provision of free education, *Minutes*, Baptist General Association of Virginia, 1865, p. 22; advertisement for Randolph-Macon College, *Richmond Christian Advocate*, 24 January 1867. For quote, editorial, *Religious Herald*, 19 July 1866, p. 2. For children, *Richmond Christian Advocate*, 27 May 1869 and 24 November 1870.

62. In late 1865, Northern missionaries arrived in Richmond to open a training school for black ministers. "A School for Training Colored Preachers," *Religious Herald*, 30 November 1865, p. 2.

63. Twenty-eight students are listed. Education Board of the Virginia Baptist General Association, located at Richmond, 1868.

64. "List of Graduates, 1849–1896" in Richmond College Catalogue, 1896, VBHS.

65. William E. Wiatt of Gloucester Courthouse reported that thirty members joined the church, ten of whom were soldiers he had baptized during the war. *Religious Herald*, 1 February 1866.

66. "The Sabbath School," *The Baptist* (Memphis), 10 August 1867, p. 3; see also J. B. W. in "Sunday Schools," *Religious Herald*, 11 January 1866, p. 1.

67. "An Appeal to the Friends of Little Children," *Religious Herald*, 8 March 1866, p. 2. For other examples of the benevolent aim of Sunday schools, see editorial, *Richmond Christian Advocate*, 24 January 1867, p. 2.; letter of D. F. Hodges, Franklin County, Va., *Richmond Christian Advocate*, 18 March 1869; "Home Sabbath Schools," *Religious Herald*, 5 May 1870, p. 3; "Are Sunday Schools Scriptural?" *Religious Herald*, 3 February 1870, p. 2; Memorandum Book, Dorcas Society of Court Street Methodist Church, Lynchburg, LOV; "Dorcas Societies," *Richmond Christian Advocate*, 22 July 1869, p. 3.

68. W. R. Vaughn to Brother [Thomas W.] Sydnor, 13 January 1871, Sydnor Papers, UVa.; Daniel, *Virginia Baptists*, pp. 70–72.

69. "Baptist State Sunday School Convention," *Religious Herald*, 19 March 1868, p. 2.

70. Letter of "J. M.," *Richmond Christian Advocate*, 22 July 1867, p. 2.

71. *Minutes*, Virginia Annual Conference, 1873 and 1876.

72. *Religious Herald*, 17 May 1866, p. 3. On the need for books, see also letter from Goldsboro, N.C., *Religious Herald*, 26 July 1866, p. 1; letter of W. R. Vaughn,

Mathews County, Va., *Religious Herald*, 31 May 1866, p. 2; "The Sabbath School," *The Baptist* (Memphis), 27 April 1867, p. 4; Sunday School Record Book, Acquinton Methodist Church, King William County, Va., 1872, "List of Books in Library Session 1872," R-M.

73. "The Way to Secure Sunday School Books," *Religious Herald*, 17 May 1866, p. 2.

74. "Sunday School Literature, An Important Question," *Religious Herald*, 12 April 1866, p. 2.

75. Letter of W. M. Mason, Caroline County, *Religious Herald*, 8 February 1872, p. 2.

76. Letter of W. W. R., West Point Circuit, *Richmond Christian Advocate*, 1 March 1877, p. 2.

77. Virginia city schools generally adopted uniform curriculum, while rural schools relied on local choice. Link, *A Hard Country and a Lonely Place*, pp. 9, 64–65.

78. *Richmond Christian Advocate*, 5 April 1877, p. 2.

79. "Report on the Sabbath School," *Quarterly Conference Minutes*, Trinity [Methodist] Church, Richmond, 10 November 1879, R-M.

Chapter 7

1. Daniel Witt to Thomas W. Sydnor, 20 September 1870, Sydnor Papers, UVa.

2. Ibid.

3. Editorial, *Richmond Christian Advocate*, 12 October 1871, p. 2. On fashionable churches, see "Stray Baptists," *Religious Herald*, 11 January 1866, p. 2; "A Virginia lady . . . ," *Religious Herald*, 25 January 1866, p. 2; "Rich and Poor Churches," *Richmond Christian Advocate*, 2 March 1871, p. 1; letter of John E. Edwards, *Richmond Christian Advocate*, 20 April 1871, p. 3; "High Notions! Church Respectability," *Richmond Christian Advocate*, 8 May 1873, p. 1; "One Thing and Another," *Religious Herald*, 7 April 1892, p. 2.

4. *Proceedings*, First Baptist Congress of Virginia, 1883, pp. 101–4.

5. Ibid., 1883, p. 53.

6. "Rich and Poor Churches," *Richmond Christian Advocate*, 2 March 1871, p. 1.

7. Letter of C. G. Wilkinson of Chesterfield County, *Religious Herald*, 15 February 1872, p. 2; letter of M. A. T., Henry Circuit, Martinsville, *Richmond Christian Advocate*, 8 September 1881.

8. Reply to editorial, "Civil Service in the Conference," by "A Circuit Rider," *Richmond Christian Advocate*, 6 January 1881; "Elmorino," "Facts for Thought," *Richmond Christian Advocate*, 12 March 1885.

9. Assessments of clerical income in this chapter are based on a close study of the annual salaries of one hundred Methodists between 1873 and 1907, chosen at random from those included in this study. Salary figures were taken from the *Minutes*, Virginia Annual Conference for the Methodist Episcopal Church, South. Baptists did not publish pastoral salaries.

10. "Big Salaries vs. Small Men," by "Content," *Richmond Christian Advocate*, 27 January 1881, p. 1.

11. "Are Preachers to Be Pitied?" *Religious Herald*, 6 March 1884, p. 1.

12. Ibid., 18 September 1875, 5 October 1876.

13. Ibid., 18 September 1875.

14. Ibid., 5 January 1875.

15. Ibid., 11 September 1876. See also the entry for 25 September 1876. For salary, see *Minutes*, Virginia Annual Conference, 1875, p. 29.

16. Account of the wedding of Stephen Putney and the daughter of Senator Withers, Steel Diary, 5 and 6 November 1877, UVa.

17. "A New Year's Letter from a Scolding Old Maid," by "S. G.," *Religious Herald*, 6 January 1876, p. 2.

18. C. H. Ryland, Letterbook, 1868, and Notebook 1859–1860, Southern Baptist Theological Seminary, Greenville, S.C., VBHS.

19. Letter of A. J. Sadler of Matoaca Village, Chesterfield County, *Religious Herald*, 16 June 1870, p. 3; A. A. Dance to T. W. Sydnor, 1 July 1873, Sydnor Papers, UVa; letter of A. Bagby of Stevensville, *Religious Herald*, 3 April 1884, p. 2; R. W., Farnham, Va., "Ecclesiastical Polygamy in Virginia," *Religious Herald*, 16 January 1896, p. 1; "The Report of the Committee on Co-operation," *Minutes*, Virginia Baptist General Association, 1905, pp. 25–26; J. W. Hart, King and Queen County, *Religious Herald*, 4 September 1884, p. 2; "The District Association: A Review and a Plea," address delivered before the Dover Baptist Association, Williamsburg, 10 July 1900, by Charles H. Ryland, D. D., n. p., VBHS.

20. D. A. Woodson to "Dear Brother Sydnor," 28 February 1872, Sydnor Papers, UVa.

21. "Boomfield Circuit Divided," by "Rambler," *Richmond Christian Advocate*, 11 January 1877, p. 2.

22. At the death of his father, Sydnor received about $10,000 worth of land and slaves. "Plan for Dividing the Negroes of the Dungarvin Estate," Sydnor Papers, UVa.

23. On poverty in the postwar Southside and churches' inability to pay full-time pastors, see A. F. Davidson to "Dear Brother Sydnor," 16 December 1869; letter from a committee of Jonesboro Church, 16 January 1870; Ken Craig to T. W. Sydnor, 20 October 1872; R. H. Dowdy and J. W. Jenkins to T. W. Sydnor, 10 November 1873; receipt, Concord Association to T. W. Sydnor, 1 June 1884, all in Sydnor Papers, UVa. For Sydnor, see "Thomas W. Sydnor," in Taylor, *Virginia Baptist Ministers*, Fourth Series, pp. 71–75; Moger, *Virginia: Bourbonism to Byrd*, pp. 80–81.

24. In 1868, the combined tuition for his daughter and son was more than $300. The Albemarle Female Institute charged $130 tuition for the January to June session; Richmond College, meanwhile, charged $265. See advertisements, *Religious Herald*, 23 January 1868.

25. I. B. Lake and Thomas Hume Jr., principals of the Roanoke Female College, to T. W. Sydnor, 15 January 1869, Sydnor Papers, UVa.

26. Robert Ryland to T. W. Sydnor, 25 December 1865, Sydnor Papers, UVa.

27. Letter from Committee of Jonesboro Church, 16 January 1870; R. H. Dowdy and J. W. Jenkins to T. W. Sydnor, 10 November 1873; and Ken Craig to T. W. Sydnor, 20 October 1872, Sydnor Papers, UVa.

28. Sydnor was paid $1,000 annually. But this position lasted just one year.

29. T. W. Sydnor to Col. R. F. Dillard, 4 March 1870, Sydnor Papers, UVa.

30. J. William Jones to "My dear Brother Sydnor," 10 June 1870, Sydnor Papers, UVa.

31. Joseph D. Giles to Mr. Thomas W. Sydnor, 21 August 1871, Sydnor Papers, UVa; Lucie A. Hamilton to Mr. Sydnor, 13 May 1870, Sydnor Papers, UVa.

32. The number of pastor-superintendents fell by half by 1900. Of those pastors from this study who served as superintendents, all were Baptists; see *Report of the Superintendent of Public Instruction of Virginia*. On pastors seeking superintendent's positions, see Rev. T. M. Beckham to Rev. T. W. Sydnor, 8 January 1872, Sydnor Papers,

UVa. "Written Report for Year Ending August 31st 1874 for Nottoway County Schools," 15 September 1874, Sydnor Papers, UVa. On religious leaders' opposition to public schools in Virginia, see Link, *A Hard Country and a Lonely Place*, pp. 18–19. State Superintendent William Ruffner was a Presbyterian minister.

33. R. R. Burton of Chase City, Va., to Thomas W. Sydnor, 16 October 1873, Sydnor Papers, UVa.

34. One Baptist pastor took the superintendency at a time when "an influential portion of the community was hostile to the system, and a tax of 10 cents on the hundred dollars . . . was all that had been grudgingly given for its support." Within a few years, he had persuaded his neighbors to agree to a tax increase. "Written Report for the Year Ending August 31st 1874 for Nottoway County Schools," 15 September 1874, Sydnor Papers, UVa; sketch of H. D. Ragland, Superintendent for Goochland County Public Schools, *Virginia School Journal*, April 1894; Link, *Hard Country and Lonely Place*, pp. 24–26.

35. A. F. Davidson to T. W. Sydnor, 16 December 1869, 28 October 1872, and 8 January 1873. For quote, D. A. Woodson of Modest Town, Va., to T. W. Sydnor, 28 February 1872, UVa.

36. George Mann Wright to Josie Wright, 2 April 1877, R-M.

37. Haber, *The Quest for Authority and Honor in the American Professions*, p. 8.

38. On leaving the pulpit, see Perry Pringle, "Is There a Way Out?" *Richmond Christian Advocate*, 30 April 1891, p. 1; "Are Men Called out of the Ministry?" *Religious Herald*, 6 October 1898, p. 8.

39. Bernice Foushee Bryant, *Reminiscences and Talltales of a Preacher's Kid, 1870–1934*, typescript, 1965, VHS; Lafferty, *Sketches of the Virginia Conference* (1901), pp. 159–63. For salary, Minutes, *Virginia Annual Conference, 1877–1908*.

40. "Methodist preachers . . . ," *Richmond Christian Advocate*, 19 February 1885, p. 2.

41. Edward Portlock Wilson Diary, 3 May 1884, R-M.

42. On Edwards, see open letter of laymen's committee, *Richmond Christian Advocate*, 7 March 1867, p. 2; Edwards's signature on life insurance policy of John William Woolfolk, 7 July 1868, Woolfolk Family Papers, VHS. A. F. Davidson became a salesman for the Maryland Life Insurance Company of Baltimore in the 1880s after years of trying to make a living in rural pulpits in southside Virginia. A. F. Davidson to T. W. Sydnor, 20 July 1889, Sydnor Papers, UVa. Also, report of 1868 Virginia Annual Conference, printed in *Richmond Christian Advocate*, 3 December 1868, p. 2; "Insure Your Churches," *Richmond Christian Advocate*, 24 April 1873; $1,000 life insurance policy of H. D. Ragland, Valley Mutual of Staunton, 1881, Ragland Papers, VHS; receipts for payment of $10 premium for $1,000 home insurance policy to Petersburg Savings and Insurance Company, 30 April 1880 and 1882 renewal in the name of Rev. E. P. Wilson, Wilson Diary, R-M; note of payment of 1889 insurance policy on Hermon (Methodist) Church, Essex Circuit, *Minute Book*, Hermon Church, Essex Circuit, 1889–1901, R-M. For insured value of parsonages and churches, see *Minutes*, Virginia Annual Conference, 1900. The total insured value was $780,695.

43. *Methodist Recorder* (Farmville), April 1895, p. 1; John McDowell, *The Social Gospel in the South*, pp. 6, 7, 11, 12; Sweet, *Virginia Methodism*, p. 385. Parsonage numbers from *Minutes*, Virginia Conference, 1875 and 1900. Also see letter of Laura W. Hank, pastor's wife of the King and Queen Circuit, *Richmond Christian Advocate*, 15 January 1874, p. 2; D. G. C. Butts, *From Saddle to City*, p. 75; and the following from the *Richmond Christian Advocate*, 1877: letter of B. F. Ball, 25 January, p. 2; "Women's Department of Church Extension," 10 February, p. 1; letter of John W. How-

ard, 22 February, p. 2; "We are pleased to learn . . . ," 1 March, p. 2; letter of C. E. Watts, King George Circuit, 1 March, p. 2.

44. An 1877 piece urged pastors and laymen to consider leaving funds for the Methodist Preachers' Relief Society in their will. "Have You Made Your Will," *Richmond Christian Advocate*, 25 January 1877, p. 1; "Virginia Conference Brotherhood," *Religious Herald*, 24 September 1896, p. 2; "Thoughts pro and con on retiring from the active itinerant work," Edward Portlock Wilson, penciled page stuck inside 1879 diary, R-M; "William B. Pedigo (c1803–1891)," in Taylor, *Virginia Baptist Ministers*, Fourth Series, p. 108.

45. T. W. Sydnor to Col. R. F. Dillard, 4 March 1870, Sydnor Papers, UVa.

46. Donald M. Scott has used the term "sacred vocation" to explain the peculiar fervor of antebellum abolitionists (in his "Abolition as a Sacred Vocation," in Perry and Fellman, eds. *Antislavery Reconsidered*).

47. Twain is quoted in R. Laurence Moore, "Religion, Secularization, and the Shaping of the Culture Industry in Antebellum America." Second quote, "The Press," *Religious Herald*, 4 January 1872, p. 2.

48. *Methodist Recorder*, March 1895, p. 1.

49. Of the pastors included in this study, approximately thirty-two published works in the nineteenth century.

50. A Lynchburg businessman said he was "called" to become the secretary of the local YMCA. Letter of J. S. Felix of Lynchburg, *Religious Herald*, 16 October 1890, p. 1.

51. Letter of M. W. of Taylorsville, *Religious Herald*, 23 November 1865, p. 1.

52. On church fairs, see Rev. R. N. Sledd to Frances Patterson Early, 24 December 1874, Early Family Papers, Section 19, VHS; Rev. George Mann Wright to "My Precious wife," 7 August 1884, R-M. For the rise of entertainment and the decline of church discipline, see Ownby, "Mass Culture, Upper-Class Culture, and the Decline of Church Discipline in the Evangelical South."

53. "Baltimore Conference," *Richmond Christian Advocate*, 11 September 1879, p. 2. A writer in 1873 had denounced the display of "mammon and fashion" at the Greenbrier. "The Contrasts," *Richmond Christian Advocate*, 18 September 1873, p. 2. On Baptists at White Sulphur Springs, see Rev. Cornelius Tyree (1814–91), in Taylor, *Virginia Baptist Ministers*, Fourth Series, pp. 120–23. A Methodist editor urged Methodists to meet at resorts like the Episcopalians and Presbyterians were doing. "Why Not?" *Richmond Christian Advocate*, 26 November 1885, p. 2.

54. For figures on conference entertainment, see *Minutes*, Virginia Annual Conference, 1897, pp. 133–34; Rev. J. C. Granbery to "My Dear Queen," 14 June 1889, R-M. On tourism in the New South, see Elizabeth Ann Atwood, " 'Saratoga of the South': The Development of Tourism in Luray, Virginia," in Ayers and Willis, eds. *The Edge of the South*; and Ayers, *Promise of the New South*, pp. 60–61.

55. "The Contrasts," *Richmond Christian Advocate*, 18 September 1873, p. 2.

56. Ownby, *Subduing Satan*, chapter 10.

57. On tobacco, "It Shows Bad Taste," *Religious Herald*, 15 February 1872, p. 1; and *Virginia Conference Annual* 1879, p. 16. On theater and the circus, see "Wordly Amusements: The Opera," *Religious Herald*, 31 May 1866, p. 2; "Did You Go to the Circus?" *Richmond Christian Advocate*, 1 October 1885, p. 1; "Resolution," *Virginia Conference Annual* 1887, p. 15; on worldliness in the church, "Growing Tendency to Blend Amusement and Religion," *Richmond Christian Advocate*, 24 January 1867, p. 2; "Sunday Excursions," *Richmond Christian Advocate*, 12 August 1869, p. 2; William Henry Christian to Willie [William Edmund] Christian, 31 July 1878, Scott Family

Papers, VHS; "Worldliness in the Church," W. J. Twilley, *Richmond Christian Advocate*, 4 April 1889. Quote from John E. Edwards, "Once More and Finally," *Richmond Christian Advocate*, 21 March 1889, p. 1.

58. Letter from Cearsley's Church, *Richmond Christian Advocate*, 13 May 1880, p. 2.

59. Another complained that the point of giving money was self-denial, not entertainment. "The Church and the World," *Richmond Christian Advocate*, 8 February 1877, p. 2. For quote, R. N. Sledd to Frances Patterson Early, 24 December 1874, Early Family Papers, Section 19, VHS.

60. "Lectures, Rev. Oscar F. Flippo of Virginia," broadside, Sydnor Papers, UVa.

61. William Leander Fitcher, 1839–1917, in Taylor, *Virginia Baptist Ministers*, Sixth Series, p. 56.

62. T. S. Pleasants, Librarian, to Rev. J. C. Granbery, 14 March 186(8)?, R-M.

63. Letter of William E. Hatcher, *Religious Herald*, 8 September 1892, p. 2. He railed against "slovenly, ugly and impractical churches."

64. The Baptist Social Union was organized in Richmond in the 1880s. Members paid $5 annual dues and were approved by two-thirds of the club's members. Women were invited only on special occasions. See "The Social Union," *Religious Herald*, 4 March 1886, p. 2; "Baptist Social Union of Richmond," *Religious Herald*, 12 April 1888, p. 2; "Baptist Social Union—Autumn Meeting," *Religious Herald*, 3 November 1892, p. 2; and *The Baptist Social Union of Richmond and Vicinity* (1900?).

Chapter 8

1. B. C. Henning, D.D., "The Pastor's Relation to the Enterprise of His Denomination," *Religious Herald*, 18 January 1906, p. 2.

2. "Missions—yes Foreign Missions—are the lifeblood of the churches" ("Functions and Values of Local Churches," *Religious Herald*, 6 September 1894, p. 2); "A Woman to Women," *Religious Herald*, 17 May 1888, p. 1.

3. Mrs. W. E. Hatcher, printed flyer, "Central Committee for Virginia, to the Women's Missionary Societies of Virginia," Richmond, July 1888.

4. "Functions and Values of Local Churches," *Religious Herald*, 6 September 1894, p. 2. On the question of the local churches, see also "The Autonomy of the Local Church," *Religious Herald*, 5 April 1888, p. 1; "The Proposed Civic Church," *Religious Herald*, 11 January 1894, p. 1; and "The Place of Authority," *Religious Herald*, 17 February 1898, p. 2.

5. "The Autonomy of the Local Church," *Religious Herald*, 5 April 1888, p. 1.

6. Letter of Rev. Edward J. Willis, *Religious Herald*, 21 December 1865, p. 2.

7. Women were an average of 60 percent of church membership for the whole of the nineteenth century. Ownby, *Subduing Satan*, p. 129.

8. Women were far more likely than men to will money to the church, and they took a critical part in fund-raising. See Lebsock, *Free Women of Petersburg*, p. 224.

9. Letter of William H. Wren of Lynchburg, *Religious Herald*, 3 February 1876, p. 3.

10. Butts, *From Saddle to City*, pp. 23–24.

11. Martha A. Fowlkes to "My dear Brother Sydnor," 12 November 1871, Sydnor Papers, UVa. Mrs. Fowlkes was a regular correspondent of Sydnor and took special care to report problems in the congregation to him. See also letter of 18 January 1875, Sydnor Papers, UVa; correspondence of various Methodist ministers to Miss Lizzie

Smith of Mathews C. H., R-M; and correspondence of Rev. R. N. Sledd with Frances Patterson Early of Lynchburg, Early Family Papers, Section 19, VHS.

12. Mary R. (Walker) Hilliard to Thomas H. Early, 16 January 1874, Early Family Papers, Section 7, VHS.

13. G. W. Beale, Notebook, n.d. (c. 1867), VBHS. See also "Conduct of Unmarried Ministers towards Females," editorial, *Religious Herald*, 9 July 1868, p. 2.

14. Manuscript minutes, trial of P. W. Archer (1863) and trial of Wilbur Robins (1877), R-M.

15. Manuscript minutes, trial of M. L. Bishop (1874), R-M.

16. Minutes, trial of Rev. C. D. Crawley, 7 August 1878, West Brunswick Circuit, R-M.

17. William Brooking Rowzie to William Gray, 26 December 1855, William Gray Papers, VHS. Pastors were also charged with violation of contract and embezzlement of church or denominational funds. John K. Littleton was convicted of embezzling $300 in missionary funds in 1862 and was dismissed from the pastorate. Minutes, trial of John K. Littleton (1862), R-M.

18. Anonymous, "From a Parsonage," *Richmond Christian Advocate*, 6 March 1873.

19. Letter of Tennessee Presiding Elder's wife, *Richmond Christian Advocate*, 23 March 1893, p. 2; Eaton, *The Itinerant's Wife*.

20. "To Southern Women from a Southern Woman," *Religious Herald*, 19 October 1865, p. 4.

21. "Normal Instruction for Young Ladies," *Religious Herald*, 30 November 1865, p. 1.

22. On postwar marriage rates, Bardaglio, *Reconstructing the Household*, pp. 130–31; Friedman, *Enclosed Garden*, pp. 94–95.

23. *The Baptist* (Memphis), 27 April 1867, p. 3; Charles L. Cocke to Bettie Sydnor, 5 September 1866, Sydnor Papers, UVa; "Give Your Daughters an Education," *Religious Herald*, 20 March 1884, p. 1.

24. "Should Women Speak in Public," *Religious Herald*, 20 February 1868, p. 2; "Queries," *Religious Herald*, 19 March 1868, p. 2; "J.A.B.," "Should Women Speak in Public Meetings?" *Religious Herald*, 2 April 1868, p. 1; letter of W. M. of Grafton, W. Va., *Religious Herald*, 23 April 1868. See also Rev. James W. Compton, "May Women Speak Publicly?" *Richmond Christian Advocate*, 29 July 1875; "Women Preaching," *Religious Herald*, 5 March 1874, p. 2; "May Women Speak in the Churches," *Religious Herald*, 14 May 1874, p. 1.

25. See comments on women in the *Richmond Christian Advocate*, 1867, especially "Criticizing Sermons," 7 February 1867, p. 1.

26. "Roanoke Female College of Danville," from the meeting of the Danville Association, *Religious Herald*, 15 February 1866, p. 2.

27. "Endowment of the Hollins Institute," *Religious Herald*, 8 January 1874, p. 1; "Normal Instruction for Young Ladies," *Religious Herald*, 30 November 1865, p. 1.

28. Report Card of Mary Ellen Pollard [Clarke], [daughter of Rev. John Pollard, Jr.], 1877–1880, for a Four-Year Course at the Female High School of Baltimore, Clarke Family Papers, VHS.

29. "Alumnae of Wesleyan," J. C. Granbery address to Wesleyan Female College, Murfreesboro, N.C., 1884, R-M.

30. "Some Thoughts," *Religious Herald*, 8 January 1880; "The Limitations of Woman," J. W. Moore of Amherst, *Richmond Christian Advocate*, 2 February 1893, p. 1.

31. "Equal Education for the Sexes," Alexander Eubank, *Religious Herald*, 1 June 1882, p. 1; "Is the University Carrying Out Jefferson's Ideals?" *Religious Herald*, 30 June 1898; "Man's Inhumanity to Woman," by "A Virginia Woman," *Religious Herald*, 5 April and 12 April 1894, p. 1.

32. "The Education of Girls," *Religious Herald*, 1 February 1900, p. 2.

33. The Baptists' Southwest Virginia Female Institute in Bristol, opened by Virginia Baptists aimed to educate poor young women. "A Plain Talk on How Best to Help the Women of the South," address of A. E. Dickinson to the Lebanon Association, reprinted in *Religious Herald*, 4 October 1888, p. 1.

34. Ella W. Granbery to "My Dear Mother," 13 May 1884, Granbery Papers, R-M. On student exhibitions, Horace G. Campbell, *The Campbell Story*, (Mesa, Ariz.: n.p., 1970).

35. The campaign fell short of its goal. Letterhead, "Office of the Memorial Committee," on letter of J. S. Burrows to "Dear Brother Sydnor," 17 January 1873, Sydnor Papers, UVa.

36. The women of First Baptist Church of Petersburg held a fair to raise money for the rebuilding of their church, destroyed by lightning in 1866. *Religious Herald*, 17 May 1866, p. 2.

37. Subscribers to the Dollar Roll received an 8-×-12 certificate on stiff paper suitable for framing. "The Virginia Dollar Roll for Richmond College," *Religious Herald*, 6 January 1876, p. 3. Rumsey and Brockman letters quoted in "Interesting Letters," *Religious Herald*, 24 February 1876, p. 3.

38. Charles Ryland, "The Baptist Women of Virginia," *Religious Herald*, 20 January 1876, p. 2. See also another untitled piece by Ryland, the Secretary-Treasurer of the Baptist General Association of Virginia, on the same page. W. W. Bennett, president of Randolph-Macon College, *Richmond Christian Advocate*, 18 December 1879.

39. "Address to Southern Women," *Religious Herald*, 24 February 1870, p. 1; "Female Missionaries," *Religious Herald*, 25 April 1872, p. 2. On women and foreign missions, see Hill, *The World Their Household*; and Hunter, *Gospel of Gentility*.

40. "Organization of the Women's Foreign Missionary Society in the Virginia Conference," *Richmond Christian Advocate*, 5 January 1899, p. 7; "Woman's Work in Virginia," *Richmond Christian Advocate*, 11 December 1879, p. 1.

41. Baker, *Southern Baptist Convention*, pp. 297–98. On Lottie Moon, see "Woman's Missionary Union of Albemarle Baptist Association, 1886–1974, typed mss., no author, 10 pp., VBHS; Hyatt, *Our Ordered Lives Confess*.

42. "Suggestions as to Women's Missionary Societies," printed flyer, n.d. (1888?), Central Committee for Virginia, Virginia Baptist General Association.

43. V. T. of Goochland County, "Working Women," *Richmond Christian Advocate*, 8 March 1883, p. 1.

44. Rosalie Josephine Whitter Anderson (1841–) Diary, 1881–82, VHS.

45. Anderson Diary, 1881–82, VHS; Mrs. May Leachman Dogan, "Early History of the Women's Missionary Society of Sudley Methodist Episcopal Church, South," 1928, Sudley Church Archives, reprinted in Elizabeth H. Johnson, *History in a Horseshoe Curve*, (Princeton, N.J.: Pennywitt Press, c 1982), p. 107. Rosalie Anderson's diary ends just as she noticed that her feelings for Hannon had caught the public eye.

46. Mary Pollard Clarke, undated entry, Diary, 1898, Clarke Family Papers, VHS.

47. Report of the 7 February 1898 meeting of the Main Street Auxiliary Missionary Society of Danville, *The Methodist*, Danville, Va., March 1898, pp. 1–2.

48. "A Midsummer's Sermon, by a Woman," *Religious Herald*, 12 July 1888, p. 1.

49. *Minutes*, Virginia Annual Conference, 1879, pp. 76–77.

50. "Women Preachers," by "L.," *Richmond Christian Advocate*, 14 March 1889, p. 2.

51. For a woman who opposed women's organization, see "A Mississippi Woman Replies to Ruth Alleyn," by L. V. of Vicksburg, *Religious Herald*, 2 February 1888, p. 1.

52. The report was published as "To the Baptist Women of Virginia," *Religious Herald*, 16 February 1888, p. 1. H. H. Harris published a rebuttal supporting the women's missionary society, "To the Baptist Women of Virginia," *Religious Herald*, 1 March 1888, p. 1.

53. Proceedings of the Virginia Baptist General Association, Bristol, Va., printed in *Religious Herald*, 22 November 1888, p. 2.

54. Woman's Missionary Union of the Albemarle Baptist Association, 1886–1974, typed manuscript, 10 pp., n. author, VBHS.

55. Editorial, "Women Preaching," *Religious Herald*, 5 March 1874, p.2.

56. "Prospects of Womanhood," *Richmond Christian Advocate*, 5 July 1883, p. 2; "Woman's Work," *Richmond Christian Advocate*, 30 April 1885, p. 1.

57. "A Bright and Cheerful Letter," by "A Member" of N.C., *Richmond Christian Advocate*, 1 March 1883, p. 1.

58. "A Member," "Notes from the Bertie Auxiliary," *Richmond Christian Advocate*, 21 June 1883, p. 1.

59. "A Few Tattling Women," *Religious Herald*, 31 July 1884, p. 1.

60. "Is the Woman's Committee Self-Appointed?" *Religious Herald*, 18 October 1888, p. 1.

61. "The Result for Four Years," *Richmond Christian Advocate*, 15 February 1883, p. 2; letters, *Richmond Christian Advocate*, 4 October 1883, p. 1; letter from Middle Tennessee woman, *Religious Herald*, 19 April 1888, p. 1.

62. The most vocal public criticism coincided with the depression of the early 1890s. On women and debt, see "Baptist Ladies of Richmond," *Religious Herald*, 30 March 1882, p. 2; "Woman's Board Finances," *Richmond Christian Advocate*, 3 September 1891, p. 2; "Women As Collectors of Church Money," *Richmond Christian Advocate*, 6 July 1893, p. 2; Mrs. E. C. Dowdell of Auburn, Alabama, "The Women Excel," *Richmond Christian Advocate*, 20 April 1893, p. 1.

63. Mrs. C. H. Hall, "The WFMS of Virginia," *Richmond Christian Advocate*, 5 January 1899, p. 7.

64. "Woman's Department of Church Extension," *Richmond Christian Advocate*, 10 February 1887, p. 1.

65. "Some Thoughts for Virginia Baptist Laymen," *Religious Herald*, 23 February 1882, p. 1.

66. "Richmond Methodism," *Richmond Christian Advocate*, 17 October 1889, p. 2.

67. *Richmond Christian Advocate*, 23 January 1879, p. 2.

68. *Religious Herald*, 1 January 1880, p. 1.

69. "Remittance Form—WMU of Virginia," used when B. A. Jacobs was treasurer (1897– 1919), VBHS.

70. "Financial Plan of a City Church," *Richmond Christian Advocate*, 14 August 1873; "Improvement of Church Finances," *Quarterly Methodist Review*, January 1889, p. 336.

71. Contribution envelope of Second Baptist Church, Richmond, Sunday, May 25, 1873, Box 9, Sydnor Papers, UVa.

72. "Money Is Power," *Religious Herald*, 17 May 1866, p. 1.

73. "A Layman's View," *Richmond Christian Advocate*, 10 August 1893, p. 1. See also letter of "Alpha" of Fluvanna County, *Richmond Christian Advocate*, 30 May 1867. On Waynesboro, see letter of B. F. Ball, *Richmond Christian Advocate*, 25 January 1877, p. 2.

74. Letter of Rev. J. O. Moss, "Statistical Illusions," *Richmond Christian Advocate*, 5 January 1899, p. 4.

75. "Some Small, But Important Items," *Religious Herald*, 3 May 1894, p. 2.

76. "Baptist Layman's Union of Virginia," *Religious Herald*, 8 February 1888, p. 1. See also in the *Religious Herald*, Charles L. Cocke, "To Virginia Baptist Laymen," 20 July 1882, p. 1; "The Layman's Movement and the General Association," 28 October 1886, p. 2; "A Layman to Laymen," 5 January 1888, p. 1; "Union Laymen's Meeting at Hardware," 2 August 1888, p. 1; Charles L. Cocke, "To Baptist Laymen," 30 January 1890, p. 1. Also, "Ministers and Laymen's Meeting," *Roanoke Baptist Union*, June 1893, p. 2. For Methodists, see "A Vigorous Laity," *Richmond Christian Advocate*, 17 September 1891, p. 2.

77. Editorial, *Richmond Christian Advocate*, 19 February 1891, p. 2.

78. Rev. John E. Edwards, *Richmond Christian Advocate*, 11 April 1889, p. 1.

79. Letter of J. E. DeShazo, *Richmond Christian Advocate*, 29 June 1893, p. 2.

80. In 1895, 129 of 871 churches in the state were, in the committees words, "derelict." Quotes from "Report of Committee on Co-operation," *Minutes*, Baptist General Association of Virginia, 1882, pp. 30–32. See also "The Fourteenth Annual Report of the Committee on Co-operation," *Minutes*, Baptist General Association of Virginia, 1895, pp. 20–22; and "The Report of the Committee on Co-operation," *Minutes*, Baptist General Association of Virginia, 1905, pp. 25–27. See also letter of Charles L. Cocke, *Religious Herald*, 19 November 1896, p. 1; letter of I. M. Mercer of the Committee on Co-operation, *Religious Herald*, 5 April 1900, p. 5.

81. 1899 Statistics for Woman's Missionary Societies, *Religious Herald*, 15 February 1900, p. 7.

82. Ted Ownby, "The Decline of Evangelical Church Discipline in the Rural South, 1865–1915: Changing Communities, Changing Moral Strategies," paper delivered at the Southern Historical Association annual meeting, November 1990, New Orleans; Ownby, *Subduing Satan*; Waldrep, " 'So Much Sin': The Decline of Religious Discipline and the 'Tidal Wave of Crime.' "

83. "The Poor of Our Churches," reprinted from the *Danville Methodist* in the *Richmond Christian Advocate*, 14 June, 1900, p. 3.

84. Joseph F. Kett ("Women and the Progressive Impulse in Southern Education") has argued that Southern progressivism was social progressivism and was "fundamentally an educational movement" in that it sought to change people through education.

85. Frederick A. Bode (*Protestantism and the New South*) has noted how this attitude, particularly prevalent among the Populists, shaped public opinion in North Carolina.

86. Ibid., p. 39.

Chapter 9

1. "Changes among Baptists," *Religious Herald*, 17 February 1870, p. 2.

2. On pastors and the Lost Cause, see Foster, *Ghosts of the Confederacy*; Wilson, *Baptized in Blood*.

3. Woodward, *Origins of the New South*, p. 157.

4. Daniel Witt to Rev. T. W. Sydnor, n.d. (late 1860s), Sydnor Papers, UVa; *Reli-*

gious Herald, "Conventionalism," 8 February 1866, p. 2; "To Young Ministers," 8 March 1866, p. 2. On a new generation of pastors, see also James A. Riddick to William Gray, 4 January 1870, William Gray Papers, VHS; letter of William F. Broaddus of Fredericksburg, *Religious Herald*, 8 February 1866, p. 2.

5. "From Our North Carolina Correspondent," *Religious Herald*, 22 March 1866, p.1.

6. Speech quoted in the Proceedings of the Virginia Annual Conference, *Richmond Christian Advocate*, 26 November 1868, p. 2.

7. Granbery to Ella Winston Granbery, 6 April 1866, Granbery Papers, UVa.

8. *Minutes*, Virginia Annual Conference, and *Minutes*, Virginia Baptist General Association.

9. Harry S. Stout, "The Life and Death of the Confederate Jeremiad," the James A. Gray Lectures, Duke Divinity School, Duke University, October 1992, in the author's possession.

10. "Power in Preaching," *Richmond Christian Advocate*, 14 September 1871, p. 2.

11. D. S. Doggett, "Introduction," to Lafferty, *Sketches of the Virginia Conference* (1880).

12. Southern Methodists adopted biographies during the 1870s; Northern Methodists did so in 1892. Patterson, "Ministerial Mind," pp. 174–79.

13. "Our Obligations to the Baptist Fathers," *Religious Herald*, 1 March 1866, p. 2.

14. "Power in Preaching," *Richmond Christian Advocate*, 14 September 1871, p. 2.

15. J. William Jones's account of the revival appeared a decade later. It borrows heavily from Bennett and was far less pious: it ends with a celebration of New South progress. Bennett, *Narrative of the Great Revival*; Jones, *Christ in the Camp*.

16. Bennett, *Narrative of the Great Revival*, p. 9. On the Virginia Movement, see Foster, *Ghosts of the Confederacy*, chapter 4.

17. Lost Cause leader J. William Jones was an ordained Baptist, but he left the pulpit in the 1870s, played only a marginal role in the denomination, and did not hold a regular preaching appointment in this period. See Wilson, *Baptized in Blood*, pp. 119–38.

18. James, *Four Years of Methodist Ministry*, p. 43.

19. A. E. Dickinson, "The Plain Old Preacher," *Religious Herald*, 14 September 1882, p. 1.

20. W. Hatcher, *John Jasper*.

21. Ibid., "Introduction," p. 8.

22. Ibid., chapter 2, "Jasper Has a Thrilling Conversion," pp. 28–29.

23. See editorial series on "Protracted Meetings," *Religious Herald*, 8 March, 22 March, and 5 April 1866, p. 2. On revivals in 1865 and 1866, see the following in the *Religious Herald*: "Revivals," 16 November 1865, p. 2; "A Revival of Religion the Great Want of the South," 23 November 1865, p. 2; "An Outpouring of God's Spirit," 14 December 1865, p. 1; letter of Rev. W. M. Mason of Caroline County, 14 December 1865, p. 2; "Editorial Gleanings," 4 January 1866, p. 2; letter of G. F. A. of Accomack County, 11 January 1866, p. 2; letter of Rev. John W. Jones of Loudoun County, 18 January 1866, p. 3; letter of Rev. V. T. Settle of Nelson County, 25 January 1866, p. 2; letter of C. E. W. Dobbs of Norfolk, 3 March 1866, p. 2; letter of Rev. Thomas E. Skinner of Raleigh, N.C., 5 April 1866, p. 2.

24. *Richmond Christian Advocate*, 1 August 1889.

25. "Tramps Ecclesiastic," *Richmond Christian Advocate*, 22 April 1897, p. 8.

26. "Revivals," from Charles H. Ryland, notebook, Southern Baptist Theological Seminary, 1859–1860, VBHS.

27. *Methodist Quarterly Review*, July 1889, p. 417.

28. "Were the Apostles Illiterate?" *Religious Herald*, 24 May 1888, p. 1.

29. "The periodic war on the D.D.s," *Religious Herald*, 10 August 1882, p. 2.

30. On study, see also Wilson diaries, R-M. On the General Conference, see Lafferty, *Sketches and Portraits of the General Conference of the Methodist Episcopal Church.*

31. See comments on the novel of "a Miss Gay of Georgia," Steel Diary, 19 April 1874, UVa.

32. "Is the Pulpit Losing Its Power?" *Religious Herald*, 10 June 1880, p. 2; Rev. J. C. Hiden, D.D., "Cramps on the Modern Pulpit," *Richmond Christian Advocate*, 12 December 1895, p. 2; "The Old Respect," *Religious Herald*, 19 April 1894, p. 2.

33. "Report on Education," *Minutes*, Albemarle Baptist Association, August 1873, p. 14.

34. "Baptist Progress," *Religious Herald*, 3 January 1878, p. 1.

35. *Richmond Christian Advocate*, 26 May 1881, p.1.

36. *Richmond Christian Advocate*, 28 April 1881, p. 1.

37. Editorial, *Richmond Christian Advocate*, 15 January 1885, p.2.

38. W. H. O., "Sam Jones," *Religious Herald*, 24 July 1890, p. 2.

39. Moody appeared at the University of Virginia the following year and returned to Richmond in 1894. Sam Jones, meanwhile, visited Richmond during the 1880s, Danville in 1889, Richmond in 1890. *Richmond Christian Advocate*, 15 January 1885, p. 2; "Thoughts Suggested By Mr. Moody's Recent Visit to Richmond," 5 March 1885, p. 1; "Gentle Hints," 12 March 1885, p. 2; "Earnest and Direct Preaching," 30 April 1885, p. 2; editorial, 4 June 1885, p. 2; "Cannot the Preachers Learn Something from Sam Jones' Mode of Preaching," 6 August 1885, p. 1.

40. *Southern Methodist Review*, January 1888, pp. 380–81, 384.

41. "Are Revivals Out of Date?" *Religious Herald*, 12 May 1904, p. 4.

42. Richey, *Early American Methodism*, p. 21; Robins, "Vernacular American Landscape"; Jones, *Perfectionist Persuasion.*

43. Leonidas Rosser (1815–92) attended Wesleyan University in Connecticut and received his D.D. from Emory & Henry College in 1858. He traveled as an evangelist in the mid-1870s and again in the early 1890s.

44. "Eastern Shore Camp," *Richmond Christian Advocate*, 23 August 1877, p. 2.

45. "Concessions to the Spirit of the Age," *Richmond Christian Advocate*, 18 January 1883, p. 2.

46. Wilson Diary, 5 August 1881, R-M.

47. Ayers, *Promise of the New South*, p. 178.

48. "The Temperance Movement in Virginia—What Next?" *Religious Herald*, 4 March 1886, p. 1; "State Local Option Convention," *Religious Herald*, 25 March 1886, p. 3.

49. "The Civil Rights Bill—Extremes in Government," *Religious Herald*, 11 June 1874, p. 2; "The Gospel the Only Hope of the South," *Religious Herald*, 14 May 1874, p. 2.

50. *Richmond Christian Advocate*, 11 January 1877, p. 2.

51. Pearson and Hendricks, *Liquor and Antiliquor in Virginia*, p. 181.

52. Bishop McTyeire, *Journal* of the Methodist Episcopal Church, South General Conference, 1890, quoted in Pearson and Hendricks, *Liquor and Antiliquor in Virginia*, p. 204.

53. "Politics and Religion," *Religious Herald*, 15 February 1882, p. 2.

54. Woodward, *Origins of the New South*, p. 111; Moger, *Virginia: Bourbonism to Byrd*, p. 124.

55. Pearson and Hendricks, *Antiliquor in Virginia*, pp. 193–94; Moger, *Virginia: Bourbonism to Byrd*, pp. 76–94; 122–44.

56. "Brunswick Circuit," *Richmond Christian Advocate*, 26 January 1871, p. 2; advertisement for *Journal of Industry*, *Richmond Christian Advocate*, 23 January 1873, p. 2; "Our Business Directory," *Richmond Christian Advocate*, 14 April 1887, p. 3.

57. *Richmond Christian Advocate*, 16 June 1881, p. 2; 10 July 1879, p. 2.

58. William Henry Christian to "Willie" [William Edmund] Christian, 20 May 1878, Baldwin Family Papers, VHS.

59. *Richmond Christian Advocate*, 10 May 1883, p. 2; "My Father's Business," *Religious Herald*, 24 June 1880, p. 2.

60. Daniel, *Virginia Baptists*, pp. 130–31.

61. "Religion and Business," *Richmond Christian Advocate*, 20 May 1880, p. 1.

62. "He who commands the most money holds the strongest hand," Richmond *Whig and Advertiser*, 4 April 1876, quoted in Woodward, *Origins of the New South*, p. 151.

63. "C" of Humanity Hall, *Richmond Christian Advocate*, 7 January 1875, p. 1.

64. *Richmond Christian Advocate*, 16 December 1869; 23 October 1873, p. 3.

65. *Richmond Christian Advocate*, 23 June 1881, p. 2.

66. "Repudiation of Debts," *Religious Herald*, 1 February 1872, p. 2. For state debt and readjustment, see letter of John W. Todd of Staunton, *Religious Herald*, 31 January 1878, p. 3; "The State Debt—Shall It Be Paid or Repudiated?" *Religious Herald*, 3 January 1878, p. 2; comments in *Richmond Christian Advocate*, 28 August 1879, p. 2; "The Beam in Our Own Eye," *Richmond Christian Advocate*, 20 February 1879, p. 2; and "The New American Era," *Richmond Christian Advocate*, 16 January 1885, p. 2.

67. Against gambling, see "Virginia State Agricultural Society," *Religious Herald*, 18 June 1874, p. 1; "Jacobus," and "Modern Gambling—What Is It?" *Richmond Christian Advocate*, 1 April 1875, p. 1; *Religious Herald*, 6 April 1876, p. 2.

68. "Morality of the Country," *Richmond Christian Advocate*, 15 March 1883, p. 2.

69. "Moral Law in the Secular world," W. F. Tillett, D. D., *Richmond Christian Advocate*, 27 July 1893, p. 1.

70. "The Presidential Nominees," *Religious Herald*, 15 July 1880, p. 1.

71. "Local Option Alliance of Virginia," *Religious Herald*, 9 November 1882, p. 2.

72. "The English Liberals and Dissenters," *Religious Herald*, 3 June 1880, p. 1.

73. Rev. A. J. Kern, D.D., "Politics in the Pulpit," *Richmond Christian Advocate*, 2 November 1893, p. 1; Bode, *Protestantism and the New South*, pp. 39–60.

74. On corruption in politics, see "Better Times," *Richmond Christian Advocate*, 20 September 1877, p. 2; letter of "Moltke," *Richmond Christian Advocate*, 28 June 1877, p. 2; letter of W. C. E. of Richmond, *Richmond Christian Advocate*, 26 April 1877, p. 1; editorial, *Richmond Christian Advocate*, 13 May 1880, p. 2; "Evil Times," *Richmond Christian Advocate*, 3 November 1880, p. 2.

75. Editorial, *Richmond Christian Advocate*, 30 June 1881, p. 2.

76. "The Christian's Part in Politics," *Religious Herald*, 28 October 1880, p. 1.

77. Professor J. T. Averett, "Religious Principles and Business Practices," speech before the Laymen's Union meeting, Suffolk, Virginia, *Religious Herald*, 23 February 1888.

78. "Protection for Girls," *Religious Herald*, 26 January 1888, p. 2.

79. "The Regeneration," *Religious Herald*, 19 January 1882, p. 2.

80. Pearson and Hendricks, *Liquor and Antiliquor in Virginia*, pp. 185–87.

81. Thompson, *The Life of John R. Moffett*; *Was J. R. Moffett Murdered? Clark vs. the Commonwealth of Virginia*; and Richard D. Hamm, "The Killing of the Rev. Moffett: The Politics of Power in Danville," delivered at the annual meeting of the Southern Historical Association, Atlanta, November 1992, in author's possession.

82. Thompson, *Life of Moffett*, pp. 62–64.

83. The Baptist press, oddly, was not outraged by the murder. "Rev. J. R. Moffett shot," *Religious Herald*, 17 November 1892, p. 2; editorial, *Religious Herald*, 24 November 1892, p. 2; W. P. Averett, "Danville Dots," *Religious Herald*, 1 December 1892.

84. Thompson, *Life of Moffett*.

85. Letter of J. R. Moffett, *Religious Herald*, 23 October 1890, p. 1.

86. "Paul, Politics, and Society," *Richmond Christian Advocate*, 21 March 1889, p. 1.

87. "The Christian's Part in Politics," *Religious Herald*, 28 October 1880, p. 1.

88. Beth Barton Schweiger, "Putting Politics Aside: Virginia Democrats and Voter Apathy in the Era of Disfranchisement," in Ayers and Willis, eds., *The Edge of the South*.

89. "An Exhortation in Politics," *Richmond Christian Advocate*, 31 May 1883, p. 2.

90. W. L. Richardson of the Holston Conference, M. E. Church, South, in *Richmond Christian Advocate*, 22 January 1891, p. 1.

91. "The Virginia Conference," *Richmond Christian Advocate*, 13 December 1877, p. 2.

92. Letter of J. J. L., reporting on the Danville District Conference, Rocky Mount, Franklin County, Virginia, *Richmond Christian Advocate*, 16 June 1881, p. 2.

Selected Bibliography

Manuscripts

Library of Virginia, Richmond
    Robert Wilkins Berryman, Marriage Register, microfilm
    Centenary Methodist Church, Richmond, Records, microfilm
    Court Street Methodist Church, Lynchburg, Dorcas Society Minute Book
    Philip Courtney, Marriage Register, microfilm
    Ettrick Methodist Church, Records, microfilm
    Monumental Church, Portsmouth, Records, microfilm
    Shiloh Baptist Church, Charlotte County, Minute Book
    William E. Wiatt Diary, photostat

Virginia Conference (Methodist Episcopal Church, South) Archives, McGraw-Page
Library, Randolph-Macon College
    Disciplinary Trial Proceedings, scattered manuscript transcripts
    Early Family Papers
    John C. Granbery Papers
    Hiram Meyers, Account Book
    Alpheus W. Potts, "The Potts Family of Preachers in the Virginia Conference,"
        Charlottesville, 1975, typescript
    Report of the Committee to Examine the Candidates for Admission, Raleigh,
        N.C., 1828
    Edward Portlock Wilson Diary
    Leonidas Rosser Papers
    Trinity Church, Richmond, Minutes
    Acquinton Methodist Church, King William County, Sunday School Record Book
    George Mann Wright Papers

University of Virginia, Alderman Library, Charlottesville
    John Cowper Granbery Papers
    Samuel A. Steel Diary
    Thomas W. Sydnor Papers

Virginia Baptist Historical Society, University of Richmond
  Noah Carlton Baldwin Diary
  R. R. Burton Diary
  C. H. Ryland Notebook, Southern Baptist Theological Seminary, Greenville, S.C.
  Richmond Female Institute–Woman's College of Richmond, Records, Vol. 1
  Robert A. Ryland Papers
  William F. Broaddus Diary
  Jeremiah B. Jeter, Sermonbook
  C. H. Ryland, Letterbook
  G. W. Beale, Notebook
  Woman's Missionary Union of Albemarle Baptist Association

Virginia Historical Society, Richmond
  Rosalie Josephine Whitter Anderson diary
  Baldwin Family Papers
  Early Family Papers
  Clarke Family Papers
  Mary Pollard Clarke Diary
  Richard Andrew Fox Sermons
  William Gray Papers
  Gregory Family Papers
  Gwathmey Family Papers
  Ragland Family Papers
  Robins Family Papers
  Scott Family Papers
  Woolfolk Family Papers

Newspapers and Magazines

  The Baptist (Memphis)
  The Methodist (Danville)
  The Methodist Quarterly Review
  The Methodist Recorder (Farmville)
  Quarterly Review of the Methodist Episcopal Church, South
  Religious Herald (Richmond)
  Richmond Christian Advocate
  Theological and Homiletical Monthly (Richmond)

Published Sources

Albemarle Baptist Association, *Minutes*, 1865, 1873.
Bagby, George W., *Selections from the Miscellaneous Writings of Dr. George W. Bagby*, Vol. 1. Richmond: Whittet & Shepperson, 1884.
Baptist General Association of Virginia, *Minutes*.
The Baptist Psalmody: A Selection of Hymns for the Worship of God. Charleston: Southern Baptist Publication Society, 1850.
The Baptist Social Union of Richmond and Vicinity. n.p. (1900?).
Bennett, W. W., *A Narrative of the Great Revival Which Prevailed in the Southern Armies during the Late Civil War between the States of the Federal Union*. Philadelphia: Claxton, Remsen, and Haffelfinger, 1877.
Brunner, Edmund deS., *The New Country Church Building*. New York: Missionary Education Movement of the U.S. and Canada, 1917.

Butts, Daniel Gregory Claiborne, *From Saddle to City by Buggy, Boat, and Railway: Fifty Years of Itinerancy in Virginia.* n.p., 1922.

Crane, William Carey, *Literary Discourses.* New York: Edward H. Fletcher, 1853.

Dickens, Charles, *American Notes and Pictures from Italy* (1842). Reprint, New York: Oxford University Press, 1957.

Doggett, David S., *The Responsibility of Talent, An Address Delivered before the Franklin Literary Society of Randolph-Macon College.* Richmond: Christian Advocate Office, 1844.

————, *The Destiny of Educated Young Men, An Address Delivered before the Literary Societies of Emory and Henry College, June 21, 1848.* Richmond: Methodist Office, 1848.

Eaton, Rev. H. M., *The Itinerant's Wife.* New York: Lane & Scott, 1851. Reprinted in Carolyn De Swarte Gifford, *The Nineteenth-Century American Methodist Itinerant Preacher's Wife.* New York: Garland Publishing, 1987.

Education Board of the Virginia Baptist General Association Located at Richmond. Richmond: Dispatch Steam Press, 1868.

Edwards, Rev. John E., *Random Sketches and Notes of European Travel in 1856.* New York: Harper & Brothers, 1857.

First Baptist Congress of Virginia, *Proceedings.* n.p., 1883.

Goss, C. C., *Statistical History of the First Century of American Methodism.* New York: Carlton & Porter, 1866.

Hatcher, Eldridge B., *William E. Hatcher, A Biography.* Richmond: W. C. Hill Printing Company, 1915.

Hatcher, William E., *Life of J. B. Jeter, D.D.* Baltimore: H. M. Wharton & Co., 1887.

————, *John Jasper, The Unmatched Negro Philosopher.* New York: Fleming H. Revell Co., 1908.

Hatcher, Mrs. W. E., *Central Committee for Virginia, To the Women's Missionary Societies of Virginia.* Richmond, n.p., 1888.

Hoge, Peyton Harrison, *Moses Drury Hoge: Life and Letters.* Richmond: Prebyterian Committee of Publication, 1899.

Hundley, Daniel R., *Social Relations in Our Southern States.* New York: H. B. Price, 1860.

James, John T., *Four Years of Methodist Ministry, 1865–1869.* Staunton, Va., n.p., 1894.

Jeter, Jeremiah Bell, *The Life of Rev. Daniel Witt, D. D., of Prince Edward County, Virginia.* Richmond: J. T. Ellyson, 1875.

————, *The Recollections of a Long Life.* Richmond: Religious Herald Co., 1891.

Jones, J. William, *Christ in the Camp, or Religion in the Confederate Army.* Richmond: B. F. Johnson & Co., 1887; Atlanta: Martin & Hoyt, 1904.

Keeling, Henry, *The Colporteur's Commission: A Tract for the Times, in Several Scriptural Hymns.* Richmond, n. p., 1862.

Lafferty, John J., *Sketches and Portraits of the Virginia Conference.* Richmond: Christian Advocate Office, 1880.

————, *Sketches and Portraits of the General Conference of the Methodist Episcopal Church, South Held in Richmond, Virginia, May 1886.* Richmond: n.p., n.d.

————, *Sketches and Portraits of the Virginia Conference.* Richmond: Christian Advocate Office, 1890.

————, *Sketches and Portraits of the Virginia Conference.* Richmond: Christian Advocate Office, 1901.

A Map of the Baptist Churches of Virginia with a Catalogue Containing the Churches, Their Pastors, Associations and Statistics Compiled from the Minutes of 1850. Petersburg: O. Ellyson, 1851.

Olmsted, Frederick Law, *A Journey in the Seaboard Slave States*. New York: Dix & Edwards, 1856. Reprinted as *The Slave States*. New York: G. P. Putnam's Sons, 1959.

Peterson, Peter A., *Hand-Book of Southern Methodism*. Richmond: J. W. Fergusson & Son, 1883.

Report of the Superintendent of Public Instruction of Virginia. Richmond, 1871, 1881, 1891.

Richardson, Frank, *From Sunrise to Sunset: A Reminiscence*. Bristol, Tenn.: King Printing, 1910.

Richmond College Catalogue.

Roanoke Baptist Union, n.p., 1893.

Sands, Alexander Hamilton, *Recreations of a Southern Barrister*. Philadelphia: J. B. Lippincott and Co., 1859.

Sketches of History of the Baptist Churches within the Limits of the Rappahannock Association in Virginia. Richmond: Harrold & Murray, 1850.

Smith, William A., D.D., *Lectures on the Philosophy and Practice of Slavery*. Nashville: Stevenson and Evans, 1856.

Stringfellow, Thornton, *A Brief Examination of Scripture Testimony on the Institution of Slavery*. Richmond: Office of the Religious Herald, 1841.

———, *Slavery: Its Origin, Nature and History*. Alexandria: Virginia Sentinel Office, 1860.

Suggestions as to Women's Missionary Societies. Central Committee for Virginia, Virginia Baptist General Association, n.d. (1888?).

Taylor, George Boardman, *Kenny*. New York: Sheldon & Co., 1859.

———, *Cousin Guy*. New York: Sheldon & Co., 1860.

———, *Claiborne*. New York: Sheldon & Co., 1861.

Taylor, George Braxton, *The Life and Times of James Boardman Taylor*. Philadelphia: Bible and Publication Society, 1872.

———, *The Life and Letters of George Boardman Taylor, D.D.* Lynchburg, Va.: J. P. Bell Co., 1908.

———, *Virginia Baptist Ministers*. Third Series. Lynchburg, Va.: J. P. Bell & Company, 1912.

———, *Virginia Baptist Ministers*. Fourth Series. Lynchburg, Va.: J. P. Bell & Company, 1913.

———, *Virginia Baptist Ministers*. Fifth Series. Lynchburg, Va.: J. P. Bell & Company, 1915.

———, *Virginia Baptist Ministers*. Sixth Series. Lynchburg, Va.: J. P. Bell & Company, 1935.

Thompson, Rev. S. H., *The Life of John R. Moffett*. Salem, Va.: n.p., 1895.

Tocqueville, Alexis de, *Democracy in America*. J. P. Meyer, ed., George Lawrence, trans., Garden City, N.Y.: Anchor Books, 1969.

Virginia Annual Conference, *Minutes*.

Virginia [Baptist] Educational Society, *Minutes*, Tenth Annual Meeting, 1840.

Virginia School Journal, Richmond, 1903.

Was J.R. Moffett Murdered? Clark vs. the Commonwealth of Virginia. Richmond: Taylor and Dalton, n.d.

Secondary Sources

Ahlstrom, Sydney E., *A Religious History of the American People*. New Haven: Yale University Press, 1972. Reprint, 2 vols. Garden City, N.Y.: Image Books, 1975.

Alley, Reuben E., *History of the University of Richmond, 1830–1871*. Charlottesville: University Press of Virginia, 1977.

Andrews, Matthew Page, *Virginia: The Old Dominion*. Richmond: The Dietz Press, 1949.

Ayers, Edward L., *Vengeance and Justice: Crime and Punishment in the Nineteenth-Century American South*. New York: Oxford University Press, 1984.

———, *The Promise of the New South: Life After Reconstruction*. New York: Oxford University Press, 1992.

Ayers, Edward L., and John C. Willis, eds., *The Edge of the South: Life in Nineteenth-Century Virginia*. Charlottesville: University Press of Virginia, 1991.

Bailey, David T., *Shadow on the Church: Southwestern Evangelical Religion and the Issue of Slavery, 1783–1860*. Ithaca: Cornell University Press, 1985.

Bailey, Kenneth K., *Southern White Protestantism in the Twentieth Century*. New York: Harper & Row, 1964.

Baker, Robert A., *The Southern Baptist Convention and Its People, 1607–1972*. Nashville: Broadman Press, 1974.

Bardaglio, Peter W., *Reconstructing the Household: Families, Sex, and Law in the Nineteenth-Century South*. Chapel Hill: University of North Carolina Press, 1995.

Beeman, Richard R., *Evolution of the Southern Backcountry: A Case Study of Lunenburg County, Virginia, 1746–1832*. Philadelphia: University of Pennsylvania Press, 1984.

Bellah, Robert N., "Civil Religion in America." *Daedalus* 96 (Winter 1967): 1–21.

Bender, Thomas, *Toward an Urban Vision: Ideas and Institutions in Nineteenth-Century America*. Baltimore: Johns Hopkins University Press, 1975.

Bennett, Floyd S., *Methodist Church on Shockoe Hill: A History of Centenary Methodist Church Richmond, Virginia, 1810–1960*. Richmond: Whittet & Shepperson, 1962.

Beringer, Richard E., Herman Hattaway, Archer Jones, and William N. Still Jr., *Why the South Lost the Civil War*. Athens: University of Georgia Press, 1986.

Bledstein, Burton J., *The Culture of Professionalism: The Middle Class and the Development of Higher Education in America*. New York: W. W. Norton & Company, 1976.

Bode, Frederick A., *Protestantism and the New South: North Carolina Baptists and Methodists in Political Crisis*. Charlottesville: University Press of Virginia, 1975.

Bogger, Tommy L., *Free Blacks in Norfolk, Virginia, 1790–1860: The Darker Side of Freedom*. Charlottesville: University Press of Virginia, 1997.

Boitnott, John W., "Secondary Education in Virginia, 1845–1870." Ph.D. diss., University of Virginia, 1935.

Boles, John B., *The Great Revival, 1787–1805: The Origins of the Southern Evangelical Mind*. Lexington: University of Kentucky Press, 1972.

———, *Masters and Slaves in the House of the Lord: Race and Religion in the American South, 1740–1870*. Lexington: University Press of Kentucky, 1988.

Boylan, Anne M., *Sunday School: The Formation of an American Institution, 1790–1880*. New Haven: Yale University Press, 1988.

Bremner, Robert H., *The Public Good: Philanthropy and Welfare in the Civil War Era*. New York: Alfred A. Knopf, 1980.

Brown, Richard D., *Knowledge Is Power: The Diffusion of Information in Early America, 1700–1865*. New York: Oxford University Press, 1989.

Bruce, Kathleen, *Virginia Iron Manufacture in the Slave Era*. New York: Century Company, 1931.

Bushman, Richard, *The Refinement of America: Persons, Houses, Cities*. New York: Knopf, 1992; New York: Vintage Books, 1993.

Byrne, Donald E., *No Foot of Land: Folklore of American Methodist Itinerants*. Metuchen, N.J.: Scarecrow Press, 1975.

Carter, Dan, *When the War Was Over: The Failure of Self-Reconstruction in the South, 1865–1867*. Baton Rouge: Louisiana State University Press, 1985.

Carwardine, Richard, *Transatlantic Revivalism: Popular Evangelicalism in Britain and America, 1790–1865*. Westport, Conn.: Greenwood Press, 1978.

Cash, Wilbur J., *The Mind of the South*. New York: Alfred A. Knopf, 1941.

Cornelius, Janet Duitsman, *When I Can Read My Title Clear: Literacy, Slavery, and Religion in the Antebellum South*. Columbia: University of South Carolina Press, 1991.

Crofts, Daniel, *Old Southampton: Politics and Society in a Virginia County, 1834–1869*. Charlottesville: University Press of Virginia, 1992.

Dabney, Virginius, *Virginia: The New Dominion*. Garden City, N.Y.: Doubleday & Company, 1971.

Daniel, W. Harrison, "An Aspect of Church and State Relations in the Confederacy: Southern Protestantism and the Office of Army Chaplain." *North Carolina Historical Review* 36 (January 1959): 47–71.

———, "Chaplains in the Army of Northern Virginia, A List Compiled in 1864 and 1865 by Robert L. Dabney." *Virginia Magazine of History and Biography* 71 (July 1963): 327–40.

———, "The Genesis of Richmond College." *Virginia Magazine of History and Biography* 83 (April 1975): 131–49.

———, "Bedford Baptists, 1840–1860," *Virginia Baptist Register* 23 (1984): 1160–72.

———, *Virginia Baptists, 1861–1902*. Bedford, Va.: The Print Shop, 1987.

Davis, Richard Beale, *Intellectual Life in Jefferson's Virginia, 1790–1830*. Chapel Hill: University of North Carolina Press, 1964.

Doyle, Don Harrison, *The Social Order of a Frontier Community: Jacksonville, Illinois, 1825–1870*. Urbana: University of Illinois Press, 1978.

Dvorak, Katherine L., *African-American Exodus: The Segregation of the Southern Churches*. Brooklyn, N.Y.: Carlson Publishing, 1991.

Eighmy, John L., *Churches in Cultural Capitivity: A History of the Social Attitudes of Southern Baptists*. Knoxville: University of Tennessee Press, 1972.

Ernst, William J., "Urban Leaders and Social Change: The Urbanization Process in Richmond, Virginia, 1840–1880." Ph.D. diss., University of Virginia, 1978.

Farish, Hunter D., *The Circuit Rider Dismounts: A Social History of Southern Methodism, 1865–1900*. Richmond: Dietz Press, 1938.

Farmer, James O., *The Metaphysical Confederacy: James Henley Thornwell and the Synthesis of Southern Values*. Macon, Ga.: Mercer University Press, 1986.

Faust, Drew Gilpin, "Evangelicalism and the Meaning of the Proslavery Argument: The Reverend Thornton Stringfellow of Virginia." *Virginia Magazine of History and Biography* 85 (January 1977): 3–17.

———, "Christian Soldiers: The Meaning of Revivalism in the Confederate Army." *Journal of Southern History* 53 (February 1987): 63–90.

———, *The Creation of Confederate Nationalism: Ideology and Identity in the Civil War South*. Baton Rouge: Louisiana State University Press, 1988.

———, "The Peculiar South Revisited," in John B. Boles and Evelyn Nolen, eds., *Interpreting Southern History: Historiographical Essays in Honor of Sanford W. Higginbotham*. Baton Rouge: Louisiana State University Press, 1987.

Ford, Lacy K., *Origins of Southern Radicalism: The South Carolina Upcountry, 1800–1860*. New York: Oxford University Press, 1988.

Foster, Gaines M., *Ghosts of the Confederacy: Defeat, the Lost Cause, and the Emergence of the New South*. New York: Oxford University Press, 1987.

Fox-Genovese, Elizabeth, *Within the Plantation Household: Black and White Women of the Old South*. Chapel Hill: University of North Carolina Press, 1988.

Freehling, Alison Goodyear, *The Virginia Slavery Debate of 1831–32*. Baton Rouge: Louisiana State University Press, 1982.

Freehling, William W., "James Henley Thornwell's Mysterious Antislavery Moment." *Journal of Southern History* 57 (August 1991): 383–406.

Friedman, Jean E., *The Enclosed Garden: Women and Community in the Evangelical South, 1830–1900*. Chapel Hill: University of North Carolina Press, 1985.

Genovese, Eugene D., *Roll, Jordan, Roll: The World the Slaves Made*. New York: Pantheon Books, 1974; New York: Vintage Books, 1976.

———, *The Slaveholders' Dilemma: Freedom and Progress in Southern Conservative Thought, 1820–1860*. Columbia: University of South Carolina Press, 1992.

Goldfield, David R., *Urban Growth in the Age of Sectionalism, Virginia, 1847–1861*. Baton Rouge: Louisiana State University Press, 1977.

———, "Communities and Regions: The Diverse Cultures of Virginia." *Virginia Magazine of History and Biography* 95 (October 1987): 429–452.

Gray, Richard, *Writing the South: Ideas of an American Region*. New York: Cambridge University Press, 1985.

Haber, Samuel, *The Quest for Authority and Honor in the American Professions, 1750–1900*. Chicago: University of Chicago Press, 1991.

Hall, David D., *World of Wonders, Days of Judgment: Popular Religious Belief in Early New England*. New York: Alfred A. Knopf, 1989.

Hall, Jacquelyn Dowd, and Anne Firor Scott, "Women in the South," in John B. Boles and Evelyn Nolen, eds., *Interpreting Southern History: Historiographical Essays in Honor of Sanford W. Higginbotham*. Baton Rouge: Louisiana State University Press, 1987.

Hall, Timothy D., *Contested Boundaries: Itinerancy and the Reshaping of the Colonial American Religious World*. Durham: Duke University Press, 1994.

Haltunnen, Karen, *Confidence Men and Painted Women: A Study of Middle-Class Culture in America, 1830–1870*. New Haven: Yale University Press, 1982.

Harvey, Paul, *Redeeming the South: Religious Cultures and Racial Identities among Southern Baptists, 1865–1925*. Chapel Hill: University of North Carolina Press, 1997.

Hatch, Nathan O., *The Democratization of American Christianity*. New Haven: Yale University Press, 1989.

Heyrman, Christine Leigh, *Southern Cross: The Beginnings of the Bible Belt*. New York: Alfred A. Knopf, 1997.

Higginbotham, Evelyn Brooks, *Righteous Discontent: The Women's Movement in the Black Baptist Church, 1880–1920*. Cambridge: Harvard University Press, 1993.

Hill, Patricia R., *The World Their Household: The American Women's Foreign Mission Movement and Cultural Transformation, 1870–1920*. Ann Arbor: University of Michigan Press, 1985.

Hill, Samuel S., *Southern Churches in Crisis*. New York: Holt, Rinehart and Winston, 1966.

———, *Religion and the Solid South*. Nashville: Abingdon Press, 1972.

Holifield, E. Brooks, *The Gentlemen Theologians: American Theology in Southern Culture, 1795–1860*. Durham: Duke University Press, 1978.

————, "The Penurious Preacher? Nineteenth-Century Clerical Wealth: North and South." *Journal of the American Academy of Religion* 58 (Spring 1990): 17–36.

Howe, Daniel Walker, "The Evangelical Movement and Political Culture in the North during the Second Party System," *Journal of American History* 77 (March 1991): 1216–1239.

Hunter, James Davison, *American Evangelicalism: Conservative Religion and the Quandary of Modernity*. New Brunswick, N.J.: Rutgers University Press, 1983.

Hunter, Jane, *The Gospel of Gentility: American Women Missionaries in Turn-of-the-Century China*. New Haven: Yale University Press, 1984.

Hyatt, Irwin T., *Our Ordered Lives Confess: Three Nineteenth-Century American Missionaries in East Shantung*. Cambridge: Harvard University Press, 1976.

Isaac, Rhys, *The Transformation of Virginia, 1740–1790*. Chapel Hill: University of North Carolina Press, 1982.

Jaffee, David, "Peddlers of Progress and the Transformation of the Rural North." *Journal of American History* 78 (September 1991): 511–535.

Jones, Charles E., *Perfectionist Persuasion: The Holiness Movement and American Methodism, 1867–1936*. Metuchen, N.J.: Scarecrow Press, 1974.

Kaser, David, *Books and Libraries in Camp and Battle: The Civil War Experience*. Westport, Conn.: Greenwood Press, 1984.

Kenzer, Robert C., *Kinship and Neighborhood in a Southern Community: Orange County, North Carolina, 1849–1881*. Knoxville: University of Tennessee Press, 1987.

Kett, Joseph F., *Rites of Passage: Adolescence in America 1790 to the Present*. New York: Basic Books, 1977.

————, "Women and the Progressive Impulse in Southern Education," in Walter J. Fraser and Jon L. Wakelyn, eds., *The Web of Southern Social Relations: Women, Family, and Education*. Athens: University of Georgia Press, 1985.

Kett, Joseph F., and Patricia McClung, "Book Culture in Post-Revolutionary Virginia." *Proceedings of the American Antiquarian Society* 94 (Part 1, 1984): 97–147.

Kierner, Cynthia A., "Woman's Piety within Patriarchy: The Religious Life of Martha Hancock Wheat of Bedford County." *Virginia Magazine of History and Biography* 100 (January 1992): 79–98.

Kimball, Gregg David, "Place and Perception: Richmond in Late Antebellum America." Ph.D. diss., University of Virginia, 1997.

Kirby, James E., Russell E. Richey, and Kenneth E. Rowe, *The Methodists*. Westport, Conn.: Greenwood Press, 1996.

Kuykendall, John W., "*Southern Enterprize*": *The Work of National Evangelical Societies in the Antebellum South*. Westport, Conn.: Greenwood Press, 1982.

Lebsock, Suzanne, *The Free Women of Petersburg: Status and Culture in a Southern Town, 1784–1860*. New York: W. W. Norton & Company, 1984.

Levine, Lawrence W., *Black Culture and Black Consciousness: Afro-American Folk Thought from Slavery to Freedom*. New York: Oxford University Press, 1977.

Lewis, Jan, *The Pursuit of Happiness: Family and Values in Jefferson's Virginia*. Cambridge: Cambridge University Press, 1983.

Link, William A., *A Hard Country and a Lonely Place: Schooling, Society, and Reform in Rural Virginia, 1870–1920*. Chapel Hill: University of North Carolina Press, 1986.

Loveland, Anne C., *Southern Evangelicals and the Social Order, 1800–1860*. Baton Rouge: Louisiana State University Press, 1980.

Lukes, Steven, *Power: A Radical View*. London: Macmillan Education, 1974.

Maddex, Jack, "Proslavery Millennialism: Social Eschatology in Antebellum Southern Calvinism." *American Quarterly* 31 (1979): 46–62.

Marsden, George M., *Fundamentalism and American Culture: The Shaping of Twentieth-Century Evangelicalism, 1870–1925*. New York: Oxford University Press, 1980.

Mathews, Donald, *Slavery and Methodism: A Chapter in American Morality, 1780–1845*. Princeton: Princeton University Press, 1965.

———, "The Second Great Awakening as an Organizing Process, 1780–1830: An Hypothesis." *American Quarterly* 21 (Spring 1969): 23–43.

———, "Charles Colcock Jones and the Southern Evangelical Crusade to Form a Biracial Community." *Journal of Southern History* 41 (August 1975): 299–320.

———, *Religion in the Old South*. Chicago: University of Chicago Press, 1977.

McCurry, Stephanie, *Masters of Small Worlds: Yeoman Households, Gender Relations, and the Political Culture of the Antebellum South Carolina Low Country*. New York: Oxford University Press, 1995.

McDowell, Patrick, *The Social Gospel in the South: The Woman's Home Mission Movement in the Methodist Episcopal Church, South, 1886–1939*. Baton Rouge: Louisiana State University Press, 1982.

McPherson, James M., *Battle Cry of Freedom: The American Civil War*. New York: Oxford University Press, 1988; London: Penguin Books, 1990.

———, *For Cause and Comrades: Why Men Fought in the Civil War*. New York: Oxford University Press, 1997.

Mead, Sidney E., "The Rise of the Evangelical Conception of the Ministry in America," in H. Richard Niebuhr and Daniel C. Williams, eds., *The Ministry in Historical Perspectives*. New York: Harper and Brothers, 1956.

Miller, Thomas E., Jr., "A Religious Press in Time of War: The Religious Herald, 1860–1865." *Virginia Baptist Register* 23 (1984): 1139–59.

Mitchell, Mary H., *Hollywood Cemetery: The History of a Southern Shrine*. Richmond: Virginia State Library, 1985.

Moger, Allen W., *Virginia: Bourbonism to Byrd, 1870–1925*. Charlottesville: University Press of Virginia, 1968.

Moore, John S., ed., "A Nineteenth-Century Minister's Problems." *Virginia Baptist Register* 21 (1982): 993–997.

Moore, R. Laurence, "Religion, Secularization, and the Shaping of the Culture Industry in Antebellum America." *American Quarterly* 41 (June 1989): 216–242.

Moorehead, James H., *American Apocalypse: Yankee Protestants and the Civil War, 1860–1869*. New Haven: Yale University Press, 1978.

Oakes, James, *The Ruling Race: A History of American Slaveholders*. New York: Alfred A. Knopf, 1983; Vintage Books, 1983.

———, *Slavery and Freedom: An Interpretation of the Old South*. New York: Vintage Books, 1990.

O'Brien, John T., "Factory, Church, and Community: Blacks in Antebellum Richmond." *Journal of Southern History* 44 (November 1978): 509–536.

O'Brien, Michael, "W. J. Cash, Hegel, and the South." *Journal of Southern History* 44 (August 1978): 379–398.

———, *Rethinking the South*. Baltimore: Johns Hopkins University Press, 1988.

Owen, Christopher H., *The Sacred Flame of Love: Methodism and Society in Nineteenth-Century Georgia*. Athens: University of Georgia Press, 1998.

Ownby, Ted, *Subduing Satan: Religion, Recreation, and Manhood in the Rural South, 1865–1920*. Chapel Hill: University of North Carolina Press, 1990.

———, "Mass Culture, Upper-Class Culture, and the Decline of Church Discipline in the Evangelical South: The 1910 Case of the Godbold Mineral Well Hotel." *Religion and American Culture* 4 (Winter 1994): 107–132.

Owsley, Frank L., *Plain Folk of the Old South*. Baton Rouge: Louisiana State University Press, 1949; 1982.

Patterson, Louis Dale, "The Ministerial Mind of American Methodism: The Courses of Study for the Ministry of the Methodist Episcopal Church, the Methodist Episcopal Church, South, and the Methodist Protestant Church, 1880–1920." Ph.D. diss., Drew University, 1984.

Patterson, Orlando, *Slavery and Social Death*. Cambridge: Harvard University Press, 1982.

Pearson, C. C., and J. Edwin Hendricks, *Liquor and Antiliquor in Virginia, 1616–1919*. Durham: Duke University Press, 1967.

Pease, William H., and Jane H. Pease, *The Web of Progress: Private Values and Public Styles in Boston and Charleston, 1828–1843*. New York: Oxford University Press, 1985.

Perdue, Charles L., Jr., Thomas E. Barden, and Robert K. Phillips, eds., *Weevils in the Wheat: Interviews with Ex-Slaves*. Charlottesville: University Press of Virginia, 1976.

Perry, Lewis, and Michael Fellman, eds., *Antislavery Reconsidered: New Perspectives on the Abolitionists*. Baton Rouge: Louisiana State University Press, 1989.

Phipps, Calvin H., "Legislation Affecting Secondary Education in Virginia from 1619–1845." Ph.D. diss., University of Virginia, 1932.

Pope, Liston, *Millhands and Preachers: A Study of Gastonia*. New Haven: Yale University Press, 1942.

Porter, Alfred Ogden, *County Government in Virginia: A Legislative History, 1607–1904*. New York: Columbia University Press, 1947.

Rable, George C., *But There Was No Peace: The Role of Violence in the Politics of Reconstruction*. Athens: University of Georgia Press, 1984.

Raboteau, Albert J., *Slave Religion: The "Invisible Institution" in the Antebellum South*. New York: Oxford University Press, 1978.

Richey, Russell, *Early American Methodism*. Bloomington: Indiana University Press, 1991.

Robertson, James I., Jr., *Civil War Virginia: Battleground for a Nation*. Charlottesville: University Press of Virginia, 1991.

Robins, Roger, "Vernacular American Landscape: Methodists, Camp Meetings, and Social Respectability." *Religion and American Culture* 14 (Summer 1994): 165–191.

Romero, Sidney J., *Religion in the Rebel Ranks*. Lanham, Md.: University Press of America, 1983.

Rosenburg, R. B., "John Davis Williams: A Forgotten Virginia Baptist Minister," *Virginia Baptist Register* 22 (1983): 1092–1106.

Ryland, Garnett, *The Baptists of Virginia, 1699–1926*. Richmond: Whittet & Shepperson, 1955.

Scanlon, James Edward, *Randolph-Macon College: A Southern History, 1825–1967*. Charlottesville: University Press of Virginia, 1983.

Schlotterbeck, John T., "The 'Social Economy' of an Upper South Community: Orange and Greene Counties, Virginia, 1815–1860," in Orville Vernon Burton and Robert C. McMath, Jr., eds., *Class, Conflict, and Consensus: Antebellum Southern Community Studies*. Westport, Conn.: Greenwood Press, 1982.

Schneider, Greg, "The Ritual of Happy Dying among Early American Methodists." *Church History* 56 (September 1987): 348–363.

Schultz, Stanley K., "Temperance Reform in the Antebellum South: Social Control and Urban Order." *The South Atlantic Quarterly* 83 (Summer 1984): 323–339.

Scott, Donald M., *From Office to Profession: The New England Ministry, 1750–1850*. Philadelphia: University of Pennsylvania Press, 1978.

Sernett, Milton C., ed., *Afro-American Religious History: A Documentary Witness*. Durham: Duke University Press, 1985.

Shade, William G., *Democratizing the Old Dominion: Virginia and the Second Party System, 1824–1861*. Charlottesville: University Press of Virginia, 1996.

Shattuck, Gardiner H., *A Shield and a Hiding Place: The Religious Life of the Civil War Armies*. Macon, Ga.: Mercer University Press, 1987.

Silver, James W., *Confederate Morale and Church Propaganda*. New York: W. W. Norton & Company, 1967.

Snay, Mitchell, *Gospel of Disunion: Religion and Separatism in the Antebellum South*. New York: Cambridge University Press, 1993.

Sobel, Mechal, *Trabelin' On: The Slave Journey to an Afro-Baptist Faith*. Westport, Conn.: Greenwood Press, 1979.

Sparks, Randy J., *On Jordan's Stormy Banks: Evangelicalism in Mississippi, 1773–1876*. Athens: University of Georgia Press, 1994.

Stowell, Daniel W., *Rebuilding Zion: The Religious Reconstruction of the South, 1863–1877*. New York: Oxford University Press, 1998.

Stroupe, Henry Smith, *The Religious Press in the South Atlantic States, 1802–1865*. Durham: Duke University Press, 1956.

Sweet, William Warren, *Virginia Methodism: A History*. Richmond: Whittet & Shepperson, 1955.

Sydnor, Blanche White, *First Baptist Church of Richmond, 1780–1955*. Richmond: Whittet & Shepperson, 1955.

Thornton, J. Mills, III, *Power and Politics in a Slave Society: Alabama, 1800–1860*. Baton Rouge: Louisiana State University Press, 1978.

Turner, Elizabeth Hayes, "Women's Culture and Community: Religion and Reform in Galveston, 1880–1920." Ph.D. diss., Rice University, 1990.

Tuveson, Ernest Lee, *Redeemer Nation: The Idea of America's Millennial Role*. Chicago: Chicago University Press, 1968.

Tyler-McGraw, Marie, *At the Falls: Richmond, Virginia and Its People*. Chapel Hill: University of North Carolina Press, 1994.

Tyler-McGraw, Marie, and Gregg D. Kimball, *In Bondage and Freedom: Antebellum Black Life in Richmond, Virginia*. Richmond: Valentine Museum, 1988.

Tyrell, Ian R., *Sobering Up: From Temperance to Prohibition in Antebellum America, 1800–1860*. Westport, Conn.: Greenwood Press, 1979.

Vinovskis, Maris, ed., *Toward a Social History of the American Civil War*. New York: Cambridge University Press, 1990.

Waldrep, Christopher, " 'So Much Sin': The Decline of Religious Discipline and the 'Tidal Wave of Crime.' " *Journal of Social History* 23 (Spring 1990): 535–552.

Walters, Ronald G., *The Antislavery Appeal: American Abolitionism after 1830*. Baltimore: Johns Hopkins University Press, 1978; New York: W. W. Norton and Company, 1984.

Weber, Max, "The Social Psychology of World Religions," in H. H. Gerth and C. Wright Mills, eds., *From Max Weber: Essays in Sociology*. New York: Oxford University Press, 1946.

Weisiger, Benjamin B., III,, *Old Manchester and Its Environs*. Richmond: William Byrd Press, 1993.

Wigger, John H., *Taking Heaven by Storm: Methodism and the Rise of Popular Christianity in America*. New York: Oxford University Press, 1998.

Wills, Gregory A., *Democratic Religion: Freedom, Authority, and Church Discipline in the Baptist South, 1795–1900*. New York: Oxford University Press, 1996.

Wilson, Charles Reagan, *Baptized in Blood: The Religion of the Lost Cause, 1865–1920*. Athens: University of Georgia Press, 1980.

Wilson, John F., "Modernity," in Mircea Eliade, ed., *The Encyclopedia of Religion*, Vol. 10. New York: Macmillan, 1987.

Woodward, C. Vann, *Origins of the New South, 1877–1913*. Baton Rouge: Louisiana State University Press, 1951.

Wyatt-Brown, Bertram, "The Antimission Movement in the Jacksonian South: A Study in Regional Folk Culture." *Journal of Southern History* (1970): 501–529.

————, *Southern Honor: Ethics and Behavior in the Old South*. New York: Oxford University Press, 1982.

Index

abolition, 41, 80. *See also* antislavery sentiment

abstinence. *See* temperance

Adams, Armaci, 15

affidavits, use in church trials, 152–53

African American churches: antebellum, 31; historiography of, 210n. 7; white views of, 172. *See also* segregation, slaves

African American churchgoers, relation to white churchgoers, 15–16

African American pastors, white pastors' views of, 114–15, 175–77

Albemarle Female Institute, 64, 155

Alexandria, Virginia, 135, 136

alienation, as goal of Christian life, 6, 39–40, 193–94

Allen, Littlebury, 29

ambition, of pastors, 55–57. *See also* education, denominations

Amelia County, 115

American Baptist Antislavery Convention, 80

American Sunday School Union, 73

American Tract Society, 140

Amiss, Joseph H., 27–28, 59

Anderson, Rosalie Whitter, 159

Anglicans, dissenters' stance toward, 6

annual clerical meetings, 49

Anti-Liquor (Danville), 192

Antimission Baptists, 11, 47–48, 162, 194

antislavery sentiment, in Virginia, 79. *See also* abolition

appointment, of pastors, 30. *See also* pastors, presiding elders

Appomattox, surrender at, 104, 106

apprenticeship, pastors', 21. *See also* education

Archer, P. W., 152

architecture, rural church, 16–17. *See also* First Baptist Church (Richmond), taste, urban style

Armistead, Robert, 159

army. *See* chaplains

Army of Northern Virginia, 104–106

Asbury, Francis, 14, 79

Bacon, Herbert Tyree, 18

Bagby, A., 137

Bagby, George, 26

Bainbridge Street Baptist Church (Manchester), 118

Baldwin, Nancy MacMillan, 77

Baldwin, Noah Carlton: conversion of, 11–12; spiritual life of, 25–26; conflict with congregation, 29; and creek baptism, 43; missionary sentiment of, 48; and slavery, 77–79

Ball, B. F., 165

Bangs, Nathan, 39

baptism: as community ritual, 17–18; service of, 17, 42–43

Baptists: identification with lower classes, 130; growth of in Virginia, 14, 15

Baptist Foreign Mission Board. *See* Southern Baptist Foreign Mission Board

Baptist Sunday School Relief Society, 125

baptistery, 43

Battle of Seven Pines, 97

Beale, George, 152

Bedford County, 16, 17, 36–37

benevolence: and clerical professionalism, 48–49; coopting of domestic responsibilities, 160; denominational context of, 87, 122; distaste for interdenominational agencies, 87; during Reconstruction, 121–127; increased commitment to, 86–87; urban context of, 48–49; women's skill at bureaucracy of, 159–160. *See also* pastors, Sunday schools, temperance, women

Bennett, William W., 100, 157, 175, 186–87

Berlin Circuit, Virginia Conference, 140

Bethany College, 61

Beulah Baptist Association, 58

Bible, study of, 25, 66, 67–68

Bible Belt, 4

biography, pastors' interest in, 144, 174

Bishop, M. L., 152

Blunt, Jabez, 188

books: market for, 68–69; in Sunday schools, 126–27. *See also* colporteurs, libraries, print culture, reading

bookselling. *See* colporteurs

Border War, 93, 225n. 9

Botetourt County, 37

Boylan, Anne, 73

Broad Street Methodist Church (Richmond), 132–33

Broadus, John Albert, 72

Broaddus, William, 24, 30

Brockman, Betty, 157

Brunswick County, 187

Buena Vista, Virginia, 191

bureaucracies: denominations as, 5, 7; enthusiasm for, 166; ethos of, 149–50; jobs in, 143–48. *See also* denominations, pastors, women

bureaucratization: of churches, 85, 163–170; and the Progressive movement, 169. *See also* bureaucracies, denominations, pastors, women

Burton, Robert, 23, 31, 138–39

Bushman, Richard, 42, 45

business, pastors' criticism of unethical practices in, 188

Butts, Daniel Gregory Claiborne, 151

call to preach: community's authority in, 18–19, 32; declining importance of, 140; family's interest in, 19–20; meaning of, 11–12, 18, 32; social context of, 19. *See also* pastors

Campbell, Alexander, 14, 61

Campbell County, 140

Carey, Lott, 14

Caroline Circuit, Virginia Conference, 151

Caroline County, 83, 126

catechism, in Sunday schools, 72

Cearsley's Methodist Church, 146

Centenary Methodist Church (Richmond), 44–45, 132

Chapin, Sarah, 22

chaplains, military: age of, 98–99; ambiguous status of, 98–100; as civil servants, 92; feminine image of, 99; masculine image of, 100; number of, 97; poor pay of, 98; prominence after war, 92, 97; and public authority, 95; relations with soldiers, 98–99, 101; submission to officers, 100–101. *See also* William Wiatt

charity. *See* benevolence, class, Dorcas societies, orphans, veterans, women

Charlotte County, 139

Charlottesville, Virginia, 3, 133, 191

Chesterfield County, 74, 137

Children's Preachers' Education Society, 124

China, missionaries in, 158. *See also* foreign missions, Virginia School

Christian Association, of the Twenty-sixth Virginia Infantry, 105

Christian citizenship, 109–12, 116–18. *See also* patriotism

Christian, William Henry, 187

Christian, Willie, 187

church courts, power of, 152–53. *See also* church discipline

church discipline: of members, 30, 214nn. 63, 64; of pastors, 30–32; and pastors' authority, 169–70; and pastors' reputations, 153. *See also* pastors

church growth: in early antebellum period, 14–15; in 1850s, 86; increase in postwar cities, 135. *See also* cities, denominations

church membership: in antebellum cities, 41; antebellum diversity of, 15; social benefits of, 129–30. *See also* church growth, cities, denominations

cities, influence in denomination, 41–42. *See also* denominations, city pastors, pastors

city pastors: different to rural, 35–36, 38–39, 46–47, 50–51; salaries of, 49–50, 131–32, 124–35; sermons, 53–54; social position of, 135. *See also* cities, pastors, salaries

Civil War and religion, 4, 92, 107–08. *See also* chaplains

Clark, J. T., 192

Clarke, Mary Pollard, 159–160

class: churches' appeal to "better," 45; entertainment as an index of, 145, 147–48; popular religious culture and, 147; and race in worship, 115. *See also* cities, city pastors, education, pastors, revivals, salaries

Clay Street Methodist Church (Richmond), 45, 132

clergy. *See* pastors

clerical authority: challenges to, 27; consensual nature of, 29. *See also* pastors

Clerical Club of Richmond College, 124

Clopton, J. C., 71

Cocke, Charles L., 167

colleges: antebellum enrollment in, 57–58, 63; and clerical profession, 6; as institutional expression of religion's influence, 74; postbellum enrollment in, 173–74. *See also* education, pastors, women

colporteurs, 24, 68–72, 111, 140. *See also* books, reading, libraries, print culture, printers

Columbian College (George Washington University), 60, 179

Confederate nationalism, and religion, 4, 5, 92, 107. *See also* patriotism

congregations: pastors' declining interest in, 149; malaise of during war, 96. *See also* denominations, localism, pastors

conversion: age of pastors', 19; meaning of, 11, 17, 18; by reading, 66; in schools, 53; black Christians', 176–77. *See also* call to preach, libraries, pastors, print culture, sermons

Cooper, James Fenimore, 103

Courtney, Philip, 24

courtship, 22. *See also* pastors, women

Crawley, C. D., 152–153

Crowder, Thomas, 30

Culpeper, Virginia, 191

Culpeper County, 84

cultural captivity thesis, 210n. 8

curriculum, uniform, 127. *See also* education, Sunday schools

dancing, 74, 146

Danville, Virginia, 169

debt: in building churches, 42, 44–46; as a sign of social decay, 188

defeat, pastors' reaction to, 106, 112–13

deference, to preachers, 28. *See also* clerical authority

denominations: bureaucratic reform of in the 1850s, 87–88; business habits of, 165–66; and clerical authority, 169–70; as conduit of urban culture, 6, 35, 36, 40; declining public influence of, 169–70; and efficiency, 169; growth after the war, 168–69; growth as a response to slavery, 78, 84–86; growth during war, 107; as modern institutions, 5, 47; modest goals of before the war, 81–82; opposition to, 168; poor state of postwar, 124; and print culture during the war, 101; and professionalism, 85; and progress, 4; and color line, 113. *See also* antimission Baptists, bureaucracies, pastors, sectarian conflict

DeShazo, J. E., 168

destruction, postwar, 111

Dickens, Charles, 41

Dickinson, Alfred E., 144, 175
discipline. *See* church discipline
disfranchisement, 176
Doctors of Divinity, popularity of
    honorary, 178
Doggett, David, 117, 174
Dollar Roll, for Richmond College, 157
Dorcas Societies, 125. *See also*
    benevolence, class, women
Douglass, Frederick, 67
Dover Baptist Association, 72, 73
Dowdell, Mrs. E. C., 163
drinking. *See* temperance

Early, John, 50, 100, 151–52
Early, Gen. Jubal, 100
Early, Thomas H., 100
Eastern Shore, 137, 181
editors. *See* newspapers, publishing
education: as central metaphor for
    religion, 75; charity for ministers, 61,
    124; as chief work of religious
    benevolence, 67, 72–74, 121–27; and
    cultivation of taste, 65; early pastors'
    attitudes toward, 6, 21–22; elite
    connotations of, 66; erosion of revival
    culture, 74; fundraising for, 7; of
    freedmen, 122, 125–26; and
    gentrification, 62; inseparable from
    religion, 65, 67–68; little support for
    public, 156; number of pastors in
    antebellum colleges, 57–58; as priority
    for pastors' families, 137–138; and
    professional prestige, 57–60;
    prohibitive cost of, 61–62, 64; public,
    debate over, 58, 139; role in "making"
    ministers, 58–59; and self-
    improvement, 62, 122–27; and social
    mobility, 65; shift from revivalism to, 7;
    support for postwar, 139; in
    historiography, 66–67; as vocation for
    ministers, 63–64; for women, 63, 154–
    56. *See also* colleges, pastors, reading,
    print culture, Sunday schools
Edwards, John E., 141–42, 146, 168
Edwards, William, 111
Eleventh Virginia Infantry, 92
emotional lives, of pastors. *See* pastors
emotional religion. *See* revivals

entertainment: as source of clerical
    income, 146; as index of taste, 145, 147–
    8; moral content of, 146–47; postwar
    interest in, 144–148; religious
    strictures on, 145–46
Ettrick Methodist Church (Chesterfield
    County), 74
Eubank, Alexander, 155
evangelists: denominational, 181; pastors'
    disdain for, 177–181; appeal of, 180.
    See also Sam Jones, Dwight Moody,
    revivals, Leonidas Rosser

farming. *See* pastors
festivals, church, 146–47. *See also*
    entertainment
finance, publishing of denominational
    figures, 165–66. *See also*
    denominations, pastors
financial costs of war, for pastors, 111–12
financial security, importance to pastors,
    139, 141–47
First African Baptist Church
    (Richmond), 43, 51–52, 72. *See also*
    African American churches, Robert
    Ryland, segregation, slaves
First Baptist Church (Richmond), 3, 37,
    42–44, 51–52, 191
Fitcher, William, 146
Fitzgerald, A. S., 114
Flippo, Oscar, 130, 146
foreign missions, Virginia's importance
    to, 14. *See also* benevolence, missions,
    women
"founding fathers," of eighteenth-century
    churches, 174
Foushee, Nathan Bangs, 140–41
Fowlkes, Henry, 114–15
Fowlkes, Martha A., 115
Fowlkes, P. A., 114–15
Fox, Richard, 26
Fredericksburg, Virginia, 191
Friends of Temperance, 184–85
fundraising: during Reconstruction, 123;
    as index of success, 165; success of
    postwar, 164; for Sunday school books,
    126; systematizing, 164, 165, 192; for
    women's benevolence, 159. *See also*
    denominations, pastors, women

General Conference of Methodist
Episcopal Church, South. *See*
Methodist Episcopal Church, South
generations, tensions between postwar,
173–74
gentrification, of churches, 54. *See also*
denominations, education
gentility, Christian ideals of, 117–18
George Washington University. *See*
Columbian College
Gilded Age, 183
Giles, Joseph, 138
Gillfield Baptist Church (Petersburg), 31
giving, rates of, 165–167. *See also*
benevolence
Gloucester County, 103
Gloucester Point Circuit, Virginia
Conference, 166
Goggin, Thomas, 26
Goochland County, 159
Good Templars, 184, 185, 192. *See also*
temperance
Grace Street Baptist Church
(Richmond), 77
Granbery, Ella, 156
Granbery, John Cowper, 91–92, 95, 145,
155, 173
greed, 122, 185, 188–89
Greenbrier Hotel, 145
Griswald, C. G., 31
Gwaltney, James, 67

Hall, Mrs. C. H., 163
Hamilton, Lucie A., 138
Hampton Roads, Virginia, 186
Hannon, John, 159
Hargrove, Sam, 177
Harris, William, 17
Harrison, W. P., 26
Harrisonburg, Virginia, 191
Hatch, Nathan O., 6, 195
Hatcher, Harvey, 17
Hatcher, Jennie, 150, 162, 176
Hatcher, William E., 17, 115, 118–121, 176–
177
Haynes, T. H., 111
Henning, B. C., 149
Henrico County, 140
Henry Circuit, Virginia Conference, 131

Hill, Samuel S., 5
Hilliard, Mary R. Walker, 151–52
Holifield, E. Brooks, 49
Hollins College (Valley Union
Seminary), 64
Hollywood Cemetery (Richmond), 97
honor, 27–29; 100
hotels, clerical meetings held in, 145
Hughes, Mrs. S. G., 125

insurance. *See* financial security, life
insurance, property insurance
intellectual defense of Christianity, 179
intellectual life, pastors, 24. *See also*
books, libraries, reading, sermons
institutions, religious, importance to
South, 195–96
irreligion, in army, 99. *See also* chaplains
Isaac, Rhys, 6

Jackson, Thomas J. "Stonewall," 116–18
James, Charles, 124
James, Henry, 99
Jasper, John, 115, 175
Jeter, Jeremiah Bell: career and
ambitions of, 3, 36–44, 129, 135; as
editor, 147; and education 59–60, 64;
estimation of forebears, 171–72; on
patriotism and religion 95, 96; and
rural churches, 16; and slavery, 51, 53,
73, 77–78, 85; and temperance, 83; and
travel, 49
Jim Crow, 116, 172, 176
Jones, Beverly, 28
Jones, J. H. C., 123
Jones, J. William, 138, 241n. 17
Jones, Martha, 152–53
Jones, Sam, 179–180, 181–182

Kern, A. J., 190
King and Queen County, 123

Lafferty, John James, 162, 187, 189
laity. *See* lay authority, denominations
Landrum, William, 130
Law, William, 25
lay authority, 28, 150–51,167
lectures, 146–48. *See also* entertainment
Lee, Robert E., 97, 105–106, 116–18

Leland, John, 79

liberal theology, 7

libraries: camp, 103; Sunday school, 73–74. *See also* books, colporteurs, print culture, reading, Sunday schools

life insurance, 141–142. *See also* financial security

literacy: rates of, 66–67; teaching of slaves, 73; teaching of soldiers, 102. *See also* books, education, print culture, reading, Sunday schools

localism, 7, 183

local option, as critique of New South, 185, 186, 188–89, 190–91. *See also* temperance

Local Option Alliance, 185, 190. *See also* local option, temperance

Lost Cause, religion's role in, 4, 5, 171–72, 175, 230n. 31

Lumsden, James, 59

Lynchburg, Virginia, 191

Magoon, Elias Lyman, 93

Manchester, Virginia, 118–20, 191

Manchester Board of Health, 120

Manly, Basil, Jr., 64, 72

Mann, Horace, 67

Martin, James, 77

Martin, Joseph E., 102

Mason, John Young, 46

Mason, W. M., 126–27

Market Street Methodist Church (Petersburg), 132

market revolution, in South, 4, 40

McClellan, Gen. George, 117

Mecklenburg County, 55, 60

memory: of the Civil War, 174–75; of "founding fathers," 171–74; of revivals, 177–83; of slavery, 176–77. *See also* "founding fathers," nostalgia

men, value to congregations, 19

Methodist growth in Virginia, 14–15

Methodist Episcopal Church, South: created, 80–81; General Conference of 1882, 178

Methodist Recorder (Farmville), 144

Middlesex County, 124

millennialism, 196, 87. *See also* proslavery millennialism

mills, textile, 118–120, 191, 192

ministers. *See* pastors

ministry: as brotherhood, 22; as full-time job, 46; social mobility in, 54. *See also* denomination, pastors

mission to the slaves. *See* slaves

missionaries, northern, 111

mission societies. *See* foreign missions, missions, women

missionary Baptists. See antimission Baptists, Noah Baldwin, Baptists, denominations

missions: financial success of, 157–59; and women, 160–63. *See also* foreign missions, women

modernism, pastors' denunciation of, 7

modernity, and religion in the South, 4, 5, 209n. 4

modernization, and churches in the South, 217n. 37

Modest Town, Virginia, 137

Moffett, John R., 191–93

Montague, Gov. A. J., 176

Montague, Thomas, 104

Moody, Dwight L., 179–80

Moon, Charlotte "Lottie," 158

Moore, R. Laurence, 68

Mooreland Baptist Church (Albemarle), 162

Moorman, Samuel, 29

Myers, Hiram, 71

A Narrative of the Great Revival in the Southern Armies, 175

national benevolent societies. *See* benevolence

Newbill, James, 124

New South, religion in, 4

newspapers: circulation of, 69–70; congregational, 161; in army camps, 102; doctrinal content in declines, 144. *See also* chaplains, colporteurs, denominations, print culture, printers, publishing, reading, *Religious Herald*, *Richmond Christian Advocate*

Nicholson Street Methodist Church (Richmond), 132

Norfolk, Virginia, 186, 191

North: capitalism and religion in, 4; comparison to South, 5

North Danville, 191–193

nostalgia: lack of for Old South, 153; of pastors, 196; for old-time religion during war, 108; for spiritual authority over slaves, 176–77. *See also* "founding fathers," memory

Nottoway County, 115, 137–39

novels: attitudes toward popular, 70; as prescriptive literature, 69. *See also* pastors, George Taylor

Ocean View, Virginia, 145

O'Kelly, James, 14

Old Point, Virginia, 145

old-time religion. *See* "founding fathers," memory, nostalgia

Olmsted, Frederick Law, 16

oratory, 79

ordination, of black pastors, 114–15

orphans, education of, 122–23

Our Business Directory (Richmond), 187

Panic of 1873, 138

parsonages: scarce in rural areas, 141; women's campaign to build, 142

pastors: as administrators, 167–168; ambition of, 12, 37, 39, 133–35; ambivalence about women's authority, 154, 161; angst over declining authority, 180; as authors, 69, 144–45; and class, 6, 118–21; declined to serve as chaplains, 97; different career from fathers, 20–21; disagreement over history, 172, 175; divisions between, 8, 131; emotional lives of, 25–26; finances of, 23–24, 96, 137–39; as former merchants, 186; as fundraisers, 168; image in historiography, 8; as scholars, postwar, 178; and local option, 191; investment of denominational funds, 187–88; more income than farmers, 141; increase in number, 1850s, 89; as newspaper correspondents, 118–21; numbers ordained postwar, 173; and political reform, 118–121; postwar generation, 173, 74; poverty of, 60; professional ethos of, 3, 6, 40; as public figures, 7–8; qualifications for ordination, 59; relations with black people, antebellum, 31; relations with congregations, 8, 11, 24; relations with

women, 151–53, 161–63; role in war, 91–92; rural—urban tensions, 130–31; as school superintendents, 138; scorned by army, 107; and self-improvement, 3, 6, 40; sexual offenses of, 31–32; social mobility of, 132–35; spiritual authority over black people after war, 114–15; status after war, 111; ties to New South business, 186–87; unity of, 8; and work outside the pulpit, 137–39

patriotism: confusion with religion, 95; rationale for war, 94. *See also* Christian citizenship

Paul, Saint, 163

peddlers, 68, 70–71. *See also* colporteurs

Pedigo, William, 142

Peninsula Campaign, 92

pensions, Civil War veterans, 121

Petersburg, Virginia, 31, 137, 184, 186

Petersburg, siege of, 105

pew rents, 43–45

Philologian Debating Society (Manchester), 119

Pittsylvania County, 142

politics: disdain for, 88–89, 94, 118, 121, 190, 193–94; and moral law, 189; pastors' definition of, 189; pastors' influence on voters, 191–93; voter apathy, 193. *See also* A. J. Montague, Readjusters, temperance

Pollard, John Garland, 159

poor relief. *See* benevolence

popular literature, and religion, 67–68

popular religious culture: and denominational identity, 148; and clerical authority, 147–48; and urban-rural gap, 148; postwar, 143–48. *See also* lectures, libraries, novels, print culture, reading

Portsmouth, Virginia, 45, 141, 186

Potts, Joseph E., 20

Powell, James, 45

Powhatan County, 50

Preacher's Aid Society, 142

preachers. *See* pastors

preaching: in army camps, 103; as profession, 12; reinterpretation of history of, 178. *See also* evangelists, nostalgia, sermons, revivals

premodern, religion as, 4, 209n. 3

presiding elders (Methodist), 30

Princess Anne County, 140

print culture: and education, 65–72; in
army camps, 101–03, 105; competition
with preaching, 144–45; conduit of
urban culture into countryside, 71;
postwar importance of, 144–45;
printers' relations with churches, 69.
See also colporteurs, education,
libraries, publishing, reading, Sunday
schools

printers. *See* print culture

Pritchett, Edgar, 21, 111

progress: experience of in antebellum
period, 13, 41; ideas of, 3, 4, 7, 119;
material, 4, 119; and pastors, 171–72;
pastors' vision of, 194; religious, 196;
social, 4, 6, 38, 119. *See also* pastors

Progressivism, Southern, 240n. 84

prohibition. *See* temperance

Prohibition Party, 192

property insurance, 142

proslavery Christianity: and
millennialism, 223n. 7; and spiritual
doctrine of Southern churches, 84–89;
public nature of, 84–85. *See also*
millennialism, slaves

Prospectus of the Journal of Industry
(Richmond), 186–87

public sphere, churches' role in: during
Reconstruction, 110–13; during war,
107

publishing, as "sacred vocation," 68

Randolph-Macon College, 14, 60–63,
73

Rappahannock Baptist Association, 72

Rappahannock Circuit, Virginia
Conference, 140

reading: as means of conversion, 102–03;
pastors' postwar, 144; by soldiers, 101–
03, 105; and study, 25. *See also*
colporteurs, libraries, literacy, print
culture, women

Readjusters, 188

Reed, Lemuel, 21

refinement: in church style, 42, 43–46;
disputes about, 130–31; in
entertainment, 147–48; in postwar
worship, 179; in preaching, 115–116;

and women's education, 64. *See also*
education, social mobility

religion, as instrument of social
consensus, 109

Religious Herald, 14, 69, 70, 96, 144, 171,
185. *See also* Jeremiah Jeter,
newspapers, William Sands

Republican Methodists, 14, 94–95

respectability, pastors and, 6, 32–33, 38,
139

retirement, 142. *See also* financial
security

revivalists. *See* evangelists

revivals: criticism of postwar, 177–181;
and emotionalism, 196; and "old-time"
religion, 181–183; tarnished reputation
of, 180–181; source of church
members, 15; in the army, 103, 107;
decline of interest in, 35; wartime
effects of, 125. *See also* evangelists,
nostalgia, pastors, preaching, sermons

Rice, Luther, 14

Richardson, W. L., 193

Richmond, Virginia: antebellum, 3, 40–
46; local option in, 191; postwar, 111;
slavery in, 41; social divisions in, 41

Richmond Christian Advocate, 14, 69, 70,
96, 127, 129–30. *See also* William
Bennett, John Lafferty

Richmond College: early history of, 60–
63; decline in ministerial students, 124–
125; and general education, 65;
postwar, 138; postwar fundraising, 156;
president of, 51, 72, 74, 111

Richmond Dispatch, 118–20. *See also*
William Hatcher, "Struggle" letters

Richmond Female Institute (Richmond
Woman's College), 64, 74, 156

Riddick, James A., 50, 93, 94, 99

risk, financial, 143

Roanoke, Virginia, 186, 191

Roanoke Female College (Danville), 155

Robertson, Lelia Anne, 141

Robins, Wilbur F., 152

Rockingham District, Virginia
Conference, 71

Rosser, Leonidas, 94, 181

Rumsey, Fannie, 157

Ruffner, William, H., 138–39. *See also*
education

rural areas, lack of schools in, 137. *See also* education
rural churches: decline of postwar, 136; shortage of pastors in, 136
rural pastors, isolation of, 137
rural vs. urban, differences: clerical responsibilities, 35–36, 46–47, 129; professionalism in, 36; salaries, 136; simplicity in, 50–51; urban disdain for countryside, 37–38, 136
Ryland, Charles Hill, 53, 157
Ryland, J. W., 111
Ryland, Robert, 32, 51, 52, 72, 74, 111. *See also* First African Baptist Church, Richmond College

sabbatarianism, 145
Sadler, A. J., 137
salaries, pastoral: increase of for average pastor, 140–41; and pastors' aspirations, 141; disparity urban vs. rural, 131–32, 134–35; significance of, 49–50, 139–40; as sign of congregation's aspirations, 132. *See also* cities, city pastors, pastors
salvation. *See* conversion
Sand, George, 70
Sands, William, 95
Sawyer, Walter, 18
schisms, denominational: and slavery, 80–81; role of Virginians in, 81. *See also* denominations, slavery
schools, churches as, 5. *See also* education
Scott, Sir Walter, 70, 103
secession: change in views of, 97; pastors oppose, 93–94; in Virginia, 91–92
Second Baptist Church (Richmond), 55, 93
sectarian conflict, 29–30, 48
secularization theory, 4
segregation, of churches: sign of social sophistication, 51–53, 116; during Reconstruction, 110, 112, 113–16, 127; speed of 113; urban vs. rural, 113–14; in urban churches, 43–44
self-discipline, as goal of education, 122
self-education, attacked, 59

seminaries, 63. *See also* education, pastors
sermons: in army, 105–106; change in, 53–54; decline of in print, 147; different standard for slaves, 51–52; to slaves, 15. *See also* preaching, revivals
sexual misconduct, pastors, 152–53
simplicity: appeal of postbellum, 181–83; gentry's attitude toward, 16–17, 37; spiritual significance of, 16, 36–37, 43
Sixth Mount Zion Baptist Church, 175–76. *See also* John Jasper
Skinquarter (Chesterfield County), 130
slave traders, 79
slavery: legacy for postwar churches, 172; reform of, 79–80
slaves: in churches, 51–53; and white pastors, 15, 28; literacy rate among, 67; laws banning literacy, 67, 72; as majority of antebellum church members, 72; mission to, 72–74, 110; pastors' reasons for owning, 77–78; rate of ownership among pastors, 78–80. *See also* segregation
Smith, William A., 73, 81, 84
Snead, George, 26
social elevation. *See* class, pastors, salaries, social mobility
social hierarchy, in church seating, 44
social mobility, pastorate as avenue of, 6
social reform: conversion vs. legislation, 185–86, 188–89, 189–93; through voting, 190–91. *See also* education, benevolence
social status: in neighborhood city churches, 47; contiguous with denomination, 216n. 31
Sons of Temperance, 83, 185
Southern Baptist Convention, 80–81, 88, 161
Southern Baptist Foreign Mission Board, 14, 56
Southern Baptist Publication Society, 70, 71–72
Southern Baptist Theological Seminary, 53, 59, 72, 179, 192
Southern Christian Advocate (Charleston, SC), 102
"Southern evangelicalism," 4, 8–9

sovereignty of God, in history, 94–95, 112–13

spirituality of church. *See* proslavery Christianity, public sphere

Starke and Ryland, Printers (Richmond), 165

Staunton, Virginia, 50

Sledd, Robert Nelson, 20

Steel, Samuel A., 3, 132–35, 139

Stevensville, Virginia, 137

Stone, Mary, 152

Strawberry Baptist Association, 17

Stringfellow, Thornton, 72, 77, 84–85

"Struggle" letters, 118–121

Sunday School Board of the Southern Baptist Convention, 125

Sunday schools: for African Americans, 125–127; antebellum, 5, 17; catechisms in, 52–53; postbellum, 125–27; sectional bias in literature, 126; use of standard curriculum in, 126–27; women and, 160; as works of benevolence, 72, 125–27. *See also* books, education, literacy, reading, slaves

Surry Circuit, Virginia Conference, 146

Sydnor, Bettie, 154

Sydnor, Thomas White: correspondence with Daniel Witt, 129, 148, 173; courtship of, 22; and mission to the slaves, 73; and postwar education, 137–39, 141; relations with freedmen, 114

taste, as a religious value, 147–48

Taylor, George B., 56, 69, 100

Taylor, James B., 6, 55–56, 59–60, 64–65, 121

teachers: antebellum status of, 212n. 9; army chaplains as, 102–103, 105; majority of pastors as before ordained, 20–21; pastors as, antebellum, 55, 62, 63–64, 65; pastors as, postbellum, 123, 125–127, 137–139; in Sunday school, 125–27; women as, 154

technology, as a metaphor for reform, 122, 123

temperance: advocates and the Prohibition Party, 184; antebellum failure of, 82–84; local basis of ministerial authority in, 82–84; local option, 184–86; made drinking disreputable, 184; opponents of local option, 185; postbellum, 183, 194; societies, African American, 83; role of pastors in, 82–84. *See also individual organizations by name*

Tennille, Benjamin, 21

theology, and ministerial education, 60–61

Thomas, Bettie, 152

Thornwell, James Henley, 39, 84

Tillett, W. F., 189

Tocqueville, Alexis de, 41

Tombes, J. B., 65

Tonsler, Horace, 16

tracts, Confederate, 102

travel, in profession, 26–27

Trinity College (Duke University), 179

Turner, Nat, 13, 41,

Twain, Mark, 144

Twenty-sixth Virginia Infantry, 104

Tyree, Cornelius, 25, 53

urban pastorate: benefits of, 134, 135; aspiration to, 42. *See also* pastors

urban style, 42

University of Virginia, 3, 24, 56, 58, 61, 133, 156

Vanderbilt University, 179

veterans, education of, 123–24

violence, against black churches, 114

Virginia: Baptists and Methodists as majority of church members in, 14; declining political influence of, 13; economic decline of, 13, 41; economic importance of, 12; economic prosperity in 1850s, 85–86; political division in, 13, 37; postbellum prosperity, 186–87; postbellum rural decline, 136–39; postbellum population growth, 135; religious folkways of, in westward migration, 8; rural nature of, 13; slavery in, 13, 78–79

Virginia Baptist Education Society, 60, 65, 73

Virginia Baptist General Association, 37–38, 55, 68, 81–82, 88, 123, 124, 161–63

Virginia Baptist Layman's Union, 167

Virginia Baptist Ministers Relief Fund, 187
Virginia Baptist Preacher (Richmond), 69
Virginia Beach, Virginia, 145
Virginia Conference of Methodist Episcopal Church, South, 126
Virginia Constitutional Convention of 1829–30, 43
Virginia Local Option Bill, 184
Virginia School, Hochow, China, 158
Virginia Temperance Society, 82–83
Virginia Tract Association, 68. *See also* colporteurs, reading, print culture
voter apathy. *See* politics

Walker, John Stewart, 103
Walton, Lizzie, 151
Washingtonians, 83. *See also* temperance
Watts, Isaac, 179
Waynesboro, Virginia, 165
wealth, concern over unequal distribution of, 188–89
Wesley, Charles, 25
Wesley Methodist Church (Petersburg), 132
Wesleyan Female College, 155–56
West Point Circuit, Virginia Conference, 127
Wiatt, William E.: career, 103–107; as chaplain, 106–107; losses during war, 104; postwar, 122, 228n. 73; as school teacher, 104; slaves of, 104
Wiles, Alfred, 46
Williams, John Davis, 31
Williamsburg, Virginia, 191
Wilson, Edward Portlock, 24, 26, 32, 184
Winston, Miss Ella, 91–92
Witt, Daniel: career of in rural area, 38–39; disdain for politics, 88; ordination

of freedman, 114–16; postwar views of, 129, 148, 173; and professional travel, 49
Women's Missionary Society (Methodist), 163
Woman's Missionary Union (Baptist), 150, 158, 161, 164
women: aversion to debt, 163; as beneficiaries of lay leadership, 7, 150–163; congregational authority of, 19; as critics of preaching, 154; desire for official role in denomination, 157–59, 161–63; as efficient fundraisers, 151; financial support for education, 63; fitness for education equal to men, 155–56; frequent mention of religion by, 210n. 14; generosity for education, 156, 157; liberal giving among, 151; limits of intellectual ability, 155; as majority of church members, 236n. 8; in marriage, 22, 153; outnumber men in church, 15, 19, 151; pastors opposition to organizing by, 161–63; in publishing, postwar, 160–61; schools for in postwar Virginia, 154–56; as teachers, postwar, 138; vocation as pastor's wife, 22–23, 153. *See also* benevolence, foreign missions
Women's Christian Temperance Union, 161, 184–85
Woodson, D. A. 137
Woodward, C. Vann, 172
Woolsey, Elijah, 49
Wright, George Mann, 139, 145
Wright, Josie, 139, 145
Wright's Chapel (Caroline County), 151

Young, W. M., 102
Young Men's Associations, 123–24